POST-COMPULSORY EDUCATION

A New Analysis in Western Europe

Edmund J. King
Christine H. Moor
Jennifer A. Mundy

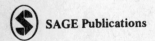 **SAGE Publications**

London/Beverly Hills

For information address:

SAGE PUBLICATIONS, LTD.
St George's House / 44 Hatton Garden
London EC1N 8ER

SAGE PUBLICATIONS, INC.
275 South Beverly Drive
Beverly Hills, California 90212

Printed and Bound in Great Britain by: Burgess & Son (Abingdon) Ltd

International Standard Book Number 0-8039-9900-3

Library of Congress Catalog Card No. 74-76709

FIRST PRINTING

POST-COMPULSORY EDUCATION:
A New Analysis in Western Europe

In October 1970 the Comparative Research Unit was established at King's College, University of London, with a grant from the Social Science Research Council to conduct a 3-year inquiry into the educational and social implications of the expansion of upper-secondary education in England and four other Western European countries (France, the Federal Republic of Germany, Italy and Sweden).

Personnel

Dr. Edmund J. King, Research Director, was concerned with the comparative study of institutional change and educational policy, and with co-ordination of the research programme.

Mrs. Christine H. Moor, Research Associate, was concerned with upper-secondary students' educational and occupational ambitions, expectations and opportunity perceptions. She has also investigated the provision of counselling and careers guidance in schools, and students' attitudes towards it.

Miss Jennifer A. Mundy, Research Associate, was concerned with curricular change, and with evolving arrangements for teaching and learning, with particular reference to the needs of today's upper-secondary school population.

Books by E.J. King

OTHER SCHOOLS AND OURS, 4th ed., 1973
WORLD PERSPECTIVES IN EDUCATION, 1962, 1965.
COMMUNIST EDUCATION (Ed.), 1963.
SOCIETY, SCHOOLS AND PROGRESS IN THE U.S.A., 1965.
EDUCATION AND SOCIAL CHANGE, 1966.
COMPARATIVE STUDIES AND EDUCATIONAL DECISION, 1968.
EDUCATION AND DEVELOPMENT IN WESTERN EUROPE, 1969.
THE EDUCATION OF TEACHERS—A COMPARATIVE ANALYSIS, 1970.
THE TEACHER AND THE NEEDS OF SOCIETY IN EVOLUTION (Ed.), 1970.
(With William Boyd) HISTORY OF WESTERN EDUCATION, 10th ed., 1972.

By E.J. King, C.H. Moor and J.A. Munday

THE DEMOCRATISATION OF SECONDARY EDUCATION
(Unesco: Series B. Opinions, No.8), 1971.

POST-COMPULSORY EDUCATION:
A New Analysis in Western Europe

CONTENTS

SECTION A: INTRODUCTION

SECTION B: COMPARISONS OF BACKGROUND AND TRENDS

SECTION C: CONTEXTUAL STUDIES OF STRUCTURE AND POLICY

SECTION D: CURRICULUM AND TEACHING-LEARNING RELATIONSHIPS

SECTION E: SOCIOLOGICAL ASPECTS

SECTION F: CONCLUSIONS

ACKNOWLEDGEMENTS

Erratum:

The histograms on pages 243 and 272 have
been transposed.

SECTION A

INTRODUCTION

CHAPTER 1

INTRODUCTION TO THE RESEARCH

The number of students staying on in upper-secondary full-time education beyond the age of compulsory attendance has grown rapidly in recent years, and in some countries has doubled or trebled since 1945. During the past decade or so the growth of voluntary enrolment has accelerated; and it seems likely to go on doing so within the next decade until the ordinary child (if not 100% of the population) may expect to be "in school" after the age of 16, perhaps to the age of 18 or 19.

Voluntary enrolments at this level have usually anticipated official moves to raise the minimum school-leaving age. In most countries more than half of the age-group were already staying on well beyond whatever age was legally defined as the minimum for leaving full-time education. By the early 1970s enrolments at 17-18 were already over 80% in Sweden and Japan. Such figures would have been quite exceptional (if perhaps not unthinkable) little more than a decade ago; but now they are anticipated for many other highly industrialised countries by the end of the present decade or soon after.

The rate of increase in full-time enrolments at the upper-secondary level is more remarkable than the absolute numbers. At the beginning of the 1960s less than 14% were so enrolled in England at the age of 17-18; in 1971 the corresponding figure was more than 27% in schools alone (not counting "further education"); and at the time of writing the figure for full-time students in school or "college" at this age and level exceeded 36%. Official extrapolations suggest that in the early 1980s about one-quarter of the age-group will obtain the minimum standard required for university admission in Britain; and this forecast undoubtedly presupposes a much larger population staying on in full-time education to about that age, without however obtaining university admission requirements.

The size of the further increase soon to be expected in Western Europe as a whole is shown by rising figures in all neighbour countries. Belgium and the

Netherlands rose from about 20% to well over 40% in the recent past, and France from about 23% at the beginning of the decade to approximately 46% in 1973. These figures, already representing a doubling in a decade or a little more, may soon expand further to Swedish and Japanese proportions. The expansion is all the more striking for being both voluntary and extended over an increasing number of years. Countries which still have relatively small proportions enrolled at this age may well experience rapid acceleration in the near future.

Problems of providing accommodation for an expected enlargement of enrolments at that age within the next decade are serious. In some cases new institutions have been specially established, or old-established schools have been greatly modified. At the same time (for other reasons) the structure and orientation of the *early* years of secondary education have also been reformed and diversified in most countries since the late 1950s. Thus the size, structure, and orientation of upper-secondary provision have been brought into question everywhere.

The increasing student body now in full-time education at the upper-secondary level between the ages of about 15 and 20 in the various Western European countries claims attention for many reasons. It may perhaps represent a wider range of social backgrounds (as many countries have hoped). It certainly represents more varied attainment levels, interests, and expectations than did previous generations of upper-secondary students. To cater effectively for the needs of today's student body and its wider range, the traditional content, organisation, and relationships for this age-group are being earnestly reviewed.

The "educational explosion" has sometimes necessitated hasty measures. Uncertainty about aims, curriculum, examinations, teacher supply, and teaching-learning relationships at all levels of education is magnified in the problems of the upper-secondary school. There the enlargement of enrolments and the increased scope of schooling would by themselves have challenged previous assumptions and practices. Yet new ideas and demands add another dimension. We see the need for a new concept of upper-secondary education catering for a majority of young people rather than a minority.

This new concept alone would clearly entail a re-thinking of the structure, content, and external relationships of education at this level. Yet re-thinking the nature, needs, and accommodation requirements of a new majority in upper-secondary education is all the more radical because it forms part of much general re-thinking. The articulation between the various phases of anyone's educational progress is now being constantly reconsidered. The interconnection between the various programmes and institutions designed to provide education at *this* age-level is itself undergoing great modification so as to ensure flexibility and interchange, as well as greater accessibility. Many previous school arrangements had presupposed a well-defined population proceeding towards well-defined (if not statutory) objectives, under instruction from a well assured supply of teachers who had specialised in largely unchallenged areas of knowledge.

All older assumptions are now assailed. Therefore the need to reconsider the entire upper-secondary level is both unprecedented and complete. Serious questions are raised because of changes in the whole context of discussion, since in technologically advanced countries the *average young adult* (a description already marking a difference in the climate of re-thinking) increasingly stays on in full-time education to the age of about 18; and the extended education or training to that age which was once the career expectation of a few (well under 5% in Britain before World War II, for example) is now the birthright of the ordinary citizen. It is now expected for all but the humblest careers in the more sophisticated "service occupations" which absorb anything up to half or more of the employed population in technologically advanced countries. Furthermore that extended initial period of education is not merely demanded as a necessary basis for job-preparation or civic and personal fulfilment on a vaster scale than hitherto; it also carries with it the expectation of lifelong renewal.

The importance of this alteration in the context of discussion can hardly be over-emphasised. It is perhaps as important for the proper understanding of any research or re-programming as is attention to careful measurement of the enrolled population in its dimensions and orientation. How rapid the change has been in the nature of enquiries about the enrolled population over the age of about 16 can be seen by looking back a little.

In the early 1960s the most favoured kind of research for the over-16s concentrated on academic schools' curricula and new kinds of examination. A new type of research was proposed to the Council of Europe; namely, a more structural and sociological kind of study which would show alterations in schools' achievements and possibilities by examining the following factors:

Changes in the background of pupils and teachers, and in the supply of teachers able to teach the subjects now required to pupils of perhaps less familiar types.

Changes in what was expected from schools by:

(i)   the expansion, diversification, and re-structuring of higher education;

(ii)   the altered relevance of what was done in schools to after-school prospects in education or occupations, especially in countries where occupational changes were rapid, and where consequently the subjects and training offered were being reconstituted in a different hierarchy of importance.

Changes caused by the use of alternative media, by "outside learning", and by lifelong renewal of early education and training.

This field of research was described in Council of Europe documents as being "of capital importance"; but, understandably, existing programmes of enquiry continued to absorb attention and support. In 1970, however, the Comparative Research Unit was established at King's College in the University of London by the generosity of the Social Science Research Council of the United Kingdom. By concentrating on the educational and social implications of the expansion of upper-secondary education in England and four other countries in Western Europe, the research team obviously concerned themselves with a wider range of students, schools, curricula and teachers than had previously been studied in pre-university schools; and their interest centred clearly on the implications of enrolling more *ordinary* (as well as selected) students, and also of educating all students of the 16-20 age-group in new school circumstances and with new contacts and perspectives.

Throughout much earlier discussion, "non-traditional" students increasingly found in upper-secondary schools or courses had usually been discussed in terms of concessions to frailty, or of "more practical" studies leading to certificates of technical proficiency, or at the best in terms of a *zweiter Bildungsweg* which might somehow *assimilate* them to existing school requirements. Few questions were asked about the wisdom of this interpretation, or about applying different research questions to the *increase* in enrolments which it is the task of the present survey to appraise.

Indeed, the 1950s' preoccupation with assimilating newcomers to respectably academic courses, or with recognising the relevance of technically oriented courses for university admissibility *within the same general perspective,* gave place in the 1960s to another kind of concern. During the 1960s researchers and administrators became more concerned to expand higher education and to "democratise" secondary education in several ways — quantitatively by increasing enrolments, socially by expanding recruitment from less familiar backgrounds, and educationally by re-constituting curricula and methods of study.

Indeed, during the 3-year lifetime of the Comparative Research Unit itself, there has been a marked change. Early preparation for fieldwork and the making of contacts overseas had to be prefaced by careful explanation of what it was intended to investigate. The research team were frequently told that much or all of the necessary work had been done in collecting and analysing data relevant to the educational circumstances and needs of the upper-secondary population — even in its new circumstances — though it was conceded that a comparative study might throw light on trends and possibilities. It was seldom acknowledged, however, that changes in the enlargement of enrolments, in students' self-awareness and expectations (especially after 1968), and within higher education itself, were already full of generic implications for *the entire post-compulsory period of full-time education* in all countries. Moreover, apparently non-educational changes of circumstances such as the extension of voting powers, of the right to marry, and the right to own property, had greatly altered the outlook of young people as they remained in full-time tutelage under the age of university admission, as well as within higher education.

The members of the Comparative Research Unit began their investigation with some attention to the educational impact of these changes, and proceeded with growing appreciation of the different climate surrounding their researches. They proceeded with their intention to investigate the situation *as perceived inside the schools* by all participants, as well as the prospect for further studies or other kinds of self-development around and after school. As a necessary corollary to the research programme, the investigators were brought into discussions with colleagues in several of the countries concerned. These sharpened their appreciation of the quickly changing context within which their enquiries were taking place. From time to time requests for special papers as "working documents", and participation in international research conferences, brought new definitions or refinements of purpose.

These shifts were not merely methodological refinements; nor did they depend only on new educational expedients to meet unforeseen circumstances such as student discontent or structural reform. They depended much more on an appreciation of what may be essentially desirable, feasible or necessary in education for the 16-20 age-group — itself a changing span of activity in a context of social and technological transformation.

Objectives

The general research intention has been to undertake a predominantly *educational* study.

School structures and programmes are often made to serve governmental or similar intentions. Every examination of schools in the modern world takes place in a social and occupational perspective. The aspirations, motivations, and prospects of the students themselves are inseparable from observable trends in the environment surrounding the schools, and awaiting the students when they leave. Curricular and teaching-learning preoccupations reflect the world outside, both in order to portray it and to serve society. Questions about what goes on in schools, what might go on there, or what might be done contextually to improve the general learning prospect inevitably take account of changes in the world's expectation of education. Nevertheless, the special focus of this research programme has been on the educational and social implications of increasing enrolments *as perceived in schools and/or colleges** by administrators, teachers, and students.

For obvious reasons the investigation takes account of re-organisation or re-orientation of education outside the chosen age-range, including lower-secondary school reorganisation, and evolving post-secondary and lower-tertiary structures. Likewise, the research team took careful account of other surveys and researches (national and international), especially those with a bearing on the upper-secondary age-range. Within the general study of trends and problems affecting the 16-20 age-group, they decided initially to focus on specific interests within the concept of "newness" in the schools or other full-time education at this level.

While endeavouring to discern factors within the school system which contributed most obviously to students' decisions to stay on in full-time education and to a sense that their needs are satisfied, the researchers found two aspects of "newness" particularly important:

(a)   **Newness of provision** (structure and organisation; curriculum; and teaching-learning relationships);

(b)   **Newness of the student population** (social background; educational and occupational aspirations and expectations; and opportunity perceptions).

In some ways, however, because of the changing social and occupational context within which the school system operates all students at this level must be considered as "new". An important conclusion here is that earlier studies of adolescence and indeed many current studies of young people undergoing education or at work or at leisure have not quite related their inquiries to the consequences of being in such a rapidly changing environment for youth. Young adults' personal, social, and educational needs have now been thrust into the

* Throughout this Report the word "schools" is used generically to include colleges, institutes and other establishments for the age-group surveyed.

very foreground of important decisions. Previously, they were often supplementary to overriding decisions about other matters in the educational, occupational, or communications field.

From the standpoint of the present investigation, the least satisfactory consequence of that shortcoming has been that many studies of young people's changed life and expectations overlook the newest aspect of all — that so many are in full-time education. In the midst of educational transformation at all levels, the very presence of these *young adults* in such numbers transforms the institutions in which they are found — in addition to changes otherwise induced. Moreover, the ordinary young adult's learning today is acknowledged to be the first stage of a lifelong continuum of education in which older people learn simultaneously with the young.

Other alterations of view are caused by a different school structure (such as a common school), often with curriculum re-orientation and an altered supply of teachers and other aids.

It therefore seemed important to look for "newness" not simply as something externally observable, or needing administrative response, but especially as perceived within the school situation. The best way of pursuing this objective seemed to be by securing the constructive and subjective partnership of students, teachers, and administrators in an enquiry designed to give an "inside view". All questionnaires, interviews, and other contacts have had this objective made explicit to participants, who have regarded themselves as partners in research. In sometimes very delicate or difficult circumstances, this research stance won co-operation and elicited information and insights not otherwise attainable.

Within the general framework of this intention, the researchers decided at first to concentrate on five specific questions:

(i) What new institutions, curricula and teaching-learning arrangements have been made or are being devised for the expanded upper-secondary population?

(ii) What student needs have been recognised by teachers and the students themselves?

(iii) What arrangements so far devised (e.g. with regard to institutions, curricula and teaching-learning arrangements) seem to teachers and students most helpful in meeting these needs?

(iv) What alternative arrangements are recommended by teachers and students?

(v)   What are the implications of these data for other levels of educational provision and for further developments within upper-secondary/lower-tertiary education (that is, for the immediately post-compulsory range of provision)?

Some implications for teaching and for the supply and preparation or re-orientation of teachers were also considered, as were some aspects of accommodation which had a direct bearing upon students' perceptions and responses at this age-level.

Modification of objectives

The researchers gradually decided not to adhere strictly to the five main questions outlined above, for the following reasons:

(a)   Current educational discussions and judgements affecting the future of the enrolled 16-20 population continuously altered the *context* of research, and therefore required realignment of sights.

(b)   It was found inadvisable to retain *priorities* possibly implied in those five questions (for example, by implying that it was always desirable to retain and "satisfy" increasing proportions of the age-group in school; or that new provision should necessarily reflect "upper-secondary" education in any form recognisable at present, rather than "post-compulsory" education in perhaps novel forms). A new dimension of education might be required.

(c)   Contacts "on the ground" in interviews, as well as in the open-ended parts of the questionnaires, helped to refine perceptions of what was feasible and desirable in this kind of *participant research* — in which students and teachers were not merely observed, but also observing educational problems and possibilities in partnership with the research team. That change of perception grew on both sides.

(d)   It was gradually realised that the present investigation differed in important respects from some others:

    (i)   It focussed on the modern concept of *education* for the upper-secondary age-group, implying acceptance by the student of educational intentions, rather than "effective" *instruction* or job-preparation.

(ii)   It was *multiple* in its attention to currently accepted curricular subjects, and was therefore innovative in its search for growth-points *between* school subjects, and in new teaching-learning relationships.

(iii)   In its search for possible growth-points the investigation was sometimes drawn to numerically unrepresentative parts of a system if they yielded valuable *interpretative insights* for that system or for the 16-20 age-group as a whole.

(iv)   The research was internationally *comparative*. Field experience increasingly illustrated the force of the cultural milieu on each of the educational systems and subsystems examined, especially among young adults; and this in its turn showed limitations in the five "type" questions first drafted.

(v)   The research was *interdisciplinary* both in educational interest and in using the specialised resources of the research team (attending to structural, curricular, and sociological aspects respectively). Throughout the survey and in the analysis of findings frequent discussions took place not only to clarify interpretation of data but to secure deeper or more sensitive penetration with new questions.

(e)   For reasons perhaps distinctive to the present research, therefore, the five questions initially proposed failed eventually to reflect the whole spectrum of the team's concerns and data. Furthermore, concentration on them would have over-restricted the content of the enquiry and of a Final Report to responses to the questionnaires.

However, the five basic questions and the questionnaires and interviews based upon them provided an important framework for the research questionnaires and for making contacts. They also had the advantage of focussing interest on the schools or institutes on the one hand, and on students and their teachers on the other, rather than on largely circumstantial matters or on what was officially supposed to happen (instead of what actually happened or was *perceived* to happen).

The prepared questions and statements of intent, furthermore, were in appearance sufficiently objective to secure generous co-operation from Ministries, local school organisers, and the school population — often in circumstances which were daunting, if not forbidding. Goodwill was assured because of the declared objectives of the research, and reinforced by its "personal" approach. Co-operation was clinched, however, by the confidentiality, partnership, and otherwise *subjective* aspects of the respondents' participation.

A change overtook the concept of "newness". It was not always easy to identify in any methodical way particular aspects of "newness". The sample of areas, of schools, or of students (not always within the researchers' power of choice) did not always represent the whole field; and evidence was incomplete in important respects. On the other hand, the expressed concern for "newness" did capture the imagination of many administrators, students and teachers. Furthermore, the researchers' commitment to educational "newness" led them, in response to feedback, to discern less expected aspects of "newness" in the population as a whole, and especially in evolving attitudes and expressions of need at the upper-secondary level.

The comparative dimension of this work also served to refine the concept of "newness". Administrators and teachers looking for new ideas and methods often find that their proposed innovations are old stuff somewhere else, or that their pressing problems have already been analysed and experimented with. However, simple importations and criteria from abroad tend to take on a different role in a new context, and nobody seriously imagines that this is worth-while comparative activity. Yet in relation to the 16-20 age-group's education, something of the same kind has been going on. Ideas, methods, programmes and institutions have been recommended from other countries — or from quite alien circumstances in the same country — to cope with enrolments and training needs that are not merely new in size, location, or origin but are new in unprecedented and often unsuspected ways. Problems arising in a variety of contexts where this mistake is repeated have revealed recurrent and comparable evidence of "newness" in hitherto overlooked forms. This evidence challenges education widely, but especially in the "post-compulsory" phase where all countries' existing provision is undergoing unprecedented strain.

Old (or new) institutions, methods, and ideas are now being applied to a 16-20 population made "new" by several distinctive yet generic features — by being enrolled in full-time education or training; by its size and rapid growth; by problems of new learning and new teaching; by a growing sense of special identity in relation to the domestic scene; and by a new sense that many of the world's most important questions are being asked afresh in relation to the 16-20 age-group. Thus international as well as inter-institutional or curricular questions bear directly on the concept of "newness" at this level.

Though the investigators fell short of some expected material evidence on "newness" in their formal enquiries, they were overwhelmed with evidence of the need for "newness" as a general recognition-point or criterion to be applied to the population surveyed — across national boundaries as well as within them.

CHAPTER 2

RESEARCH METHOD

It was originally intended to centre the research work as far as possible on a series of questionnaires and interviews in schools, in connection with which all information given to the researchers would be confidential and anonymous, and would also be "participant research" in the sense described above.

In each of the five countries included in the survey three cities or districts were chosen as centres of enquiry, and in each of these attention was concentrated as far as possible on the 17 — 18 age-band. This narrow age-band was chosen because it fell roughly in the middle of the upper-secondary phase in most countries; but it obviously came relatively late for the English sample, and relatively early for some of the continental samples, partly because of different school structure, and partly because on the continent a number of students repeat classes and are therefore to be found in any given class at a rather older age than that formally provided for. For administrative reasons, too, it was not always possible to match this age-band everywhere.

The reasons for these choices are set out below:

(a) **Choice of countries** — England obviously was the researchers' operational base, and the basic criterion by which the inclusion or exclusion of any research topic might be decided. Indeed, it is hoped that a major outcome of the research programme will be indications for policy — or at least hypotheses for enquiry — in the researchers' own country, where so many opportunities exist for varied experimentation.

On general grounds too the choice of England has much to recommend it. The English educational system is notable for decentralisation of responsibility, not only in a general administrative sense, but also for adaptation and innovation at the level of the school itself — indeed, in the individual classroom. Likewise, curricular innovation and changes in teaching-learning methods in England owe much to the contribution of unofficial foundations, to professional groups within and outside the teaching profession, and to an unusual degree of co-operation between public and voluntary enterprise.

A further consideration is that in the provision made for the 16 — 20 age-group there is a rich variety of structures and programmes. These may well represent not only local variation but sometimes different developmental stages or experiments within one locality. For historical reasons, too, they sometimes represent distinct educational concepts. They may, for example, embody different ideas about the relationship between general education and "training", about specialisation or expanding the curriculum, about retaining students in extended secondary education or branching out into a new form of education for young adults.

While it is true that the institutions catering for the education of the 16 — 20 age-group in all the countries surveyed are more multifarious than establishments and practices at levels preceding and following this critical period of education, diversity in England is greater than elsewhere. Some reasons for difference are purely historical, reflecting a hierarchy of occupations and studies which may no longer exist. On the other hand, that great diversity of institutions also represents repeated attempts at adaptation — to jobs, to local conditions, to necessary compromises between ambition and prudence, between investment and parsimony, between the actual supply of teachers and more elaborate response to learning needs. British diversity represents in miniature, though in one single range of idioms, criteria which may be of special importance for the present international debate.

England has a special importance for the research project in yet another respect. Britain's formal accession to the European Economic Community in January 1973 brought a special sense of challenge to many institutions and practices. Though astonishingly little effective attention was paid to the educational implications of that membership before 1973, probably because of the unawareness of continental norms and experiments which was widely revealed during the fieldwork, nevertheless Britain's impending membership of the European Community introduced new criteria.

France and Italy were chosen as representing a strongly "intellectual" tradition in education, with an emphasis on theoretical study and a largely centralised administration. They were also countries where an array of formal certificates and other legal entitlements for students and teachers alike was closely identified with particular official courses, syllabuses, and enrolment requirements.

Sweden, and at least some parts of the Federal Republic of Germany, were thought likely to reflect some consequences of technological and social change within a different cultural heritage, and with a great variety of institutions or courses catering for the education of the upper-secondary age-group. Both of these countries are technologically advanced and economically prosperous, and in some ways have much in common; nevertheless for the purposes of the present survey they seemed to be a contrasting pair in other respects. A useful point of possible contrast might be found between the centralisation of Sweden and the devolution of responsibility to the *Länder* and city states in the Federal Republic of Germany. Another point of contrast could be the headlong educational and social reform of Sweden, as against the cautious educational development of most of the German *Länder* — a contrast mirrored in the markedly different rates of upper-secondary and lower-tertiary enrolment in the two countries.

Furthermore all the countries selected are responding in different ways to the educational and social needs of their expanding upper-secondary enrolments. This difference in response is occasioned in part by the different scale and distribution of enrolments; but it is also associated with a different heritage of institutions. Of more interest to the researchers was the obvious variation in the different concepts of education employed to justify or re-think educational structure, practice, and orientation in the perspective of reform. Therefore, a cross-national examination of newness in the enrolled population and the provision made for it was expected to reveal points of great importance for the research.

Comparative examination of this enrolled population and response to its needs might show contrasting dimensions in global numbers, and in the proportions assigned to particular institutions and/or studies; there might be contrasts in the age- and time-span concerned; there would doubtless be differences in the status, hierarchy, and range of the teachers and courses engaged; there would very likely be differences in the measures and criteria applied, as well as in the overall dimensions of problems in individual countries. The great variety of circumstances and contexts would certainly reveal practical difficulties of many kinds, and perhaps widely usable solutions. But all the contrasts — it was hoped — would nevertheless show common features in recognising newness and catering for it.

Two other considerations carried weight in terms of method. The first was that in each of the countries chosen longstanding contact had existed with well-developed research centres. The Comparative Research Unit was assured of valuable assistance in selecting centres and schools, as well as helpful opportunites for assessing the appropriateness of research method and hypotheses in those particular contexts with the help of indigenous colleagues. The second consideration was that of language. The researchers between them speak or at least understand the languages of the countries surveyed, except for

Swedish; in that case deficiency was not so serious because of widespread competence in English in the schools of Sweden — even among students.

(b) **Areas within the countries** — As the resources of the research team were limited it was decided to examine three areas in each country in some depth instead of attempting a generalised national survey. In any case, several official national surveys of upper-secondary schools or their equivalent already existed in some form, with varying emphases (e.g. on curricula or examinations). However, such surveys as existed did not address themselves to the present research team's preoccupations. It was therefore decided simply to take account of existing surveys or of any which might be afoot, and (so to speak) capitalise the research team's limitations by focussing quite sharply on the kinds of variation (perhaps innovation) which might be observed in close, on-the-ground enquiry.

With this intention the areas were chosen according to two criteria. First, that they should ideally represent examples of educational innovation; and secondly that they should reflect a range of socio-economic backgrounds and employment opportunities. Though it was not always possible to make the two criteria coincide in particular cases, and though differences between the chosen centres were marked in varying degree in the various countries surveyed, nevertheless the researchers were shrewdly helped in their choice by senior educational administrators in the countries concerned. In this way they hoped to discern novel aspects (and perhaps disparities, problems, or internal contradictions) which seldom show up in a broader national survey.

Within the research intentions, and as far as the criteria just specified would allow, the researchers set out to examine in each country the following types of area: a favoured metropolitan suburb with a high staying-on ratio; an enterprising and rather prosperous area of perhaps new industries, with a sufficiently "self-contained" yet varied cross-section of population; and a perhaps less favoured centre of heavy industry or with a changing occupational structure still lacking many modern opportunites for school-leavers, many of whom would come from a rather mixed population.

In the event, the researchers were satisfied on the whole with the selection made; and colleagues in each of the countries fully understood what was required and were themselves satisfied with the selection. Of course, there were problems of matching. What is upper-secondary school in one country may be "further education" or "technical school" in another, working under different regulations and with different teachers and prospects. The institution observed, or others preceding it, may be comprehensive whereas in other countries there may be competitive selection or a long process of attrition in order to get there.

The kind of innovation which in one country is established right across the board is evolved piecemeal in another. Therefore there were obvious problems in trying to match school with school in terms of structure and curricular prescription.

Nevertheless, transcending the differences of cultural idiom and institutional form, a comparable climate of decision was undoubtedly found in many or most of the centres visited — at least in terms of the education of the young adults staying beyond compulsory attendance, or in some respects at any rate. Probably that similarity of concern in schools and around them was initially prompted by the need for general reorientation of schools in face of a world of continuous change; but it had become specially acute because institutions formerly intended to shape candidates specifically for university or a hierarchy of differentiated levels in careers and life-style were now being adapted or paralleled so as to provide education for a larger, different, and questioning population.

That similarity of concern for reorientation (sometimes anxiety because of reorientation) ran right across the formal differences between cultures, administrative patterns, and even distinct socio-economic levels or school types in one and the same country. Inequalities and different levels of development are to be found everywhere, of course; they result in differential rates of staying-on according to social class, occupational background, or even chance access to information and encouragement. Thus, technically speaking, they make the problem of matching schools and circumstances very difficult. Moreover, the researchers did not have an altogether free hand in selecting schools or courses, though colleagues in the countries visited were astonishingly frank and helpful. Educationally, however, the same kinds of questions were being repeatedly asked — in different "languages", in different circumstances, but with similar people and similar long-term prospects in mind. The general terms of reference which the researchers had set themselves were fully intelligible variants of other people's concerns or anxieties — and for similar reasons.

Therefore, while the members of the Comparative Research Unit strove for institutional and socio-economic representativeness, and also sought possible innovations in curricula and teaching/learning relationships, they resolved to concentrate on *characteristic* and perhaps widely useful criteria applied to post-compulsory education by its various participants, so as to reveal recurring issues and promising lines of development. With sympathetic advice from officials and research colleagues in all the countries, they sought access to a complete spectrum of upper-secondary institutions in each of three chosen centres in the five countries included in the survey. Objectivity and anonymity of comment were safeguarded, with full support by teachers and administrators.

But the enormous bonus which the researchers received came from the welcome and amazing openness on the ground. This to some extent compensated for the team's inability, for example, to visit genuinely "disadvantaged" schools; but they were unlikely to do that anyway because of being concerned with students "staying on". Within the sample — and in connection with more "applied" studies — it was possible to reach out and make real contacts with at least some recognisable "newcomers".

Access to institutions and courses in characteristic variety was thus assured, with personal sympathy, confidence, and co-operation from almost all participants. In fact, many of them said they were helped by the enquiry; and everywhere the results of the research were eagerly asked for.

To return to method — it was felt that 300-500 students and 3-5 institutions in each centre would suit the researchers' purposes and would give as much material as they could handle. Though the questionnaires were indeed of great importance, it was recognised that they could not stand alone. Matching questionnaires designed to give complementary pictures of students' and teachers' views on problems of common concern were backed up by interviews with the teachers. They were enriched and supported by being preceded by conversations or explanations in individual schools. In particular, one or more fairly lengthy interviews were usually arranged with the principal and officials.

This procedure was adopted as far as possible. Naturally, the researchers were introduced wherever appropriate by the staff of the schools or by official or semi-official representatives of education from outside. These details are given here simply to illustrate the extent to which the research intentions were translated into *personal* contacts — and mutual confidence — from the level of the highest administrators to that of the teachers and students.

(c) **Questionnaires** — There were three questionnaires for the principal or head teacher.

(i)   K   This questionnaire was concerned with admissions, transfers, and staffing. It also sought information about school and college structure, and about the hierarchy (official or perceived) of institutions, courses, teachers, certificates, and educational attainment.

(ii)   CM1 The second questionnaire was concerned with the social and the geographical catchment area of the school or college, and the patterns of education and occupations followed by students (or expected by them) after they left school.

(iii)   JM3 This was a request for a statement of the courses and/or subjects offered by the institution. (In countries abroad, this information was usually available in the form of an official curriculum; a special questionnaire was devised for Heads of English schools).

In all these questionnaires, and in the others soon to be described, a certain amount of factual information was sought which could be obtained only in the individual schools. Variations on the "official" theme of organisation, enrolment, and destination of students, were thus revealed in the enquiry. Problems associated with differential staffing, and the absence or impermanence of staff, and a good many other important details of this kind were revealed in responses even to the more tightly structured parts of the questionnaires. Yet in every questionnaire a gradual transition was made from enquiries about factual details, through questions leaving a certain amount of interpretative latitude, to fully open questions inviting a flexible answer and indeed personal comments. Though the latter type of question introduced considerable complications in the final compilation of material and its analysis, such answers have supplied the researchers with some of the most interesting information received.

There were two questionnaires for staff:

(i)   *CM2* This questionnaire was for staff specially concerned with careers guidance and counselling. In many school systems no special officer exists, and even staff responsible part-time for guidance and counselling may be hard to find. Yet every attempt was made to distribute this questionnaire to any members of staff (such as ordinary teachers) who felt that in some way they recognised a responsibility for giving careers or personal guidance or counselling.

(ii)   *JM1* This was concerned with staff perceptions of students' reasons for staying on in full-time education, perceptions of students' educational needs, and the ways in which these needs were met by school or college. There were also questions on the development of curricula and teaching methods. As many as possible of the teachers actually instructing the student sample, and all "heads of departments" (where these existed), were asked to complete this questionnaire.

There were two questionnaires for students:

(i)   *CM3* This was concerned with the students' social background, their experience of counselling and guidance in school or college, and their educational/occupational aspirations, expectations, and opportunity perceptions.

(ii)   *JM2* A questionnaire concerning reasons for staying on in full-time education, subjects studied, and students' perception of their educational needs and the ways in which these needs are met.

(d)   **Interviews** — To obtain supplementary information and insights the researchers conducted structured interviews with teachers and officials in the way described earlier. In some cases important supplementary information was received in this way; but the main intention was to elucidate possible misunderstandings of research questions or information on either side.

In order to prepare and to some extent validate the content and style of the questionnaires, initial exploratory work and pilot surveys were conducted in England and Sweden. In the light of that experience the questionnaires were refined and sometimes altered considerably, though without loss of general applicability or international comparability.

By way of illustration it may be mentioned that, although the translations were done and revised by nationals of the countries concerned (and indeed by people with inside knowledge of education and all its appropriate terminology) a number of questions were slightly misunderstood by teachers or students responding. Clarification was sometimes secured on the spot, or in subsequent interviews; but meticulous care had to be taken in translation and other aspects of communication in order to avoid losing the sympathy of the respondents or causing them to believe that the questionnaires did not exactly fit their local requirements and concerns.

Two more methodological points may be mentioned here. Though in every case the "voluntariness" of the student response to the questionnaires was mentioned as an aspect of the greatest importance when the researchers were negotiating permission to work in this way, the fact is that this "voluntariness" varied according to the degree of regimentation or permissiveness which characterised individual institutions. A difference could be made by the individual teacher who happened to be present when the students were answering the questionnaires. Closely associated with this problem was the "intensity" or full sincerity with which students and sometimes teachers replied to the questionnaires. Indeed it is highly gratifying that on almost every occasion in so many schools the researchers succeeded in obtaining the fullness of reply and the co-operation for which they were seeking. The limitations and risks inherent in the method used were amply compensated for by the novelty and richness of replies. These yielded information that had so far proved inaccessible to indigenous workers — especially those officially connected with the administration.

Over a three-year span the researchers obviously read a vast amount of material on education, both documentary and reflective, national and international. During the same period an increasing amount of educational attention has been paid everywhere to the 16 — 20 age group, since the crisis of education for the over-16s has been more and more seen as the end-product of features in the lower-secondary school structure (if not earlier); and at the same time the 16 — 20 age-range is the point of decision for higher education, vocational preparation, and lifelong education and re-education. It was the task of the researchers to concentrate on perceptions in the school context; but these could not be appreciated without reference to perceptions carried into the school by all participants.

Consequently the research could not be isolated from awareness of background forces which bring school activities or intentions into question, or justify them. Every national pronouncement, each international review (like those of OECD and the Council of Europe), prominently displays the wider issues. Furthermore, each local and topical comment on education for the over-16s presumes deep familiarity with the entire system and its setting. The present research, therefore, took account of general influences considered by the local participants to be important factors in decision — the more so because an "inside view" was sought. To clarify critical points in the education of the over-16s, therefore, and to place them in perspective, contextual studies precede particular studies of curricular and social aspects in the body of the Report.

SECTION B

COMPARISONS OF BACKGROUND AND TRENDS

CHAPTER 3

INTERNATIONAL COMPARISONS

This Report's intention is to provide relevant evidence on the present position and self-perception of the over-16s in the matter of education, complemented by the views of teachers and others concerned with their education, and related (wherever possible) to significant trends or phenomena in the European countries surveyed. Those trends and phenomena permeate education — or at least educational questions. Some trends relevant to present decision are *in* education; but the majority are outside or all-pervading. It is those which make for comparability of concern, and sometimes of response; and comparability is most marked at the point where young adults have already ventured beyond compulsory schooling and are half out in the world.

Yet it is in school — "school" of some sort — that the most sustained and skilful support to young adults' education must be offered, even when education is vocationally based or socially linked. Such a remark by no means implies that the school in the foreground is a suitable instrument or even a suitable locus for education as now required. But it does mean that systematic and continuous public provision is needed if successive interests and training are to form part of a really educational continuum. As far ahead as can be seen, the basis for such systematisation will be links with schools, universities, colleges, training and information centres, and the formal media — in other words, a public educational system.

New demands on old provision

Public educational systems are in full transformation in all developed countries. They are bursting with people, with new learning and training demands, and sometimes with ideas. Simply because they are systems, they have a structure, a frame of contacts, and practised personnel. The truism that they became systems in quite other connections from those required today need not be laboured. Anyone with a conscience about education knows that the present system will not do, whatever it is, because no system has been built and no staff have been fully trained to do the things now possible or necessary.

On the other hand, no one would have got to where he is without some system to expedite his way. The people surveyed here are young adults enrolled voluntarily in full-time education. Obviously, not all their education is received in school; but it is being in full-time school that makes full-time education possible. The "alternative educators" outside or penetrating school are potent, sometimes destructive and always critical in the sense of demanding a justification. Yet it is largely in school or "college" alternatives that young adults and their teachers seek a more justifiable formula. Some of the sample actually demand more school (a "full-time day", a better course, a wider range of subjects). In any case, supplying them and their teachers with new educational growth-points will be mainly undertaken through schools and colleges — modified, of course.

Modified in which way? All educational reform is in some sense a venture into the dark, because a new social situation is made which introduces its own unfamiliar problems. But no one thinks of it in that way. Would-be improvers look around for better performance elsewhere, or a more suitable institutional framework — perhaps even better ideas and attitudes. In a world where education is many countries' biggest industry, a sort of industrial espionage or research and development programme has taken the place of amateur comparisons of education. Manpower considerations, cost-effectiveness and socio-economic wellbeing loom larger than the theory of education in many ministries. That is especially so when planners reckon up the enormous costs — not to speak of wastage and counterproductiveness — of upper-secondary and tertiary education. The work of OECD and its researchers, always in collaboration with countries' ministerial experts, will be frequently referred to in these pages; but that is only one of many research agencies, national and international.

Such reviews are international in membership; but they are still more international in adopting a comparative perspective for future development. The purposeful language of today's educational reformers is an international comparative discourse — and so is the language of the young adult, already with one foot in the future. Thus pedantic tabulations, juxtapositions, and "predictions" — as though on a drawing-board or graph — are a long way behind the modern kind of comparative study, both historically and logically. Of course the raw materials of evidence are needed (if it is possible to find "raw" evidence that has not been "cooked" by the process of selecting it); but the real need is to bring it *to the point of decision.* That is the real function of comparative studies today — with facts and problems "relevant" to other people's decisions, and using methods of analysis which have proved their worth elsewhere. There is no more critical point of decision than that at which young adults and their mentors decide on educational relevance.

Comparative aspects of this enquiry

The questionnaires, interviews, and other evidence of this Report are comparative and functional in that sense. Obviously they do not "predict" — much less command — any conclusions. With all possible sensitivity they do convey evidence seen to be relevant and critical by the central participants at the point of decision about post-compulsory education in the five countries studied. Yet the task is not one of reporting. As in any research, the researchers have pursued their own interests, in a continuity of evolving hypotheses for further enquiry and interpretation.

The evidence and appraisal have been internationally comparative, and that makes a difference. In each national or local context there have been perceptions and priorities different from those of the researchers, yet fed into the data and interpretations by the participant nature of the research. This feature has enriched and sensitised understanding of the educational problems of the over-16s; but it has made more than usually necessary some careful insulation of the local and non-comparable from the comparable and recurrent questions of education for the post-compulsory phase.

Some reasons are obvious. The contexts of discussion and degrees of development differ. So do cultural sensibilities and financial resources — to say nothing of the school systems themselves and the students and teachers in them. The mesh of indigenous entanglements is what first strikes the eye in each sovereign locality where education is perhaps the most touchy of topics. Yet even cultures and administrative systems have similarities. The school systems which have developed in step with industrialisation, while still reflecting social systems and traditions, show patterns of convergence and awareness of future-building. Therefore characteristic constellations of intention or hope are recognisable; and friction between these and local characteristics produces crisis-points which in their turn are comparable.

Unskilled "comparison", however, is often an alignment of incomparables. Latin in England is not Latin in France or Italy — as curriculum item, as social index, as a mark of "intelligence". Even line-for-line the same text has different connotations in different contexts, ideologies, teaching methods, or school structures. Yet comparable questions run through these particular differences and can be sharpened by them, if comparison is well informed and practised.

The comparative studies and analytical enquiries of this Report are consistently addressed to one set of questions — those of post-compulsory education in five highly urbanised and culturally developed countries perplexed about their educational future. Countries will severally decide that future. Very likely they will decide it in domestic discourse and programme study with their own educators and students; but in the European community — as never before — even domestic questions about an educational topic are sensitive to neighbours' larger decisions and their implications. Therefore it is essential to know what has been decided, in what context, for what reasons, with what implementation, and with what outcome.

Background information

Information is here provided on the educational context of each country, with its cultural legacy, its priorities, its structure of schools and promotions, its operations and problems. Challenges to those legacies by technological, social, and political change will be seen in their varied impact, and in responses evoked for the future. The particular challenge of the upper secondary school's increasing and changing population will be followed throughout.

In each educational system, care is taken to distinguish a general idea (like "excellence") from particular institutional forms (like the *lycée* or an examination) in which it may have hardened; and institutions are sometimes distinguished from operations (which might be better done somewhere else, or by new means). Anatomising concepts, institutions, and operations in this way clarifies comparison internationally; but it is always in the home context that decisions must be reached and implemented.

The case-studies of this Report show idiomatic responses made in each system. Here there is a dilemma. If decisions and programmes are not contextually true they are unacceptable or unworkable. The existing apparatus, system of aspirations, and legacy of skills and subtlety must be used in the local idiom. Yet those idioms — precisely because they are analysed comparatively — are beginning to provide comparable evidence and sometimes a new common language of discussion. It is precisely where there is no prescribed formula — notably in the "new world" of the over-16s — that a more nearly common discourse can take place. A new organisation of young adults' education can be discussed and brought to joint fulfilment.

The young adults do not live entirely in a new world. Their education is firmly entrenched in this one — very often constrained by ideas, institutions, and habits — for three reasons. The first is that the old prestige of learned status and university graduation has combined with ever-growing enrolments in the upper-secondary ranges of school to make protracted education seem more desirable if not inevitable, perhaps with corollaries of increasing competition and ever more elaborate examinations.

A second reason is that, in addition to real upgrading of content and skills in a course for technicians and the like, the glamour of universities and university-type "graduation" seems more essential than previously for a much wider range of technical and "service" occupations. Consequently unspoken considerations of life-style and rewards influence the content and expectation of particular kinds of technical and commercial education, as much as the genuine needs of modernisation.

A third and very important factor on the continent is that upper-class expectations of "learning" rather than of "training" (for which in continental languages there may be no proper translation at this level) has left many school and college courses so theoretical that they seem inevitably to lead only to universities or whatever new partners the universities may have.

The problem of "unusable" university graduates is of worldwide concern now. In continental countries over-enrolment in university faculties with a restricted employment prospect has long presented the problem in an acute form. Though we shall see that in some countries a small minority of students repudiates the university's supposed inevitability, the general situation reflects tendencies set in motion long ago. These still strongly influence the outlook of typical students in school over the age of about 16. In all countries "newcomers" to extended education are less likely to be aware of the variety of opportunity available in higher education; they are less venturesome in the professions and possible new careers than students from more favoured backgrounds. They seem readier to "join the competition" on traditional terms without too many questions. In continental circumstances this means that more eyes than ever are turned towards higher education in the traditional sense.

That is not surprising if we take just one example. In a typical recent year over 90% of the boys obtaining the *Abitur* in Germany went to higher education in a university or teachers' college, and over 80% of the girls so qualifying. A similarly high percentage of higher education enrolments also characterises Italy; there, however, passing the *maturità* is an easier matter than obtaining the *Abitur* in Germany and is therefore within easier reach of those who stay on.

The main point here is the very large enrolment in higher education of those formally entitled to enter. It is this figure which affects the immediate outlook of the young adults still at school before the university threshold. On the continent the university seems an essential step to success.

The result has been not only a steep rise in the numbers enrolled for usual "matriculation" courses, but an earnest search for formal "equivalents" guaranteed by the state. These are sought in parallel school types, in sections and sub-sections of an examination like the *baccalauréat* (where there are now 18 varieties), in "alternative paths to the university", and also in legal upgrading of minor qualifications, or perhaps even in the removal of necessity for a particular examination for admission to higher education (as in Sweden). As far as the present research is concerned, it all adds up to more young men and women staying on almost inevitably — perhaps without a clear realisation of why, or to what end.

Points of contrast: old and young

Talk of age and youth is trite. Yet contrasts in educational expectations are the reason for comparing teachers' views with those of students, for example. A similar comparison is implied if we try to measure educational expectations generally against the real possibilities of existing institutions and programmes. Differences of view are bound to arise in the education of young adults because of changes in education itself, over and above the influence of technological and social developments.

Leaving aside differences in general expectations and life-style which have developed in the years since the second world war, some account must be taken of factors directly affecting school, even though there is no possibility within the present research of comparing their impact from country to country. Two such factors reinforce one another: urbanisation and the surge in the birthrate which has made the average Frenchman, for example, a young person instead of an ageing one. In French cities — and especially in the suburbs or areas with new industries — people of school age and their parents predominate. Elsewhere, votes at 18, military service in some countries, and the international repercussions of "the events of May 1968" in their different ways underline the importance of young people who in any case are less willing to be treated as of conditional status. The contrast with previous attitudes is more marked in countries which have had a traditional authoritarianism at home and in school.

Everywhere there are uncertainties of relationship between old and newer kinds of secondary school, especially among the teachers. Teachers in the schools which have traditionally set the pace (grammar schools, *lycées, Gymnasien* and the like) formerly enjoyed high social status and pay and favoured working conditions, and many still do. Perhaps the main feature to emphasise, however, is their "learned" status. In several countries such teachers can be part-time university "professors", and it is in the university that they take their measure. The fully established university professor in Italy, for example, has an average age of around 60; and many of the other university or school specialists who want to "maintain standards" are also very senior. Furthermore, they were recruited by fierce competition based on scholarship when university intake was much smaller — for example, little more than 1% of the age-group in Britain at the beginning of the war. Without conscious restrictiveness they are nevertheless thinking of an educational structure and order of employment that has passed away.

The "Great Charter" for English education was the 1944 Act — a generation ago. By contrast, neighbouring countries have had much more recent overhauls, including several countries in the survey. France undertook substantial educational reforms in 1956 and 1959, following them with big alterations in higher education in 1966 and still more important reforms in 1968. Italy had a large consolidating reform of the lower secondary school in 1963, as did the Netherlands. Sweden had big reforms of structure and curriculum in 1962, 1966, 1969, and 1971; and the U68 proposals for reform in 1973 are indeed radical across the whole upper-secondary stratum as well as in higher education. Where change has not yet come or is still in full swing, as in some German *Länder,* the turmoil in the upper-secondary school can be greater still.

Everywhere there are Reports and public debates to stimulate discussion. Britain has had these in the Newsom and Robbins Reports (1963), followed by Plowden (1967), James (1972), and the 1972 White Paper, *Education: A Framework for Expansion.* Together, these have affected education from pre-school to university level. They have borne on the social aspects as well as the education and reorientation of teachers. The same reformative commitment is found right across Europe.

Though students in schools and university seldom know details of any such reform plans, they are at home with the outside circumstances which have prompted them — if only in a casual way. They live in a world where it is now normal to stay a long time beyond compulsion in school and college, yet where the careful scholarship or conscious "culture" of their older teachers seems alien to many. Moreover, the upgrading of many secondary schools and vocational courses has brought challenges to teachers and schools previously enjoying high prestige. This sometimes results in hardening of attitudes — and therefore of student resentment. Events like the War in South-East Asia and student disturbances since 1967-8 are often referred to in a confused medley of criticism aimed at schools and the "system" of which they are part.

Of course, much student criticism is to be expected; but it is noteworthy that university professors assembling at Caen (1956 and 1966) and at Amiens (1968) also spelt out radical criticisms of the university system (and, by implication, of the schools). So did the French government itself in the reform legislation of 1968, and the Joxe Commission's Report on the role of teachers in 1972. Therefore huge enrolments in upper-secondary schools and higher education by no means indicate efficiency in the schools or satisfaction with them. In fact, they accentuate misgivings and accelerate the search for remedies — increasingly with the example of other countries in mind.

Other contrasts, and some similarities

Young adults still enrolled in continental schools very often exceed the formal age for taking the university admission examination. Protractedly juvenile status in terms of curriculum and teaching-learning relationships inside school contrast markedly with the adult-life experience of the young man out of school hours, and indeed with the conditions in which he may be paid employment during the early morning or late afternoon. It all goes to show how fierce is the pull of formal education in an upper-secondary school or an institute of the same status on the continent, usually in rigidly defined conditions of study.

In marked contrast we observe the "Anglo-Saxon" counterpart. First, because it is unusual in Britain or North America to "repeat a class" for reasons of unsatisfactory performance. Secondly, there are usually wide curricular choices for any student within one and the same establishment. Examination systems are also flexible enough to meet personal or institutional requirements — indeed, to an extent which is seldom utilised to the full. Thirdly, in Britain a wide range of *types* of institution in the upper-secondary/lower-tertiary range offers similar or alternative syllabuses and examinations, so that students can seek alternative environments, different teaching systems, or a variety of personal objectives. Nothing like this is to be found on the continent. Yet it is an important aspect of education for the present survey, since students often show clearly which style of learning they prefer. That is a matter of moment not only when considering the expansion of enrolments numerically; it is vital when we reflect on the effectiveness of the education received. *Participant* education and education for a self-directing life ahead require a conviction that the provision made is fully appropriate.

Yet we must not make too much of such contrasts — for several reasons. In the first place there is much international comparing of notes. Serious comparative studies inevitably query whatever may have worked well enough before for a different population in other circumstances. It seems certain that traditional "Anglo-Saxon" make-do-and-mend will not survive the rapidly increasing flood of enrolments in the upper-secondary or lower-tertiary institutions designed for other things; and students and employers want "effectiveness" of a different kind from old-fashioned productivity in qualifications. Both on the continent and in English-speaking countries a new educational style demands a new dimension, in addition to provision for students or an increased teacher supply. Those very countries which seem to have an assured supply of teachers in quantitative terms may be most out of touch with today's teaching-learning needs.

All of this should be related to the long-term prospect ahead. In some countries post-graduate research and the feedback of information from practice have at least for many decades been part of the professional scene. More recently, the necessity for re-training and in-service re-education has been taken for granted — in principle. In the past few years the example of the Open University has reinforced the century-old practice of university extension education and other forms of adult education. It exemplifies the realisation that l'éducation permanente in some form is not only desirable but feasible. Though we now use a French phrase to describe lifelong education and re-training, and though some kinds of adult education have long flourished in Denmark and neighbouring countries, any such prospect of educational reinforcement or reorientation has generally been out of the question on the continent of Europe for the traditional student educated in the university.

Indeed, it is paradoxical that university systems (like that of Germany) which placed great emphasis on professorial research did not develop for students that provision of "graduate schools" for research leading to higher degrees which has been such a strength in the United States. Many European university systems have nothing like an adequate opportunity for research — even for staff; and some have none at all. Therefore, prospects for future advancement are concentrated in the upper-secondary phase, or in those professionally predictive parts of higher education to which access is most competitively gained by rigorous coaching in schools. The supreme example is found in the grandes écoles in France — those highly specialised establishments in which students live a charmed and already rosy life as probationary civil servants in an academically specialised field, but only after success in a fiercely competitive examination preceded by 2 or 3 years of special coaching. Though France is outstanding in this respect, nearly all university systems elsewhere have their counterpart hierarchies, with the faculties of medicine and law at the top and the faculty of teacher-education at the bottom (if it exists).

These background considerations — though not at first sight evident — reveal the different expectations affecting upper-secondary and post-secondary choices. Such differences in the countries included in the present survey need to be spelt out if we are to understand what contributes to the continental tendency to stay on in formal education.

Reinforcing this tendency are two other important factors which might be overlooked. The first consideration is that in some countries craftsmen's certificates, and even licences to run a business, are obtained as a rule after attendance at a course. Sometimes these certificates are required by law. In other cases they matter very much in the competition for employment. Any such training carries with it more of the aura of learned status than would be expected in more casual countries. Understandably, therefore, much of the "less academic" work in schools at the upper-secondary level may also be motivated by considerations of certificated status or by demand for academic "equivalence", rather than for skill as such.

A second consideration may be the fact that in at least the remoter parts of many continental countries the "peasant" is still distinguishable — sometimes by clothing, always by life-style. Centuries of disdain in literature and fine manners cannot disappear overnight. They are embedded not only in school-books but in the very words of everyday contempt. Aids to transport or mobility often mean turning away from the countryside. France's longstanding rural denudation has in recent years become a crescendo of townward movement. The movement of the young must be through the schools which prepare them for another way of life. In Italy whole regions are left behind, as the schoolboys of Barbiana showed in their *Letter to a Teacher*. More recently, the vast immigrations of foreign "guest workers" into European cities have accentuated the contrast between the menial jobs they take up and the white collar expectations of the ordinary town child.

The irony is, of course, that many European countries (and especially the hitherto underprivileged in them) are becoming plagued by old-fashioned kinds of competition and ambition when more developed and richer countries like the U.S.A. and Sweden are beginning to show a different attitude. On the continent a crescendo of pre-university competitiveness seems likely to persist for a while, with upgrading of courses and colleges to satisfy ambition — at the very time when "recurrent education" in its varied forms is welcomed as a panacea elsewhere.

CHAPTER 4

STRUCTURE AND POLICY – TRENDS AND CONSTRAINTS

The present chapter is intended to prepare for separate studies of the five countries included in the survey. Each of the countries was selected for particular characteristics affecting preferences and priorities in the development of education for the 16-20 age-range; but obviously general trends are discernible across all national settings.

The present stage of development in any one country may perhaps be regarded as a point of progression along the path of its own national evolution; on the other hand, sociologists and students of development tend to look for aspects of "convergence" in systems overtaken by technological change and social or political demands. It is not part of the task of the present Report to engage in these wider considerations; but it is obviously necessary to remember them in relationship to the needs, expectations, and possibilities of educational change in the post-compulsory phase.

Some of the educational systems of Europe were deliberately planned; and most have had a strongly guided evolution. Others appear to have developed as so many bits and pieces, like that in England and Wales. Nevertheless, even apparently spontaneous growth has generally been in response to specific requirements or convenience, or in accordance with what has been deliberately allowed to happen or prevented from happening. The allocation of finance, the grading of teachers, the articulation between institutions by means of examinations or otherwise – all these hidden or overt controls have imposed constraints.

The educational systems of Europe, especially in secondary schools and above all at the level of upper-secondary education and in higher education, have thus been established to preserve and develop a professional/occupational system which has largely passed away. Most older European universities are public universities set up to do a public duty: they have been the avenue to preferment in government; they have instructed and occasionally trained people for the professions $\div$ lawyers, doctors, and so forth; they have handed on and sometimes enlarged the fields of knowledge approved or required for current purposes; and in some countries at any rate they have developed research and enlarged the areas of speculation.

Educational change as a reflection of national reorientation

Nevertheless, many schools and university systems re-developed their logic afresh under the influence of officialdom, particularly in the nineteenth century. University qualifications and some school certificates then acquired juridical status. The *Abitur* and the *baccalauréat* in principle give the right of admission to a university. A degree gives the right to practise as, for example, a doctor, or to enter the civil service at a particular level. This juridical status and the need for specific qualifications for admission to careers reach far down in the societies of Europe. In considering close links between the structure and hierarchies of education on the one hand and the development of educational policy on the other it will be remembered that in some countries the professor, the doctor and the teacher, and sometimes researchers too, are civil servants. In these circumstances the retention or reform of a school system and its hierarchies reflects a view of the "ideal structure of society", or of inherent priorities and values, if not of something inherent or immanent in "the natural order of things".

Looking back on comparative studies of education, it is easy to see intensified public use of such studies to shape educational policy and practice. In the nineteenth century particular institutions such as universities, technical colleges, and teacher education programmes were established on the basis of comparative study. In the twentieth century three more phases of using comparative study are clearly distinguishable: the universalisation of particular institutions (such as secondary schools); attempts to co-ordinate and make more logical the national school and college systems of particular countries; and finally the attempt since 1945 (particularly since 1960) to guide what are essentially *political, economic and social decisions* in an international perspective by using comparative *researches*. Of these, O.E.C.D. provides conspicuous examples; but UNESCO studies and many national surveys of education also illustrate this new intent.

Changed technological patterns: changing educational idioms

In line with the preoccupations of O.E.C.D. experts referred to above, attention has recently been focused on the implications of three technological stages, matching three phases or styles of educational development.

The *earliest educational idiom* (still with us in many countries) reflects the requirements of pre-industrial times or the early industrial stages of development in less advanced societies. It relies heavily on a formal system of schooling preparing the children of the well-to-do during youth to assume positions of relatively easy responsibility but of high status in later life. In this style, the content of education is a possession for life and a badge of status, rather than a tool for *renewable* responsibility. Emphasis is on perennially "liberal" studies and detachment from practical concerns, especially of a commercial or technological kind.

The *second stage or idiom of education* is more closely associated with an industrial-commercial society. It often has an urban origin in the middle-class concerns of the "new men" rather than the upper class. Its "virtues" are those of diligence, competitiveness, and the kind of ethic which postpones gratification in the pursuit of reward — preferably here on earth, but possibly in another world. This educational idiom is often socially expansive in its recruitment; but ideologically it insists on "convergence", management, control, and "law and order". The characteristic preoccupations of school and college are those of increasing attention to *"applied"* science or management *techniques*. The school system and its examination pattern are those emphasising competitiveness and a linear progression from one objective to another in an approved series.

A *third technological and social phase* is now developing in conjunction with what is increasingly described as a "communications society" — dependent on a much greater sharing of knowledge and experience, and with interchange and feedback as characteristics of widely diffused responsibility. Instead of being "engineered", such a social pattern is open to growth. It is sometimes described as "permissive", casual, and intermittent or spasmodic in its attention to study and other fields of concern. It is recognisable in much recent talk of "recurrent education", of "modules" of learning, and of feedback from experience.

Tentative and incomplete though these classifications are, there is no doubt that the school systems of Western Europe reflect them to some extent in the pattern of evolving needs. Early "second stage" improvements on the traditional elementary school showed first of all the need to supply growing industry and commerce with humbly educated and submissive clerks and supervisors or light machinists. They also revealed an evolving awareness of social values. Insistence was gradually placed on the need to recruit an increasingly *responsible* labour force, and to diversify technology and commerce by encouraging creativity. More recently the approach to the "third stage" has emphasised developing the entire population in all aspects throughout life — not only to benefit individuals but to improve the "quality of life" in the entire community.

Implications for structural reform

Some implications for structural reform are obvious. Some countries have long insisted on providing a common primary education for all (like Germany), though variations are allowed in particular regions. Likewise, the growth of common lower-secondary schools reflects the wish to retain a common trunk of schooling, which may ramify later into different branches of upper-secondary school. These branches still usually cater for distinct academic futures, but now less frequently than before separate the future "academics" from vocationally oriented studies. The simplest way of presenting an overview is to begin with structural changes, to consider policy implications, and then move to the life-style of people in school, especially the over-16s and their teachers.

The development of "middle" schools

The term "middle" school is itself subject to confusion. In some countries this represents simply a secondary school, as in the Soviet Union. In Germany it traditionally meant a lower secondary school better than the upper part of the elementary school but inferior to the much more academic Gymnasium. However, in recent years the concept is of an *intermediary* stage in every child's development between the relatively simple work of the primary school and the more complex or differentiated part of the upper-secondary school.

Probably the most potent consideration has been the difficulty of deciding what, if any, selection should be made at any transition point between primary and secondary education (including questions of who, by what means, to what end, and so forth). It is also recognised that, no matter what criteria are applied, children from less privileged regions and homes do far worse in any test. In any case, the value of the selection test as a predictor has been increasingly doubted.

Therefore a process of postponing "selection", and of substituting self-differentiation, has in many countries taken place between the age of break-off from the primary school and the beginning of a distinctively secondary phase. In Italy, for example, the immediately post-primary phase after the age of 11 is called the "middle school" (*scuola media*). In Britain since the Plowden Report on *Children and their Primary Schools* (1967) that same term has been used for a school bridging the 3- or 4-year period between the first school and the "secondary" kind of school beginning about the age of 12 or 13. (It depends on the part of the country where the child happens to live). Yet something very similar had already been established in the famous Leicestershire scheme, whereby *all* children were transferred without examination from primary to a lower-secondary school for 3 years until the age of 14.

The "middle school" as a phase of observation

These details are given only to show a widely characteristic stage of educational evolution. The "common middle school" is in principle a period for diversified growth which reveals the interests and career possibilities of the children.

At a later stage, the obvious fact that a "middle school" is really an extension and enlargement of the "basic school" is recognised when, as in Scandinavia, the former elementary school or "people's" school is combined with the former middle school to become a single-span "basic school" to the age of 16. That administrative and pedagogical device comes more easily to the Scandinavians, since their primary school does not begin until the age of 7; and even then it does not offer the children a complete school day until the age of about 11.

In countries where an earlier and more formal start is made, as in France and Italy, it has seemed more reasonable to adopt a separate lower-secondary "middle school" as in Italy or a secondary "observation cycle" as in France. In France, the "first cycle" lasts for 4 years from about the age of 11 as an integral part of the secondary structure. It was intended to be a pre-selective phase for the upper-secondary school — and indeed for higher education, where a rapidly increasing proportion of the school population will go. In this Report no recommendations one way or the other will be ventured on at this stage; but it seems important to recognise a difference in concept between a lower-secondary school which is already intended to be diagnostic for the future, and one intended to prolong "common basic schooling" though providing opportunities for personal diversification. However, from the general standpoint of this Report's observations, the main point is that a common lower-secondary element is now in an increasing number of countries the usual precursor to a more differentiated upper-secondary school structure.

It should be mentioned that continuous assessment (rather than single-try pass-fail examinations) is more usual in these newer types of lower-secondary school. Indeed, the concept of a single-try examination simultaneously examining all subjects is generally on the way out. It has been repudiated at even higher levels in several countries. Reliance is placed instead on a school record, or an examination on several levels, or an *examen bilan* (an educational "balance sheet"). In all of this the finality of selection or personal categorisation is either avoided or in some way mitigated. At least, that is so in theory; but within any selective system the old subtleties of career prediction usually survive in some form.

Levels of school and the hierarchy of teachers

The intricacies of teacher supply, the hierarchies of the teaching profession, and the "noble" or "ignoble" subjects taught all continue to affect a student's progress. The traditional teacher for the academic secondary school has been called *"professeur"* or the equivalent in other languages. His education has been very similar to that of university teachers. The usual recruiting-ground for continental university teachers is the staff of the academic secondary school. Thus any attempt to combine the upper part of a secondary school with the lower part, or to blend esteemed academic subjects with those of a more practical or applied nature, runs foul of statutory hierarchies in the teaching profession and the curriculum.

The "middle school" as a change in policy

In addition to the administrative headaches and consequential reorientation of teacher-preparation which school reform entails, questions of policy are introduced. Is the primary school's offering to be "elementary" in the old sense of providing a low-level sufficiency? Or is it to be *basic* for lifelong development for the majority of the population? The answer seems clear. Such questions lead to a provisional regime in the middle part of school life, no matter what follows in the upper-secondary school or later.

Indeed, the provisional regime of a middle school may be extended — at least for some students — over a much longer period. On the basis of present evidence, it seems probable that by about the end of the present decade there will be widespread adoption of general education in a "middle" or comprehensive "secondary" school until the end of compulsory school attendance, followed by greater variety in an upper-secondary school or school-college hybrid between the ages of about 16 and 20.

New dimensions of "post-compulsory" education

A very familiar pattern of providing education in variety in the post-compulsory phase is to provide several main branches after the "common trunk", some more weighty and extended, others of shorter duration and with reduced prospects of bearing fruit educationally or occupationally. Yet, with the "ennoblement" for commercial and industrial purposes of subjects previously deemed "ignoble", many institutions and courses once considered inferior have been formally granted "parity of esteem". Likewise, qualifications once not considered to be adequate for admission to higher education receive a new ennoblement for that purpose, either by themselves or after supplementation with an additional year. Thus the upper-secondary school in many countries is undergoing the process of assimilation which overtook the lower-secondary school during an earlier period.

Scholastic snobbery being what it is, the time-honoured process of "making respectable" has very often taken the form of making practical institutions and courses "academic". Such upgrading may in some cases be little more than a matter of re-naming — at least during the early stages; but after a while course and examination requirements may be extremely rigorous. Thus rigidity sets in though flexibility and evolutionary openness are really required. Some systems have attempted to produce genuine diversification at this level. However, lengthy courses and technical specialisation may really be out of place, since what modern industries and society require is "polyvalence", or multipurpose adaptability. Moreover, if there is detailed specialisation, the old hiatus between the generally "learned" and the specifically "trained" may be perpetuated. Fragmentation can be further aggravated if highly specialised institutions take on a monotechnic character.

Some post-compulsory institutions (like the *instituts universitaires de technologie* in France) were originally intended to bridge the upper-secondary and lower-tertiary levels. But sooner or later many of them, like the IUTs and the *höhere Fachschulen* in Germany (and in a different way the various teacher-training colleges across the world) eventually "made the grade" by being recognised as higher education in the conventional sense. In other words, they become universities or parts of universities, or else they have university equivalence in some way for students who migrate from one to the other.

This is an important phenomenon in its own right, at present undergoing very careful study by O.E.C.D. and other international agencies; but it is less important here (except as part of students' awareness) than a new kind of educational development which is intended to make more permeable the boundaries between upper-secondary and "higher" education.

New "hybrid" institutions for the post-compulsory phase

In the United Kingdom the junior departments of technical colleges and colleges of commerce have for a long time really been equivalent in many ways to the concluding years of the academic secondary school in so far as they have prepared candidates for university entrance examinations and equivalent qualifications. Sometimes they have enrolled students because the academic secondary schools did not have sufficiently strong teaching, or adequate facilities for practical work in the sciences, or some special field of study. Sometimes, too, students who have been at boarding or other schools with rigid discipline have welcomed the opportunity to enter a more adult atmosphere. Many think they find a "true to life" approach in an establishment catering for young adults from about the age of 16 to the age of 22, 23, or later.

Furthermore, young people entering a "college" about the age of 16 have before them the vista of continuing in full-time or part-time education far beyond the ordinary boundaries of "school" as commonly understood, a possibility made more attractive for some because it allows a slower and more practically linked approach to examination objectives. In addition, such institutions often represent a wide variety of social backgrounds, interests and perhaps working experience. A change of attitudes in the post-adolescent stage is often worth a lot in personal terms and learning. For administrative and educational reasons there is a trend towards "all-inclusive" (but not uniform) institutions of new types in the post-compulsory phase.

Thus an attempt is made to provide a common basis of culture in a combined upper-secondary school or college of some kind, together with polyvalence for the future. Countries of every ideological complexion are coming to this solution. "Short-cycle institutions" (or "SCIs") are currently undergoing special consideration by national and international study groups and commissions.

Mistrust of "linear progression" and eliminatory selection

Since the 1950s students in colleges, and sometimes in schools, have made clear their attitude towards educational rituals and older forms of "linear" progression-through-competition.Richard Hoggart observed some years ago that these challenges should be expected, since the "Puritan ethic" was no longer accepted in the very countries where the "managed" and "convergent" pattern of protracted juvenile education was most marked – for example, the U.S.A. As recently as the 1960s Ministers and administrators advocating reform of school structure still thought mainly in terms of conveniently housing the ever-mounting number of those eager to stay on, while improving methods of selection-by-observation. It was believed that curriculum reform would provide sufficiently for varied growth and openness. Within and around the schools, however, the realisation has been growing that structure and policy are inescapably interrelated. A structural change often accompanies a change in social attitude, which further entails a change in teaching-learning relationships.

New structures, new patterns of organisation, often impose new roles on students and teachers. A serious problem is how to make administratively convenient school structures serve the evolutionary process. In addition to ordinary questions of teacher supply comes the problem of increased sharing between the various kinds of teachers who in many systems have juridically distinct roles and quotas of hours. This is no abstract speculation, but has provoked much inter-union feuding and has caused the establishment of weighty commissions. A difference expected in teacher attitudes, and in the length of time over which teachers' education extends, logically entails changes not only in institutions directly responsible for the preparation of teachers but in the entire pattern of higher education.

None of the upheavals referred to above takes place simultaneously even in one country. There is much asynchronous self-contradiction in many systems. A "sense of crisis" may be very local – confined to a particular type of school, or one region. Yet a "sense of crisis" generally develops in a crescendo until a particular conclusion must be reached.

Countries with a diffused pattern of responsibility and longstanding permissiveness to teacher experimentation do not experience this so directly. In centrally administered systems without a mechanism for sharing ideas and experiments, a sense of crisis may erupt in a positive decision by officials, or by students, or by teachers meeting at a conference. Alternatively it may produce a widespread feeling of impotence. The question of how much is already permissible and feasible within a school system makes a big difference to the strength of opinions expressed in various parts of the present survey.

Politicisation in schools

It should be understood that politicisation of the student body is much more powerfully marked on the continent than in the United Kingdom. "Party lines" identifiable with political life outside the schools are only to be expected in countries where there has been a long tradition of student involvement in politics at the university level. Association of the Church or of a particular government with resistance to moderate educational reform is frequently seen as a frustrating impasse. Then a solution seems attainable only by political means.

Moreover, hierarchies of subjects, of teachers, of occupations and life styles outside the school, are more easily recognisable as political issues by continental students, who are not cushioned by paternalism as in the British school system. Students in continental schools, though coerced by examination requirements and by the formalities of the curriculum, in some ways enjoy freedom to develop their own tastes and preferences simply because they are not subjected to close invigilation. There are often gaps in the daily timetable. Many students are free to come and go, just as teachers are. Students therefore feel that, though only passive juniors in the classroom, they are fully adult outside school or in timetable intervals.

The extent of some politicisation is best shown perhaps by a simple account of what happened to the researchers when they sought admission to some of the schools to be included in the survey, after careful preparation of the ground in advance. In Italy formal permission was given, and admirable assistance and advice were also given by Italian colleagues at the highest level. However, after the practical arrangements had been set in order, the very sight of some of the questionnaires was sufficient to produce the following reply from one of Italy's leading representatives:

"It is clearly understandable that you do not fully appreciate the situation in Italian secondary schools, especially in the upper age-range (15-19 years). To propose to a school today that it should administer questionnaires to 100 or 150 students presupposes the agreement of the head of the institution or at least of a group of teachers, which is in the present state of affairs impossible to achieve. The teachers themselves would not do it willingly. On the other hand it would be extremely difficult at the present moment to obtain from the school authorities an order or indeed a simple authorisation. Furthermore, even if the opportunity were presented, you will understand that it would not be easy to secure the students' acceptance. In the present situation of ideological and political tensions tearing apart the fabric of the school, an initiative of this kind would undoubtedly meet very strong resistance — by forces external to the school as well, but with repercussions within the school itself. Therefore I cannot feel confident of being able to further a plan like that proposed by you, of entering schools with a group of researchers. The situation in the schools is almost of a "Northern Ireland" type, in which I must have serious doubts about your personal safety, since there might be accidents of a type encountered not infrequently in schools and often in unforeseeable situations. In an extreme case, some teacher or pupil would implicate the CIA".

As things turned out, there was only one institution in which the researchers were not welcomed. In most cases the questionnaires and interviews were arranged to the satisfaction of the team, and in one "greatly disturbed" institution students stayed behind afterwards for a peaceful discussion with its members.

Education in the wider political context

In considering the relationship between structure and policy generally, therefore, it is clear that we cannot confine our thoughts even within a research project strictly to the schools' own programmes. The situation *as perceived within the schools* by many of its participants already includes the perspectives of politics at large. All the subject-matter's relevance tends to be subjected to real-life criteria at this age-level.

Students in schools make common cause with many of the students in the various forms of higher education, and sometimes even with their own teachers. As shown by demonstrations against the cancellation of military service exemptions in France in 1972, the political field itself is of immediate concern during the concluding years of what was once an intensely scholastic phase but increasingly is a phase where experiences are shared with other young adults. The young German who obtains his *Abitur* does so at an average age of 20.6; and even if he were exempted from military service he would be unlikely to obtain graduation or a state examination certificate before the age of about 25 − 27. Students everywhere are likely to repudiate the protracted conditional status which was endured grudgingly enough when the universities seemed the only way to a decent living.

The prospect of lifelong or "recurrent" education

Several times already in this Report reference has been made to the prospect of lifelong or "recurrent" education. Before starting on the national case-studies, it seems important to bring together further aspects of organisation and planning which are already influencing the countries reviewed. General uncertainty about how to cope with education in "a communications society" and in a perspective of ever-increasing knowledge is aggravated when administrators consider the post-compulsory phase of education.

The prospect of lifelong or "recurrent" education has stimulated a variety of responses. At the simplest level, it has caused those chiefly concerned with vocational preparation to envisage much more in-service training and factual updating than has previously been familiar. Likewise, still at a simple level, the idea of breaking down the generation-gap in educational opportunity by providing late-comers with a kind of Open University service extending far beyond "scholastic" knowledge, and reaching into the wider fields of social understanding, has also exercised many minds. Within the parameters of this Report too it is necessary to take account of "recurrent" education as an *alternative* to the end-on monopoly of upper-secondary/higher education. At least four main aspects of thinking on these matters must be mentioned, however briefly.

Lifelong or "recurrent" education is now often spoken of as a way of avoiding an increasingly crowded upper-secondary school or "college". Responsible thinkers as well as those who doubt the value of continued mass education believe that many young adults would enjoy being at work, or in some combination of work-and-study, rather than at school. Many students might thus more readily acquire a general competence of knowledge and responsible attitudes. Even in "higher" or "further" education no one any longer believes in the "portmanteau" view once unquestioned: namely, that one could acquire during the early adult phase a competence of knowledge for learning and skill throughout a professional life.

An early consequence of this realisation was an extended provision of postgraduate and even post-doctoral courses; but even along channels of rather narrow specialisation the value of that expedient has been questioned — both for itself, and for its financial and social costs. Hence there has been so more talk of a *return* for re-training or in-service supplementation. The 1973 Ontario Plan and the U68 Commission in Sweden proposed doing away with a formalised, sequential structure of higher education as it has been understood in the past. They proposed instead to recognise a "birthright" of higher education or whatever supplementation may be necessary at later stages throughout life. Several other countries seem to be following suit, and adapting studies at the upper-secondary level so as to prepare for recurrent education.

Preparing for recurrent education

During recent years writers dealing with the immediately post-compulsory phase of education have insisted that young adults must be prepared for the long vista of re-education ahead. It is notorious that a relatively small proportion of those leaving school until recently ever took up any formal education later. In any case, there is little point in switching abruptly from juvenile preparation to a much more adult style at the age of 16 or so. That has been one of the bugbears of much vocational preparation and training in the past.

It goes without saying that new *preparatory habits* of teaching and learning are needed still lower down the school if this more modern view of lifelong learning is to be held. That means not only a different pattern of subject matter or new methods during the juvenile phase, but initiation into self-directing resourcefulness of a kind that has seldom been achieved so far, except among those we tend to call "born scholars". "Born scholars" have always been few. In any case they have sometimes turned into pedants or specialists in some fixed field. By contrast, the outlook for nearly everyone in future will be of lifelong readjustment and learning without necessarily having the enthusiasm which motivated a small number of experts in the past.

This consideration not only affects the methods of learning and teaching; it requires a greater provision of varied learning resources, and also reappraisal of the fields of knowledge considered to be basic for long term planning of education. This implies curricular reform in yet another sense. Former distinctions between the fields of "training" and of "scholarship" – and even between allegedly "distinct areas of knowledge" or phases of progress – may be due for early, radical review.

Formerly well-marked barriers between different kinds of school, between secondary and higher education, or between "higher" and "further" education have all been breaking down in recent years. It would not be surprising if the distinction between pre-service and in-service education and training were soon to be broken down as well; and other distinctions between "liberal", "vocational", and social education might crumble too.

"Strategy", practical politics, and planning

No reform of this nature can start *de novo*. Existing systems are marked by legal requirements such as a compulsory age of school attendance. They also have juridical definitions between the various types of school and teachers. Learned bodies and trade unions have deeply rooted problems of demarcation, and are likely to have for some time. No matter what may be considered socially or politically desirable, there is obviously a lag between the time when ideas are recognised in principle as useful and the time when they become practical politics.

Those who in the last decade or so have been talking about "deschooling" and its desirability very often overlook the fact that simultaneously many parents are withdrawing their children from public school systems considered to be rather slack and sending them to tightly managed and conventional private schools. The same thing has been happening at the university level. Indeed, unofficial universities are planned in countries like Britain which have never previously known them. The private sector and unofficial privilege tend to be overlooked in many public surveys.

Public planning is marked by laws and financial commitment, and by the allocation of plant and staff over long periods. It is not enough simply to devise a long-term strategy, though that is undoubtedly needed. It is one thing to discuss ideas in principle, quite another to achieve them in practical planning, and to benefit by feedback as the programme proceeds.

Perhaps the clearest recognition of this point has occurred in Sweden, in an attempt to co-ordinate national policy with the co-operation of industry, teachers and educational planners, and politicians at every level.

The Swedes have in many ways been fortunately placed to conduct their experiment. Neutrality in two wars, rapid technological progress, cultural homogeneity and the pursuit of prosperity have all favoured acceptance of educational and social planning by the majority of the population. That is neither here nor there from the viewpoint of this chapter. The important observation is that — for them — realism at the upper-secondary phase (where now well over 80% of the age-group enrol) necessitates new perspectives of recurrent education throughout life. Other countries are likewise reconsidering structures and policy for upper-secondary education, long before reaching the high enrolment levels already characteristic of Sweden, the United States, and Japan.

SECTION C

CONTEXTUAL STUDIES OF STRUCTURE AND POLICY

CHAPTER 5

STRUCTURE AND POLICY IN FRANCE

Introduction

Since the Revolution of 1789 France has often been studied as a model for other educational systems. Though the rigorous Jesuit colleges in France and some of the innovations of other religious orders had previously given rise to many striking educational ideas and forms, there was much in the revolutionary idea of the infinite perfectibility of man — especially by the pursuit of reason and the exploitation of technological resources — that caused other ambitious countries to look earnestly at France.

The intellectual tradition in France has been powerful, indeed paramount. It remains so today. "General education" *(culture générale)* is still the aim of even the most technological and practical development. The French educator usually wants a short cut to the "principles". In all of this, the Roman Catholic consciousness of austere asceticism survives in today's secular schools to curb the waywardness of youth and cultivate mind and spirit (the same word *esprit* is used in France for both); but it is the Cartesian or rational denial of man's animal propensities which is found there rather than any religious piety.

This same kind of austerity almost to the point of ruthlessness has supported fearless application of scientific principles to technological and political use. Faction-ridden though they may seem, the French have always concurred in the dedication of such resources to the strengthening of their own country. All this is implied from Revolutionary times onwards in the educational prescription of Diderot and Condorcet. The latter always envisaged education (including vocational education and training) as a lifelong influence in all human growth, and that view persists today in the highest counsels of France. But it was actually the Napoleonic prescription that French education followed, especially from 1808 onwards, as the framework of a perennially rigid system, though the underlying philosophy officially invoked is always that of a humanity that is

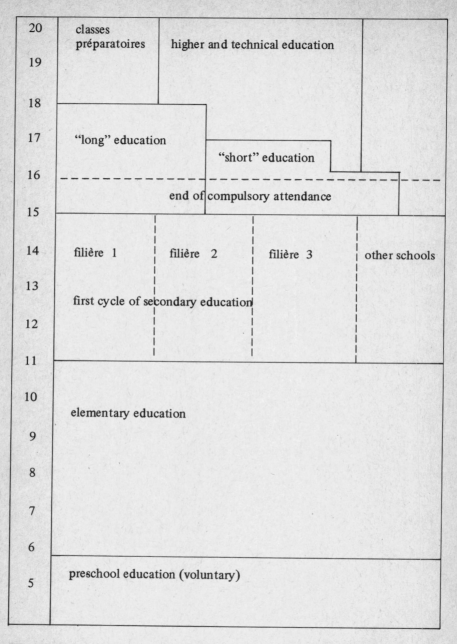

FRANCE: Simplified diagram of school structure. (Ages are nominal).

rational above all else.

"Freedom, equality and brotherhood" were the clarion call of the Revolution; but "meritocracy" in the form of *la carrière ouverte aux talents* has certainly ruled the recruitment of French genius from Napoleonic times onwards by means of harshly competitive *concours*. Even before that time the establishment of the *Ecole Polytechnique* for future engineers in 1794 and the *Ecole Normale Supérieure* to build up a corps of schoolmasters and university teachers shows very clearly what kind of technocratic "general staff" was to be recruited by these means.

Competition and Educational Planning

The incubus of a massive examination system, and the brooding sense of competitiveness within narrowly defined courses, continue to oppress the youth of France today — especially beyond the age of 16 and among the young adults with which the present Report is concerned. Likewise, the intense centralisation which still persists, despite notional acknowledgement of the need for more flexibility and more "personal" variations, was intended in the post-Revolutionary period to serve both quality and equality together. Theoretically, in every school in every town in the 95 *départements,* and throughout the 25 *académies* by means of which France is administered educationally, the intention has been to provide a common French heritage of culture and skill, with access to all the prizes of excellence.

Thus at every point administrators, teachers, and parents too think constantly in terms of competition within a system so strongly constructed and so efficient in some respects that the young people on the threshold of adult life often feel absolutely trapped.

France has produced excellence in many fields. Most of the world is conscious of France's literary, dramatic, and artistic contributions to human refinement. Most of the great political principles of mankind have undergone a further refinement in France. They have been proclaimed as universal manifestos, valid across all space and time. In addition, the French remember their country's remarkable contributions to human prosperity through science and technology. French people are aware that in 1972 France for the first time surpassed Britain in terms of world trade. They are confident, too, of outstripping the rest of Europe and all but the most advanced countries elsewhere by means of technological, commercial, and educational achievements within the next decade or two.

The Hudson Institute in the United States has predicted that in 1985 France will achieve the third highest place in the world in terms of *per capita* income. A recent Japanese judgement supports this prediction. This material progress of France has been based upon the careful calculations of central planning authorities since 1946. A series of Plans (of which the sixth ends in 1975) has marked out the stages by which progress and prosperity may be assured for France. From the inception of the third Plan in 1958 the interplay of education with socio-economic progress has been minutely considered.

Initially, such relationships were largely construed in economic and technocratic terms. During the life of the fifth Plan (1966-1970), more emphasis was placed upon "democratisation" by increasing the number of boys and girls staying on, and widening access to important careers. That Plan also faced the task of enlarging the social span of intake, and sought to ensure "qualitative democratisation" through a larger spread of subject offerings and improved relationships in school.

Nevertheless, what most powerfully strikes both French students and the external observer is careful calculation of evolving employment patterns in France, and the endeavour to secure proper placement of skill. The inauguration of a National Office for Information on Education and Careers in 1970 (ONISEP from its French initials) has been felt by students, teachers, and parents alike to be far more closely concerned with straight employment prospects than with orientation or guidance of any other kind.

After experiencing the lowest birthrate in Western Europe in the inter-war years, France has had a far higher birthrate than demographers anticipated. People are marrying earlier and having more children. The under-20s now form one-third of France's expanding population. In 1972, more than 40% were under 25. In that year there were twice as many people under the age of 25 as in 1939, though the population increase during that time had been only 15%. This is a feature that French writers on education always point to, since the contrast with pre-war days is so great; but they also point to their young people's successes.

That youthful population represents a great increase in certificate-holders. Despite the fairly steady rate of failure in notoriously harsh school examinations (as well as the obviously more competitive *concours*), the fact that so many are staying on at school meant that by 1970 the percentage of the age-group passing the *baccalauréat* exceeded 23%, and by 1978 it is expected to reach 35% of the entire working force. Such calculations are not merely scholastic predictions, but part of France's carefully calculated modernisation. In 1971-1972 the percentage of 17-18 year olds in full-time education was already 46.1%; and 26.3% over the age of 18 were also enrolled in full-time school. Furthermore, it is the expressed intention of the French authorities to enlarge vocationally linked education and training, in addition to making a considerable increase in the number of "preparatory classes for the higher professional institutions" (that is, to prepare for competitive entry to *grandes écoles* such as the *Ecole Polytechnique*).

The Checkered Progress of Reform

The meticulous and often successful planning just described nevertheless has left in France a very great deal of uncertainty, and sometimes profound self-contradictions. Important reforms of secondary education began in 1947, with the establishment in some experimental secondary schools of a common two-year period of observation (11-13). This was later extended to 4 years. At the same time new curricular experiments and teaching-learning relationships were fostered. Ever since, a number of quite revolutionary proposals have come and gone, leaving behind a cumulative sense of theoretical directions for radical reform, not always seen as feasible programmes. No fewer than ten Ministers of Education in about a decade had charge of French education. New kinds of classes, courses, and diplomas, and proposed new arrangements for veteran examinations such as the *baccalauréat*, have checkered the progress of France towards educational modernisation. They have induced a certain cynicism about gradual but feasible reform.

Even the large-scale reforms of 1959 which really formed the basis of today's secondary structure with its 4-year observation cycle, and the development of all-inclusive common lower-secondary schools, nevertheless left some impression of attempting to adapt an effete framework for modernisation of which it was incapable. Partly concealed within the new organisation are the remains of a rigid hierarchy of structures, the formalism of curricula tightly bound to varied examinations, and teachers' long-established professional hierarchies and carefully graduated privileges. It seems important to acknowledge the *malaise* frequently voiced in journals, books, and indeed in answers to questionnaires of the present research.

The "Events of May 1968"

In France university professors and teachers themselves demanded fundamental overhaul of the university and school system at Caen and Amiens 2 years before the final outburst of near-rebellion in schools and higher education in the 1967-1968 period. The publicity given to the "events of May 1968" made many French and foreign observers suppose that what occurred was primarily a student manifestation; but student demonstrations were just the most outstanding of many symptoms of disquiet, obvious to anyone looking at French education in its wider context.

At the end of 1967 one of the recurrent strikes in Paris induced students from 8 *lycées* to join in demonstrations on behalf of the workers. Those *lycées* contained students taking extended classes leading to competitive examinations about the age of 20. The Ministry of Education punished the demonstrators, and a student was dismissed. In January, 1968, 500 *lycée* students gathered in front of the Lycée Condorcet and secured the reinstatement of the dismissed student.

From that time on *lycée* students repeated their demonstrations until great assemblies of 50,000 assorted young adults manned barricades in Paris and elsewhere. In May 1968 no fewer than 10,000 *lycée* students assembled in the streets during a general strike. *Lycée* action committees published a manifesto on the 13th May declaring their right to political action in the *lycées* and the right to go on strike during the "second cycle", which includes the age-group from about 15 to 18, 19 or 20. The students also criticised what they call the "university system" — words which in France include the entire educational system.

As everyone knows, there was violent conflict with the civil authority as well as with the representatives of the educational system. It is less well known that there were many constructive and pertinent diagnoses of the educational sickness at the heart of student discontent. Some manifestoes were general statements of intention or need, and possible reform. Some, however, dealt carefully with the reform of the entire structure, the curricular pattern, examinations, relationships between educational institutions, and contacts between these and working life or society at large.

A number of these declarations have been collected in what are to all intents and purposes serious manuals of educational discussion. Some observations made which seemed particularly relevant to France were officially incorporated in hasty reforms of schools, universities, and teaching-learning relationships by means of a multiplicity of laws, administrative edicts, and explanations at the highest level.

The Higher Education Law or *Loi d'Orientation* of 1968 could not have been more explicit in its self-identification with the very points made by the students when condemning the remoteness, unreality and lack of humanity of French higher education (and by implication upper-secondary education). The impact upon vocational education, guidance, and support for disadvantaged students has also been profound. Perhaps the most striking consequence has been official reconsideration of teaching/learning roles.

The Joxe Report of 1972, the teachers, and school relationships

The very important Joxe Report of 1972 (*La fonction enseignante dans le second degré* – Paris, 1972) made significant recommendations of a practical kind for the re-organisation of teachers' education, in-service training and in-school relationships. However, the outstanding contribution of that report may be described as a spiritual one. It stated: "It is absolutely essential that every school shall be made a centre of life, of friendly exchanges, of easy contacts, and not merely a place where a teacher finds pupils at fixed times in the classrooms". Such a statement might seem to be little more than a pious declaration of intent or hope; yet it could be found paraphrased in, for example, a manifesto of the students' action committee called *Les lycéens gardent la parole* (1968) written by a student team. To say so much by no means belittles the Joxe Report, but rather commends it.

Likewise, the Joxe Report recalls that in previous times secondary schools used to be places where selection had been made before the moment of entry, whereas at the present time social and career selection takes place within the school system itself, with an infinite array of subtleties associated with uncertainties on the part of students and parents, and in an incomprehensible pattern over a long period. These sentiments are echoed at many points in replies to the research questionnaires.

The Joxe Report continued: "A new pedagogical style is necessary; yet that is impossible without changes in the socio-professional role of teachers. A new way of looking at the profession becomes a new method of conceiving the institution, of administering it, and of conducting its professional relationships. It is impossible to deal with one element of the system without repercussions on every other element. The crisis of teacher relationships is inseparable from the crisis of school institutions". The Joxe Report obviously demands multiple reorganisation in school structure and policy too.

On the other hand, "it is useless and impossible to define for tomorrow a single model of secondary school". The secondary school of tomorrow will be quite unable to deal with educational situations, resolve its internal tensions, or cope with its varied tasks unless teachers take upon themselves the responsibility for establishing an educational change which is at the same time a social change. That social change is both internal to the school, and external in its real-life connections.

That is exactly the burden of much student criticism and also of the O.E.C.D. Report: *Reviews of national policies for education – France* (1971). Despite their examination of detailed points of possible reform, the O.E.C.D. examiners recur constantly to their conviction that an examination simply of structure and/or performance in French education would miss the point unless there was a radical alteration in attitude and policy.

The French people as a whole were given an unprecedented opportunity to express their opinions on education by means of a series of public opinion polls in July, 1973. This was part of a three-stage enquiry organised by the Ministry of Education. More than 7,200 interviews were arranged, not only with parents, teachers, administrators and employers but with students too at school and higher education levels. After a committee of 11 experts had analysed the preliminary findings, six main themes were selected as topics for a "National Discussion on Education" attended in Paris in November, 1973, by 600 delegates representing the whole spectrum of opinion. This final stage was intended to guide the Minister in the formulation of a 1974 *Loi d'orientation* for secondary education; but from ministerial pronouncements and other inspired documents in advance it was clear that much interest was felt in "bringing the schools into closer touch with the outside world" – not least by the inclusion of new kinds of technological and occupation-oriented studies at the upper-secondary level, and perhaps in new short-cycle provision overlapping the upper-secondary and lower-tertiary ranges as hitherto constituted.

From the viewpoint of this Report, it was interesting to observe that the French experts chosen to advise the Minister had been closely connected with innovations in the 16 to 19 age-range or with recent surveys of educational and social need at that level, while the few foreign specialists brought into the deliberations were likewise known for their special responsibilities or researches in this field. But whatever new structures and plans are introduced in 1974 will derive their significance over the next decade or so from the way in which the present school system has developed since about 1959, bringing ever-growing enrolments and ever-widening demands into the post-compulsory period.

The present school system in France

The structure of the school system now looks fairly simple on paper, compared with the official pattern before 1959 – and still more when contrasted with the transitional arrangements made between that year and 1972-3, when the 10-year period of compulsory schooling inaugurated in 1959 was expected to be achieved. (In 1958-9 54% of all children aged 15 were still at school; by 1969 85% of the 15-16s were enrolled). Four years of optional pre-elementary education are also provided from the ages of 2 to 6, when compulsory attendance begins. In 1972-3, the 5-6 year age-group was stated to be "almost entirely at school".

Elementary education (the present name for what until recently was called "primary") lasts officially for 5 years between the ages of 6 and 11. Frequent "repeating" makes it necessary to think of 5 classes rather than the pupils' chronological ages.

The secondary level's "first cycle" begins about the age of 11 in the "sixth class" (the French count backwards in numbering classes), and ends at the age of 15. The first cycle is one of observation. Officially all children of the appropriate age-range are in one or other of the "first cycle" courses; but some rural children, and some of the slower ones elsewhere, are still to be found in what is to all effects a survival of the old upper-elementary classes. In 1972-3 not more than 17% of the lower-secondary ("first cycle") enrolments were in such classes. Moreover, that number is dwindling fast.

The lower-secondary school of the future is the comprehensive lower-secondary school *(collège d'enseignement secondaire or CES)*. Of these there were 2,376 during the current school year, accommodating almost 80% of first cycle enrolments. A CES includes all the three sections (or *filières,* most readily understood in English as "streams") which are still distinguished from one another at this level of schooling. Section I is really the "first cycle" of a *lycée* or academic course. Section II is still known — at least unofficially — as *cours type CEG* and represents a "secondary modern" programme of less academic character, but nevertheless a secondary school in a real sense. Section III is markedly less favoured. A tremendous effort has been made to build new comprehensive lower-secondary schools of CES type, or to transform existing establishments into this new 3-stream common lower-secondary school.

Originally, it was intended to provide a common curriculum during the "observation cycle". Official pronouncements still sometimes leave the impression that the first secondary year does have a mainly common curriculum; but inside any establishment it is quite clear that it does not. The pupils are selected officially or unofficially, by previous school records or otherwise. Retardation and class-repeating in the elementary school not infrequently mean a difference in chronological age of 3 or even 4 years between the brightest and slowest pupils at this level; and this difference is accentuated by differences in the qualifications of teachers even in the first two years of the "first cycle" of secondary school.

Retardation is a severe problem, often hard to detect. Despite the near-universality of pre-elementary classes, an astonishingly large number of children have to repeat the very first elementary school year. The O.E.C.D. examiners in 1971 reported that only one child in four completed the five elementary classes at the official age of 11. The chances of completing the elementary school's five years at the official age are 76% for upper-class children, and only 36% for the working classes.

This obviously has a direct effect on access to the first secondary cycle and on progress there; and that in turn affects prospects of upper-secondary education and training. An official report to the Council of Europe on the education of the 16-19 age-group showed that in 1970-71 in all the last-year classes of the lower-secondary cycle there were over 61,000 pupils aged over 16 (when they ought to be aged between 14 and 15). All the statistical evidence, and all the information which it has been possible to gather from the schools, indicate the differential influence of social backgrounds. This is shown in admission to the several "streams" or *filières* of a supposedly "comprehensive" lower-secondary school like a CES.

The "second cycle", or upper-secondary phase

Though compulsory education extends to the age of 16, many pupils obviously do not complete the "first cycle". On the other hand, when a 10-year period of compulsory schooling was introduced for those beginning school in 1959, well over half the 16-year olds were already in full-time school on a voluntary basis. The number has grown since, as shown by 1971-72 figures. In that year 64.8% of the 16-17 age-group were in full-time school and 46.1% of the 17-18s.

The same legislation envisaged three possibilities at the end of compulsory education:

an immediate start on a working life, with or without the certificate of compulsory education;

a "shorter education" — either "general" or "vocational" — for one or two years leading to various technical or vocational certificates (in a *collège*);

a longer "second cycle" leading to one of the varieties of *baccalauréat* or technician's certificate *(brevet)* in a *lycée.*

The academic school *par excellence* is the *lycée* — and not only for France. Its example has been widespread throughout the world. Since its development by Napoleon it has served as the model for cultivating "talent" by intellectual rigour and a firm foundation of knowledge, sufficient for the service of the state and for training in the professions. Of course it owed much to the Jesuit colleges before it; but in its Napoleonic form it appealed to governments everywhere as the seminary for official *cadres*.

Some important features of the *lycée's* development are often overlooked. It grew to eminence at a time when French universities had all been officially disbanded; and therefore the *lycée* in some ways served the function of a "liberal arts college" preparing for public life, or for higher studies in one of the *grandes écoles* (institutes of professional higher education). For many years, until the official restoration of the universities, the *lycée's professeurs agrégés* were the only "professors" that higher education had to serve the re-developing faculties; and this fact enhanced their already high status. *Lycée* students might be taught by such scholar-specialists from the age of 11 to the age of 18 or 19, for that was their span until the reforms of 1959. (Even in 1972-1973 there were still 610 *lycées* beginning at the age of 11). To this day, *professeurs de lycée* may also teach in universities part-time, and it is from them that permanent university teachers are normally recruited. Thus the *lycée* has very close connections with the university, which have grown stronger with the development of the second-cycle's "long general education" since 1959.

It is the *baccalauréat* which justifies and crowns the *lycée's* strenuous academic exercises. It is officially declared to be the first "degree" *(grade)* of the state. The state's monopoly of examinations tightens the bond between school and official life. The *baccalauréat*, like most of its counterparts in continental countries, confers the legal right to enter university. At one time, when the classical *baccalauréat* stood alone or paramount, its possessors were entitled to enrol in any university faculty. Since university fees have always been low, entering a university presented few problems to middle-class students who formed the majority of those passing the *baccalauréat*. But that was always difficult. For decades the pass rate for already thoroughly selected and re-selected candidates was about 50% or less. In 1966 it was only 31%. The floodgates were opened in the troublesome year of 1968 to let 80% through; in 1969 68% passed, and in 1970 73%.

It is not surprising, therefore, that the *baccalauréat* is the criterion for the *lycée's* exercise in the recruitment of talent. "Talent" in many more varieties has been recognised in recent years; so has the need to recruit from a wider social background and for a wider range of careers. But for most French people it is well-nigh unthinkable that the measure of real success in school should not be a *baccalauréat*. Hence, at the latest count there were already 18 varieties (many new), with more expected. Other kinds of certificate and course are understandably upgraded by receiving *baccalauréat*-equivalence or by translation into a new *baccalauréat*. No schooling can escape this measure in France.

At this point it is convenient to turn to the post-*baccalauréat* classes in *lycées*. All of these people must have triumphed in a series of arduous examinations, of which the *baccalauréat* itself has so far been the most formidable. Students enrolled in the post-*baccalauréat* classes have before them the ordeal of competition for admission to the *grandes écoles*; yet they know that they are privileged already, and indeed their circumstances at home and at school show it. Several of the students in the present survey formed part of what schools now usually call their "third cycle" and definitely count as being on the higher education level. That is quite legitimate, since the work done in these "preparatory classes" carries exemption from one or two of the undergraduate years at a *university* when once successful candidates enter higher education.

The effect on a school of possessing such an important "top storey" can well be imagined. In one of the cities examined, a *lycée* included in the survey had no "first cycle" of secondary education, but did have a two-year post-*baccalauréat* course whose complement of 300 students was recruited from other *lycées* as well as from the *collèges* making up the "second cycle" in other establishments. Another renowned *lycée* in the same city had almost 3,000 students in the first and second cycles of secondary education, together with another 300 in the "third cycle" of "preparatory classes". Yet a third *lycée*, more modern and well equipped materially, had no "third cycle" or prospects of having one.

Interviews with the teaching staff and principals showed keen awareness of the prestige conferred by having strong "preparatory classes" – and the carefully recruited top-level teachers to match. As mentioned already, it is the intention of the government to expand the "preparatory classes". In 1972-3 there were 843 "preparatory class" sections in the public sector of education, with over 30,000 students. The significance of this body is that it is almost impossible to secure admission to one of the *grandes écoles* within higher education unless one has been specially coached in this way.

Work in the "preparatory classes" is of higher education level by most international criteria. The O.E.C.D. examiners, however, detected important consequences. The "preparatory classes" cream off the most able students. Even before the *baccalauréat* they focus student attention on themselves. They divert attention from the general faculties of the university and especially from the "university institutes of technology" (IUTs) which have recently done so well, though not as well as the Ministry of Education expected. Some school courses (especially that for *baccalauréat* C — strongly mathematical) are considered to be pre-selective both for the *grandes écoles* and for any kind of career success.

Technical education in the second cycle

In 1972-3, 722,000 students were in the long "second cycle"; and of these 310,000 were in technical education, which is beginning to be officially called "technological education". In the past decade or so much emphasis has been placed on the need to develop technological and medium-level technical education in France. Some of the new *baccalauréats* (in addition to the *baccalauréat de technicien*) include an impressive range of technological studies as well as their always strong "general education" component.

Ever since 1919 under the Loi Astier, a commercial and industrial levy has been used to encourage the development of technical and technological courses both within the full-time system of general education and on a part-time apprenticeship basis. Sometimes, elaborate equipment and facilities have been made available; and even today some parts of a school's programme are conspicuously better endowed than the other courses in consequence of benefits derived from the Loi Astier.

To match growing industrial sophistication, a number of intermediate qualifications and studies have been upgraded. The intention is to accelerate and intensify this process. The relatively new *baccalauréat de technicien* in 1971 showed well over 12,000 passes on the industrial side; nearly 20,000 on the business and economics side; and 175 for the very new section of "information science". In 1972, there were 63,000 candidates in all for the *baccalauréat de technicien*, representing almost a 12% increase over 1971. (The general kinds of *baccalauréat* attracted 228,300 candidates). The *baccalauréat de technicien* now admits to higher education. It has also become easier for people holding a technician's certificate *(brevet de technicien)* to continue vocational or academic studies.

The short "second cycle"

The shorter upper-secondary cycle is much more vocationally oriented than the longer cycle. In the latter, even the "technological" courses leading to *brevet* and *baccalauréat* are more theoretical and concerned with fundamental learning, whereas in the shorter "second cycle" very down-to-earth practicality is given a firm basis in hard study and systematic training. Some of the latter is conducted according to trade union specifications, and students may work to the same kind of job-sheet as technicians outside.

At the lowest level there are certificates of vocational skill (*certificats d'aptitude professionnelle* or CAP). These were originally intended for people leaving school at the age of 14 under previous laws, and pursuing part-time studies or training while in employment. Since 1959, however, "vocational education sections" or "technical secondary schools" *(collèges d'enseignement technique)* have formed part of public secondary establishments. In three full-time years they train students aged not less than 14 (often 16 or older when they begin) for very specific trade qualifications. In 1972-3 344,000 students were preparing for a CAP.

For those who have really completed studies in the "first cycle" of secondary education it is possible to take a 2-year course for a more advanced "certificate of vocational study" (*brevet d'études professionnelles*, BEP). In the current school year 164,000 students were preparing for such a *brevet,* of which there were 34 distinct varieties in 1973. Six new BEP courses were instituted in 1972 to be examined in 1974.

There is great pressure to enter the *collèges d'enseignement technique.* Understandably in continental circumstances, the CETs in the schools visited were less impressive in general atmosphere than the more theoretical courses, whether long or short. Some schools gave the impression that they were soon going to lose their CETs. Nevertheless, in 1971 over 240 different kinds of *certificats d'aptitude professionnelle* were still offered, and the *brevets d'études professionnelles* seem likely to grow.

There is no doubt that technician-level workers are needed in great variety, especially when we remember that in French terminology that also includes medico-social workers, musicians, and workers in the clothing trade and graphic arts. Nevertheless, some dissatisfaction with the perhaps overspecialised character of these lower-level certificates is indicated by the occasional official comment that the content and focus of training are being modernised to take account of changes in occupations.

Moreover, the ancient dictum of Condorcet is now being frequently invoked to secure public acceptance of the principle of "lifelong" or at least "recurrent" vocational education, together with a complement of broader education to suit the modern worker-citizen's roles. Indeed, much attention is given at a research or theoretical level to combining the traditional principles of "general education", with a more "polyvalent" approach to specialisation by means of options, round a core of interests, whether in general studies or in those of a vocational kind.

In the French government report to the Council of Europe on the 16-19 age-group in 1972 it was said: "In the present system students from the fifth "secondary" year onwards are restricted by rigid sections; streaming must be more flexible to make it easier to change courses if necessary". In keeping with this general aim, teachers in technical subjects, and the colleges which prepare them, are promised equivalence with their counterparts in "general education" by the law of the 16th July 1971. In France however, the requirements of law are not always fulfilled at once. There are difficulties in securing equivalence of teaching standards, and doubtless of attainment in the students opting for these courses.

Any possibility of upgrading on the technological side must in any case be considered against the background of ancient reverence for the philosophy-arts *baccalauréat* sections. In 1969 when the general pass rate was 68% these arts sections maintained their own normal pass rate of about 80%, whereas the newer technician *baccalauréat* pass rate was little over 50% — and even lower on the industrial side. As part of the overall picture it may be mentioned that in 1970, 23.5% of the entire age-group in France obtained the *baccalauréat*, while a total of 75% of French pupils were said to have obtained "some kind of paper qualification". Pressure to compete and to qualify — even in an outmoded specialisation — seems inescapable to many of the young.

The long shadow of higher education

In France, the entire educational system is described as the *Université de France* — a title likely to be found on official stationery. The men from the Ministry not infrequently refer to people in education as *universitaires.* Napoleon pre-empted that title when he disbanded the old universities, to suggest that from the elements of education to the very top there was a unitary system. Ever since, the pattern of administration for education has been pyramidal. The pyramid was even more clearly marked before university reform in 1968, because until then the administrative head *(recteur)* of each of the *académies* or educational regions in France was also the academic head *(recteur)* of the university in its capital; and the two functions combined to show the direction of all educational endeavours — towards the perfecting of "the mind" in the university, preceded by the *lycée* in very close connection.

Apart from the formal structure, French education's concentration on the recruitment and polishing of talent always did focus attention on university-type studies at the upper end of the *lycée*, and on the *baccalauréat* which was its only real "sanction". Many continental school-leaving certificates serve little else but to prepare candidates for the university; but that was specially so in France because the *baccalauréat* is at the same time the first university "degree". Thus many well conceived reform proposals in recent decades have been abortive because of the tremendous pull of the university, and with so many set on obtaining the *baccalauréat*. To reform the upper-secondary school it was also necessary to reform the university.

Hence, a French 1972 communication to the Council of Europe declared: "A revised secondary course must be matched by an adapted higher education system; otherwise there is a serious risk of distortion". In September 1964 the then Minister had declared that the *baccalauréat* would no longer give automatic right of entry to the university; and the possibility of having a restricted entry or *numerus clausus* was again revived. However, pressure of public opinion and student demand for admission has long since swept all that away. Other devices had to be thought of to rationalise the transition from school to higher education.

In any case, 1966 reorganisation introduced into university studies three 2-year cycles. The first of these led to a diploma in Arts or Sciences (DUEL or DUES). A new diploma of general university studies (DEUG) was introduced in 1972 to supersede these, amid loud protests from students and employers too. The former thought they were being side-tracked from real higher education, while the latter could not see the relevance of that new diploma to their own immediate needs. By the end of 1973 the DEUG existed in seven varieties, reflecting some response to the demand for specialisation, but still attempting to preserve a "general" complexion of first-cycle higher education. The second university cycle can lead to a *licence* after one more year (the third) for most students, especially those intending to teach; while a further year can lead to a master's degree *(maîtrise)*, especially for those intending to pursue research careers or to aspire to university teaching. The third university two-year cycle may lead to a *doctorat*.

There had already been a number of attempts to "filter out" students. The most obvious was by heavy failure rates at the *baccalauréat*. When examination severity was mitigated there, a preliminary year was instituted in the university, and followed by an examination which again failed about half of those entering for it. That has now been ended; but, even after being admitted, persistence in higher education is no simple matter. Many drop out, and many have financial difficulties. Some students now receive bursaries of various kinds.

Every French student aspiring to higher education is vividly aware of a hierarchy of establishments. At the highest level there are the *grandes écoles* specialising in distinct fields of applied learning, such as the *Ecole Polytechnique,* the *Ecole Normale Supérieure,* and others preparing for the learned professions. All of these depend upon a very exacting competitive examination for entry, assure their students of a probationary civil servant's salary, and have a very low failure rate (about 5%).

On an entirely different plane, as far as the students are concerned, are what used to be called the university "faculties" but are now called "teaching and research units" (*unités d'enseignement et de recherche* or UERs). Here vast numbers of students are enrolled in overcrowded conditions, with a very poor student-staff ratio, and with little or no guidance of any kind on what is really to be expected of them. In 1970 more than 650,000 students were already enrolled in universities — 3 times as many as in 1960, and with about two-fifths of them in arts subjects ("letters"). Every year 90% of those gaining the *baccalauréat* register for higher education.

The 1968 *Loi d'Orientation* ("Orientation Law") tried to redistribute the lopsided student population and the choice of academic studies by reorganising the existing faculties and universities into approximately 700 "teaching and research units", associating groups of academic interests, and encouraging interdisciplinary studies. Thus, at the end of 1972 there were 13 universities in Paris, and 45 in the provinces, making a total of 58. There were also 9 "university centres" *(Centres Universitaires)* where university studies could be begun, and 3 National Polytechnic Institutes *(Instituts Nationaux Polytechniques).* This adds up to 70 institutions of higher education, not counting the *grandes écoles.*

A significant innovation (potentially more important still) has been the establishment since 1966 of *Instituts Universitaires de Technologie.* At their inception, the status and role of the university institutes of technology was not altogether clear, since some announcements gave the impression that the IUTs would overlap the upper-secondary and higher education ranges. However, since 1966 it has become quite clear that the IUTs have fallen squarely in that post-*baccalauréat* range of "third cycle" studies which are not altogether recognised as being genuinely "higher education" since some may actually take place in *lycées.* Nevertheless, it is at this level that growth possibilities and future adaptation seem more plausible.

Recognition has been slow to come to the IUTs. There is uncertainty about the status of the diplomas acquired. A world where retraining is inevitable argues for at least flexible contacts in future between institutions like the IUTs and the other institutions of higher education — especially if they are short-cycle institutions. From about 1970 onwards no fewer than 11 former *brevets de technicien* (technicians' certificates) have been transformed into *baccalauréats de technicien,* and those in turn have now been given "equivalence" for admission to higher education. It seems likely that this kind of permeation process will continue.

However, the present gulf between the IUTs, the universities, and the *grandes écoles* marks a great social hiatus as well as differences in attainment and style of study. Young men and women at school are acutely aware of these social and economic facts of life in their country; and if they were tempted to ignore them, the minutely differentiated hierarchy in the teaching profession would be certain to remind them.

The teaching profession

In many countries the teachers are sharply divided from one another into two or three main groups according to the institution and length of time in which they were educated and/or trained — itself very often a reflection of the social background from which the teachers have come. Universally, there has been a tendency for secondary teachers to have their education in a university, and to have originated from upper-middle class or even superior backgrounds. The ordinary elementary-school teacher has very often been to a teachers' college or school of sub-university status.

Since the second World War there has been a universal tendency to promote all teacher-preparation to the higher education level. Such a move has been easier in countries like the United States, where "higher education" has been a house with many mansions, few of which have been as academically distinguished or as socially privileged as those in Europe. In France itself, to serve school reform the process of postponing teacher-preparation to the post-*baccalauréat* phase began in 1970 and culminated in the 1973 elimination of all pre-*baccalauréat* classes from the *écoles normales.*

The *écoles normales* had previously been training-schools for primary school teachers, recruiting students competitively at the end of what would now be the "first cycle" of secondary education but used to be called "supplementary classes" within the upper-*primary* framework of courses and institutions. After the second World War, the *école normale* course took the "pupils" (they were never called students) to the *baccalauréat,* and held them for one more year of theoretical and practical preparation for the teaching profession within their own *départment* (roughly equivalent to a county). The post-*baccalauréat* period was later extended to two years.

After the school reforms of 1959, and especially after the establishment of the CES or comprehensive lower-secondary cycle in 1963, there was an urgent need for better-qualified teachers to cope with the new conditions. A hasty re-training and upgrading process was embarked upon. With the gradual removal of pre-*baccalauréat* classes, the *écoles normales* could concentrate on a new role — that of providing in-service opportunities for teachers. A bewildering array of halfway-house qualifications has thus developed over the past decade, with courses, examinations, and titles to match.

Many of these new secondary teachers are former *instituteurs* or elementary school teachers. Despite the best efforts of the Ministry there has so far been an inadequate supply. The task of staffing the CES and even the CEG in the lower-secondary cycle is far from being satisfactorily completed. The already deeply divided teaching profession in France has been further sub-divided through these improvements. In 1969 the important intellectual journal *Esprit* maintained that there were over 20 different categories of secondary school teacher, each with its own salary scale, its own career prospects and its own kinds of isolation from other teachers. This point claims attention because of its serious effects on the relative chances of a student's staying for the second cycle, and on his career opportunities.

The preparation of teachers for "real" secondary education is quite another matter. Traditionally, these have obtained a university degree *(licence)* in an approved subject, followed in more recent years by courses of theoretical and practical training for the secondary school teaching career, which may lead (by competition) to the award of a certificate approximately equivalent in value to a master's degree. Those who hold the certificate (CAPES) are specialists teaching for not more than 18 hours a week. Beyond that time they do not stay on the school premises. Even so, they are not as lofty and "remote" as the *agrégés*.

The most powerful teachers in France are the *agrégés* — specialists recruited by severe nationwide competition for permanent appointment to the highest (and well paid) positions in *lycées,* with permanent tenure, and also with entitlement to teach in universities or other institutions of higher education if an opportunity offers. They teach 15 hours a week, or may have some of that time set aside for other advanced academic responsibilities. It is not surprising that the new proposals for the reform of teacher education in 1972 drew heavy fire from the "Society of *Agrégés*", which declared itself determined that the new arrangements for building up a profession of schoolmasters and schoolmistresses (instead of scholars) would never be allowed to work. These are the facts of life in French upper-secondary education, thoroughly understood by all students as well as teachers, and affecting the outlook at that level. They divert the energies and ambitions of brilliant young men and women who see where success and power actually lie.

The mixture here is explosive in France; but a comparable situation exists or may be anticipated in several other countries where school and higher education systems do not move quickly enough to meet the needs of a world quite different from that for which they were established in a different technological and social age.

CHAPTER 6

STRUCTURES AND POLICY IN THE FEDERAL REPUBLIC OF GERMANY

Introduction

People look at education in Germany from many different angles — perhaps more so than in the case of other highly industrialised Western nations. It is not only from outside Germany that these different viewpoints are marked. Within Germany itself there are distinctly different views of what ought to be the future shape of German society at home and the role of Germany in relation to the outside world. These different standpoints immediately affect education — especially that beyond the basic level, and more especially at the level of the over-16s.

Discrepancies are not surprising in a federal country returning in some ways to ideals cherished before the time of Hitler, perhaps even before the first World War. Moreover, it is a country where at one extreme we find the conservative Catholicism of Bavaria, while at the other extreme we have intense industrialisation in the Rhineland and the Ruhr, or the mercantile self-sufficiency of Bremen and Hamburg.

In the matter of education regionalism is still of great importance. Education in the Federal Republic of Germany remains the responsibility of the individual Ministries in each *Land* or city-state, despite growing co-ordination in the closing years of the 1960s and the early 1970s. In effect, as one German commentator recently put it, his country contains eleven "Frances" or self-sufficient, centralised units. Still, in 1949 a Permanent Conference of *Land* Ministers of Education (KMK) was set up to co-ordinate plans; and the Federal Government has since set up a programming federal "Ministry of Education and Science", whose Education Council *(Bildungsrat)* was established in 1969 and produced powerful policy documents in 1970 and 1973. Agreement has now been generally reached on important matters — not least, on the need for widespread radical reform in the educational system; but the extent to which any reforms

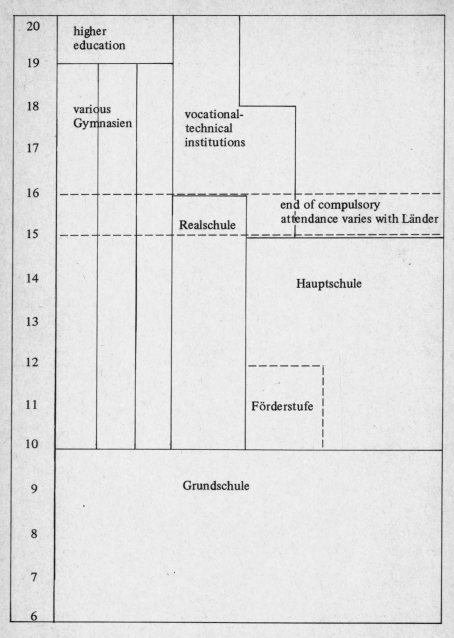

FEDERAL REPUBLIC OF GERMANY: Simplified diagram of school structure. (Ages are nominal).

are implemented has remained a *Land* matter from the inception of the Federal Republic to the present day.

Furthermore, many of the *Länder* are far from homogeneous internally. Most of them comprise rural and urban districts, districts differing greatly in the levels of urban and industrial development, favoured residential areas as distinct from disadvantaged areas, and sometimes fundamental differences of religion or philosophy associated with distinguishable sectors of the population.

The divisiveness of German education

German education, it is often said by the citizens of the Federal Republic itself, not merely reflects ancient social distinctions and strongly demarcated vocational categories; it actually perpetuates and enhances them. The words "Dual System" in Germany refer not to religious divisions but to the clear demarcation between extended "general education" and vocational training. The first leads to higher education (as parents and pupils hope) in an unbroken line from the age of 6 to the age of 19 and through the *Abitur* to the university. The alternative has been a much more truncated education in the primary school, the upper elementary school (or perhaps a slight improvement on that), followed by vocational training and then permanent relegation to one of the lower-middle occupations as a technician, clerical worker, or craftsman. The inherited system, moreover, is further sub-divided into a great variety of segments and levels, especially at the secondary stage. It will be a major part of the present introduction to consider how far these affect the present position and future prospects of the 16-20 age-group.

The mention of age-range introduces a further split. In the German Federal Republic — as in Japan — the generations have lived their lives in distinct realms of experience for political and international reasons even more than for social and educational reasons. Hitler came to power 40 years before the time of this Report. Those Germans who experienced the earnest heart-searching and striving for democracy of the Weimar Republic are now old indeed; but it was largely they who in the immediate aftermath of war from 1945 onwards sought to re-establish in a democratic Germany the norms and aspirations of the pre-Hitler period. Such men, often idealists respecting the intellectual pride of 19th century Germany, sometimes sought to revive its ancient academic traditions.

In marked contrast, during the very same post-Hitler period, younger Germans seeking to construct a more liberal and internationally responsive Germany were often genuinely attracted to "Anglo-Saxon" or other "reformed" secondary school models. Democratic ideals and new teaching concepts or methods appealed to many Germans. Some were spontaneously drawn towards structural reforms which would democratise social access, and generally open up the school system to new personal qualities and attitudes.

Reform   Their main obstacle lay in the rigidities of the inherited school system and the too well categorised structure of occupations and esteem in Germany. Structure is relatively easy to change on paper. It is difficult to change associated curricular content and teaching-learning attitudes. It is still more difficult to change the expectations of parents and employers. It is most difficult of all to break down the scholastic "Establishment", with its hierarchies of institutional pride and rewards — not least those in the teaching profession itself.

How different from the latter must be the outlook of today's *average* German in the Federal Republic! He knew nothing of Hitler or what he stood for. He has always lived in a post-war world in which France and the Americans seem in many ways closer and more congenial than those neighbours immediately to the East. Besides, the European Economic Community and the "Economic Miracle" have literally brought an embarrassment of riches that seem in no recognisable way dependent upon the ancient disciplines which authority imposed upon young people a generation ago. The Federal Republic of Germany, like France, is now a predominantly young country.

Those who know Germany only from abroad, or have for that matter never travelled much further than the great cities of the North and North-West, can have little idea of the extensive farmland, heaths, and ancient fairy-tale towns which remind today's observer of a parochial and orderly life-style not so long ago. Then every garden, field, and small-town street was a lesson in order, thrift, and hard work. The very rapid urbanisation of Germany and the "Economic Miracle" have brought much easier prosperity to any young native German, and also brought an influx of two million "guest workers" to do the menial tasks which no young person wants.

The call for an altered system

All these changes have by themselves introduced a quite different context for thoughts about education and its future. They are, of course, heavily reinforced in Germany as elsewhere by the huge spread of new specialisations both in learning and in industry or commerce. They are further reinforced by the need for flexible preparation for ever-changing occupational perspectives throughout life, and by social expectations of a differently ordered society. In the circumstances it is not surprising that Germans are acutely conscious of the need for widespread, radical, and large-scale educational reform. They wish to end the "Dual System" divorcing general from vocational education, and spread reforms not only across upper-secondary education but in a much wider range of "higher" education than had ever been envisaged before.

After what Professors Saul B. Robinsohn and J. Caspar Kuhlmann in 1967 called "Two decades of non-reform in West German education", a spate of recommendations at the federal level has been produced in the last 4 or 5 years. Goodwill has been shown towards many of these within the individual *Länder*. Implementation varies, however; and in the individual school or classroom some projects of reform may indeed seem far away. Implementation is bound to be difficult in a deeply divided country with so many entrenched privileges, where even courtesy titles perpetuate a minor feudal system – not least in the schools with their surprising array of tightly prescribed courses with certificates to match. The irrelevance of many of these courses has been admitted by leading German spokesmen, and still more by outside observers.

To the young German keenly conscious of the frustrations of protracted adolescence and intrinsically questionable authority, additional domestic perspectives introduce reasons for profound disquiet. The overcrowding of universities is grievous, yet it has arisen during a time when German universities still enrol a smaller proportion of the age-group than do countries which are at a similar technological stage but a much lower level of prosperity. The further student increase expected not merely makes nonsense of many cherished traditions in German universities themselves; it also brings into question the content of much schooling and the minutely specialised array of upper-secondary schools with their "Cinderella" neighbours, the vocational institutions. Over all is the examination-monopoly imposed on access to satisfying careers. Thus the outlook from the position of the 16-20 age-group in Germany is of particular significance.

The Comparative Research Unit was unable to administer questionnaires in more than one city-state in the Federal Republic of Germany, though it had also been intended to investigate two quite different regions in the same way. Nevertheless, information more widely gathered and some insights in answers to the questionnaires may throw general light on problems of developing and reforming education in the upper-secondary/lower-tertiary range.

The Federal Republic of Germany, like England, has a bewildering multiplicity of institutional and curricular types at this level of education. In England, however, flexibility is the order of the day, and the instruments for guaranteeing a reasonable standard positively encourage variety of teaching and learning. The opposite is characteristic of Germany. There sharp differentiation exists, partly because of the diffusion of administrative responsibility to the various *Länder*; and this is intensified in vocational education because of the wish to serve industrial and commercial needs in an ever-proliferating variety of courses and certificates, all of which must however be "official".

Whether flexibility and adaptability for the future can be built out of the existing system — for a different technological order and a "communications" society — is a problem causing much heart-searching both among the young people and their elders. Perhaps for the very first time in German educational history, questions are being asked about education *as a whole system*, instead of being addressed to problems of a particular kind of institution such as the *Gymnasium*. Questions are also asked about the structure of education in relation to the entire social structure and the national distribution of opportunity. Perhaps more significantly questions are being asked in all-German terms, in terms of comparison with the German Democratic Republic, and also with the example of other countries constantly in mind.

The inherited system

Exceptions can be found to many of the statements below in one or other of the *Länder* or city states. However, a family likeness is preserved.

Under the Weimar Republic, most *Länder* established a four-year compulsory primary school (*Grundschule* or *Volksschule*) for all children, either of a public or a "confessional" (Church-attached) type. Those selected for academic secondary school or other institutions were transferred at the age of 10, or 12 in some places. This basic structure still remains, except that during the 1960s in the churches had to give up their control over primary schools and teacher-training. Tax money is no longer available for providing denominational schooling.

Compulsory education on a "full-time" basis is provided for 9 years. This should mean to the age of 15. However, class-repeating and local or social disadvantages meant that at the end of the 1960s an average of 20% of all upper-primary school leavers left without successfully completing the final year of the course; and that figure in a few places reached 50%. When the phrase "full-time education" is used, however, it simply means not being in paid employment. The O.E.C.D. examiners reported in 1972 that "at the moment the proportion of children enrolled in whole-day schools is negligible".* By that the

* O.E.C.D.: Reviews of National Policies for Education: Germany, 1972, page 75.

examiners reminded readers that German schools (secondary schools especially) resemble most others on the continent in starting very early in the morning and finishing in the early afternoon after concentrating instruction into a packed time-table, instead of maintaining an easier pace of learning with more opportunity for creativity and self-directed education.

There is much talk of extending the compulsory period of schooling to ten years. In any case, a further period of part-time school at least to the age of 18 is insisted upon for those who leave "full-time" school before that age. That period must be spent in vocational training supplemented with general education of various types. The basic school *(Grundschule)* still generally comprises the school years 1- 4 or 1-6; but some pre-school establishments have recently been established and more are being developed. Secondary education now officially begins at the age of 10 or 12 (according to the *Land*) with three alternatives: the *Hauptschule* or main school, which does not represent much change on the old upper-elementary school; the *Realschule* or *Mittelschule*; and the *Gymnasium*.

In the late 1960s, roughly 63% of all 13-year-olds were attending an upper-elementary school; 15% or so were in a middle school; and a little more than 17% were in a *Gymnasium*. At the age of 16 some 23% were still attending some form of non-vocational school, including 8.8% in a *Realschule*, and some 13% in a *Gymnasium*. At the age of 18, some 10.3% were in general education schools, and the vast majority of these (9.8%) were in *Gymnasien*. Proportions in these schools and others varied from state to state, and indeed from area to area and social class to social class. It has also been shown that girls and Roman Catholics are at some disadvantage, especially if they live in rural areas.

Because of the "Dual System", at the end of compulsory full-time school the majority of young Germans have traditionally moved from "general education" to part-time vocational education in the *Berufschule* or part-time continuation school until the end of vocational training. They must continue such education or training until at least the age of 18. A few students have transferred to full-time vocational schools (*Berufsfachschulen* or *Fachschulen*). If all the vocationally-linked part-time establishments are counted in, in 1969 some 94% of all 16-year-old Germans were receiving education, as against 23% of the 19-year-olds.*

The choice of schools at the early age of 10 or 12 to all intents and purposes has traditionally determined future access to opportunity. It is only within the "general" type of school that students have been able to obtain the *mittlere Reife* or intermediate certificate that can admit eventually to other kinds of academic preferment, or the much higher award of the *Abitur* or

* Council of Europe DECS − EGT (72) 87 page 1.

Hochschulreife admitting to higher education proper at the age of nineteen-plus. (In fact, the average age of attaining the *Abitur* was 20.7 years in 1969, because of class-repeating, even after a good deal of private coaching paid for by the parents).

Alternatives to the traditional Gymnasium, and their prospects

Following the so-called Hamburg Agreement of 1964 between the *Länder*, a large variety of secondary school types dealing with trade *(Handelsgymnasien)*, or otherwise vocationally oriented schools, was established very widely; and further varieties of establishment were envisaged in a number of the reform plans currently discussed. Yet the traditional type of *Gymnasium* definitely held pride of place over all of these newcomers, with its curriculum based upon the classical languages, modern languages, and a solid core of other general subjects to a total of 9 or 10 pursued throughout. It was more successful in obtaining funds and better-qualified teachers. All this forms part of the inheritance which must be reckoned with when reform plans are appraised. It is always important to recognise the simple distinction whether the years after age 15-16 are spent in a type of "general education" or not as the essential criterion for later opportunity.

The "general" institutions of secondary education all maintain a solid core of studies which is almost identical for the first six years of the course. Thereafter, differentiation is made mainly on the basis of the foreign languages studied. For example, the classical *Gymnasium* starts English as a first foreign language at the age of 10 as a rule, adds Latin at the age of 12, and Greek at the age of about 14. In the modern languages *Gymnasium* the three languages would probably be English, Latin, and French. In the maths/science *Gymnasium* students are unlikely to take a third foreign language but will have more mathematics. Such *Gymnasien* still enjoy pre-eminence.

The newer types of upper-secondary school which have developed since about 1955 often confer an *Abitur* or *Hochschulreife* which is restricted for higher education purposes to the particular field of specialisation (such as economics or social sciences). However, they do still offer right of entry to a university (subject to the proposed restrictions under discussion since about 1970 in order to cope with ever-mounting pressure of numbers). The question of admission to higher education (vitally important in German social esteem and career perspectives) therefore depends not merely on obtaining an *Abitur*, but on the type of upper-secondary school attended.

Recent reforms or proposed reforms in higher education have officially included within the term "higher education" not only the university, but also the teacher-training establishments known as *Pädagogische Hochschulen*, and quite a range of establishments roughly corresponding to what in Britain would be called "further education". These had not hitherto enjoyed recognition on this plane. For example, the former *Ingenieurschulen* or *Höhere Fachschulen* (higher vocational institutes) are at present in process of transformation into *Fachhochschulen* or colleges of advanced technology – in principle of university status. It is only in these establishments for higher and applied studies that those who have moved up the vocational line of the "Dual System" can really secure admission to higher education – and that as a rule in two moves – first from the upper-elementary school to a vocational school, and then from that into a higher establishment in something corresponding to British "further education" or technological higher education.

In all of this there are discrepancies between the various *Länder* and city states. For example, the city-state of Hamburg is readier to admit into its own university people with qualifications from the former *Ingenieurschulen* than are some other *Länder*. In consequence, the graduates of Hamburg University in some faculties are not recognised as of graduate status in some of the other *Länder*. Thus the much-cherished concept of "permeability" or "transferability" *(Durchlässigkeit)* is far from easily embodied in actual practice. Equivalence or acceptability still has far to go.

The foregoing remarks show that it would be relatively easy to transfer from one older type of *Gymnasium* to another because of the large spread of common course-work in them. During the post-war years a number of reform plans envisaged that a "common core" of at least 2 years' work would be established as the basis for all secondary education. This innovation was best known under the name of *Rahmenplan* or framework plan from 1959 onwards. According to this pattern, the basic school would end at the age of 10 and then be followed by an observation period or promotion stage to the age of 12, called a *Förderstufe*. However, even that 2-year period had exemptions made in it to enable the really "bright" boys and girls to move straight away into a selective *Gymnasium* at the age of 10. Despite the intense interest aroused by the *Rahmenplan* and parallel proposals, very few *Länder* have adopted it fully.

However, some *Länder* or cities have gone even further and established comprehensive schools for the whole or part of the secondary phase, at least for the junior part now usually known as *Sekundarstufe I*, to the age of 16. In April 1972, for the very first time, the comprehensive secondary school at Gelsenkirchen had its first pupils entering for the *Abitur*. The Gelsenkirchen comprehensive school was perhaps the only one of more than 200 "comprehensive experiments" then regarded as really successful. It will undoubtedly be followed by many others, not only as experiments but as models for the future. Indeed, at the university level itself the *Gesamthochschule* or "comprehensive university" has already been established in a number of *Länder* as a combination of a university, a *Pädagogische Hochschule* (teacher training college), and the "further education" type of college. Thus in this instance the university seems to be setting the pace for the secondary schools.

Yet a further possibility is the *Oberstufenkolleg* or senior secondary college, established experimentally on a comprehensive pattern in a number of *Länder* or cities. Once again there is an attempt to provide within a common establishment an opportunity for boys and girls coming from different schools, different types of course, and different social backgrounds to complete the secondary range of studies to a level where they compete on roughly equal terms for jobs at least, and perhaps also for continued studies or higher education. The *Oberstufenkolleg* at Bielefeld in North-Rhine-Westphalia (1974) in fact combines the last three years of school and the first years of the university course *(Grundstudium)* — a very significant innovation for upper-secondary/lower tertiary education in any country.

The proliferation of new types should not mislead us about the actual numbers of establishments or enrolments. The number of students enrolled in all kinds of comprehensive or multilateral schools is still relatively tiny compared with those in older types of establishment. Nevertheless, the example of these newer types is officially stated to be of great importance for the future. Not only German and overseas experts but young people themselves are well aware of these possibilities. There are constant discussions in the increasingly politicised student movements — a point not to be underestimated.

Of course, the establishment of comprehensive-type schools or "permeability" does not mean equivalence socially or in other respects. All the evidence continues to show that admissions to *Pädagogische Hochschulen,* for example, or to recently upgraded parts of a "comprehensive university", are of lower attainment and less favoured social background than are students admitted to the older prestige-enjoying institutions. In fact, there have been complaints that the new types of establishment are used as filters or "sumps" for that half of the enrolments who are likely to leave the university altogether before completing the course (as often happens in Germany).

The proposed shortening of all university courses to provide for shorter undergraduate work might do something to ease this fear of being enrolled in a "short cycle institution" deliberately used as a kind of sieve for the "real" higher education levels; but such "short courses" would need to be developed right across the spectrum of higher education, not confined to the less favoured segments of it. At this point useful comparisons could be made with France and England.

Such then is the "field of force" within which the sensibilities of young men and women in Germany between the ages of about 16 and 20 are being polarised personally, socially, and politically. It is appropriate to say more about reform proposals and the instrumentation envisaged. Obviously, these are not only plans for the future; they reflect Germans' observations on current experiments, and also some dissatisfaction with the state of affairs preceding reform — more especially at the upper-secondary and tertiary levels.

Reform plans — especially since 1970

The year 1969 marked a substantial change in nationwide attitudes towards the development and reform of the school system. Whereas Germans have frequently criticised the piecemeal nature of reform proposals, and the general lack of will to carry them out if they required social or other consequential reforms, from the beginning of 1969 the recommendations of the *Bildungsrat* rapidly gathered momentum and far-reaching force.

In January 1969 the *Bildungsrat* proposed a broad experimental programme with comprehensive schools, recommending that at least 40 of the genuinely comprehensive or integrated type should be established in the various *Länder*. However, it did not at that time recommend their widespread adoption. Later in the same year some constitutional amendments were passed which made it easier for the Federal Republic as a whole and the *Länder* to undertake certain programmes in common, especially in long-term planning and research. The new Chancellor, Dr. Brandt, emphasised the importance of bringing closer together the general and the vocational aspects of education and training, and the importance of research in this direction.

In April 1970 the *Bildungsrat* produced an Education Report *(Bildungsbericht)** covering every level and aspect of the educational system except higher education. (The latter fell within the special purview of the *Wissenschaftsrat* or Science Council, though the Education Report clearly had implications for higher education in its recommendations on the future structure of the upper-secondary school). A number of subsidiary studies followed. Notably, a number of the *Länder* and city states published their own

* Available in an official English translation as: *Report of the Federal Government on Education 1970.*

interpretation of the *Bildungsbericht '70*, usually filling in the framework with practical illustrations of how the scheme might work locally, and very often adding a stronger recommendation for the extension of a comprehensive school system even to the concluding years of the upper-secondary school.

Among implications for the upper-secondary school, a major point to emphasise is the new concept of an all-round, interlocking system. This should offer greater possibilities of access to any type of education from which a student may profit, without predestination to a particular level of learning or life-style. The ideal would be for more "permeability", to allow students to modify or amplify whatever type of learning they had begun.

Few Germans now disagree with the essential intentions of this programme. However, an apple of discord has been thrown down by a very few simple phrases. Wholesome emphasis on the need to provide education in variety, according to present aptitudes and inclination, is construed by some as sanctioning a wide diversity of upper-secondary schools and courses.

Between the various *Länder* and cities at present there is a miscellany of school types. Some *Länder* acknowledging the need for "comprehensiveness" in the long-term future nevertheless regard such a possibility as dependent upon a varied "multilateral" system ("additive", as the Germans say) rather than on a really integrated comprehensive *Gesamtschule*. They therefore propose to exploit or even expand provision for all types of people and interests in the present variety of upper-secondary schools (for example the many types of "trade" or practical *Gymnasium*, together with the *Fachoberschule* or technical upper-secondary school). That could be a "first step" towards essential integration. In complete contrast, some *Länder* have established really integrated comprehensive schools, while elsewhere there may be an integrated *Kolleg* serving the entire upper-secondary range.

Bildungsbericht '70 — The main points

The main points were as follows:

Kindergarten or pre-school education to be provided for all three- and four-year-old children.

Compulsory school attendance to begin at the age of 5, instead of 6 as at present, with new programmes and teacher-preparation to match.

Compulsory education to last for 10 years, instead of 9 years of full-time school as at present.

Reorganisation of the structure and curriculum of 4-year primary schools *(Primarstufe)*.

A two-year Orientation level *(Orientierungsstufe)* will occupy the fifth and sixth classes, before the beginning of secondary education proper at the age of 12.

Secondary Stage I *(Sekundarstufe I)* will last for 4 years (12-16) and be available to *all* pupils, with a more or less common curriculum subject to minimal variations. It will lead to a first school certificate *(Abitur I)*, available to every pupil of Secondary Stage I on successful conclusion of the basic educational phase, and will give access to later studies of a general or vocationally-linked type in the next secondary stage.

Sekundarstufe II will continue education in far greater variety until *Abitur* II by means of a widespread range of courses, with (it is hoped) increasing integration of non-vocational and vocational education. *Abitur* II is expected to be achieved after two years − i.e. at age 18, instead of 19 for the present *Abitur*.

Both the *Bildungsrat* (concerned with schools) and the *Wissenschaftsrat* ⌉ *defn's* (the Science Council concerned with higher education and research) agreed ⌋ on the need for much broader access to higher education in increased variety, and an ever-stronger link between academic learning, practical training, and research and development programmes. This intention is simply stated; but some difficulties in the way of its achievement are clear because of previously mentioned demarcation lines between courses and certificates which still lead to quite distinct careers, and also because the different levels of teacher and teacher-preparation have been so sharply marked off from each other.

Likewise, the various schools and courses have been strongly linked not only with particular social classes, but sometimes also with industrial or commercial concerns such as factories or banks for the implementation of part of the school's programme. Any breaking down of barriers between institutions and studies must also take account of the fact that "academic" lessons have traditionally been on a morning-only basis, followed by diligent homework in the afternoon, whereas other types of course (especially vocational) have been part-time, characterised by the aura of old-fashioned apprenticeship.

Some misgivings

The new proposal for *Abitur* I will recall for many the somewhat inferior connotation of the *mittlere Reife* at present. That certificate is obtained at the end of the *Realschule* course. It is largely preliminary to employment or to some sort of sandwich programme of education and in-service training. More recently, this certificate has come within the reach of students of the *Hauptschulen*, now that a ninth or even a tenth year has been instituted in several *Länder*. The newly proposed *Abitur* I will seem to many to approximate to the *mittlere Reife* rather than to the "noble" studies associated traditionally with the *Gymnasium*. Nevertheless, it is expected that plans will go ahead strongly and that by 1980 about half of the entire age-group (having obtained *Abitur* I), will be attending full-time the two years of Secondary Stage II and so within reach of *Abitur II*.

In some city-states like Hamburg, with a compact population and a tradition of educational and commercial enterprise, the progress of reform seems more likely. It is relatively easier there to ensure co-operation between (for example) neighbouring *Berufsschulen* and other centres of practical education and training, or between these and new types of upper-secondary school. Progress will probably be much slower in rural areas, in those with strongly conservative governments, or under pressure from parental conservatism. That remains a strong influence in Germany.

It cannot be taken for granted that even young German men (not to speak of young women) readily assert themselves against parental and magisterial domination. In the upper-middle classes traditionally associated with extended studies, conformity in public and in scholastic choice imposed by parents has been a socio-economic necessity. Authority still counts for a great deal in Germany, not least the father's authority. Within schools, continuous assessment by homework and classwork marks throughout the year (rather than occasional written examinations) has added up to a rather strict system of control. In the concluding appraisals of the *Abitur* (which is an internally administered examination) this makes a big difference to prospects of admission to higher education or desirable jobs.

There are still structural and assessment controls at work which the outsider might not appreciate. For example, students with a leaving-certificate from some of the more "applied" upper-secondary institutions such as a *Wirtschaftsgymnasium* (commercial grammar school) have found it difficult to get admission to the more coveted faculties of the university not only because of the curricular content of a *Wirtschaftsgymnasium*, or because of queries about the quality of the "internal" *Abitur*, but because that school is suspect since it admits pupils from a *Realschule*. That perhaps explains why greater "freedom" in experimental or comprehensive schools has caused anxiety even among the students, because of the uncertain standing of alternative courses or "sets". In a few cases the students themselves have expressed a wish for more "drill" in the familiar type of school subjects. Of course, the general shortage of specialist teachers in Germany may have something to do with this. A number of German education authorities have actually advertised on a large scale for foreign teachers of ordinary school subjects.

Problems of teacher supply and competence

There has long been a shortage of fully qualified teachers in West German *Gymnasien*, and the prospect is not comfortable despite some return of popularity to the teaching career in 1972 and 1973. The past decade had shown an increasing shortage. In 1963 the lowest shortage was 8.1% in Schleswig-Holstein and the highest 30.4% in Niedersachsen — for *Gymnasium* teachers alone. For 1970-1971 the estimated deficit for West Germany as a whole was 21.8% in *Gymnasien* or equivalent institutions, although the ratio of pupils to teachers has been slowly mounting.

The teacher shortage has not been anything like as severe in the *Realschulen*; but, despite recently improving facilities for teachers of every kind to take higher education courses which will qualify them for higher levels of teaching, a real shortage may be expected before long when practically the entire age-group will stay on until at least the equivalent level to the *Realschule* in the new *Sekundarstufe I*, at the same time as the curriculum is increasingly diversified and also intensified to reach a reputable level in the new *Abitur* I.

In these circumstances it is not surprising that in-service teacher education has concentrated somewhat on upgrading subject-matter. Some of the *Länder* and city states have for some time had special opportunities for teachers to improve their qualifications and competence in particular subject matter. These institutes or workshops are to be found especially in such educational power houses as Hamburg, Bremen, Berlin and Hessen. Teachers' subject-associations also help with publications and conferences. It seems very likely, both from German experience and from the example from other countries, that the new reforms will stimulate widespread experiments for the improvement of teachers' capacity for service in the new types of *Gymnasium*; that is, in both of the new Secondary Stages I and II.

Politics and educational attitudes

While most of the in-service provision for teachers has concentrated on academic knowledge and professional competence, in Germany there has always lurked in the background some concern for questions of civic understanding and "democratic" relationships. Over and above any influence which memories of the pre-war period might have, a change-over from rigid authoritarianism and a tightly academic school system to a more relaxed one would necessitate some alteration in teaching-learning relationships.

Ordinary inter-union rivalries over such matters as teacher status, salaries, and working conditions traditionally linked with teaching particular subjects in particular places, may in Germany be additionally invested with socio-political overtones. Moreover in a country as provincially loyal as Germany still is, and so divided by religious traditions, questions of curricular preference and attitudes sometimes tend to be linked with fidelity to a particular church or with questions of secularism.

The separate existence of the German Democratic Republic, with its Communist ideology and somewhat ostentatious development of universal basic education and new forms of secondary school organisation and curriculum, can never be far away from discussions of the secondary school system of the Federal Republic of Germany. The signing of a treaty between the two Germanies and the developing *détente* seem bound to raise questions of comparison.

The near-comprehensive *Kolleg*, now to be found in a number of *Länder* for the upper-secondary age-range, has already come close to demonstrating that there can be many paths to higher education, that many kinds of competence require intellectual ability and perseverance, and that the teacher of the future must be assessed by criteria other than those which in the past tended to identify him with a university-style *Wissenschaftler* (academician or "scientist"). Furthermore, the more manifold kinds of "applied" upper-secondary school curriculum in Germany encourage local diversification in future – in rather marked contrast to the strict regulations of France.

One main problem is having enough teachers sufficiently self-directing and basically competent to ensure growth for the future, unless a well-sustained service of in-service education and updating can be provided.

New proportions for new plans

Germans themselves have already begun to say that the Federal reform plans mean the twilight of *Land* responsibility. In June 1970 a *Bund-Länder Kommission* for educational planning was given the task of preparing a long-term skeleton plan for developing the educational system, and intermediate structural plans for organising schools which would facilitate the development of educational policy. Late in 1971 the Commission produced an interim report on the "overall educational plan". This was finalised in June 1973 and later published as a *Bildungsgesamtplan* already agreed in principle by the Federal Chancellor and the heads of *Land* governments; but all Germans recognise that it may be one or two decades before proposed reforms are widely and effectively implemented.

With particular regard to the 16-20 age-group the Commission envisaged the following developments:

(i)   reduction of the numbers of pupils in part-time vocational schools from 57% of the age-group in 1970 to 39% or 37% in 1985;

(ii) a corresponding increase in the proportion of the age-group at *full*-time schools leading to vocational qualifications from 15% in 1970 to 21% in 1985;

(iii) increase in the percentage of students proceeding to the *Abitur* II with the intention of entering higher education from 14% in 1970 to 20% or 22% of the age-group in 1985;

(iv) an increase in the number of those in "non-academic" or vocational courses (the "dual system" at present, but in future with the possibility of access to higher education) from 4% of the age-group in 1970 to 14% or 15% of the age-group in 1985.

To facilitate this growth, financial assistance for students over 16 is proposed at some future date. A "Federal Education Act" came into force on August 27th, 1971, to cover the whole field of general and vocational upper-secondary school for this purpose.

Obviously, the various *Länder* of the Federal Republic of Germany are now watching each others' experiments with the *Sekundarstufe II* with profound interest. It is hard to assess what forms of upper-secondary school seem likely to secure the most general adoption. The recommendation of the KMK to the

Ministers of Education in the *Länder* in 1969 that they should begin to experiment with comprehensive schools has met with some success. The initial figure recommended was 30 or 40; but in 1972 an official report to the Council of Europe from the Federal Republic of Germany mentioned that 113 school experiments of this type were already under way, and that 8 of those included the upper-secondary stage (classes 11-13).

Some indication of trends in enrolments during the 1960s is given by the following table:

Educational establishments for 16-19 year old pupils
(*Sekundarstufe* II)

Enrolments

	1961	1969	Increase Decrease 1961-69
Berufsschule (part-time within the "Dual system")	1,638,671	1,635,864	− 0.2%
Berufsaufbauschule (part-time or full-time vocational extension school, beyond *Berufsschule*)	42,298	48,489	+14.6%
Fachoberschule [1] (Technical *upper*-secondary school, after *mittlere Reife*)		21,903	%
Berufsfachschule (Full-time vocational school, at lower-secondary level, after 14)	128,805	195,725	+52.0%
Fachschule (Technical school or institute − usually after age 19)	98,936	103,722	+ 4.8%
Gymnasium grades 11-13 (nominally ages 16-19)	207,814	296,708	+42.8%
Total	2,116,524	2,302,411	+ 8.8%

[1] Set up since 1961

Source: Ministries of Education and Culture; Federal Statistical Office, reported to Council of Europe, 1972.

CHAPTER 7

STRUCTURE AND POLICY IN ITALY

Introduction

A little information has already been given about the Italian "middle school" (*scuola media*). Apart from Sweden, this example of a combined middle school is really the sole instance in Western Europe of a comprehensive school applicable to all children in the lower-secondary age-range. That alone is rather surprising. Yet Italy in several other ways can be an educationally surprising country.

Within the upper-secondary range surveyed in this present Report Italy has had a long-standing tradition of very systematic instruction-and-training leading to diplomas and certificates in the technical and vocational fields. To those remembering the immense prestige of the classical tradition in Italy, and the traditional respect for the written and spoken word as well as the fine arts, some of the more down-to-earth kinds of educational provision available in Italy come as rather a surprise. They should not really do so in a country which has maintained the ancient Roman emphasis on huge buildings, fine roads, and skilful land use. Nor can anyone forget the science of Bruno, Galileo, Leonardo, Volta, Marconi and Fermi.

Evidence of all the arts, sciences, and humanities of the ancient world, of the Renaissance, and of post-Risorgimento modernisation, surrounds every Italian as he reappraises education today in terms of fitness for life. There are also clearly parts of Italy where re-gearing for modern industries is proceeding apace. There are abundant signs of wealth and sophistication on a scale comparable with that of the most prosperous developed countries. Much of the socio-economic change that has reduced the agricultural population from about 60% of the working force immediately after the first World War to under 25% at the beginning of the 1960s, and has also brought about huge internal migration and an altered life-style, is still relatively recent. Nevertheless it has transformed

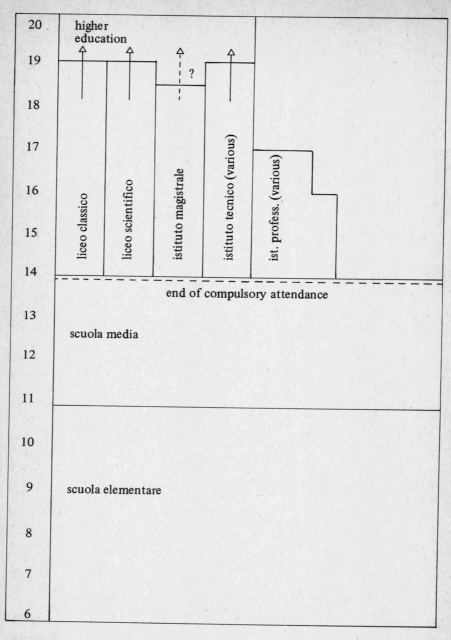

ITALY: Simplified diagram of school structure. (Ages are nominal)

the expectations of that fast-growing population in schools and higher education. By contrast, the universities are deeply conscious of their mediaeval and Renaissance roots; the schools which lead to them (or perhaps to modern industry) are still shaped by a legal framework dating back nearly 50 years to the rise of Fascism. Any alternatives that may be considered are generally evaluated in terms of either the Roman Catholic Church's authoritarian conservatism or else the theoretical radicalism of the extreme left wing. (The Communist Party in Italy has the largest percentage of membership outside Eastern Europe).

Stalemate and paradox

In the circumstances it is hard to look for educational reforms of a gradual and empirically justified kind. An endless succession of Ministries has proposed one reform after another in education, only to have them all rejected or neglected though interminably discussed — except for the *scuola media* (1963) and a few similar innovations. Despite all the plans and indeed an ever-mounting enrolment of pupils (10,500,000 in 1972-3, representing a full one-third increase in the middle school and a doubling of enrolments in upper-secondary schools within less than six years) — a new Minister of Education in 1972 might well exclaim: "There is dust everywhere in the Ministry". So little has changed for so long. Every new proposal leads to a filibuster in parliament.

Yet the Italians constantly talk about education, and are keenly interested in it for itself as well as for political reasons. Some of the comments received in reply to the questionnaires in Italy reflect this characteristic more clearly than replies from most other countries. From the point of view of typology, furthermore, Italy provides the researcher with perhaps the clearest example of a "Latin model". As a matter of history it has been the French system that has served as the "Latin model" of schooling in many parts of the world — reaching far beyond the "Latin" tradition into the Arab world, the Russian empire, and even into Japan. However, recent reforms in France and French independence itself have together made France's educational ventures more uniquely Gallic than traditionally Latin, even though both France and Italy and many other countries throughout the world have been joint inheritors of the traditions of imperial Rome, the Roman Catholic Church, and the Renaissance which gave new life to these legacies.

This is the conceptual world in which older people — especially teachers — live in Italy. That is all the more true because the schools and the universities following them have long had a monopoly of access to the ruling and professional careers in Italy as in nearly all similar countries. However, the rise of prosperity through other channels, and the impact of new economic and educational examples from abroad, have introduced challenges which the older people find almost unthinkable.

It was in Italy on January 1st, 1958, that the European Economic Community first came into operation as the result of the Treaty of Rome. Businessmen, consumers, taxpayers and most young people in Italy are specially aware of being members of an economic community which already numbered 170 milllion people before the accession of three new member States in 1973. Italy's precarious economy and internal problems ensure that. The emigration (and sometimes the return) of Italian workers, and the internal migrations too, have unsettled previous assumptions, especially that persistent regionalism which reminds us how recently the country came to nationhood.

These remarks so far refer to Italy generally. Inside the country there are marked discrepancies in the success or indeed the availability of education between North, Central, and Southern Italy. There are also social inequalities on a marked scale, as well as between the sexes, and also between the various types of upper-secondary education with which the present survey is mostly concerned. In fact, across the wide range of upper-secondary institutions it is sometimes hard to remember that what is observed is all officially part of the upper-secondary school. The tokens of privilege and the stigmata of poverty or lower achievements are still very marked, even though all the institutions' leaving certificates after a 5-year course beyond the middle school now give access to the university, where enrolments mount uncontrollably. (Higher education enrolments rose from 261,358 in 1965 to 474,727 in 1970 and have continued to increase — to approximately 900,000 in 1972-3! That means almost a doubling since 1970, and trebling in six years.

Italy has the highest rate of youth unemployment in the Common Market, even though the Ministry of Labour recently calculated that more than half a million children of compulsory school age (under 14) were illegally employed. Such children work long hours for a pittance — impairing their own scholastic prospects — while older, qualified students find it hard to get a job. Despite all the progress, the official Italian statement for the O.E.C.D. examiners reviewing national policies for education in Italy in 1969 frankly admitted that: "Numberless inequalities persist in Italian society". These are some of the paradoxes surrounding education at the upper-secondary level in Italy, nominally between the ages of about 14 and 19, though often extending well beyond that upper age-limit.

Organisation of the school system

The present school structure, apart from the *scuola media* (introduced in 1963), is based upon laws passed long before. Previously, in the period after the second World War, the pattern had been as follows:

> 5 years' compulsory primary school for children between the ages of 6 to 11, followed (in principle) by one of the following alternatives:
>
> an academically oriented "middle school" then monopolised by socially favoured or unusually bright young people intended for an academic career or the professions;
>
> a firmly vocational training school (from the age of 11);
>
> an art school;
>
> an upper-primary school.

The upper-elementary school was really the lot of most children if, indeed, they actually stayed until the required age of 14 instead of going out to work or helping with the parental occupation. Statutory compulsion was not insisted upon. Class-repeating in any case meant that even 14-year-olds might not complete the work of the basic five classes.

The law of 31st December 1962 combined the different streams after the age of 11 in a common 3-year middle school. Yet towards the end of the same decade the official Italian report to O.E.C.D. said: "The unitary middle school scheme (up to age 14) will continue to require great efforts over a number of years before it can be regarded as being accomplished", even though that same middle school had already been introduced experimentally in a number of places some time before 1962. Middle schools can, where necessary, now be set up in communities with fewer than 3,000 inhabitants — the nominal minimum; but there are many towns and villages in Italy where even that concession must be hard to apply.

Though the new middle school was intended as a general opportunity for personal growth for everyone, it has also been frequently described as a period of observation or orientation towards different careers. In the circumstances, optional instruction in Latin from the second year onwards, and varied rates of progress through the school (influenced by parental background), introduce clear elements of selectiveness. The real importance of the middle school for many people lies in the fact that success in an examination at its conclusion is essential for admission to upper-secondary education's varied institutions and courses.

Upper-secondary education: general schools

Traditionally "liberal" education is available in the *liceo classico* (5 years), the *liceo scientifico* (5 years), and the *istituto magistrale* or teacher-training college (4 years).

For many years, boys and girls obtaining the leaving-certificate of the classical *liceo* have had the right to enter any faculty of the university. Those with a similar certificate from the *liceo scientifico* were long restricted in university access, being debarred from the literature and philosophy faculties of the university because they have no Latin. At the end of the 4-year *istituto magistrale* course students are allowed to enter the *facoltà di magistero* (educational studies) but can be admitted to other faculties only after taking a further one-year course (5 years in all).

It is worth while to consider striking differences between these officially parallel upper-secondary schools. Ostensibly most of them begin with a two-year general course (linked with their field of specialisation), and then take students for another 3 years towards a maturity examination (*maturità*) about the age of 19. But in fact, both general schools and specialised or technical schools are arranged in a recognisable order of esteem and attainment. Compared with any other upper-secondary general school or even a vocational institute of one of the types soon to be described, almost every *istituto magistrale* looks particularly down-at-heel. The students often seem to be of lower intelligence — let alone attainment — and more poorly dressed. In one large *istituto magistrale* visited, the entire student body consisted of girls, except for one young man. Principals of *istituti magistrali* interviewed or replying to questionnaires described their students as coming from the families of craft workers, small shopkeepers and minor business men, with a fair sprinkling from families where the parents were in domestic service or some poorly paid Civil Service job, as on the railways. In several replies the *istituto magistrale* was referred to as an "escape hatch" (scappatoio) towards the university. Such students do not take it seriously as a teacher-training school, but rather think of it as a poor man's upper-secondary school, near the bottom of the hierarchy. That fact illustrates Italian upper-secondary education's preoccupation with the university; but it also bodes ill for the pupils whom those students may soon have to teach.

Although the primary purpose of the *istituto magistrale* is to train people directly for the teaching profession, it assuredly does not, as the Italian spokesmen in the O.E.C.D. book on Italy explain. It gives a mainly academic and theoretical course, and simply entitles its successful certificate-holders to compete in the competition (*concorso*) for "qualified status" (*abilitazione*); in virtue of that they can further compete for whatever appointments may be available. Far more appointments should be made, to satisfy the schools' needs; and many primary and middle school teachers are out of work. But questions of teacher supply must come later. At the moment the important thing is to illustrate the disparate levels of general-education upper-secondary schools. The *liceo classico* is paramount; the *liceo scientifico* (modern) comes next; whether the commercial and vocational institutes take precedence over the *istituto magistrale* or not can be argued, though many would maintain that they do.

It will be observed in passing that Italy still follows the ancient European tradition of preparing all primary and most lower-secondary school teachers in an establishment which itself falls within the secondary (and not the higher) range of studies. Any upward change in status for the *istituto magistrale* is "in the remote future" as far as practical plans are concerned, though there has been talk of following the French example (since 1970) of transferring all teacher-preparation to the post-secondary phase (where it already is in the other countries surveyed in this Report).

Upper-secondary education: Technical Institutes

In Italy the technical institutes have a long-established reputation. Though teaching and learning conditions in them are often austere, to say the least, these establishments are highly prized because they endow the successful student with qualified status as a craftsman (*perito*) after a 5-year course, consisting of a basic 2 years of extended general education in a vocational perspective, and a further 3 years with a markedly technical or vocational slant.

The present 5-year length was established in 1961 when the curricula were re-defined; but technical education as a whole is still governed by a law of 1931, with probably inadequate response to the changing technical and social demands of today. Thirty-four per cent of the successful candidates in the *scuola media* leaving-certificate examination enrol in an *istituto tecnico* of some sort. There are 7 basic types of technical institute, such as *istituto tecnico industriale* and *istituto tecnico commerciale*; and these in turn are divided into many specialised branches. The industrial sector alone for example has 29 specialised branches.

When a student seeks admission to any technical institute he knows he is choosing, or being chosen for, a particular narrowly defined *course* or series of courses within it, from which there is no possibility of transfer within the institute, or any possibility of combining or adding subjects. This point is emphasised in many answers to the questionnaires.

Recent alterations in the regulations governing access to universities have made it possible for students from any kind of technical institute to enter any faculty in the university. Therefore in recent years this upper-secondary complex of narrow avenues to the sub-professions is also used as an access to the more general kinds of higher education. For those students the *istituto tecnico* is clearly a second-best.

The main clientèle of the technical institutes, however, is that large number of determined medium-level technical or administrative aspirants whose ambitions are clearly vocational. Indeed, some of these have returned to education after a period in paid employment, while others are actually so employed in the early morning or afternoon of the same days on which they are attending the technical institute. Some of them refer to the strain which this imposes. Far more hanker for a system of "full time education" (*a tempo pieno*) in which all their energies could be devoted to study.

Neither the students nor their teachers seem to recognise that the 30-hour week already spent in school would qualify them for "full-time" status by international criteria, perhaps because they are all too conscious of the inroads made on their time and faculties by being in paid employment while they study. (It is relevant to mention here that shops, offices, and many other types of enterprise in Italy close during the early afternoon hours, employing the same or perhaps a different staff when they re-open at 4 or 5 o'clock in the afternoon). Though the official age-range of the technical institutes is obviously from 14 to 19 (if there has been no delay on the way), a number of respondents gave their ages as well over 20 even in rather favoured institutions for surveyors, accountants and the like, and identified themselves as being in the half-worker/half-student category just described.

Clearly, by international comparison, the *istituto tecnico* in Italy roughly corresponds to a great deal of what would be called "further education" in Britain or "higher education" in the U.S.A., Japan, and the Dominions of the British Commonwealth; but in Italy and many parts of Europe generally these institutions are locally reckoned as part of the *upper-secondary* system — in esteem, in the student body enrolled, and in the level of competence of the teachers who serve them. Two types of argument therefore surround them, the first one influenced by foreign example, and the second by native considerations.

Critics sensitive to international trends and example often doubt the wisdom of preparing students so specifically for any occupation at a time of enormous change. They sometimes say that if specific preparation is to be given it should be "short and sharp" for the job but open to renewal and change later. In actual Italian circumstances, it is often surcharged with obsolescent detail and "dignity-conferring" subjects over a full 5-year length.

Italians thus differ markedly from outside critics on this point, since instead of thinking only of technical adequacy they often pay more regard to considerations of university access and "educated" status. In many recent reform proposals, therefore, they have recommended enlargement of the "general" curriculum content at the expense of "applied" elements. (In Italy, enlarging the "general" element would almost certainly mean more *instruction* of a theoretical or literary kind).

Upper-secondary education: Vocational Institutes

Vocational institutes (*istituti professionali*) were first instituted on an experimental basis in 1950, to provide a 3-year course in 112 specialised branches of study, each awarding a vocational diploma. (In agriculture, the courses last for 2 years). As with the technical institutes, the courses are indeed highly specialised. For example, girls may be trained as fashion models, seamstresses, or theatrical designers, while boys may prepare for the hotel trade, commerce and industry, or for the merchant navy. Though the vocational institutes are state-controlled, they sometimes have strong support from local employers and comunities. Thus they have enjoyed more liberty in introducing new courses or modifying old ones than other educational establishments. Nearly all the funds have been provided by the Ministry of Education, though subventions for specific purposes from the communal authorities have introduced a slight possibility of variation.

From 1969, however, on an experimental basis, a system of vocational training lasting for five years was introduced, again giving access to the university like all the other upper-secondary courses.

This last move was in direct opposition to the recommendations of the O.E.C.D. examiners on Italy as reported in the policy document of 1969. These examiners also observed that the 3-year vocational institutes were already in competition with *one*-year courses, followed by a one-year probationary "apprenticeship", which were available under the aegis of the Ministry of Labour. These appealed greatly to boys eager to qualify quickly, and especially to the rather large percentage who drop out from technical institute courses because they find the theoretical content overloaded or remote from present requirements.

Upper-secondary education: prospects of re-organisation

It is generally agreed that modern employment and indeed social and private life require a high *general* level of education and a postponement of vocational restrictiveness. On the other hand enlargement of intake from "less studious" homes, and the inclusion of many young men and women with a strong sense of vocational urgency, have brought into question the protracted perspective of "general education" which administrators and teachers like to insist upon. In Italian circumstances debates on this dilemma often founder in arguments about the meaning of "culture" and "humanity", while the evidence of research and development studies elsewhere goes unheeded. Indeed, many plans actually drafted for reforms in the upper-secondary levels of education have much to recommend them if only they were feasible in Italian circumstances, as by common agreement they are not. Nevertheless, it is worth reviewing some of them here because these arguments are part of the daily discourse in and around the schools. They are therefore reflected in answers to the questionnaires and interviews.

Many responsible Italians believe that in the interests of educational adequacy and social justice all upper-secondary education (after the middle school) should be based upon a 2-year general course (*biennio*), followed by a further 3-year course of more specialised study and/or training. This was the position taken in the recent reform proposals of Misasi and Biasini, and actually approved in principle by the Council of Ministers on 31st March, 1973. It goes without saying that the present right of admissibility to higher education would be attached to every kind of maturity certificate awarded at the end of a total 5-year course. In Italy this means admissibility to *any* faculty, in principle though not in practice.

Universities have been swamped in recent years. For example, the University of Rome has maximum accommodation for about 25,000 students; but about 100,000 are enrolled. In a recent university year (1972-1973) more than 1,000 modern history students were in the care of one teacher, without assistance, at the University of Turin; and two professors who helped to arrange the current research have comparable numbers, though with some assistance to mark the students' work.

For more than two decades now attempts to find a policy for the universities have focused on two alternatives: either to impose a *numerus clausus* officially (as the Minister of Education proposed in 1972) or to diversify faculty structure while providing an adequate supply of university teachers in all fields of specialisation. Talk of a *numerus clausus* creates a furore, since the widely canvassed "right to study" really means "the right to become a student" – a matter of status rather than learning. Moreover the Bank of Italy recently estimated that 6 out of 7 university places are already occupied by students from professional, business, or white collar backgrounds; and it is believed that well-intentioned, rational selection would actually aggravate social selectivity.

As in the case of Germany it is important here to consider the hierarchical structure of university teaching and its effect upon the schools. A permanently appointed professor needs to lecture only for a few hours each week (in some cases for only one term in the year) and to examine students in their thousands with the help of assistants. Such an examination may represent as little as a quarter of an hour's contact, though the assistants will have examined beforehand many thousands of pages of dissertation. The assistants almost always begin as unpaid workers, being allowed to give a few lectures or perhaps a course, but also undertaking a variety of quasi-clerical or administrative chores in the hope of one day being put officially on the list (*di ruolo*) and at a later stage being actually paid. Some of the more distinguished professors have 20 or even 30 "vassals" of this kind. Many of them are teachers in various kinds of secondary school, but still frequent the university in the hope of recognition. (In many continental countries the "habilitation" qualifying a teacher for a post as a specialist in a secondary school also gives the right to teach in a university faculty if a post is available).

The large-scale university reforms proposed for Italy during the early 1970s would have altered the structure of university institutes and faculties, reorganised the teaching, and granted tenure to those who actually taught the courses; but in 1972 the proposed reforms were abandoned by the newly elected government. With the preponderance of professors on any reform commission, and the academic loyalties of any non-professorial members, the prospects of reform would be slim in any case. On the one hand, fully established professors have an average age of around 60. On the other, many of those most eagerly seeking to reform the university are known to be of the Left, which does not do much good to the prospects of agreed reform.

The implications of these all-pervading sensibilities make an immediate impact in the upper-secondary school, especially in a country where many of the teachers have their eyes on the possibility of a university post in due course. One of the consequences has been insistence on making all courses more "scientific" (i.e. academic or theoretical, since the continental languages usually do not distinguish between practice-oriented "science" and the "liberal" or cultural "sciences"). The amount and type of theoretical content in an upper-secondary course must therefore seem respectable in the local idiom.

To take things one stage further – just as all university degrees must be equally respectable in principle, so must all the alternative institutions and courses at the upper-secondary level. The argument is not really about education, but about social structure and career prospects in Italy. No matter how devious the route, that is where the argument finally rests. It was pointed out to the researchers that a *laurea* (degree) is always a *laurea* – that is; even from the *facoltà di magistero,* and even if it results in unemployment anyway.

In the circumstances it is not surprising that such a high proportion of those who obtain the school-leaving certificate register in university courses. Some 70% so registered in recent years, even though about half the students enrolled in the most popular faculties never obtain a degree, and about half of those who eventually do so will on present showing take two or three years longer than the official four-year period in order to graduate. It is this social demand for student status which the Biasini Report of 1971 and the Andreotti-Scalfaro proposals approved by the Council of Ministers in 1973 really had in mind. Likewise the discussion on whether the proposed "unitary" *biennio* should be followed by a multilateral upper-secondary school (*pluricomprensiva*) or a unitary upper system (*onnicomprensiva*), whenever circumstances permit, is conceded by Italian observers to be really about politics rather than about content and methods of learning.

Sociological and educational evidence from Italy in the present Report should be interpreted in the light of these considerations, which shape the priorities of the over-16s in school. It is not surprising that university enrolments are still rapidly expanding. They rose from 4% of the 19-22 age-group in 1952 to some 15% in 1970, and expansion continues. Over 7,000 of some 16,000 students at the University of Turin were *new* enrolments, on a more recent showing; and in Milan new enrolments were over 5,800 out of a total of nearly 15,500. Making allowance for dropouts, the pressure is clearly mounting.

The structure of the teaching profession

Some 70% of Italian teachers are women, the majority in primary schools, but with a substantial proportion also in the *scuola media*. The proportion of women is higher in North and Central Italy, and in urban centres generally, than it is in the South and in the countryside. Feminisation is proceeding apace. In Italian circumstances this means that teaching is often a wife's job, while the husband works somewhere else. That economic point has repercussions in every kind of school — not only the *scuola elementare* or the *scuola media*. Teacher supply and competence affect every student's access to an upper-secondary school.

Rules and regulations minutely lay down numbers and precise obligations for any permanent appointments. ("Italy is a country of categories"). It is well-nigh impossible to transfer a teacher from one school or even one subject-commitment to another. If a teacher is ill, or is suddenly removed elsewhere because of her husband's change of employment, a class may be left teacherless for some time. Therefore many schools start the academic year in October without a full complement of teachers, most of them being on "supply" (*supplenza*) or in other ways provisionally engaged.

The Italian report to O.E.C.D. (prepared before 1967) admitted officially that over 100,000 persons possessing teaching certificates from the *istituto magistrale* were not teaching. Yet there were not enough teachers — partly because there were not enough posts, partly because of inflexible arrangements. A Bill increasing teachers' pay but at the same time re-defining their highly specific legal status in 1972 brought about a series of strikes. Primary school teachers earn about the same as a typist, which is discouraging enough; but one of the gravest causes of discontent was the huge unemployment of teachers and their temporary status. Even so, official figures show that well over half of the teachers in primary, middle, and some kinds of secondary school are officially "not qualified" — a phrase often meaning that they have certificates from an *istituto magistrale* and perhaps a university degree, but are not formally "qualified" within the statutory definition of the *abilitazione* required.

It is common to be told by a teacher in a school that he or she is "really a chemist" or an unemployed member of some other profession, or a student completing his course. In 1973 at least 70% of Italian teachers were employed on a casual — not even an officially "temporary" — basis (*incarico a tempo indeterminato*). They have thus no hope of career prospects or real salary increases. A really permanent appointment depends upon success in a competitive examination for a particular position, and must each be approved in Rome. In 1972, 225,000 candidates therefore competed in the state qualifying-examination; 40,000 passed as worthy of appointment, yet there were only 14,000 jobs actually available.

Obviously the mischances of the supply-and-demand position in the teaching profession affect prospects of students in middle schools on which access to upper-secondary school depends. It is, however, astonishing to find that as many as 48% of teachers in *upper*-secondary schools in the South and even 38% in such schools in the North-West are *non abilitati*. The percentage of "unqualified" teachers is higher in the *general* forms of upper-secondary education (such as the *licei* and *istituti magistrali*) than in technical and vocational institutes.

The structure of teacher-preparation introduces further problems in the upper-secondary school. The university gives secondary school teachers a general education but no training in educational theory and practice, except by voluntary attendance at particular courses in some places. Undoubtedly a number of university professors and some departments take it upon themselves to include such courses under the general provision of the faculties of Philosophy or Letters.

Until the end of 1972 no courses were officially approved or organised by the Ministry for secondary school teachers except special, occasional courses to prepare "temporary" teachers to compete for *abilitazione*. Paradoxically, in consequence of that 1972 reform in regulations, the 1972-73 academic year began with not a single state secondary school teacher in the country having the professional training which, according to the state's own definition, qualified him to teach. In fact, apart from some degrees awarded by the *facoltà di magistero* there was no secondary-school teacher training, apart from a few spasmodic and theoretical short conferences or courses arranged by a variety of bodies. Such courses were often of a hortative kind rather than practical.

It is not as though examples of a very impressive kind did not exist in Italy. The city of Milan and a voluntary agency have co-operated, for example, to run a very well equipped and efficient residential centre for the in-service training of teachers called OPPI (*Organizzazione per la preparazione professionale degli insegnanti*). A number of university teachers also, often of rather left-wing sympathies, are keenly committed to the modernisation of teaching methods and perspectives in the light of internationally available information; but they fight an uphill battle.

From the questionnaires: further points on structure and access

Within the samples surveyed, the principals of a *liceo classico* and a *liceo scientifico* indicated that it was usual for 95% of both the boys and girls leaving the school to enter a university faculty. The principals of *istituti tecnici* usually emphasised that their students could enter any faculty of the university, although those who left the more successful institutions with (for example) a surveyor's qualification (*diploma di geometra*) or one in accountancy (*ragioneria*) preferred to take a good chance of immediate employment in commerce or industry. That appeared to be particularly the case in institutions emphasising their close links with surrounding industries, which not merely took an interest in their work and advised students but sometimes provided additional facilities for visits, lectures and the like.

Financial anxiety at the university has in recent years been alleviated somewhat by the provision of a small award at the university for students who attain a final mark of more than 42 out of 60 marks in the *maturità* examination. That does not seem a very severe criterion when it is observed that 36 marks out of 60 are required as a condition of admissibility to university faculties. Most students except the well-to-do earn their way in paid employment. That is a major reason for dropouts and delayed graduation.

A comparative note

It would be a mistake to suppose that Italy's educational dilemma over the 16-plus group is either a unique problem situation or "just typical" of a particular kind of country. Indeed, it is both in some measure, as all critical decisions are; and that illustrates the two main planes of any comparative study — a horizontal examination of recurrent problems, and a study in depth within a particular context but with the application of international insights and experience. It is at the critical point where the two planes meet that the decisions must be made. Decisions about the 16 — 20 group are of peculiar significance in Italy.

The words "problem situation" were used above — not to cast aspersions but to recognise that all areas of decision start as states of confusion. In Italy, the evidence is particularly clear: contrasts of scholarship and procrastination; contrasting claims of deep classical learning, aesthetic sensibility, craftsmanship, technological enterprise, and commercial flair. Italy is particularly rich in these — but simultaneously and paradoxically in the idioms of the three different technological and educational stages described earlier. Internal self-contradictions show up nowhere more clearly than at the point of decision where the 16 — 20 student population finds itself. Perceptions of priority and long-term policy in that age-range seem in Italy to be obstinately inseparable from value-constructs implicit in the present social structure or in expected patterns of political and technological development.

Yet that situation could be full of hope — and not only for Italians. Many problems are so deep-seated that core decisions must be taken. The Italians themselves recognise in several recent reports where — for them — the pivotal point is: it is in the upper-secondary school and its links with later work or studies. Local entanglements or political manoeuvres have never obscured that point. Long traditions of training skill and developing learning in and around the school have left keen enthusiasm for the essence and the rewards of learning; but that zest is frustrated in an educational system which is the least modernised of Italy's industries. Doubtless the crisis of policy will come soon; and it will almost certainly be in the upper-secondary/lower-tertiary range on which so many Italian debates have recently focussed, in ever closer relationship to international examination of the same theme.

In almost all countries of the "Latin" tradition some or most of the characteristics observed in Italy are repeated, though never of course in quite the same constellation of social phenomena and politics. Public institutions are often strikingly similar in their formal aspects; and among the most similar are schools and their hierarchies. In other "Latin" countries such institutions are undergoing rapid change to serve new policies and, by experience, to engender them. Educators find it easier to reform institutions than ideas; but new ideas then have a chance to grow. The newness of the 16 — 20 student body — in size and outlook — brings countries of every background to a new reckoning of institutions and policy, a crisis of conscience. The intense turmoil of Italian decision at this point is of wide international relevance.

CHAPTER 8

STRUCTURE AND POLICY IN SWEDEN

Introduction

Sweden has aroused immense interest for many reasons. Among the most obvious is the development of comprehensive schools as an instrument of educational and social policy, followed by replanning of the higher education phase in a pattern of "recurrent" education to serve the entire community.

In the transition from traditional to comprehensive schools there were parliamentary debates, local and large-scale experiments, re-interpretations of principles and methods, concurrent programmes of research and development — and even national reorientation. The experimental phase began in 1950 and extended until 1962; it was based upon the structure of a 9-year compulsory school, comprising 6 primary and 3 secondary years. The experiment expanded geographically year by year until about half the municipalities were involved. By 1962 a suitable curricular pattern was decided on. After 1966 the 9-year comprehensive school was extended to the whole country; and it was then made clear that the comprehensive principle would eventually cover the whole upper-secondary range too. Various internal and minor experiments continued under close official control until the new "comprehensive *gymnasium*" was established in 1971, in fulfilment of a resolution by the Riksdag in 1964.

The implementation of this comprehensive upper-secondary school is still in progress. A number of growing-pains have been experienced. There are also problems of spreading opportunities over a very large country with a relatively small population of 8 million people; and still many questions are asked about curriculum and teacher-preparation despite the ever-careful endeavours of the National Board of Education and of researchers in many centres. Concurrently with the reform there have been co-ordinated studies at the National Board of Education, in the 15 schools of education, throughout the 24 county authorities, and in 6 Higher Training Institutes for Teachers (in Stockholm,

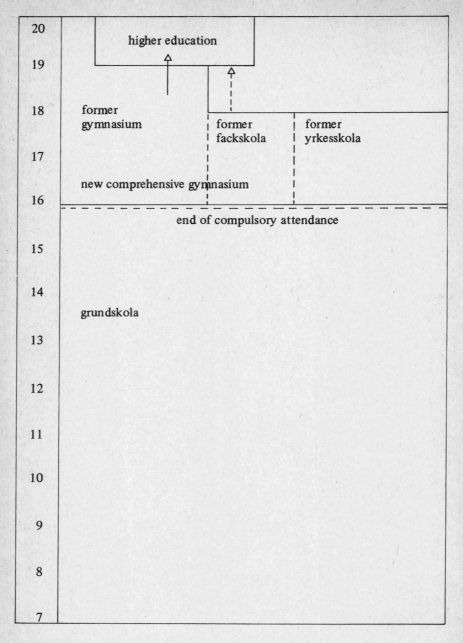

SWEDEN: Simplified diagram of school structure.

Linköping, Göteborg, Malmö, Uppsala, and Umeå).

By any standard — either of numbers, or of levels — the achievement is extremely impressive. Since the 1971 reforms, places have been available in the comprehensive upper-secondary school to the age of 19 for over 90% of the age-group. In 1971, 85% were so enrolled. Two years later after a slight drop in enrolments the figure was actually just over 80%; but official Swedish figures quoted by O.E.C.D. documents during the same year show that at least a 90% enrolment is expected and realistic.

Such figures seem realistic despite the reluctance of many able students to stay on "at school" immediately after reaching the end of compulsory attendance, because so many return. In 1972, the upper-secondary enrolment figure had again increased to 85% "of the age-group"; but only 68% were actually within the age-group. The other enrolments were of young adults returning to school or training.

The report in 1973 of the Swedish 1968 Educational Commission (U68) on *Higher Education (Högskolan* SOU 1973:3) gave even more remarkable evidence. The very reason for that Commission was the surge of enrolments not only in upper-secondary school but beyond. This is best illustrated by a simplified table adapted from the U68 Report.

Year	Number of *newly enrolled* HE students in Sweden	Total of students enrolled in HE
1940/41	2,000	11,000
1950/51	3,500	17,000
1960/61	8,000	37,000
1970/71	26,000	125,000

"Higher education" in these statistics means universities and certain colleges of equivalent status. It does not mean adult education courses or job training. Municipal adult education had 160,000 participants in 1971-1972; there were over 115,000 in job training and 1,600,000 undertaking evening studies with educational associations in 1970-1971. Many of these courses help to feed additional adult students into *gymnasium* courses or higher education. Therefore the already massive tide of upper-secondary enrolments and the further potential from supplementary courses later have understandably produced their own kinds of embarrassment for those re-thinking the entire field of post-compulsory education in Sweden.

Figures like this are all the more impressive when it is realised that in the 1930s compulsory education still lasted for only 6 years. Then only 10% of each generation went to the *realskola* ("lower-level secondary school"), and only 3% went on to the upper-level secondary school (*gymnasie*).

This rapid growth is indeed striking; but perhaps more important than simple numbers is the contrast drawn from domestic Swedish documents and personal recollections. Some of these show that the quality of education experienced in the elementary school during quite recent decades left much to be desired and often seemed remote from the people. The *realskola* and *gymnasium* were on a different social plane from most ordinary folk. The Swedish language itself still to some extent recalls the recency of the switch from a largely agricultural or mining way of life, which sent many emigrants to the United States and other places. Now in urban and educational sophistication the Swedes are in some ways examples to many of their neighbours.

So much has been written about Sweden in both a general way and in close detail that it is difficult to know what to emphasise here with reference to research conducted on the 16 — 20 age-group. Some points stand out, however. The obvious one is that the present state of provision and practice in Sweden is destined to undergo further radical changes. The Report of the 1968 Commission (U68) on the future of universities and a new-style higher education shows that the school-university end-on connection is almost certain to be broken, with important repercussions down the school system in the expectation that "recurrent education" in a multiplicity of types is bound to develop. Many of these will be vocationally linked; and periods of study will alternate with periods of work. In the immediately post-compulsory phase with which the researchers are primarily concerned new thoughts for the future are already beginning to affect practice in the present.

Policy choice and purpose

The administration of education in Sweden is strongly centralised, as are other aspects of government provision. This characteristic has encouraged the Swedes to take a global view of education, and of education's place within a generally evolving — if not directed — system of social and political reform. Everything about education in Sweden is part of a grand strategy of change. Sweden's neutrality during two world wars, especially the second, allowed a period of reflection and self-measurement against the achievements of other countries. During the second World War there were lively discussions about the desirability of the German model which tended in the past to be the favourite pattern of educational thinking, as against the model of broader access to more generalised education associated with the United States. Questions of social and economic equality were very much part of this reconsideration. The Swedes constantly declare that education and even the non-provision of education are very much political matters. Discussions about education, therefore, were debates about the kind of social and political future which Swedes wanted for themselves.

These discussions resulted in the setting up of a Royal Commission in 1946. Politicians were strongly represented on the Commission. In any case, debates in the Swedish parliament differ somewhat from those in Britain, for example, in reviewing a broad base of principles rather than the phrase-by-phrase analysis of clauses for particular legislation. Much use was also made of discussions with industrialists and social scientists, whether members of the Commission or not. Thus a kind of cybernetic instrument was set up to regulate what in recent years has come to be known as "the rolling reform", but which from the very beginning had that intention.

The very procedures for innovation in Sweden encourage this kind of relationship. When once parliament decides on a new measure, the actual implementation and much policy commitment is devolved upon the National Board of Education (not a Ministry) and upon the office of the Chancellor of Universities. In principle, especially in recent years, the intention is to devolve authority further on a number of local authorities. Before 1971 there were more than 900 local authorities with some responsibility in education, chiefly in the provision of primary schools and the maintenance of simple services. (In 1971 their number was reduced to 464, and more recently to 420). Such a multiplicity of small authorities merely left great power at the centre. Current proposals are to establish more self-sufficient regional boards (6 in number), and to charge the 24 county boards with a fairly comprehensive responsibility for ensuring a full development of educational services in their area. Alongside these, the enormous growth of post-secondary education (already a ten-fold increase in the period 1950-1970) will in future be based on 19 local areas comprising either a populous county or a group of counties. Even at present higher education of some sort is available in most of the areas.

Thus in retrospect we see a concentration of powers in recent times especially to serve the upper-secondary and higher levels of education, counterbalanced by some re-distribution of responsibility and innovation to foster the growth potential of regional or local centres. As an illustration of this process it may be observed that in 1950 only Uppsala and Lund had universities, though Stockholm and Göteborg had university-like institutions. The latter are now full universities. At Umeå there is now university-type provision too. A sixth institution for training and research is being developed at Linköping. These details do not matter so much as the clear indication of a quickly developing national system now based upon the concept of a unified structure of post-secondary studies. Almost everybody now has an education to this level or approaching it.

This development of education in Sweden of course reflects in some ways the step-by-step progress of many countries; but there is more to the picture than that if we are to understand it fully. The question is not simply one of accommodating at the higher education level the enormous upsurge of upper-secondary enrolments. Indeed, both the education authorities and many of the young people themselves already show considerable dissatisfaction with this end-on syndrome. Included in the purview is concern for those who are parents of the young people now enrolled to the age of 18 or 19, and also those older and rural people overtaken by the big changes in Sweden's industrial style and life-patterns. In answer to the questionnaires of this particular research some replies reflect uncertainties for which the new reforms are intended to provide possible answers.

Consequent on all these changes in policy and structure are questions of curriculum reform, and new teaching-learning relationships at every level, but especially in the new *gymnasium* (as the post-1971 upper-secondary school is called), and also for the in-service education or reinforcement of the teaching profession.

Within the National Board of Education there are working groups and committees concerned with curriculum in every type of school. There are also sections dealing with the preparation of texts, with the training and retraining of teachers and the preparation and distribution of new materials — in fact with everything that goes to make up the Educational Programme (*Läroplan*) for each level of education, which is supposed to direct everything that happens within the school system.

Each *Läroplan* is constantly revised. It is intended to be a book of guidance for teachers on all matters of importance, though nominally the classroom teacher and other practitioners are free to develop their own interpretation within the pattern. Sometimes the National Board of Education emphasises the importance of the *Läroplan*, sometimes plays it down. Correspondingly teachers alternatively grumble about its power or state their liberty within it. The outside observer, however, notes that the passion with which (for example) the debate on school marks and other instruments of regulation is conducted really tells how strongly the power and policy-pressing influence of the National Board of Education are felt.

Recent Structural Reforms and Progress towards the Present

It is easier to understand the present structure and discussions around it if a simple description is given of two previous systems of organisation, together with a few details showing transition from the older system to the new.

Before 1966, schooling in Sweden for most people began at the age of 7 and ended at the age of 14. For able children, especially those in the upper social classes, there was a chance of transfer at the age of 11 or 13 to the *realskola*; and this in its turn could lead to the general *"gymnasium"* or a technical or commercial counterpart. Alternatively, at the end of the compulsory school, some few able children could go on to one or other of the various vocational schools. Access to higher education depended upon passing the "students' examination" (*studentexamen*). However, as late as 1948 half of all the elementary school children were in all-age schools, and on average were taught by no more than two teachers throughout their school life. One consequence of this arrangement was a great development of individual or group work. This particular feature was continued in selective schools, despite the extreme formality of the teacher's methods and heavy reliance on book work.

The new pattern introduced in 1966 after a long period of experimentation firmly established a 9-year compulsory comprehensive school to the age of 16. There were, however, 9 optional courses available in the last (ninth) year. Differentiation at this level was done internally by the choice of school subjects of greater or less difficulty, such as additional foreign languages and more advanced mathematics. Without being exactly predictive, these alternative lines within the school system led in their turn to the academic *gymnasium* (5 "lines"), or to the "continuation school" (*fackskola*) with its 3 lines, or to a vocational school *(yrkesskola)* with many alternative and highly specific forms of training combined with general instruction.

As happens in many countries, the raising of the school leaving age really reflected the voluntary staying-on of increasing numbers of pupils. Nevertheless, during the time in which the comprehensive school was gradually established in Sweden, the number of pupils obtaining the difficult *studentexamen* doubled in the ten years after 1945, and again doubled in the ten years following 1956.

It was in 1962 that the curriculum for the developing comprehensive schools was decided upon; and this programme was expected to have an 8-year life. However, the onset of school reform and a great increase in the number of students meant that only about 40% of the teachers responsible for the 13-16 period were really prepared and competent for this age-level. It was originally thought, perhaps, that a substantial proportion of students would choose courses of a "practical" kind; but in fact the preference was the other way. General courses were sought by up to 80% of the students.

Because of practical difficulties in implementing the 1962 curriculum and securing a sufficient number and array of teachers, the 1960s were felt to be experimental. Even in 1969 the Swedish Ministry of Education referred to the *fackskola* as "almost entirely new" though it had been regularised in 1966 after a 2-year period of experiment. In a 1969 document the Ministry also said that the *fackskola* was "quantitatively not very extensive at present" and that it would not be universal throughout Sweden until the end of the 1960s. Thus, though the "continuation school" was intended to be a competitive modern alternative to the academically oriented "lines" of the *gymnasium*, it was nevertheless fairly clear that, through lack of provision, some potentially able students were unlikely to secure the *kompetens* which would admit them to higher education.

Because of the rapid growth of Swedish education, even an elementary school might be in several buildings or two or three units. One must remember that a town of 8,000 people in Sweden is quite average. There were limits to what many districts could provide, especially for a highly differentiated upper-secondary school system. Indeed, despite the choices which might be available officially, a 5- to 7-form-entry school could offer only about half of the official alternatives even for classes 7-9 (ages 13-16).

The 1966 scheme reorganised the *gymnasium* into 5 3-year lines beyond the age of 16: liberal arts; social sciences; economics or business; natural sciences; technology. This provision was coordinated with a 2-year "continuation school" (*fackskola*) with 3 lines: social sciences; economics or business; technology. These two types of schools were to be provided in the same districts and have the same administrative staff.

The vocational school (*yrkesskola*) was also to be assigned to the *gymnasium* district in the hope of securing eventual co-ordination between the three types of schools, with integrated syllabuses and administration.

In point of fact, even the *fackskola* sometimes found it hard to combine with the *gymnasium*. Staff and programmes were noticeably different in some cases, apart from the fact that the *fackskola* course normally lasted for 2 years as against the *gymnasium*'s three. It was only in the more modern buildings and in favoured districts that harmonisation appeared to be reasonably successful. Even more so the vocational school with its many courses (often with strong practical specialisation) might be distributed over a wide area and hardly ever envisaged as a single *yrkesskola*. Thus co-ordination between the three distinct types was likely to have a difficult passage.

In some ways it is surprising that so much was achieved in a relatively short time, especially as the old buildings will continue to be used for several years to come. The teachers have been prepared in previous times for quite distinct types of school*, and both the students and their parents are going through a period of intense change in which not enough guidance is available to reorientate all those concerned.

Examinations, marks and *kompetens*

Whereas there used to be selective examinations at the age of 11 and after the *realskola*, the introduction of the 9-year basic comprehensive school in 1966 led to the abolition of examinations within the Swedish school system. The 1966 *gymnasium*, the vocational school and *fackskola* were also without examinations. The formal *studentexamen* admitting students to university was finally abolished in 1968, giving way to an assessment of *kompetens* based upon marks received throughout the 3-year course of study in the *gymnasium*. The Commission for Admission to Higher Education went further in allowing people with at least 5 years' satisfactorily documented practical experience and other evidence of suitability for higher education to begin studies at a university without final marks from the *gymnasium*.

In place of the former examinations *before* the *gymnasium*, students now receive a final mark-list at the end of the basic comprehensive school (*grundskola*), showing what subjects they have studied and at what level (since there may be a general and a "special" course). These final marks theoretically qualify people to apply for any one of the *gymnasium*-level school's offerings. However, for certain lines special attainment is insisted upon — a requirement which obviously introduces a selective emphasis, but is mitigated by the possibility of acquiring supplementary marks. No entrance tests are held for the different lines of the *gymnasium*-level school. Nevertheless, there is considerable anxiety about marks both at this level and just before higher education — at least among those whose ambition or parental prodding points to a crisis immediately ahead. Thus a number of students unofficially repeat the final year of the basic school (*grundskola*) so as to obtain better marks. Principals connive at this, no doubt because they are also concerned about the reputation of their school or because they fear that "standards are slipping".

Since 1970 homework has been optional, though as late as the 1950s it

* It was in 1968 that all teachers, including secondary academic specialists, began to be trained at the same type of institution (a school of education). Many were not previously competent to teach all the subjects recently required of them, and much in-service supplementation or reorientation has been necessary.

used to be set even in primary school; now both teachers and parents complain that even older boys and girls do not always bestir themselves enough to match their abilities. Moreover, there is a good deal of truancy; and, as 1973 IEA evidence* showed, Swedish 10-year-olds were "the least interested in learning" of all the students in the 22 countries surveyed. The picture did not much improve at the age of 14, which still left the Swedes amongst "the most reluctant learners". In these circumstances it is astonishing that over 80% of pupils still continue their studies at the *gymnasium*-level school.

The New Comprehensive Upper-Secondary School (1971)

An official pamphlet published in 1971 by the Swedish National Board of Education was entitled "The integrated upper secondary school: three schools in one". It will be a long time before that ideal is attained. Nevertheless, on 1st July 1971 the old *gymnasium*, the continuation school, and the vocational school ceased to exist as separate entitites with different organisation and objectives. In principle the intention is to co-ordinate the varied types of education within one broad social purpose and one set of educational aims.

The really practical problem is to cope in satisfactory ways with the enormous enrolments of young men and women forming the student body at this upper-secondary level. The principle behind it was recognised by the 1964 enactment of parliament. It resolved to combine not only the two distinct types of establishment (*gymnasium* and *fackskola*) and their curricula but the higher education and career expectations of the young men and women in each type of course. In principle too the *yrkesskola* and its huge variety of offerings will be brought within the scheme as rapidly as possible, since in theory this type of school is already within the pattern. The 1973 U68 Commission's report is even more explicit: "To permit a real choice, on conclusion of the upper-secondary school, between continued studies and work, every line of study at the upper-secondary school should in principle prepare pupils both for further studies and for gainful employment to a greater extent than is now the case".

The post-1971 *gymnasialskole* has 22 "lines". 17 of these lines last for 2 years; 4 for 3 years; and one is a 4-year line. There may also be a number of special courses of varying lengths.

Within the new school it is easy to recognise the "family likeness" of the

* i.e. in the International Evaluation of Educational Attainment, a survey under the direction of Professor T. Husén.

courses offered. Some clearly resemble the old *gymnasium*. These include:

a 3-year "liberal arts" line;

a 3-year social sciences line;

a 3-year economics or business line;

a 3-year natural sciences line;

and a 4-year technical line (which also has a number of shorter courses).

These five lines are not affected by the recent reform. About 70% of the subjects taken are common to all students regardless of the "lines" chosen. The following subjects are studied for a longer or shorter period by nearly all the students taking the five lines: Swedish, English, another modern language, religious knowledge, history, mathematics, general science (or physics, chemistry, biology), civics, psychology, and gymnastics. (There is some difficulty in providing enough teachers for civics).

The continuation school (*fackskola*) in the integrated upper-secondary school roughly corresponds to programmes in the older *fackskola*. There are three 2-year "lines":

a social line;

an economics or business line;

a 2-year technical line.

The social line has in recent years acquired a very great popularity among girls, but not only there. Some of the *fackskola*'s studies are beginning to exercise an unexpectedly strong appeal as an alternative to the vista of university studies ahead, as students begin to doubt the advisability of protracted studies in a world of employment which seems to put a premium on work experience rather than formal qualifications. In fact a number of parents and employers told the researchers that *any* kind of work experience is an important criterion in making initial appointments. In the present climate of Swedish opinion, that emphasis is not altogether surprising.

The former *yrkesskola* used to have 22 lines by itself. The number of courses has been reduced under the new scheme, partly in consequence of incorporating more general studies and "polyvalence" in place of narrowly vocational studies.

All the courses or lines replacing the vocational school in the new comprehensive *gymnasium* will be of 2 years' duration, though a number of special courses will also be provided. Some of these vary in length. Two important innovations in this branch of instruction-with-training are insistence upon a common body of general interest studies and the grouping of even the vocational courses around a common core of "polyvalent instruction". The following subjects are compulsory: Swedish, labour market orientation, and gymnastics. Students must also choose at least one of several optional subjects of a general nature. These are: English, German, French, civics, religious knowledge, psychology, mathematics, consumer education, music or art. A student may also dispense with one of the vocational subjects in order to study a subject belonging to another "line" within the new comprehensive *gymnasium* framework.

It is said that there has been a "renaissance" of vocational education, with a marked shift of interest towards the now broader vocational side. Yet in 1971 nearly 11% of all 16-year-olds still chose the natural sciences line as the most predictive of success in higher education.

As mentioned above, since the introduction of the 1966 *gymnasium* examinations have been eliminated from the Swedish school system. Work receives a final assessment on a 1 − 5 scale, 5 being the highest mark; and the instructions carefully lay down the principle that some 38% of all the pupils in a given grade throughout the country will be awarded a 3, with the other marks according to the normal curve of distribution. Care is taken to point out that the 5-point numerical scale is now to apply to all branches of the upper-secondary school, presumably in the hope of establishing parity of esteem.

The Commission for Admission to Higher Education has proposed that all the lines of the upper-secondary school, including the 2-year courses in the *fackskola* and the *yrkesskola*, should rate equally for the purposes of admission to higher education. Officially the Commission's recommendation came into force in April 1973. The first students of the new upper-secondary school to leave after completing a 2-year course did so in the autumn of 1973, and put "equivalence" to its first acid test. Making the point in principle was not quite the same as getting it accepted. Supplementary courses enabling students from a shorter type of school course to qualify in real fact for admission to very competitive higher education courses (such as those in medicine or science) are an essential feature of many countries' systems; and Sweden provides the same.

In Sweden almost 40% of upper-secondary school leavers already go on to higher education of some sort (about 24% to university and the rest to non-university alternatives). How is equivalence for admission to be achieved? Not only is there the question of making up the future attainment level of the *fackskola* into something acceptable in higher education; there is the present obstacle that even within the programme of the older *gymnasium* type of school the "natural science" line gives the best chance of admission to higher education. A spokesman for the National Board of Education in 1973 said quite simply "the *fackskola* fulfils the general requirements for teachers' college but not for the university". Therefore, the U68 Report's proposed reorganisation entails much readjustment of the 16-19 school levels.

That is a problem independent of school marks. In recent years the debate on marks in Sweden has been fierce. An average of 2.3 out of 5 will nominally admit to the university. In fact an average of 4.8 out of 5 may be required from the very best line (e.g. natural science) to enter a medical faculty or similar. Pupils in their last year who cannot expect a high grade admit to seeking a low one deliberately so that they will have to repeat the year and perhaps end with a high mark after all. (In the *grundskola* class-repeating is not officially allowed but it can happen there too). In these circumstances it is obvious that for some time there will be little objective equivalence of marks derived from different types of schools, or from schools in different parts of the country — especially if adherence to a national distribution is required in very unequal circumstances. Yet an earnest endeavour is made to open up life-chances by breaking down regionally-linked, or socially determined, choices of school career and prospects beyond.

The geographical and social spread of opportunity

In all the Scandinavian countries a very great effort has been made to extend educational opportunity geographically. In the 1950s facilities were available for attending a *gymnasium*-type course at only some 60 places in the country. The regional spread of educational opportunity has proceeded so quickly that the 1971 integrated upper-secondary school was based upon some 120 regions. Not all of these could, of course, offer every kind of facility, as has already been observed. Each of the 19 new educational regions in future, however, is expected to offer a complete range of services up to higher education and throughout life.

It cannot be emphasised too strongly that any part of the programme in any part of the Swedish school system is envisaged in intimate relationship with other parts of the system. Its entire prospect is envisaged as an interlocking scheme of educational and social reform not only for those who can benefit by recent changes in the Swedish school system but for those parents, teachers, and workers, who under an earlier dispensation had a truncated education and training. This is not simply a matter of government planning from an office, either; questions of structural reform are accompanied by widespread and careful consideration of curriculum content, teaching-learning methods and new relationships, and the social and working conditions of "sensitising" citizens of every level and age to each other's educational needs. It would be foolish to pretend that all Swedes are satisfied with progress; but their frequently expressed dissatisfaction is an indication of the harsh criteria applied and the earnestness of their attempts at reform.

To the outsider, Swedish determination to cater for all contingencies sometimes presents a highly centralised and perhaps regimented picture. In recent years care has been taken to incorporate even into the most careful planning a certain contrived liberty or leeway. For example, in the *grundskola* a stated amount of "freely chosen activity" is actually required. The same sort of opportunity is given even in the vocationally "applied" courses in the new comprehensive upper-secondary school. To provide for "second thoughts" about education and careers, 25% of the "continuation school" places (in the *fackskola*) are reserved for older students who have completed vocational school or have at least 3 years' vocational experience behind them. There is earnest discussion also about a proposed special admission to higher education for late developers after the age of 25, with or without the evening classes and supplementary courses available in *gymnasialskole* for those who want to make up the level still required for admission to higher education, especially in some of the faculties.

None of this widespread provision should be interpreted as necessarily supposing that it is always better for people to continue their education formally in schools, college, or university. The 1973 report of the U68 Commission declares the opposite, in fact.

Admissions to the new gymnasium

The most recently available figures (for 1971-1972) show the following distribution of choices at the age of 16. The percentages given are of the entire 16-year old age-group. It will be observed that the most popular single line is the 3-year natural sciences line. A larger overall popularity is seen, however, if we add together the 2-year "social" line and the 3-year "social sciences" line. The 2-year "distribution and clerical" line and the 2-year "economics" line, both of which are really in vocationally oriented business studies, also attract many enrolments. The 3-year "economics" line is of a higher level, as well as being longer.

Upper-secondary school lines	% of all 16 year olds (1971)
1. Two-year clothing production line	0.5
2. Two-year building and public works line	4.2
3. Two-year distribution and clerical line	8.2
4. Two-year economics line	5.2
5. Two-year electrical and telecommunications line	2.7
6. Two-year motor engineering line	2.5
7. Two-year agricultural line	0.7
8. Two-year consumer line	6.9
9. Two-year consumer and social service line [1]	—

[1] Curriculum not yet established

10. Two-year food manufacturing line	0.8
11. Two-year process techniques line	0.2
12. Two-year forestry line	0.5
13. Two-year social line	9.8
14. Two-year technical line	5.8
15. Two-year woodwork line	0.5
16. Two-year workshop line	4.1
17. Two-year nursing line	3.8
18. Three-year economics line	5.5
19. Three-year liberal arts line	4.3
20. Three-year natural sciences line	10.6
21. Three-year social sciences line	4.4
22. Four-year technical line	6.3

Further points from the questionnaires

The distribution of student choices, and their availability over the whole of Sweden, clearly have a bearing on the objective validity of marks obtained in them. In addition, few marks are assessed solely on their face value in determining acceptability for higher education or jobs. A small compensation is allowed for periods of more than 6 months of full working experience, up to a maximum of 36 months. 5% of higher education places are reserved for applicants with special vocational or similar qualifications.

It is not surprising that the previously hierarchical system of schools has left Sweden at present with teachers possessing a wide range of qualifications and experience. Teachers are paid according to these criteria. Higher or lower rates are attached to a certificate, university degree, and experience. In addition to the *rektor* (principal), *studierektor* (deputy principal in charge of programmes and studies) and the *kurator* (teacher in charge of welfare and advice on student employment prospects) there are teachers responsible for particular aspects of the work. For instance in a large *yrkesskola* there are vice-principals who are teachers with special responsibility for specific lines under the general direction of the *yrkesskola* principal.

The new subject of "labour market orientation" brings in specialist teachers from outside, who are still rather hard to find; but in almost every other case teachers are attached to a particular school and stay there during the required hours. In recent years much has been made of "teacher participation" in the life and reorientation of the school; but apart from fairly recently developed staff meetings it is notorious that in many schools the teachers have never once met as a body.

The reforms of recent years introduced a good deal of student participation, too, not only for general welfare and student interest but also for recommendations and comment on the school's curriculum and general manner of life. One student represents each subject in every class on a student council. It appears to depend upon the headmaster or on the town or local government council how much influence and activity is encouraged, though it is the intention of the Swedish National Board of Education and the government generally that this kind of activity should be strongly encouraged.

Despite — or because of — sweeping reforms, there is still much to work on in Swedish education. The establishment of the upper-secondary school and new programmes in other parts of the system have understandably occasioned some strain; yet about 70% of the schools have schemes working on the integration and co-ordination of the programme, and the task of making teaching and learning more realistic. These endeavours on the ground are supported by researches and in-service conferences for teachers. Some teachers accuse the National Board of Education of focussing on spectacular centres and places where a "Hawthorne effect" is marked; but at the National Board of Education it is believed that average schools and circumstances are used as the basis for research and development studies.

Understandably there has been much criticism by teachers of what often seems to be an imposed new role; and this kind of criticism must be expected from those who enjoyed a privileged role and relatively easy teaching of more docile students in the old *gymnasium* in times when homework was compulsory, when the *studentexamen* exercised its own constraints, and when life generally was not so easy for the young. The general indifference of many students to the kinds of ambition which motivated their parents and teachers is, of course, a source of dismay to all elders.

It would be unreasonable to attribute these changes to recent scholastic reforms. When almost the entire age-group stays on in school — as Swedish administrators often remind us — the ordinary percentages of slackness and perhaps crime to be found in the older population at large will very likely be found in school as well. It is notorious that in nearly all countries the most "delinquent" or fractious age-group has traditionally been that in the last year before the end of compulsory schooling. In Sweden the situation has moved on. Staying-on which is "socially compulsory" rather than legally so has undoubtedly spread over a number of years some of the difficulties of transition from a scholastic to an adult role, particularly as the upper-secondary student in Sweden now is no longer a very "special" person, but rather the ordinary young adult.

CHAPTER 9

STRUCTURE AND POLICY IN ENGLAND

Introduction

There are several reasons for leaving the English case study until the last. Two reasons at least are subjective. It is difficult for an English observer to write about his own system with anything like the detachment possible when considering others; and, in any case, whatever may be observed about students aged 16-20 in other countries will, it is hoped, provide evidence relevant to structure and policy in England. Another reason for postponing the English study is that the complexities of English administration and experimentation stand in almost complete contrast to continental models, affording an almost limitless array of examples for appraisal and possible guidance in the future.

The Federal Republic of Germany did indeed show eleven variants in the *Länder* and city-states; and in some of these further local adaptation was possible in the vocationally linked upper-secondary schools. Yet each variation was officially approved, and linked in some way with the official formula for an examination. In England the possibilities for variation extend down to each school or college, and below that down to the individual classroom or method of instruction — still within the possibilities of assessment for examination or certification. The longstanding "partnership" of central and local authorities, of public and voluntary agencies, has nowhere led to more elastic experimentation than with the 16-20 age-group.

However, manifold British experimentation has led to much uncertainty about what actually happens (as the Schools Council Report on *16-19: Growth and response* (1972) made clear). Such evidence as is available may relate to "sixth forms" (the last two or three years in school before the age of 18 or 19); or it may refer to the same age-range catered for in one of many alternatives to traditional school, nevertheless offering full-time education of the same or similar kinds.

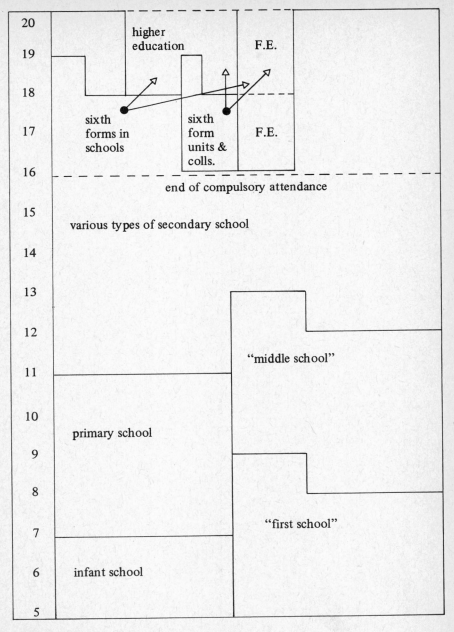

ENGLAND: Simplified diagram of school structure.

The evidence most readily and reliably come by relates to specific instances, or to a multiplicity of local variations; but it is difficult to obtain an up-to-date, overall account of the facts from any statistical service. Because of the rapidly changing shape of provision for the over-16s, it is still more difficult to discern trends that will be true for all parts of the country or every type of educational enterprise. The *least* documented aspect of education for the 16-20 population enrolled concerns the dimensions of its appeal to what the Schools Council Report just referred to calls "the new sixth formers" — even where they are in school sixth forms. The facts are still more obscure if students are in one of the new hybrid or specialised institutions growing up to serve them. Within the limits of feasibility, therefore, the researchers tried to select a reliable sample which might reveal characteristic trends and needs. They have supplemented that with the best information available from other sources.

For reasons of comparability it should also be pointed out that, whereas the British field work in the present survey was carried out entirely in England, official statistics often relate to England and Wales. Wherever figures have been broken down, statistics for England are used; but most of the averages include Welsh figures. If there seems to be any significant difference, it is indicated.

Educational Administration: The Sharing of Responsibility

Information is given here not to reveal Britain's complexities, but to show some of the variety to be anticipated in dealing with the over-16s. Attention will be also paid to perhaps unsuspected influences which affect the flow of boys and girls to upper-secondary school, or their expectations there and immediately afterwards.

Though the 1944 Education Act which is still the foundation for education in England and Wales spoke of "A *national policy* for providing a varied and comprehensive service in every area" (emphasis added), the local education authorities are generally free to organise schools as they wish. (There has been some Ministerial prodding or delaying on such matters as comprehensive school development; but that is the legal position).

In 1973 there were 163 local education authorities, mainly counties, or cities and large towns with county powers. From April 1974 there will be 104 (8 in Wales, the rest in England), mostly with new boundaries but with the same responsibilities. LEAs must fulfil certain requirements under the law; but they can and do enlarge on those (subject to certain financial limitations), and vary their school structures and style. Present variations in competence, expenditure, and commitment (despite uniform salary scales and central subvention to local taxes) are likely to be smoothed out. Special funds are available for poverty-stricken "educational priority areas".

The national inspectors (Her Majesty's Inspectors), numbering about 550, give professional advice, run courses, and prepare advisory pamphlets. LEAs also employ inspectors to visit and give advice in their own schools. Important national committees such as Robbins (1963), Newsom (1963), and Plowden (1967) have produced influential documents on higher, secondary, and primary education. Some of them have resulted in legislation, and several have affected practice profoundly. A Schools Council for Curriculum and Examinations was set up in 1964, with strong representation from schools, to give practical guidance and suggestions for policy. (Because of its terms of reference it is often somewhat cautious or formal in its "school" and "examinations" emphasis – a characteristic of some significance when the over-16s are considered). The National Foundation for Educational Research, financed by the DES and the LEAs, is perhaps the most important single organisation undertaking research in education. The Science Research Council and Social Science Research Council (especially the latter) finance important educational researches. Many of these are centred on universities, where there are also numerous research units financed by foundations. All of these bodies have a great influence on educational policy and experimentation; but none has any directive powers.

Direct responsibility for public education in schools and most colleges in Britain rests firmly with the local education authorities, subject to approval by the Secretary of State for Education and Science, and within the framework of legislation and finance. The DES (formerly Ministry of Education) does not own the schools, recruit or control the teachers, prescribe courses or texts or examinations and certificates; nor does it regulate admission to the various institutions.

These matters are in the hands of the local education authorities and teachers in the schools and colleges, in an ill-defined but well understood "partnership"; or else they are cared for by joint committees at the frontiers where interests meet (for example, where school leaving examinations also serve to show admissibility to higher education).

Universities, polytechnics, some other colleges, and a number of educational services enjoy autonomy in most respects, though tax-supported and effectively part of the public provision.

These special characteristics intimately affect the life of everyone in schools, or concerned with their output. No teacher is designated for officially assigned tasks or status, or for a particular school indefinitely. No course is officially designed to meet a legal requirement. No school or college has a character or status juridically defined, apart from universities, polytechnics and colleges of education — and even here (except in universities) there are "permeable" limits and exceptions to serve the evolutionary process.

One important consequence for upper-secondary education is that school certificates do not give legal entitlement to enter colleges or universities. (Entry to higher education may indeed be possible without them in exceptional cases). Nor are courses tightly tied to examination requirements. Even where a course is aimed, for example, at one of the several General Certificate of Education (Advanced Level) examinations, both the content and teaching method can be readily modified. Indeed, the so-called "Mode III" in several examinations puts responsibility for this kind of innovative syllabus and presentation right back among the teachers. Thus flexibility and growth are encouraged even at the formidable level of official examinations.

Teachers may apply for any post for which their qualifications and experience seem fitting. From 1973 onwards newly appointed teachers in maintained primary and secondary schools must have been trained to teach. Teachers are paid according to their degree, certificate, experience, and responsibility; but in principle the same general basic scale is applied in all types of school. (There are supplements for schools with special difficulties, and for some metropolitan areas; but those do not impair the principle). Teachers can also move from teaching one subject or class-level to another, if they are competent. In-service training and formal courses in higher education facilitate such development, particularly if there is structural or curricular re-arrangement.

Organisation: Responsibilities in School

Teachers in a school generally feel themselves "all teachers together". Excluding part-time staff, they are usually on the school premises throughout the school day, and take an all-round part in the life of the school — including much extracurricular activity. Additional commitments of this kind are not paid for. The teacher assumes that these are normal responsibilities of the teaching career, though special responsibilities may be recompensed with an annual allowance.

Responsibility for the curriculum and timetabling in a school effectively rests with the headmaster or headmistress, though the local authority may influence choice and method through its inspectorate. In some cases the board of governors or managers which each school has in a benignly custodial capacity may make observations. Generally, however, the head teacher works closely with the teaching staff in arriving at a workable distribution of the curricular subject-matter, methods, and timetabling. Some schools allow the students (through a council) to make recommendations — usually on method and relationships, or amenities. That is specially likely with senior students. All of this means that no two schools are quite alike; and a school's character may change over time, especially with a change of head teacher. All schools have deputy heads and other responsible teachers; but all the staff continue to feel that they have an all-round teaching and custodial responsibility, extending even into the time when students are not at school or college.

The rather paternalistic atmosphere thus engendered is felt to be overwhelming by some over-16s; and that is one reason for the growing popularity of colleges (a point to be considered later). However, traditional commitment to the all-round development of students extends into many colleges too. For that reason, almost all colleges and schools assume that clubs, semi-academic and/or recreational activities should be encouraged as an important aspect of the students' general education and the teachers' responsibilities.

These broadening activities are all the more valuable in Britain because the curriculum usually contains a narrower range of subjects for each individual student in the upper-secondary levels than would be expected on the continent. However, even where three main subjects are chosen for concentrated examination preparation in the last two years of school (the "sixth form"), it is usual to study several additional subjects, often optional. But whereas on the continent such enlargement of interests would probably be intellectual, the emotive and moral as well as aesthetic and cultural aspects are greatly prized in Britain. Most teachers feel they ought to take part in these commitments, and do so. In seeking promotion or official plaudits, extracurricular enterprise carries weight.

Extracurricular activities and the extension of scholastic programmes often bring about collaboration between neighbouring institutions. Sometimes these institutions are of the same general type (e.g. schools); but they may be quite different (e.g. colleges, business enterprises, social services, or clubs). When well arranged, these contacts may be admirable and may result in some sharing of staff and studies; but there is a tendency, perhaps, to rely heavily on amateur competence in some fields (e.g. guidance) where other countries recognise the need for specialist expertise. Some of the most successful and happy British schools may, indeed, be all-in-all to their students in a way that would be impossible in most other countries. The obvious benefits of a rich collective life may, however, be offset by the risks of a certain isolation or juvenility.

Schools and the Prospect of Higher Education

Although applications of qualified school leavers for admission to higher education are now processed through a nation-wide clearing-house system (with students stating their preferences in order), nevertheless schools usually maintain fairly good contacts with some universities and colleges, and formally or informally assist in the placing of students there. Personal letters of recommendation help or otherwise. Most students making the transition from school to university have individual interviews in the institution of higher education which is considering them. Thus personal appraisal counts for a lot in many cases — with the merits and failing of any such system. The point to note is the personalisation of the assessment process, itself derived from a custodial idiom of teaching/learning relationships and from the widely inclusive commitment of the teacher.

Here should be mentioned a characteristic British assumption still affecting the outlook from schools; that higher education in a university (for example) is not absolutely essential to success even in a learned profession. Though doctors (for example) are all taught and trained in universities before proceeding to the clinical part of their preparation, very many fully qualified engineers, architects, and lawyers have not been to the university or any equivalent "applied" college — though the tendency is now overwhelmingly to do so. The reason is that from medieval times onwards the great corporate bodies representing the learned professions administered their teaching and training autonomously. Nowadays many of them do so at postgraduate level, or in combination with the corresponding faculty of a university.

This legacy of former times shows itself in several ways. The university is neither as monopolistic of learned status nor as inevitable to the ambitious student as it is on the continent. The non-university or para-university colleges and some "apprenticeship-type" approaches to distinguished careers have long been in the forefront of any school leaver's "respectable" choices; and in recent years some new-style technological degrees on a work-and-college "sandwich" basis have begun to appear as alternatives to the university. Thus learning, even higher learning, has a rather different complexion for the student in post-compulsory education in Britain. Consequently, the way is open for future development of varied combinations of paid employment and higher studies, either immediately following school or after an interval.

Though it is arguable that so much trust in "applied" rather than fundamental studies has left many Britons possessed of skills without much science of the type needed for modern industries and a life of change, the traditional pattern has undergone substantial development since about 1950 with the rapid expansion of new post-secondary courses for diplomas in such fields as engineering, commerce, and the like. These provide a broad grounding in those applied fields but are careful to combine it with a foundation of general studies. A number of diplomas have achieved graduate equivalence in some fields. Some details of these qualifications are given later. It seems important to point to their increasingly "polyvalent" nature, which is in marked contrast to the sharply specific focus of many training courses on the continent. (There, indeed, they are found at upper-secondary as well as post-secondary level). The expanding diversity and increasing polyvalence of British courses and qualifications has recently attracted favourable attention from OECD, for example at the 1973 Paris Conference on new structures in post-secondary education.

Despite the long tradition of flexibility and adaptation in British "further education" (as non-university higher education has traditionally been called), some rigidities and rituals have set in which continental systems have avoided. Among these have been excessive regard for long periods of apprenticeship to satisfy trade union requirements and the "customs of the trade". Some of these made it difficult to hybridise learning and practice for a new perspective. Another problem has been over-much reliance on part-time courses stretched over lengthy periods, which have resulted in much wastage. Nonetheless, the vision of a "permeable pyramid" of secondary-level, "further", and higher education in a great variety of types has had perennial if patchy embodiment in Britain's colleges of further education. It achieved a new dignity and prospect in the 1963 Robbins Report on *Higher Education*; and a much wider range of possibilities seems open since the 1972 White Paper on *Education: A Framework for Expansion.*

Whatever happens in universities, or in the very businesslike short courses which have trained so many professionals in other parts of British "higher" education, the probability is that "further" education's essential flexibility will continue to contrive "short cycle" courses and institutions for most of the newcomers and most new needs. This provision is different from most "technical" or vocational courses on the continent, where any close counterpart to British "further" education is hard to find. On the other hand, some of the British rigidities just mentioned would certainly have to go, along with an unnecessary clutter of differentiation, if a new beginning were to be made with large-scale provision of comprehensive type for all or most of the over-16s. That has already begun experimentally in some local education authorities' areas. It finds many advocates of various political complexions as well as in the Labour Party's *Opposition Green Paper: Higher and Further Education (1973).*

Examinations

Since examinations loom large in the prospect for the over-16s, some account must be taken of them here. However, present contentions and proposals will be largely omitted. Examinations for school-leavers are conducted by independent bodies. The General Certificate of Education examinations at Ordinary and Advanced levels are conducted by eight joint boards with strong teacher representation among the examiners, and mostly connected with one or more universities.

The Ordinary Level of the General Certificate of Education (GCE) is usually taken in several subjects about the age of 16 — as many as 8 subjects being not uncommon. The O-level GCE is something of an oddity by world comparisons, since it is normally taken by students intending to go on later to Advanced Level anyway, and is therefore not a lower-level mark of attainment for those diagnosed earlier as less bright. The Advanced Level of GCE is usually taken in 3 subjects (sometimes 2, sometimes 4) about the age of 18. There are no compulsory subjects at either level; and candidates may take one subject or more. The minimum requirement for students seeking university admission is usually given as two A-level passes in highly specialised subjects to suit the university faculty admitting them; but in fact a high mark in three subjects is generally required.

In 1965 a Certificate of Secondary Education was introduced, mainly for less successful pupils after a five-year secondary course. It is administered (always by teachers) through 14 regional boards; and it is intentionally school-based rather than under the influence of external considerations or other boards. That is to say, the CSE examination was intended, while providing the incentive and reward of a certificate, to encourage evolution and independence in the schools, instead of looking outward to the possibilities of employment or the prospects of enrolment in colleges afterwards. To that end, it can be taken in three "modes" with varying degrees of school autonomy, though it is a matter of record that Mode III which confers the greatest autonomy has been the least popular choice (13% of the candidates in 1972).

Since the uppermost CSE grade counts as equivalent to a low General Certificate of Education Ordinary Level grade, the latter has very often been taken as a measure of success for abler students among those not previously thought to be "academic". Thus the brighter candidates in a class may be entered for GCE in some subjects (rather than CSE with the rest); and a certain tension or envy has grown up. Many students take some subjects for CSE and other subjects for GCE O-Level, particularly those students who voluntarily stay on at school after the age of 16 to obtain modest certification in subjects in which they have not qualified so far.

Current discussion about school examinations

Much argument has gone on in recent years about the question of examinations at the age of 16: whether there is any sense in them at all; whether there ought to be one instead of two public examination formulae; what the relationship of examinations at the age of 16 is to those taken at the age of 18 (either in prospects for higher education and jobs or in measuring educational attainment so far); and what possible alternative forms of assessment there might be. The Schools Council, teachers' associations, and influential writers on education have produced alternative schemes of examination or appraisal. All that one can say is that the pattern of examinations and the debate around them (to have them or not, and at what ages and in what form) are in full evolution. One broad conclusion is now generally accepted: that "sixth form" studies (in the immediately post-compulsory years) are much too restricted in number and range, and that in any examination at the age of 18 not less than five well-spread subjects should be assessed.

The Schools Council for that purpose proposed a new Certificate of Extended Education (CEE). At first this was clearly thought of as an examination at about 17 for those of average ability who stay on beyond compulsion for perhaps *one* year; but later the proposed CEE began to be thought of as a broad-based alternative to GCE A-level for students not suited by the older examination, with equal standards but varying "modes" in different parts of the country. Throughout 1973 consultations continued with a view to substituting a CEE-style examination (probably in five subjects at different levels) for the established two- or three-subject GCE A-level examination. The outcome is far from clear. At the time of writing students were taking courses with every one of these possibilities in view.

Confusing though the details are, the plain message for international observers is that there is remarkable flexibility if only it can be put to sensible use for the evolution of new studies and relationships. Three further points may be noted which often come up in international comparisons. The piecemeal or cumulative nature of these examinations is in keeping with the "recurrent education" emphasis now popular in educational discussion. Methods of examination which reveal a "profile" or contours of ability rather than a statutory attainment across several subjects are in keeping with "qualitative democratisation" and the development of growth-points. Radical questioning whether examinations are really worth the trouble taken over an imperfect predictor is coming closer to that "open access" now widely advocated. Indeed, many "sixth forms" and colleges at the same level already allow "open access", instead of demanding so many O-Levels. In 1970 the Committee of

Vice-Chancellors of the Universities of the United Kingdom said of university admissions too: "The criterion of A-Level passes may well cease to have practical meaning within a decade in view of proposals currently under consideration for a substantial revision of the structure of sixth-form syllabuses and examinations".

Publicly Provided and Other Schools

Once again, attention is limited to those aspects which have bearing on the onward flow of boys and girls to upper-secondary school, and affect their life expectations there. The present is a time of great changes in Britain, including the effects of comprehensive school development and new articulations of structure which introduce different age-groupings into primary and secondary school. Of more direct concern to the population surveyed in this research are new and evolving school units or colleges at the upper end of secondary education, or over-lapping that and part of tertiary education. These offer working examples for innovators in other countries, especially those concerned with similar hybrid institutions like that at Bielefeld in Germany or some of the newest vocational establishments in Scandinavia.

Two points should be promptly made for international comparison. The first is that this research is concerned only with full-time education in the publicly maintained sector. However, in England and Wales — much more than in any other advanced country — an independent sector of schools flourishes, not for religious or ideological reasons but partly because of history and partly because the best of such schools usually give preferential access to certain universities and a large array of important positions in public life. Thus the influence of independent schools as an example is considerable, though indirect.

The second point concerns church-associated schools. Schools in England and Wales initially built by churches ("voluntary schools") can also be maintained, with salaries and running costs paid, while retaining their sectarian character, if they show that they are doing the same kind of job in other respects as the local authority schools. They can also have large percentage grants for any reorganisation necessary. Such schools in most respects behave exactly like LEA schools. None was included in the present survey.

Really independent schools are financed by fees or ancient foundations. (Sometimes individual students' fees may be paid for them by local education authorities). In addition, a number of formerly independent schools (179 in 1972) receive "direct grants" from the Department of Education and Science in return for giving free secondary education to students coming from publicly provided primary schools.

No independent or "direct grant" schools are included in the present survey. Yet it would be wrong to overlook the background influence of independent or partly independent institutions on thoughts about studies for the over-16s in publicly provided schools and colleges. After all, the major independent schools (paradoxically called "Public Schools" for historical reasons, since they were once charitable foundations) usually have large "sixth forms" which in their competitiveness for university access – especially at Oxford and Cambridge Universities – set the pace and sometimes the style of study for other "sixth formers" or their equivalents everywhere. Zest for scholarship, or at least for examination-passing, is of relatively recent origin in most of the independent schools. It began to be sharply stimulated by competition from maintained schools in the years following 1945. But "Public Schools'" large "sixth forms" and favoured staffing ratios, together with very high fees and high family motivation, now offer a strongly predictive alternative to other kinds of school.

Less than 3 per cent of the whole secondary population goes to "Public Schools", which are a minority even of the independent sector; but in the early 1970s nearly 50 per cent of the students at Oxford University and 60 per cent at Cambridge came from this small sample. Approximately 20 per cent of all "academic" sixth-formers are in schools of this type; about 20 per cent of all university entrants come from them; so do one-third of all the top personnel in industry and commerce and two-thirds of those in the learned professions. Hence there is always this unacknowledged and often unhelpful yardstick in the background when people measure the suitability of examinations and curricula for "new sixth-formers" against those of the "traditional sixth form", which is not traditional at all. Preoccupation with examinations and their outcome reflects an attempt to substitute meritocratic criteria for those of favoured upbringing – at a time when informed opinion questions examination validity altogether and often deplores the identification of curricula with examinations.

Maintained Schools: New Questions of Structure

The basic foundation for British education is still the Act of 1944, developed since by minor legislation and administrative orders or legal judgements. Compulsory schooling begins at 5 and extends to 16 (since 1972-3). Voluntary pre-school education is being developed apace during the present decade, but has been the experience of very few at present in school. (12.4% of the under-5s were enrolled in 1971). Not merely has secondary education for all been free of cost (indeed, supported by student grants where appropriate) since 1944, but higher and further education too has gradually been made free of cost and supported by very generous grants according to parental income. Inflation has cut down the value of these grants, which were once ample to maintain a student in higher education. The highly selective nature and very low failure rate of higher and further education in Britain made these large maintenance grants possible; and these have certainly made it possible for students of all backgrounds to aspire to continued study for the usual 3 years of a degree course or the 4 or 4½ years of some professional and technological awards.

This bald account of free education and awards does not reveal significant differences in structure and access. Though the 1944 Act really did hold out the promise of education at any level from which students might profit, selection about the age of 11 for different kinds of secondary school was rigorously applied. (It still continues inside some comprehensive schools, which are increasingly established as the norm towards which most local authorities are moving). Selection has maintained many disadvantages of previous home background and schooling, as everywhere.

"Parity of esteem" for different kinds of secondary school and course was intended in the 1944 Act; but understandably it was never achieved, even though in Britain graduate teachers with similar kinds of qualification may teach in any kind of school. There is legally nothing to stop a local authority from developing a school or course into another, more highly esteemed or experimental type. Ministerial prodding was used in 1965 to encourage the development of comprehensive schools; and Ministerial reinterpretation and delaying tactics since 1970 have discouraged the same tendency — much to the annoyance of many LEAs. Authorities once opposed to comprehensive schools on political grounds are now in the majority committed to them for educational and social reasons.

Experience and considerations of feasibility have weighed heavily in this change of attitude. The formerly accepted tripartite division of secondary schools into "grammar" (academic, from 11 to 18 — 19), "secondary technical" (a few, from 11 or 13 to 18 — 19), and "secondary modern" (11 to the end of compulsory schooling, with a few volunteers staying on) is gradually being broken down in most LEAs. Few people think it can last much longer even where it survives.* Secondary modern schools in some instances have combined

---

* In January 1970, there were 5,385 maintained secondary schools. Of these, there were 1,038 grammar schools, 2,691 secondary modern schools (many with "academic" and otherwise enlarged courses), and 82 secondary technical schools. At the same time there were 1,145 comprehensive schools; but these co-existed with maintained selective schools in all but a few counties and boroughs. However, comprehensive development is now accelerating.

with secondary technical or other schools to form "bilateral" or multiple units. Other secondary modern schools by natural growth through staying-on or accretion of new interests have become more comprehensive.

Many schools in a large number of LEAs have been transformed into comprehensive schools by the amalgamation of all the former "tripartite" segments; but to this day the majority of so-called comprehensive schools are in important respects not really comprehensive. For historical or policy reasons a selective grammar school may exist alongside; and in all instances the existence of the booming independent sector acts as an invitation to some parents and as a possible criterion for all secondary schools. Haste and mistakes in the actual implementation of some comprehensive school schemes have accentuated this latter problem.

Despite difficulties, however, the trend to comprehensive schooling gathers momentum — for administrative as well as for educational and social reasons. Most present sixth-formers in Britain have had some of their schooling during this time of change; and a large number have experienced some of its consequences in practice. Some two-third of all the enrolled population was in local authority areas where comprehensive or partially comprehensive school programmes were being developed, even as early as 1965 when a Ministerial circular required LEAs to submit complete schemes of comprehensive reorganisation; and both administrative and public opinion has since 1965 moved steadily towards recognising the inevitability of comprehensive schools.

By "partially comprehensive" above was meant schemes whereby a comprehensive high school from 11 or 12 to 14 or 16 allows students to go on at will to a general or more specialised school afterwards. Such plans appeal to local authorities because they permit the best use of buildings and teachers for comprehensively gathered students and equipment, notably after the age of 16.

When faced with such reorganisation, and especially any which would somehow separate the "sixth form", however, many teachers and some parents regret the loss of continuity between the ages of 11 and 18 which characterised the grammar school kind of organisation which had become dominant since 1902 — at least for those students who stay in such schools to the age of 18. Head teachers and other spokesmen sometimes regret the loss of paternalistic responsibility which a minority of prefects and other senior students used to enjoy. But a fair number of grammar schools have already abolished prefects anyway. The burgeoning of sixth forms and the pressure of examination work has transformed many internal attitudes. So have questions of teacher supply — not least in sixth forms themselves.

The whole climate of discussion surrounding questions of suitable education for young adults has been altering very fast. The young adults' own views themselves are increasingly expressed; and they now have several other ways of continuing their formal studies beyond 16. Furthermore, problems of accommodating ever-growing numbers in upper schools have coincided with much re-thinking about organisation lower down the ladder. This obviously affects progression towards the top. Particularly since the Plowden Report of 1967 on *Children and their Primary Schools* there has developed a tendency to reorganise the compulsory years into "first", "middle", and secondary schools — the latter increasingly to the age of 16. In consequence of Plowden, many local authorities now follow a "middle school" with a 12 — 16 school of some sort (increasingly comprehensive), and gather up the over-16s in a separate sixth form school or college.

Accommodating the over-16s

Pressure of numbers alone demands unprecedented accommodation for the over-16s. Traditional thought concentrated on expanding sixth forms in those schools where boys and/or girls follow the trend to staying on; and that accounted for the expression "the sixth form explosion". But former secondary modern schools which had no "top" have increasingly retained their students; so the question arose whether these should develop a "sixth form" or transfer students elsewhere. And, if elsewhere, was that to be to an adjacent grammar school, to a "further education" college, or to something new — such as a special "sixth form unit" attached to a grammar school, or perhaps a separate sixth form college of some kind? And should such institutions be selective or not? Every expedient has been tried. A. D. C. Peterson, in *The Future of the Sixth Form* (1973), listed seven ways in which the sixth form might be accommodated.

For the purposes of this present survey variants for the 16-20 age-range may be rather differently listed as follows:

(a)   Attached to or part of a *school*:

    (i)   selective sixth form or unit;

    (ii)   non-selective sixth form or unit.

(b)   Part of *further education* college provision:

(i) as a "general studies" segment of a mainly vocational college for the over-16s which includes some courses extending ultimately to diploma or degree level;

(ii) as a distinctively prelinimary phase for students still below A-Level or its vocationally-linked equivalent (now often called the "tertiary" level to distinguish it from "higher", post-A-Level work).

(c) A separate *secondary sixth form college*:

(i) selective;

(ii) non-selective.

(d) A separate *comprehensive junior college* under "further education" regulations, rather like b (ii) above but consciously combining all upper-secondary and "tertiary" education below "higher education" proper. (In such a connection the latter term is generously construed).

There are seven varieties here alone, independently of whatever type of school preceded the "sixth form level" a further point which Mr. Peterson took account of. Indeed, one of the most noticeable features of recent provision for the over-16s is the possibility of ignoring or compensating for whatever schooling students have previously experienced, especially in open-access colleges.

It will not be overlooked that students entering colleges of types (b) and (d) have often had experience of employment or domesticity. Therefore in social terms there is sometimes a richly varied catchment. There is an absence of that compensatory-academic emphasis associated with the *zweiter Bildungsweg* in Germany and Austria, or formerly imposed on adult "returners" in the Swedish *gymnasium*. It is closer to the attitude expressed in Sweden's "U68" Report on *Higher Education* and in the Ontario proposals of 1973.

In the present survey it was not possible to examine — much less administer questionnaires in — every type of provision for the over-16s. Apart from questions of time and labour, there was the compelling reason that it seemed preferable to concentrate in England as elsewhere on three cities or towns, and in those to conduct close enquiries in schools or colleges across the whole upper-secondary/lower tertiary spectrum, if possible. Because several of the institutions visited had recently undergone structural reorganisation as separate institutions, or as institutions in a new relationship, the principals, staff and students were often able to contrast their own years of experience in one type of provision with current experience in another. That was also true for students who had spent their secondary years below the age of 16 in another establishment, migrating to their present institution at or after that age. Some of these migrations were noteworthy: a number of students had moved, for example, from highly selective and socially privileged independent schools to socially mixed and educationally comprehensive colleges or upper-secondary schools.

The English questionnaires thus covered, at least potentially, a wider educational and social range than might seem likely when the research programme's necessary exclusions are considered. Comments will be offered in a later chapter about the extent to which variation or a sense of innovation showed itself in the students' or teachers' responses. To the extent that it did not, the assimilative force of the "sixth form tradition" and the example of socially predictive schools should be weighed. A measure of compensation for these was sought in pursuing oral enquiries through interviews – both in the schools and colleges which answered questionnaires, and among the staff who were interviewed by the researchers in other connections. No formal account is taken of these latter contacts; but hypotheses and questions prompted by them doubtless entered into formally arranged interviews in the sample surveyed.

One detail distinguishing schools from further education should be mentioned, since it can affect teacher supply and role. It also affects the supply of statistics. Schools and further education are administered under different regulations. Very recently there has been some frontier modification because of the overlap between territories and interests; and radical reconsideration before long seems imperative.

Figures for school enrolments are given separately from further education statistics. Teaching staff in schools are required after 1972-3 to have a teacher's qualification in addition to whatever degrees or other diplomas they may possess. (Previously that rule applied in primary schools, but not in secondary schools, though even here more than half of the teachers were so qualified). In further education these rules do not apply. Furthermore, salary scales in further education are more varied and better; and promotion prospects to higher scales and responsibilities are better. Therefore there has been some migration of well qualified or ambitious teachers from schools to colleges for these reasons, in addition to any general appeal which teaching adults in colleges may exercise.

The shortage of teachers in some subjects – notably in mathematics and the sciences (but also including some languages and conventional school subjects as well as "innovative" interests) – has encouraged "linked courses" between secondary schools and colleges, and between secondary schools of hitherto different types. Considerations of cost and effectiveness have also introduced some rationalisation of resources. In the past, many courses at sixth-form level have had very small classes. Merging these is obviously more economical. One of the major reasons for an early prototype proposal for a sixth form college in England (that at Croydon in 1954) was the economy as well as the desirability of amalgamating a boys' and a girls' grammar school sixth forms, and of combining their instruction with corresponding ranges in a local college. The supply of suitable teachers and facilities seems bound to grow more acute when the growth in enrolments accelerates. Therefore, in addition to questions of educational and social desirability, considerations of attractiveness to teachers and administrators may influence a preference for further education facilities and regulations.

The Size of the Problem

Recent figures are of interest. For accurate comparison with continental statements three points should be observed. First, British figures are for full-time (i.e. all-day) enrolment of students whose programme also includes much reading and other home preparation. (Indeed, some at least of further education's *part*-time students would have to be added in if a strict comparison were to be made with some continental statistics). Secondly, in further education too — especially at this level — some of the custodial responsibilities of the teacher already described make most of the staff feel obliged to do everything possible to encourage the student. A "collegiate life" is sought for, as a rule. Thirdly, since school statistics and those for further education come under different headings in Britain, it is not always possible to obtain them in quite the same categories or for the same dates. The following are obtained from *Social Trends, No. 3*, 1972 (Government publisher, HMSO); Schools Council Working Paper 45, *16-19: Growth and Response, I Curricular bases* (Evans/Methuen), 1972; and the United Kingdom "country report" to the Council of Europe on *The education of the 16 to 19 age group*, DECS/EGT (1971).

The most recent figures available are those relating to *schools* in 1971. It is convenient to list those in comparison with 1961, and with projections for 1975, 1980, and 1985 (where possible). It will be remembered that the 17-year-olds represent the last normal year at secondary school, and therefore those aged 18 or more are a minority staying on for special work, as a rule.

Actual enrolments (whole of U.K.)   **Projections**

All schools; percentage of age-group, full-time enrolments.

	1961	1971	1975	1980	1985
Age 16	21.5	35.6	52.3	56.9	61.2
Age 17	11.7	20.3	24.1	29.6	34.4
Age 18 or over	4.1	7.0	8.2	10.1	11.8

To those must be added the full-time students in further education. Figures for 1971 were not available in the same form at the time of writing; but it is possible to use 1970 figures and compare them with 1960 for further education within the same age-groups.

Actual enrolments (England and Wales only)

Further education establishments; full-time, percentage of age-group.

	1960	1970
Age 16	3.7	7.0
Age 17	2.4	7.1
Age 18	1.5	4.4

Adding together students aged 16, 17, and 18 (i.e. including one year beyond the usual length of schooling, when enrolments are bound to diminish), the United Kingdom report to the Council of Europe, referring to the previous year (1969), gave 19.4% of the entire 16-19 age-group in *schools*, and another 5.8% full-time enrolments of the same age-group in *further education*, making a combined percentage for full-time enrolments of 25.2% of the 16-19 age-group. A more recent semi-official estimate for 1972 puts the complete full-time enrolment figure of those aged between 17 and 18 as approximately 30%, which would be in line with obvious trends. The fact that institutions catering for the over-16s in the upper-secondary/lower-tertiary overlap are in two distinct categories makes exact figures hard to come by; but from various evidence the conclusions are obvious enough.

On the basis of DES projections at the beginning of this decade, Lord Boyle, a former Minister of Education, forecast that the number of students enrolled full-time between the ages of 16 and 19 would rise from the then quoted figure of 260,000 in England and Wales to over 600,000 by 1980. (As a matter of fact, at the time Lord Boyle was speaking the actual count was already 312,700 — as later statistics showed). Enrolment increase has been faster than anticipated, and projections have risen higher. The official handbook *Social Trends No. 3*, 1972, published by the Central Statistical Office, showed that in January 1971 (for the whole of the United Kingdom, and therefore including 52,000 for Scotland) there were already 482,000 *school* enrolments between those ages. In the same document, projections for the same age-range were 916,000 in 1980 and 1,082,000 in 1985 — *in schools alone*. These figures should be increased by at least 25% to allow for those enrolled full-time *in further education*.

Nor is it a case of numbers only. The attainment level continues to rise. The Robbins Report on *Higher Education* (1963) expected that by 1980-1981 about 506,000 would enrol in higher education on the basis of attainment in A-Levels, in step with increasing social demand. A DES projection in 1970, on the same basis, anticipated a full-time higher education figure of 835,000 by 1981. The 1972 official White Paper, *Education: A Framework for Expansion*, retrenched a little with an estimate of 750,000 for 1981; but that may well fall short of actuality, if only because of increasing social demand and the example of competitor countries. Certainly, the 1970 DES projections predicted that some 23% of the relevant age-cohort would qualify for university admission on the basis of 2 A-Levels by the beginning of the next decade (1981); and that might imply a figure of perhaps 40% of the age-group with at least 1 A-Level.

Forecasts for school enrolments tentatively offered in the Schools Council Working Paper No. 45 of 1972 (Table 16) seem even more impressive in sheer numbers. Starting with a 1970 actual figure of 312,700 sixth-formers in schools ("traditional" students and otherwise), the Working Party predicted a possible 525,000 "traditional" sixth-formers by 1981, while the figure for "non-traditional" sixth-formers was "not available". All the evidence goes to suggest that the global total might be very large in schools, and perhaps much larger in alternatives to schools — that is, in the further education sector or in new types of institution rapidly evolving. Almost all forecasts have underestimated demand in all countries; and rapid changes in the sophistication of industries and the age at which they wish to recruit seem likely to enlarge educational demand generally among the over-16s.

Another factor for increase is often overlooked. Whole regions of the country, and a number of towns and cities within any region, have not yet caught up educationally with the surrounding average. Regional and socio-economic disparities are less likely to be tolerated as time goes by, not only because of higher aspirations but because urbanisation in some places and regional replanning in others are likely to stimulate educational demand. Furthermore, the provision of more accessible ("home-based") higher education facilities forecast in the 1972 White Paper, and the structural reorganisation of higher education proposed therein and in Circular No. 7 of 1973, undoubtedly make continued studies seem more accessible. That prospect will directly encourage students over 16 to stay on. However, the most potent inducement to staying on may be the attractiveness of new kinds of "college" within the 16-20 age-range itself.

"College" for the 16-20 Age-Group

Whereas the word "college" in North America is understood to mean post-secondary provision after the age of 18, in Europe it need not do so. In fact it has usually indicated some kind of school, though parts of universities are also called "colleges". In the present context, "college" is increasingly used in many languages to signify that special range of institutions or services now being developed as a new dimension of post-compulsory education.

The more adult status of the over-16s today, both socially and educationally, has contributed to public recognition of the need for new horizons of knowledge and new methods, as well as new approaches and relationships in education. Indeed, a number of current proposals in many countries no longer draw a clear distinction between upper-secondary school and higher education. (Internationally, that has always been difficult, since some countries' higher education overlaps the upper-secondary education of other countries both in age-range and — more significantly — in attainment levels). Readiness to think of "college" as something generic to the upper-secondary/lower-tertiary overlap after the age of 16 is encouraged not only by the development of short-cycle courses and "modules" in higher education but by successful innovations and new needs in upper-secondary education itself. England has much to show here.

It is convenient to recognise as a beginning that an "expanded sixth form" at the top of a grammar or comprehensive school is already a different kind of place, especially if it takes in students from other schools. Simply with its own students staying on in increasing numbers, the inclusion of those whom the Schools Council calls "non-traditional" (because not seeking A-Levels or not doing post-O-Level courses) adds to the general feeling that the "sixth" is not the same because of numbers enrolled and the general change in expectation.

If the inclusion of real newcomers from other schools at the age of 16 leads to the formation of a "mushroom sixth" disproportionate in size to the rest of the school (as often happens now), that is still more a hybrid institution. It is then an "altered sixth" for those staying on from the same school, and a new and separate place for the newcomers. (One school of this type was included in the survey). Apart from any general appreciation the students may have of educational changes around them, most have become specially aware from inter-school contacts that the future of the "sixth" is in question. They usually know of contemporaries who have gone to other places to get their A-Levels or other qualifications.

Between 1966 and 1970 the number of students obtaining their A-Levels in further education colleges doubled, from 15,800 to 31,000. Indeed, the number of students taking their O-Levels in colleges increased from 25,000 in 1966 to 32,000 in 1970 (28% increase). Not all of these were within the usual age-range; but that is not a negative point. Within the usual upper-secondary age-range 16-19, one in four full-time students were in colleges of further education in 1970, and the proportion is growing steadily. In 1970 also further education colleges provided 16.5% of all university entrants, whereas one year earlier the proportion had been 10%.

The junior or general departments of further education colleges (now frequently called their "tertiary" level to distinguish it from degree courses) were once generally thought of as havens for "repeaters" from grammar school sixth forms, or as providers of supplementary or unusual instruction. They do serve that function in some measure; but migration to college even from grammar schools now takes place for more positive reasons. Students seek better or more specialised teaching and equipment; they feel the need for a change, and a fresh start in some instances; but most frequently of all they crave for a more adult atmosphere, though in many grammar schools themselves the climate has greatly changed.

In any case, it should not be supposed that the grammar school sixth form exists for A-Levels. As Mr. Peterson showed, less than a third of even "traditional" sixth-formers go to university; almost a quarter go straight into employment; nearly a third of the "traditional" sixth-formers get only one A-Level or none; and an increasing proportion of "non-traditionals" does not take the examination at all. The DES showed them to be one-sixth of all sixth-formers in 1970.

Thus it cannot be imagined that the sixth form in even favoured selective schools should be contrasted with something less scholarly in further education, or indeed less "educational". For students wishing to prepare for examinations or simply to continue education after attending a non-selective school to the age of 16, the further education college has some advantages. In some LEAs in the West of England, the sixth form has already been abolished altogether, and all A-Level work is concentrated in further education colleges. But rather than move immediately to a conspectus of further education provision, it is more convenient first to consider separate upper-secondary colleges.

Four sixth form "secondary" colleges of the separated type were included in the English survey. Three of them were in one city. Two were single-sex, two coeducational. In each locality a further education college existed alongside. One of these was also included in the survey for the 16-20 age-range, and for studies below the equivalent of A-Level (for example, the Ordinary National Diplomas in technological subjects). All the secondary colleges surveyed, and all the further education colleges, had open access; that is, they did not require a stated number of O-Levels for general admission, though a number of colleges elsewhere do so for all or for some of their intake. In the sample surveyed, one city intends to retain its sixth form secondary colleges distinct, but in coexistence with a further education college. Another locality intends to amalgamate the sixth form college with a "further education" element in a new all-purpose college for the over-16s in 1976.

These facts alone show the variety to be found in a small sample; and that variety could be amplified by referring more fully to the 23 sixth form colleges or separate junior colleges existing in 1973. 20 more were planned for opening by 1975. In fact, of the 132 LEAs which had had their reorganisation plans approved by the Department of Education and Science in a 1972 survey, 51 authorities had introduced or proposed some kind of concentrated sixth form provision. So the tendency to develop separate sixth form colleges under "secondary" regulations is obviously strong.

Arguments of convenience or arising from teachers' preferences vie with others based upon ideology, curriculum study, or the unspoken evidence of young people who choose for themselves where to enrol, and migrate there. Most teachers in schools, especially headmasters, strongly support the retention in secondary schools of whatever sixth form units may be devised. But there is substantial and growing professional opinion in favour of a break about the age of 16.

Understandably, the representatives of further education generally feel the advantages are all on their side: specialist staff, new premises in many cases, equipment, a fresh beginning in tertiary studies, and so forth. In a very moderate stance, the Association of Teachers in Technical Institutions has recommended greater use of further education provision; but it has recognised that for the time being sixth form colleges and junior further education colleges — both of evolutionary type — should probably coexist for some time, so that neither faction should seek to pre-empt the situation. The important regional advisory council for technological education in London and the home counties at the end of 1972 strongly urged co-operation between upper-secondary and tertiary institutions, with distinctive provision in each sector.

In the long run, young adults' own preferences and problems of teacher supply for a hugely enlarged and widened demand may tip the balance in favour of separating from schools a majority of institutions for the over-16s. The evolution of a distinctive "tertiary" college (a "junior" college in the English sense only) may develop a new style. To meet the present mixed situation, it has been proposed that a new set of common regulations should be formulated for all the over-16s, more in keeping with those at present in further education.

For the time being, much experimentation is going on to make the best of both worlds. In some cases, without formal separation of the "sixth" from school or any merger of that with a neighbouring college of further education, there has been co-ordination of timetables so that students may take some courses in each institution. There may also be staff exchanges, or at least one-way traffic in specialists. Some schools also have "linked courses" whereby their students migrate to the college for special facilities on one or more days a week. Naturally, more than scholastic knowledge is gained by these exchanges; the social and humane benefits are obvious. Yet it is astonishing how some LEAs still persist in regarding schools as quite separate from further education — and, indeed, segregating school from school at a time when the students' own out-of-school contacts are more realistic.

Fading Assumptions and New Prospects

No inescapable conclusions are to be drawn from the evidence available. Some of the researchers' personal conclusions will be offered in a later chapter. What the evidence does show inescapably about England is that there is a steadily growing demand for education beyond the age of 16, which is nearly unpredictable in size and extraordinarily varied. What is on offer is multifarious, sometimes imaginative. Sometimes courses seem to be linked only with surviving demands of higher education or trade union specifications. Some of these are absent-minded, to say the least. Even if they are not, they were not designed to serve the futures of the young adults now asking to be educated.

The extraordinary variety of courses on offer — hundreds of A-Level courses, for example, and thousands of others — makes the education of the over-16s all the more of a wilderness in Britain because even within identically named courses there can be internal variation. A teacher can devise his own course within the rubric of formal examination requirements; he can even have a special syllabus approved by an A-Level board, for example. Yet this kind of personalised individuality, which was practicable when a sixth-form teacher had a small circle of diligent (and probably homogeneous) disciples, is remote from today's actuality for most students over 16. For most, the supposedly "traditional" sixth form is a tight system, with little room for manoeuvre in learning. Even structurally, it has not changed enough, despite the manifold variations which local authorities, examination boards, teachers and others have invented. In fact, from the students' or parents' angle alterations often look like a makeshift.

It is a matter of record that year after year, and often more frequently, new prescriptions are proposed for the reform of structure, curricular content, methods, relationships, and policy for the over-16s. It must all bewilder students, and even teachers, if the specialist committee writing the Schools Council Working Paper No. 45 felt compelled to say, despite all their resources, (p.46): "We have been struck at the outset by the lack of information, or even of coherence in the official statistics, when it comes to establishing such apparently simple matters as numbers of pupils, their qualifications on going into the sixth form and their objectives on leaving". Those experts went on to say that such distinctions as that between "traditional" and "non-traditional" sixth-formers were nothing more than a "stubborn old myth". Though for want of better they felt constrained to use such terms, "their dangers should by now be obvious".

In Britain more than in most other countries the range of possibilities is bewilderingly vast, — academic, vocationally linked, "sandwich", part-time, "recurrent", extra-mural, by correspondence, broadcast, intermittent with residence and so forth. But unless this structural apparatus is to be a bothersome clutter it needs firm systematisation and research — if only to supply information, resources and student opportunities.

It seems best to conclude the survey of structural and policy considerations in England with a reference to two potent statements by the government. The 1972 White Paper, *Education: A Framework for Expansion*, proposed the introduction of new two-year courses leading to a Diploma of Higher Education, with the same admission requirement as degree courses. The Dip. H.E., already adopted by some universities and colleges, may be a halfway-house for degrees or other qualifications; or for some students it might be terminal — at least for the time being. It is bound to challenge in important ways many of the assumptions which have hitherto shaped unversity recruitment and therefore have constrained the sixth form. Circular 7/73 anticipated that universities, polytechnics, colleges of education (destined to have new forms and relationships) would all prepare students for the Dip. H.E. across a basic spectrum of higher education, and that more institutions would provide courses leading to degrees.

These simple words imply a structural upheaval. In Britain the awarding of degrees was a jealously guarded prerogative of universities (which can be set up only by Royal Charter) until 1964, when a Council for National Academic Awards was established in consequence of the Robbins Report to validate higher education courses and award degrees in non-university institutions of high standing. Obviously, the polytechnics and a number of technological colleges availed themselves of this new right, and a large number of new degree courses have since been set up, often associated closely with local interests in industry and commerce. A few colleges of education came to prefer this arrangement to the post-Robbins association they have had with universities' Institutes of Education (or Schools of Education), by means of which they could prepare their students for a university's B.Ed. degree as well as teachers' certificates and diplomas.

The real breakaway came in the summer of 1973 when two of Britain's largest colleges of education decided to abandon teachers' certificate studies, to break their existing connection with a university School of Education, and to strike out independently so as to concentrate entirely on degree work from 1974 onwards under the aegis of the Council for National Academic Awards, using the same admissions criteria as universities. At the time of writing neither college was considering the Diploma of Higher Education; but both were consciously moving towards the provision of degree courses in "liberal arts" and "human sciences" as well as in educational studies. Such independent moves of large colleges of education, or new combinations of colleges of various kinds, were foreseen and blessed in the 1972 White Paper. They bring the prospect of higher education much closer to the homes and interests of many students in the sixth form — both geographically and in new complexions of study.

For over-16 institutions other than sixth forms, which have already flexed for the future, these higher education proposals mean something more. They embody the policy of keeping options open and of preparing for a prospect of replenishment rather than of once-and-for-all attainment. Although admission to Dip. H.E. courses themselves is to be conditional on good attainment (2 A-Levels), the proposed siting of some of these courses could mean that all-purpose colleges for the over-16s would include in a 16-20 continuum that first 2-year level of higher education. Comprehensive secondary schools and comprehensive sixth form secondary colleges have already shown a favourable staying-on ratio — all things taken into account. A similar organisation of "college" in the wider post-compulsory range of 16-20 is already showing a favourable effect. With a more welcoming prospect of diplomas and degrees immediately ahead, and with "recurrent" education by the Open University or other means also in the picture, a larger proportion of young men and women might stay on for higher education or take it up later. The already wide range of studies and training available in British higher and "further" education could provide that "working life" base which the Swedes and others have sought so earnestly as a corrective to previous scholastic assumptions.

SECTION D

CURRICULUM AND TEACHING/LEARNING RELATIONSHIPS

PREFACE TO THE CURRICULUM AND TEACHING/LEARNING SECTION

There have been considerable developments recently in the structure of secondary education systems. These developments, noted in the previous section, have on occasion been accompanied by changes in curriculum and teaching/learning relationships. This section of the Report is concerned with the curricular provision in upper-secondary schools and the perceptions of students and teachers of the education offered in these schools. It is not concerned with the detailed content of the curriculum. Instead this section deals rather with the *type* of provision offered, the attitudes and assumptions of the teachers who 'teach' it and the attitudes of the students who 'learn' it.

The fieldwork was based on questionnaires and interviews. 5419 students and 631 teachers from 54 schools answered questionnaires dealing with curriculum and teaching/learning relationships. Examples of these questionnaires, JM1, for teachers, and JM2, for students, will be found in Appendix 1. Many of the questions gave fixed alternatives, others were open-ended. Interviews with teachers, head teachers and officials supplemented the information given in the questionnaires.

The JM1 questionnaire asked students why they had decided to stay on in full-time education, what had attracted them to their particular school, what subjects they were studying. It then asked them what they thought school *should* be doing for them and whether they thought that their teachers were *actually* doing this. There followed a series of open-ended questions in which students were asked how the subjects they studied, the teaching methods, the internal organisation of the school and the extra-curricular activities (if any) helped them or not to achieve what they wanted from school. They were also asked how these things might be improved. These questions were also open-ended.

Open-ended questions were used here because it was felt that fixed alternatives for these questions, which, admittedly, were not easy, would at once suggest categories to the students and "teach" them the sort of replies that were expected. For example, some students saw teaching methods in terms of techniques, such as audio-visual aids or group teaching, but others saw them in terms of personal relationships.

After an initial reading of some of the questionnaires from all the countries a preliminary coding scheme was drawn up to reflect as fully as possible the students' replies. This scheme was tried out on a sample of questionnaires from all countries, adjusted and finally adopted.*

The final part of the students' questionnaire asked them what they thought were the current problems facing schools. There was also space for additional comments for those students who still had the energy and enthusiasm to write! Some students showed a keen and penetrating interest.

The JM2 questionnaire asked teachers whether they expected any changes in the student intake, whether the syllabus and/or teaching methods for their subject(s) would have to be changed as a result, and whether they anticipated any changes in syllabus and teaching methods even if the intake of students was not expected to change. These questions were open-ended. Not all of them have been coded for presentation in this Report because of lack of time. Teachers were then asked exactly the same questions as students, though again, not all the open-ended replies were coded.

By asking these "mirror-image" questions it was hoped to obtain: first, the students' view of themselves, and of their teachers; and, secondly, the teachers' view of themselves and of their students. It was thought that these varying perceptions would illuminate the *process* of education within the schools and suggest some guidelines for policy.

Results, and conclusions, from the work outlined above are in the chapters which follow:

(a)   Chapter 10 deals with the curricular provision as it exists in the countries visited. Only England is dealt with at length because in the other countries it is possible to get official descriptions of curricula from the Ministries concerned. Trends and implications for policy are outlined at the end of the chapter.

(b)   Chapter 11 gives an account of the information on students compiled from the JM2 English questionnaires. Similar accounts of student opinion in

* The authors are much indebted to Mr. J. Tandy of the Computer Advisory Centre in the University of London King's College for his help in preparing the statistics and in particular for his help in preparing the histograms used to illustrate the differences in student and teacher goals.

France, Italy, Sweden and West Germany, though prepared, would have made the Report too long.

(c)   Chapter 12 summarises the information on students from all the countries visited, noting similarities and differences. One point in particular seemed very interesting. It is practically taken for granted now that student achievement is closely linked with social class; and it will be shown in the sociological section of this Report that certain student attitudes to school itself are linked to the school system rather than the social class to which the students belong. More work than can be presented in this Report needs to be done on this point with the material available.

(d)   Chapter 13 looks at the attitudes of teachers and the way in which these contrast with those of students. There is a large gap between the perceptions of students and those of teachers when it comes to describing what actually happens in school. This, together with other findings and conclusions about the teaching/learning situation will be illustrated at the end of the chapter.

CHAPTER 10

CURRICULAR PROVISION

It is almost a truism these days that rapid social change, economic developments which change expectations in life-style and job prospects, and increasing enrolments at 16-plus have led to the questioning of the role of upper-secondary education. It is also clear that many developed countries have realised that the traditional academic curriculum and, in some cases, the authoritarian, magisterial teaching-methods which often accompany it, are not suitable for large numbers of young people in school after the age of sixteen.

As mentioned in an earlier chapter, reforms for the education of this age-group have tended primarily to be structural — an attempt at a *quantitative* democratisation at this level. Curricular studies have often been done "from outside the schools" — studies of the equivalence of diplomas, for example or a re-arrangement of the curriculum in terms of estimated manpower requirements; or a philosophical analysis of the ingredients which should appear in a balanced curriculum.

In the following pages no attempt will be made to compare lists of subjects from different countries, hours devoted to particular subjects, or the equivalence of diplomas and certificates. The curricular policy of the schools and colleges visited in England is dealt with at some length because policy decisions are made at school level rather than local or national level, and are quite diverse. Outlines only are given for the other countries. Their curricular reforms are often built into structural reforms, and this matter has been dealt with in previous chapters. In any case details of subjects etc. are available from the various ministries concerned.

A curriculum, for the purposes of this section of the research, is taken to be the collective name for those structures through which educational goals are achieved. This working definition is deliberately impersonal since educational goals may, in different circumstances, be laid down by ministries, teachers, industry, or even by students themselves! The definition not only includes the content of particular subjects and the methods involved but can also include such things as extra-curricular activities and the internal organisation of the school, where this has an educational, as opposed to an administrative, function. "Organisation", in the following chapters, refers to the internal running of the school, and is not necessarily connected with the structure of the educational system. Two schools, for example, may be comprehensive in structural terms, but, in terms of organisation, one may reflect militant authoritarianism and the other, benevolent anarchy.

A curriculum embodies the sets of educational, social and political values of those who have power to influence decisions. The *level* at which decisions are taken reflects assumptions about subject matter, students, teachers, and the nature of the learning process. The values embodied within the curriculum will be varyingly reflected or distorted by teachers (if these are not the people responsible for the decisions in the first place), and will be perceived by students as a more or less true reflection of original intentions. Student assumptions about the value of education, student perceptions and expectations will all affect the degree to which they accept or reject the curriculum which is offered to them. Thus, in describing a curriculum one is describing a dynamic process. It is therefore necessary to give some indication of the way in which decisions about the curriculum are taken and the way in which they are received.

This chapter looks at the kinds of curricular provision found in the various countries visited, and developing trends.

England

School curricula in England are legally the responsibility of the local education authority; but, in practice, this responsibility is exercised by the head teacher or principal of a school or college. Studies in the sixth form have continued to be based on the specialist study of three allied subjects at A-level, despite various recommendations for reform in the 1960s[1] and despite a growing number of non-academic students in the sixth.

This traditional pattern was illustrated in 1970 by *the Schools Council Sixth Form Survey*.[2] It showed that 69% of sixth formers were doing three or more A-level subjects. Of these, one third were studying only science subjects,

---

[1] A concise summary of these may be found in Peterson, A. D. C., *International Baccalaureate*, London: Harrap, 1972, pp. 99-101.

[2] Schools Council, *Schools Council Sixth Form Survey, Volume 1: Pupils and Teachers*, London: Councils and Education Press for Books for Schools, 1970.

one third only art subjects. Just over one tenth were doing a mixed course of sciences and arts or social sciences. However, 36% of those doing science subjects only said they would have liked to be doing a mixed course; and 29% of those doing only arts subjects said that they too would prefer a mixed course. The most frequently mentioned reasons, in their opinion, for this not being possible were, for scientists problems connected with career, and, for arts students, discouragement by staff.

A further Schools Council publication, *The Universities and the Sixth Form Curriculum*,[3] showed that mixed courses were indeed prejudicial to the chances of university acceptance for those students wishing to read for science degrees. Hence it is understandable that sixth forms with a strong tradition of gaining university places encourage conventional subject groupings. Even so, despite the influence of the universities, another study, *Working Paper No. 45*,[4] shows that the percentage of students taking a mixed arts/science course has risen considerably.

Besides pointing to a change in subject groupings, *Working Paper 45* also shows that there has been an increase in the number of students taking A-levels, together with an increase in the number of students who are doing O-levels (not A-levels) or a non-examination course. The size of this latter group will very likely increase now that the school-leaving age has been raised to 16, but there is no consensus as to the kind of curriculum which these students should follow.

Provision within the schools is therefore diverse — because of the freedom allowed to individual head teachers, and because of the changes occuring in educational thinking and in the student intake.

Fieldwork: curricular policy within the schools

Because of this diversity, it was decided to look at the curriculum of each English school and college visited. Schools Council and DES statistics give a national, general picture; but, inevitably, they do not illustrate the possibilities of growth points in the curriculum nor the influences which the traditional ethos of the school coupled with the attitudes of staff can exercise on the range of subjects offered. Furthermore, Schools Council statistics do not differentiate

---

[3]   Reid, W. A., *The Universities and the Sixth Form Curriculum,* London: Macmillan for the Schools Council, 1972, (Schools Council Research Studies).

[4]   Schools Council, *16-19: Growth and Response,* Working Paper No. 45, London: Evans/Methuen Educational, 1972.

between subjects which, according to the school, need previous study or qualification if they are to be started at A-level and those which, according to the school, do not. This last point is an important one. Sometimes it seems that it is the schools' opinion of the difficulty of a subject rather than something inherent in the subject itself which is the deciding factor as to whether a student should be allowed to do it. One selective grammar school "sixth", for example, allowed no subjects to be started at A-level without some previous study or qualification; yet one of the sixth form colleges visited offered 42 A-levels to beginners.

In order to get as full a picture as possible of the provision offered by a particular school, head teachers and principals were invited to fill in a form which listed subjects (50 in all) which the school might offer. There was space at the end of the form for heads to list additional subjects. In addition to ticking off the subjects in the list they were asked to indicate:

(1)   whether the subject was offered at A-level, O-level, CSE or for any other examination;

(2)   whether the subject could be started at A-level, O-level, or CSE without a previous qualification or course of study;

(3)   whether the subject was compulsory;

(4)   whether there was non-examination course in the subject;

(5)   whether the subject was studied by their students at another school or college, or whether other students came to their school or college.

Principals of technical colleges were asked to give a prospectus with details of their courses and admissions policy. Full details of the range of subjects in particular schools appear in Appendix II. Wherever possible, staff were interviewed so that they could give details of curriculum innovations for which they were responsible.

Findings show a great variety in provision and suggest that the devising of a satisfactory sixth form curriculum is not just a matter of sorting the range of subjects into some philosophically justifiable pattern, but of persuading staff to re-think their attitudes to their own subject, to the teaching methods they use, and to their students. When reading the following account it is as well to bear in mind that English sixth forms often have classes no larger than fourteen and, according to Simon and Benn,[1] quite a number of English teachers consider this to be quite large. Their continental counterparts may well have to struggle with thirty or more to a class. Also English schools tend to be smaller than those on the continent. Of the schools and colleges visited in England, only the technical colleges numbered over a thousand. Several heads of open-access colleges thought it would be difficult to offer a comparable service to a number much over five hundred.

Detailed notes were kept of the subjects taken by students in the sample, which illustrate differences in the allocation of students to various subjects and the degree to which mixes of various kinds are encouraged or allowed within the curriculum policy of individual schools. Students were categorised according to the number of A-levels they did, and whether they did O-levels only, a professional course, or a non-examination course. A-level subjects were classified into the following categories: humanities, human sciences, sciences, mathematics and physics, technical subjects, professional subjects, and arts and crafts. There was also a "mixed" category. To be classified as "mixed" on a three A-level course, for example, a student would have to be doing subjects from *three* of the categories mentioned above e.g. a humanities subject, a human science and a technical subject. On the other hand, if students studied three A-levels, two of which were from one of the categories listed above, they were classified according to that category.

Notes were also kept on which subjects "infiltrated" into other categories. For example, it was rare to find a humanities subject studied with two sciences, or with mathematics and physics; but it was more frequent to find a science subject studied with two humanities subjects. Figures for individual schools are too detailed to be published in this Report but trends of the general policies followed by individual schools will be outlined.

Schools and colleges visited

In all, twelve schools and colleges were visited: two grammar schools, four sixth form colleges, three non-selective secondary schools (officially called "bilateral" in that county, but resembling secondary-modern schools elsewhere), two technical colleges and one art college. It is possible to identify differences in policy between various types of institution as well as differences between institutions of a similar kind.

[1] Simon, B and Benn, C, *Halfway There – Report on the British Comprehensive School Reform,* London: Penguin Books, 1972, p. 302.

The two grammar schools were single-sex; both had a considerable record of academic success; both had a great deal of prestige. Each school had a total enrolment of about 850 students, with over 300 of these in the sixth form.

The four colleges were fairly similar in size (about 500 students). All were open-access, conscious of the problems associated with the open-access situation (particularly the problem of developing subjects and courses for the non-academic sixth former); and all were experimenting in several ways: development of new subjects, adaptation of teaching methods, new forms of assessment, provision of "vocational" courses. Despite these similarities, particularly in respect of structure, these colleges differed amongst themselves, partly because of their past tradition, partly because of the influence of individual head teachers and of the attitudes of staff; and all of them were different from the grammar schools.[1]

The three non-selective ("bilateral") secondary schools shared a catchment area with two grammar schools and two technical colleges. This made it difficult for such non-selective secondary schools to plan a sixth-form curriculum. Should they try to keep their best students, or send them to one of the larger institutions where there will often be better material facilities and a wider choice of subjects? This decision is made even more difficult by the points system which restricts the money available to schools of secondary-modern type, and by the deliberate slowness of some authorities in implementing comprehensive plans.

The two technical colleges were each surrounded by different kinds of institution: one shared a catchment area with grammar schools and non-selective secondary schools, the other with open-access sixth-form colleges and a direct grant school.

Admissions

The grammar school sixth forms demanded some evidence of academic ability before students could be admitted. The girls' school accepted girls from other schools as a matter of policy, but there was a minimum entry requirement of four O-levels. More than half of its sixth-form intake consisted of new girls drawn selectively from other schools over a wide area.

[1] In June 1968 students in sixth-form colleges accounted for only 0.5% of the sixth-form students in full-time education in schools. By 1973 there were 22 such colleges, and plans to introduce about 60 more. For more details of these see Simon, B, and Benn, C *Halfway There – Report on the British Comprehensive School Reform*, London: Penguin Books, 1972.

In all the colleges, entry and allocation of students to various subjects was done through a process of interviews and references, with some consideration given to O-level and C.S.E. examination results at the end of the fifth year in the feeder schools. Particular members of staff in the colleges were responsible for maintaining close links with the feeder schools and making arrangements for the interviews which took place at the end of the summer term prior to entry to the college. Once students were in the college, and once examination results were known, it was possible, in all colleges, to make adjustments to individual timetables.

The girls' sixth-form college was outstanding in this respect. At the end of the summer term in the feeder schools students discuss with the headmistress and staff what they would like to do, assuming that they pass their examinations. They also discuss what they might do if they were to fail. In September, new entrants to the college come a week earlier than the other students so that their timetables can be arranged. The timetable is made up in general outline but finalised only after discussion with staff and students, often on an individual basis.

Even after examination results are known final decisions can be delayed until after students have had some experience of the work expected of them. There is constant revision, and students have the possibility of asking for their personal timetables to be changed after discussion with their tutor and with the head. The headmaster of the boys' sixth-form college said, of his own college, "The main function of the school is to give a *personal service* to students, to detect a student's best qualities and foster them". Such concern for individual requirements is considerable even in comparison with the general run of English sixth forms.

Staff in all the colleges visited said that it was sometimes difficult to assess a student's potential achievement on the basis of O-level and C.S.E. results already obtained. A physics teacher in the boys' college stressed:

> "I do not have much faith in examination results as a judgement of potential, especially as the teaching methods in a sixth-form college are often so different from those in the feeder schools. It is most important that the feeder schools recognise motivation . . . . sometimes boys have potential when the feeder schools don't see it at all".

An English teacher in the same college pointed out that the flexible timetabling system which did not insist on qualifications for entry was such that:

"It enables a lot of people to fulfill themselves who would not otherwise have done so. They would have had nothing. The cleverest of them would have gone out to work and achieved similar qualifications at a tech; but many of them would not have been accepted by a technical college".

Sixth forms in the non-selective secondary ("bilateral") schools were made up of students who had decided to stay on in their own school rather than transfer to another school or college.

Students can apply to technical colleges direct, whereas sixth-form college entrance is arranged via the schools. Entrance to one of the technical colleges was determined by interview and examinations results. The minimum entry requirement was three C.S.E. passes; but many courses required a minimum of four O-levels, and there was a college entrance examination for some courses. The interview provided a screening system; for, although, according to the principal, the college is willing to accept students who have been thrown out of school, the list of courses published by the college points out that: "Applicants for all courses will be required to attend for interview and *must satisfy the appropriate head of department that they are able to benefit from the course"*. (Writer's emphasis).

Subjects and courses

The table below shows the numbers of subjects offered at various levels. The differences illustrate considerable variations in policy on the part of the individual head teachers and their staffs.

In both the grammar schools the range of subjects offered was fairly traditional. This was particularly so in the boys' school. Here over 90% of the sample were doing three or more A-levels. 42.9% of the total sample were doing three or four A-levels in mathematics and physics. The mathematics and physics, and science, categories were the "purest"; i.e. there was very rarely a subject from another category included amongst the three or four A-levels. One boy, for instance studied pure mathematics, applied mathematics, physics and art. By contrast, there was not one single "pure" humanities reply. Usually students studied two humanities subjects with either geography or economics. Similarly students doing two human sciences usually accompanied them with a humanities subject such as history or English (*not* modern languages), rather than with a science or mathematics. Hardly any of the students bothered to list any subjects other than their A-levels, e.g. General Studies, although the school listed these as compulsory. Perhaps the students felt that these were not important compared to A-level subjects. Certainly this school was criticised strongly by students because they felt that there was too much emphasis on teaching for examinations.

Grammar School A (Girls)	Grammar School B (Boys)	Sixth Form College A (Boys)	Sixth Form College B (Girls)	Sixth Form College C (Mixed)	Sixth Form College D (Mixed)	Non-selective Secondary School A (Boys)	Non-selective Secondary School B (Girls)	Non-selective Secondary School C (Mixed)	
22	16	27	31	23	27	1	0	17	A-level
5	8	0	19[1]	42	12	0	0	0	Beginners' A-level
1	0	26	34	22	23	15	19	23	O-level
10	4	15	30	34	29	0	7	0	Beginners' O-level
0	0	0	8	20	6	17	17	17	CSE
0	0	0	7	33	8	0	2	0	Beginners' CSE
0	1	2	12	7	2	2	0	0	Examination other than GCE or CSE
17	20	32	39	33	28	7	19	9	Non-examination course
0	1	0	3	32[2]	1	3	2	12	Compulsory for *all* students
0	3	1	0	5	3	0	0	2	Compulsory for *some* students
0	0	0	2	0	0	0	0	0	Studied by students *from* another school or college
0	0	1	4	1	1	4	0	7	Studied at another school or college

Numbers of subjects offered by schools visited during the course of the research programme

Notes: 1 − plus a further 9 after a short introductory course
2 − represents a course of general studies

By contrast, the girls' school was complimented by a considerable number of its students for its "progressive" teaching methods, and some students thought that their teachers did their best within the constraints imposed by the examination system. The curriculum policy seemed more flexible in the combination of subjects it allowed, and the students listed a great variety of general studies courses and some O-levels in addition to their A-levels. As in the boys' grammar school the humanities category was rarely "pure", and the most frequent "interlopers" were geography and economics. However, unlike the situation in the boys' school, the mathematics, physics, and science categories were not quite so watertight. There was, for example, a girl doing pure mathematics, applied mathematics and history, and another doing botany, zoology and art. Also, in contrast to the boys' school, science subjects were occasionally studied with arts subjects: e.g. English, French and zoology; English, Greek and biology. Compared to the timetables at the boys' school, some of the girls' timetables suggested a much wider range of interest. For instance, one girl was doing history, English, economics and art — all at A-level, together with general studies, cookery, and Latin literature in translation.

Both of these grammar schools fitted into the national picture in that there was a preponderance of A-level work (understandably, as both were highly selective), and girls tended to study the humanities rather more than the sciences while boys tended to concentrate more on science. Compared to the sixth-form colleges, which had no academic entry qualifications, the grammar schools offered few subjects to beginners despite the already proven success in O-level terms of the intake into their sixth forms. This may be due to innate conservatism or the fact that staff do not have sufficient time to develop courses for beginners because of teaching commitments in the lower school. Certainly the deputy head of the girls' school pointed out that their own tradition of success in conventional terms was a problem:

> "Our own success in terms of examination results, and the expertise we have developed in a limited range, militate against change. Examination syllabuses dominate, and teachers who have succeeded in examinations themselves and learned to live with them are not necessarily alert to needs outside them. Large schools impose greater strain and more pressure; but teachers resist radical changes in organisation and structure (which might lead to greater efficiency and less strain) through fear that they will destroy the personal touch".

The "large" school of which she is speaking has about 850 students of whom 300 or so are in the sixth form. This is small compared to the numbers of

1,000 or even 2,000-plus in some continental schools where teachers may have to cope with 30 or more "sixth formers" to a class.

The provision offered by the grammar schools contrasts with that offered by the sixth-form colleges. It is worth emphasising at this point that the percentage of students who stay on in full-time education in England is still fairly low compared to the number staying on in other European countries (see the earlier section on Structure and Policy). Therefore English sixth-form colleges are, perhaps, partly revealing the larger "pool of ability" which a low staying-on rate has previously concealed and, partly (through flexible timetabling, waiving of "minimum qualifications" and recognition of motivation) allowing individual students to develop much more fully than they would have done in a conventional setting. The previously unrecognised potential of some students, together with the willingness of staff to experiment, and the influence of individual head teachers, have led to the large numbers of subjects available to beginners in the sixth-form colleges.

The boys' sixth-form college, formerly a grammar school with an impressive record of academic achievement, offered at the time of the field-work: 27 A-levels, 26 O-levels, 15 O-levels for beginners, no C.S.E. subjects, no A-levels for beginners. This would seem to be more conservative than the range offered by the other sixth-form colleges visited. Indeed the headmaster said, in an interview, that as far as curriculum was concerned he preferred to consolidate the existing pattern and explore general and integrated courses for which it was important "to get the content right and to get the enthusiasm of the staff". Interviews with staff confirmed this impression of development within a tradition, and development of new courses as a form of experiment in expectation of a larger non-academic intake.

The student sample in the boys' sixth form college were doing fairly conventional A-level humanities and science groups of subjects; but, unlike the boys' grammar school, there were more mixed courses — some very interesting — and more willingness to allow a subject from one group to be studied with subjects from another group. For example, two boys were doing pure and applied mathematics, physics, and French. Though some students studied two humanities subjects with economics, as in the boys' grammar school, economics was found just as often, and perhaps more wisely, with mathematics and sciences. Some students were doing O-levels only, though none did less than four; but these were a minority. The college, however, was developing teaching materials and methods to cope with an expected larger group.

The girls' sixth-form college — a former grammar school — had, for a number of years previous to becoming an open-access college, accepted girls from the local secondary modern schools into its sixth form. Possibly the experience gained from this practice may have been the reason why the college was able to offer a large number of beginners' O-levels, and unlike the boys' college, a considerable number of beginners' A-levels. Many subjects were offered as either one- or two-year O-level courses, and staff were flexible in their attitude to qualifications for particular A-level subjects. As in the boys' college, staff stressed that motivation and determination on the part of students were very important. There was a growth of C.S.E. Mode III examinations,* wide use of Nuffield science examinations, and a development of vocational subjects such as animal-nursing and child care, though these affected only a small number of students at the time of the fieldwork.

Most of the student sample were doing fairly conventional A-level courses; but again, in contrast to the grammar schools, there was a larger percentage of mixed courses, more readiness to allow subjects from different groups to be studied together. This college was the only school visited to have humanities groups of subjects at A-level which were strongly biassed towards modern languages — perhaps because of the enthusiasm of the head of modern languages who had worked outside teaching for some time, and was introducing some courses which did not emphasise the literary element. Some students spanned an extremely wide range of interests both in the subjects they studied and in the extra-curricular activities offered at the college.

Sixth-form college C, a mixed college, offered the largest range of subjects. Like the other two colleges it had been a grammar school; but, unlike them, it was co-educational and did not have such a famous tradition. Perhaps for this very reason it was able to introduce a greater range of beginners' subjects, as staff would not have been concerned to protect what they considered to be "high academic standards". There was a considerable number of Mode III syllabuses and a concern to make subjects relevant and practical. More applied studies were being introduced, especially on the technical side.

As in the other colleges, staff were much concerned about their relationships with students; but, apart from some particular exceptions, discussion on curricular questions tended to rest on the question of content without veering into discussion of relationships as it had, for instance, in the two colleges mentioned above. One felt that many changes had happened, and were happening, quite fast in the college. This, while resulting in enthusiasm and excitement in some members of staff, tended to produce some resentment in others. In the two colleges mentioned earlier new subjects and internal organisational changes had been introduced at a slower rate. It seemed that staff were more united in their aims because of this. Rapid expansion of subjects and

* A method of examination which emphasises teacher participation and choice of syllabus.

courses also produced staffing difficulties; this college ran thirteen separate mathematics courses at the time of the fieldwork.

The last of the four colleges visited was similar in many respects to the other three but it was unusual in one respect — many of the student sample were doing a mixed A-level course of subjects taken from three groups of subjects, and others spanned a great range of subjects and levels of work in the mixtures of O and A-level work. For example, one student was studying music, sociology and engineering drawing, all at A-level, plus O-level German.

The colleges so far described place great emphasis on individual choice, on personal time-tables, and on recognition of motivation as a qualification to do a particular subject (not just academic attainment as measured by O-level). Combinations of subjects and sometimes even the length of course are arranged to suit individual students. But, although staff go to great lengths to ensure immediate intrinsic satisfaction as far as subject choices are concerned, they are aware, particularly those who teach boys, that many students stay on for qualifications for a job or for further studies.

Technical colleges, on the whole, provide courses (rather than subjects) which have entry qualifications and a fixed duration. In an interview the principal of one of the two technical colleges visited pointed out that the college was too big to provide individual timetables for students like the sixth form colleges in the area. The technical college offered instead a series of structured courses — even the choice of A-levels was structured. He questioned the value of tailor-made courses and wondered what students would be qualified to do after such courses, and went as far as to say, "Free choice is not in the best interests of students".

Both the technical colleges visited run link-courses with schools in their area. One of the colleges was able to report in its annual review, "Liaison with schools grows stronger and link courses are proving almost too popular. Accommodation problems will mean that a limit must be imposed". Short full-time courses run during vacation were also very well attended.

The curricular policies of the three non-selective secondary schools are rather different, as can be seen from the list of subjects listed for various schools at the beginning of this section.

Non-selective secondary school A (boys) was, at the time of the survey, intended to become the main home of a new comprehensive school by amalgamation with grammar school A mentioned earlier. The curriculum policy is that in the fifth form most students take a range of C.S.E. subjects, as many as eight or nine. In some classes boys take three to six subjects at C.S.E. level and spend two full days a week at one of the local technical colleges. Once in the sixth form they take a range of five to eight O-levels. There is only one A-level subject on offer and no beginners' courses either at O-level or in C.S.E.

In non-selective secondary school B, a girls' school, it was the policy of the headmistress to encourage her most able students to transfer to the local grammar school so as to stand a better chance of receiving the sort of education she believes they need. At the time of the survey 38 girls had been so transferred in the previous year — all with more than 4 O-levels, and some with as many as 9. Most girls who stay on into the sixth take either a mixture of O-level and C.S.E. subjects or an O-level/C.S.E. course together with shorthand and typing, and/or O-level commerce. However, A-level provision is now expanding.

The third non-selective secondary school, a mixed one, was far more distinctly "bilateral" in offering a range of examination-oriented courses. It was larger than the other two and had, again, a different policy. (In fairness it should be added that the material resources of this school were better than the other two). Students in the fifth year tended to take either eight or nine subjects at C.S.E. level or a range of O-levels, sometimes as many as ten. As in non-selective school A there are also link-courses for fifth-formers with one of the local technical colleges. Unlike the other two non-selective schools, it had a range of A-levels in the sixth form. (The local grammar schools cream off 15% of the initial intake at 11; but they are obviously not using up all the available talent). Some of the students in this school had very heavy time-tables. One student, for example, was doing English, history, and religious knowledge, all at A-level, together with O-level French, R.S.A. shorthand and typing, German, and general studies! The groupings of the various subjects at A-level seemed fairly flexible.

The headmaster looked forward to the development of more link-courses, more flexibility in the curriculum, a greater range of A-levels, an extension of the C.S.E. approach, and an acceptance that A-level was not necessarily a two-year course — it could be more, or less. In this, and the other factors mentioned above, his approach was similar to that of the heads of the sixth-form colleges. He thought too that an extended school day and provision for students to stay on in school in the evenings would be likely developments. Such an attitude was in contrast to that expressed by the head of one of the neighbouring grammar schools who thought that students transferred in the sixth form from other schools "needed a lot of remedial O-level coaching"!

Finally, the Research Unit visited a school of art and design which was in the process of moving away from the position of "art for art's sake" to the preparation of its students in general skills useful to their career, as well as in artistic techniques. The college prospectus points out:

"It is a main objective of the design courses to produce
students educated and trained in such a way as to

become effective in the industrial situation as soon as possible after leaving school . . . . Apart from a comprehensive range of craft skills and techniques . . . . the students must also learn to control complex situations comprising people and services; be capable of working within and of contributing to group situations; be capable of comprehending and utilising the effects of other technological skills and research".

It is envisaged that these very diffuse skills will be acquired through the subjects associated with each of the five main areas of study: communication design, three-dimensional design, dress and fashion design, fine art, and a general foundation course. Interestingly, when the principal of the college was asked to fill in the form which indicated the subjects offered by the college, he did not place a tick against art, but ticked economics, mathematics, metalwork, psychology and sociology and listed under "additional subjects": ecology, cybernetics, systems analysis and organisational theory!

Extra-curricular activities

All the schools and colleges encouraged extra-curricular activities though the emphasis placed on them by schools and sixth-form colleges was rather different to that placed on them by the technical colleges.

The sixth form colleges emphasised the value of extra-curricular activities by making space for them in the official time-table, usually in the form of one afternoon a week devoted to sporting or leisure activities. Sometimes colleges were open in the evenings. Taking part in extra-curricular activites was seen to be educationally beneficial. The head of sixth form college A, for example, expected teachers to encourage extra-curricular activities as part of their job: "Staff have got to go out and make things happen". He thought that the students should get to know staff not just because this made the academic content easier to teach, but also because the relationship was worthwhile in itself, "otherwise we might just as well hand over to F.E."

In "F.E.", i.e. further education in the technical colleges, students ran their own Students' Union. In one college the Union had an income of £10,000 from the local authority (£3 for each full-time student, 50p for each part-time student). The other college ran a Leisure Activities scheme on one afternoon a week, rather similar to schemes organised by the sixth form colleges. However, unlike the sixth-form college programmes, this programme was not compulsory for full-time students. It was organised through clubs affiliated to the Students' Union. Students were encouraged to play a responsible part and staff were available for help and advice. The member of staff responsible for the overall organisation of this new venture commented, in the college report: "The scheme encouraged good staff-student relationships and ensured that clubs had a keen membership. On the other hand, the aimless and apathetic students were left in a vacuum, and this might be deemed an educational failure".

This contrast in attitude between technical colleges, and schools and sixth-form colleges is a reflection of the differences in the attitude of staff towards their pastoral role. Although some individual members of staff in technical colleges take great trouble to get to know their students, there is much less emphasis on these colleges on pastoral care than there is in the schools and sixth-form colleges.

From the account just given above, it seems that curricular provision in the institutions visited during the course of the research falls into two main categories: that provided by the schools and colleges and that provided by the technical colleges. Assumptions about the subject matter and the role of staff are somewhat different.

In schools there is an emphasis on the pastoral role of staff; in technical colleges there is less emphasis on this aspect, more on a preoccupation with job preparation and industry. The technical colleges tend to provide courses rather than a free choice of subjects. These courses tend to be of specific length and aim at a particular qualification. They may have a specific entry qualification and are often related to a particular field of employment. This characteristic is in contrast to the schools. The grammar schools seemed preoccupied with offering combinations of subjects which would relate directly to university and other full-time studies. Sometimes they were flexible in allowing unusual combinations of subjects to be studied; but the sixth form colleges were far more flexible in this respect, as they were in permitting variations in the length of studies, waiving qualification requirements for strongly motivated students who wished to do particular subjects, and developing a range of subjects which could be taken by beginners.

In many ways the sixth-form colleges seem ideal — they can capitalise on student motivation, use all their available resources, give full rein to teachers' inventiveness, care, and commitment. However, one does wonder whether some of the students who leave school at eighteen, with qualifications no better than many other students have at sixteen, really do stand a fair chance on the job market, even though they have "mature" personalities and an interest in a variety of subjects. Perhaps this risk will be minimised as more people stay on who will be in the same position, and more opportunities for part-time education become available. On the other hand, although technical colleges provide specific courses, often related to a field of employment, they may turn away students whose atainment so far is low and whose potential is, as yet, unrecognised. Several staff in the sixth-form colleges made the point that they had seen students achieve highly successful grades at A-level who would have been turned away by technical colleges. These students would also, possibly, have been given much more support in terms of relationships with staff, and more individual attention.

At the time of writing, approximately one quarter of all English students receiving upper-secondary education are in "further education" colleges. Several schemes now in operation have amalgamated a technical college and all the local sixth forms so that all young people in those areas receive their education in one common institution. As a structural reform this is administratively attractive; but it raises many questions as to curricular provision and internal organisation. To what extent will the placing of responsibility for his own "life and work" be given firmly to the student himself? Will there be set qualifications for courses/subjects, or will motivation be taken into account?

From the experience of the fieldwork in England it seems clear that innovations in content are not so important as changes in attitude on the part of teachers and head teachers, and a more widespread acceptance of, and competence in, basic teaching skills. The same history syllabus, which attracts praise from students in one school because it teaches them to think and reason, will be criticised by students from another, who find that they are forced to swallow a mass of unrelated facts.

In the curricular developments in the sixth-form colleges, the innovations in the art school, and in the development of general studies in one of the grammar schools, the role of the head teachers or principal was of paramount importance in acting as a catalyst for the adoption of new policies. This was particularly evident in the case of the sixth-form colleges, especially as many of the staff had been used to a grammar school tradition. Judging the degree and rate of change in organisation and relationships is perhaps more difficult than deciding details of curriculum and teaching methods. It was a tribute to two of the heads particularly that so many of their teachers had become committed to making the idea of open access really work. Colleges such as these match up to proposals outlined in *Working Paper 45.*[1]

"The schools and colleges will have to plan for diversity,

[1] Op. cit., P. 53.

allow for the late developer and the student who changes
course and make sure that no route is a dead end . . . . It
is up to the schools and colleges, *rather than any
external body*, to see that their pupils have the right
curricula . . . . *Each school will have to decide,* and make
clear to students, *just what its resources can provide".*
(Writer's emphasis).

England is unique among the countries visited in wishing to foster such a
degree of decentralised initiative. Such a system needs really good head teachers
skilled at getting their staff to adapt and work together. It assumes a good
counselling service. It assumes, too, that research into, and development of, new
approaches and curricula will be firmly based in the schools, with teachers'
centres and the inspectoral and advisory services developing a role akin to
consultancy. Such a system encourages an individualistic approach and is in
strong contrast to what may be found in other countries.

France

In contrast to England, France has a strongly centralised system where curricula,
general directions as to teaching methods, and hours to be spent on certain
subjects are laid down by the *Ministère de l'Education Nationale.* Details are
published by the *Institut National de Recherche et de Documentation
Pédagogiques* (INRDP), formerly called *Institut Pédagogique National.*

After the lower-secondary course, students are "guided", according to
their aptitudes, results and wishes, to one of the "long" courses leading to a
baccalauréat or a technician's certificate (*brevet*), or to one of the "short"
courses which combine a vocational training with a general education. (Details of
the *baccalauréats* and *brevets* have already been given in Chapter 5). Even
though students are "guided", it is not clear to what extent it is possible for
students to change courses, nor to what extent wishes and aptitudes are taken
into account, as opposed to examination results.

This centralised system is at once France's greatest strength and weakness.
It ensures a uniform system throughout the country and can in principle insist,
for instance, that teachers of a particular subject follow several days' in-service
training if there are changes in curricula or techniques. On the other hand the
sheer massiveness of the system makes it cumbersome. The reasons given for
reforming higher education might well apply to the schools.

> "Centralisation, which was designed to ensure co-ordination, provoked suffocation. It no longer harmonised initiatives, but risked paralysing them . . . . The great currents stirring the world seemed to stop at the gates of the educational system".[1]

Educators are aware of this creeping paralysis, and the system is slowly becoming more flexible. It is possible, for example, to ask for new courses to be approved by the Ministry, *if the school can prove that there are employment opportunities* for students enrolling on such courses. One of the technical *lycées* visited during the fieldwork had started a *baccalauréat* in 1971 for socio-medical studies. It was thought that students on this course would find employment in the laboratories, the large medical faculty and thermal centres in the region. The same *lycée* also organised a new course for the vocational certificate (B.E.P.) in health and social studies, which would send students into the same range of employment but at a lower level. There was also a centre for computer studies in the school which had its own special computer and a terminal linked to the university computer. Five teachers had gone on a year's training course, paid for by the State, to the firm which supplied the computer. One of the staff who had been on the course stressed the value of close links between industry and school, but thought that industry should hire out equipment to schools to save them the enormous capital investment needed to buy it.

Technical *lycées* have an advantage over other *lycées* in that they have additional money to spend from the *taxe d'apprentissage*. It also seemed that the technical schools, perhaps because of their links with industry and the inevitable changes that this would bring in curricula and techniques, were open in their attitudes, more ready to change. This did not affect only teachers of technical subjects but of general subjects too.

The ordinary *lycées* can run experiments if the individual teachers responsible have permission from the *Institut National de Recherche et de Documentation Pédagogiques*. Not many teachers seem to want to cope with this formality. The *lycées pilotes* seem to have more teachers who are ready to experiment and undertake research but, basically, the programme and timetable for these schools are the same as for the ordinary *lycées*. A head teacher cannot select his own staff. He can encourage experiments and research but he cannot initiate them. One head teacher of a *lycée pilote* said, when pressed on this point, *"Moi, je ne peux rien"*. Teachers who participate in research and experiments which have official approval are paid for a specific number of hours.

[1] French Government, *Higher Education Act of 13th November 1968*, translation from the Service de Presse et d'Information at the French Embassy in London.

This is a double-edged bonus. The number of hours which can be paid for is limited; and several teachers said they would not experiment in new curricula or techniques, because there was no money to pay them. Again this is in contrast to England where the many hours put in by some teachers on the development of new programmes are unpaid.

The *Centres de Recherche et de Documentation Pédagogiques* are the base for research and development of two kinds: first, that imposed and paid for by the Ministry; and secondly, that which is voluntary and unpaid. The courses run by the centres also fall into the two same categories. Such centres are better equipped and have more money and staff than English teachers' centres. One centre had, for example, six full-time staff, plus a director, plus thirty part-time staff who spent half their time in the centre and half in school. English centres, however, like English schools, are more free and experimental. The director of one French centre said that it was difficult to bring about a less authoritarian and centralised system simply because of the strength of tradition: "Teachers will wait for a directive which tells them to be less directive in their teaching".

The *Institut National de Recherche et de Documentation Pédagogiques* has powers to conduct experiments, and to produce working papers for discussion; but it is the responsibility of the government to pass an appropriate law and implement any reforms which are considered necessary. For this reason reforms, according to a senior spokesman of the *Institut*, tend to be piecemeal. They deal with one small aspect of all schools at a time, and have a restricted impact. He would prefer a much more radical reform to affect a small number of schools which would then act as catalysts to other schools in the region. He proposes a completely new form of upper-secondary schooling which would unify general and technical education. It would be based on the recognition that students want to be able to spend more time on the subjects that interest them, and that they want to be treated as adults. The curriculum would be based on a small common core, and a series of options. The students would spend most of their time on the options and on independent work. At the end of the course there would be an examination, equivalent in value to the *baccalauréat,* in which the forms of assessment would reflect the kind of teaching the students had received. If such a scheme were to be accepted by the government it would be revolutionary indeed, for it implies a much greater say being given to teachers and to students. It also implies a radical change in the attitudes of teachers, and a different approach to teacher training.

France has officially accepted that its centralised system is no longer altogether satisfactory, and the Ministry has started to encourage freer teaching methods and some degree of experimentation and decentralisation. As yet, however, attitudes in many areas are a reflection of the old authoritarian system.

Any change in attitudes will need to include changes in attitudes on the part of inspectors and administrators as well as teachers.

Italy

Like France, Italy has a strongly centralised system; but, unlike the system in France, it is not being used very much at present to ensure the growth of new structures, for instance, to develop teacher preparation and an advisory and consultancy service for teachers. France is exploiting its centralised system to develop, for example, a network of teachers' centres across the whole country. These arrange courses and experiments proposed by the Ministry; but they also have a degree of autonomy to arrange courses according to local demand for the teachers in the region. One has the impression that in Italy there is much discussion, but no action. This is due, in great measure, to the political situation.

Upper-secondary schooling takes place in various *licei* and *istituti* each of which has a curriculum which emphasises its particular specialism and also offers a general education, rather like the system of *baccalauréats* in France, though in France several *baccalauréats* will be taught in one school whereas in Italy only one type of *maturità* is available from each type of *liceo*. Teacher training is minimal, curricula are encyclopaedic, and teaching methods magisterial in most cases. (Further details on these points are in Chapter 7: Structure and Policy in Italy).

As in France, any changes and experiments have to be approved by the Ministry. Technical institutes have some autonomy in that they can adapt the technical aspects of their studies to take into account recent or local developments in industrial techniques; but all other changes have to be approved via the hierarchical channels which lead to Rome. Although there is a special bureau within the Ministry which deals with the *scuola media*, there is no special office which has responsibility for initiating research and development. Each type of school has a "general director" at the Ministry to oversee curricula and teaching methods; but within the offices of these directors the officials who approve or reject innovations and experiments have not had any special training in assessing the value of such projects. Nor is there any official policy with regard to experimentation. Some schools are said to ask for permission to run experiments because of the status, money and extra facilities that this will bring rather than any genuine interest in research as such.

In Italy all kinds of *maturità* have a strongly "academic" content — sometimes for prestige reasons. The *maturità* from the *liceo classico* is, as pointed out earlier, much prized. The students may hate the teaching methods and the mass of facts they have to learn, and the *maturità* may not be much help in getting a job, but as a status symbol it is fine. In the Italian system, therefore, there are undoubtedly some students following academic courses who would be happier with a less academic content; and there are also students following scientific, technical, or vocational studies, for example, who would be happier with more of "the humanities". The absence of a flexible curriculum, the impossibility of transferring from one course to another and the absence of a counselling service all combine to make the situation frustrating to students — and to some teachers.

The main experiment in the general upper-secondary sector is a development in some places of a new kind of preliminary two-year common cycle (*biennio*) for all students in the first years of their five year course. It is thought that this experiment was backed because three of the "general directors" at the Ministry favoured it. Within the already well-defined framework of the institution attended, the common cycle enables students to delay choosing their specialist course of study until the age of sixteen. Though, as shown in Chapter 7, proposals for a *biennio* of general character are discussed as though they are to apply to all upper-secondary education, in fact they are feasible only in *general* education, and would be much more difficult in technical or vocational institutes.

The new *biennio*, in its various forms, was developed to combat the difficulties outlined above. Five schools in various regions in Italy were given permission to allow a particular number of classes to study a common core of subjects for two years. Researchers and specialists in sociology and psychology worked with the teachers to develop content and teaching methods. The five *biennio* experiments were allowed to develop individually so that the Ministry could decide on future action on the basis of the different results. At the time of writing no such decision has been made and, according to the writer's present knowledge, there has not been a directive as to whether the original classes should be continued or disbanded.

One of the first examples of a common *biennio* to be set up was that in Milan in 1970 after permission had been given from the ministry in November 1969 — which gave teachers and researchers less than a year for the detailed planning. (The English sixth-form colleges were given much longer). Full details of the *biennio* are published by the Milan authorities.[1] Briefly, three researchers worked with teachers in the school chosen. The curriculum was agreed between staff and researchers jointly. The teachers had a week of in-service training and

[1] Amministrazione Provinciale di Milano, *Il Biennio — per una Scuola Formativa Orientiva Unitaria*, ed. Scurati C., Milano: 1971.

met the researchers once a week to discuss details of progress and suggestions for further development. Changes could not be too radical as students had to continue with three years of the ordinary course after two years on the new course. As part of the present research described in this Report, a small number of JM questionnaires were given to some of the Milan *biennio* students. The number was far too small to give any real indications as to whether the different system had made any real impact; but an Italian educator, closely connected with the Milan experiment, who read through answers to the questionnaires (*not* coded with the main bulk of the Italian sample), thought that they were not very different from the replies given by the ordinary run of Italian students.

Another experimental *biennio* was started in Rome one year after the Milan experiment. As with Milan *no directions were given from the Ministry and teachers and researchers were left to "discover" appropriate measures for themselves.* The head of the school which organised the *biennio* pointed out that a number of students in his *liceo* came from a Montessori private school in the neighbourhood. For this reason the students were receptive to the new methods and the parents were keen too.

The head explained that one of their first goals was to establish what he called *homogeneity among teachers.* Italian teachers in the same school often do not know each other professionally or personally. The first eight group meetings of teachers and researchers were non-directive, with no agenda, to allow staff to get to know each other. Only then did discussion turn to educational objectives. The second goal was, according to the head, a "sensitisation" of the families. Parents were invited to come to school in the evenings. They expected a lecture but were surprised when they were invited to discuss rather than listen. Students also were invited to discuss, so that they could come to understand more fully what they wanted to do.

On the teaching side there was much innovation, including a completely experimental physics course (though mathematics was taught in a traditional way), a direct-method approach to the teaching of Latin and Greek, and the introduction of an optional sociology course, and some psychology. The main objectives were to give a broad, concrete approach to the disciplines so that students would be able to select their subsequent studies on the basis of a clearer understanding of those studies, and a clearer understanding of themselves. This was important as, in Italy, the parents traditionally chose for the children – and the principal wanted students to feel they could make their own choices. (Again this calls for a good counselling service). The school was also trying to establish links outside school so that students could go on visits, and so that people from outside could come in.

Perhaps the main thing was the attempt to change attitudes in teachers and students. Once the *responsibility* for changing attitudes was given firmly to the teachers, the principal felt that in-service training would then be directly helpful (rather than hortatory) if it could "catch the teacher at the point of trouble", and help him to solve the problems of the moment. A more open situation in the classroom took away the atmosphere of confrontation associated with the traditional classroom situation. The psychologist associated with the project thought that political extremism was a form of paranoia and came from "a too abstract way of living with other people". He pointed out that students were very keen on politics but that if they were asked questions about facts or politics they *knew* little, though their attitudes were extreme. (This was borne out in the researchers' conversations with students in several schools after the questionnaires had been completed). The psychologist thought that if the school had not developed in students a more concrete human feeling about the community in which they lived then it would have failed. A teacher who worked with the Milan *biennio* felt that the extreme position taken up by many students on questions of politics meant that people did not communicate in any real sense any more, but just shouted slogans at each other.

Although the new *biennio* experiments affect very small numbers of students and teachers they have been described as far as space allows, because they point to interesting considerations for reform in the Italian system. They are fascinating, not because of any changes in the content in the curriculum (which does not appear to be very different from what is happening now in other schools with progressive ideas), but because of the way in which changes have been initiated. In particular they are of interest because they have taken place in a rigid, centralised, and mainly static system. In Italian circumstances, several features are remarkable: the freedom from ministry directives; the use of psychologists and sociologists as consultants at the place of action (i.e. "where it happens!"); the attempts to get teachers to know each other before starting practical in-service training; the possibility for teachers to contribute to, and devise, programmes for themselves; the acknowledgement that curricular reform depends on changes of attitude and relationships more than it does on changes in content.

Sweden

Sweden is so well documented that it is almost an impertinence to present a summary of the curricular provision for the upper-secondary age-group. In any case, since many Swedish curricular reforms are linked to reforms in structure these have already been described in Chapter 8: "Structure and Policy in Sweden". It suffices here to recall that there are places in school for 90% of the age group, though 80% – 85% are actually enrolled, with the possibility that this number might fall rather than rise.

Although students can enter the now comprehensive upper-secondary school as of right, entry to particular lines depends very much on marks obtained in the *grundskola*. A 1972 investigation revealed that not more than 50% of students entered the "line" of their first choice because of the unequal demand for places, though in answer to the questionnaires most of the student sample said they were studying the subjects they originally wanted to. The system of guiding students to particular "lines" so that enrolments reflect the percentages outlines above is in contrast to the developments in English sixth-form colleges, where an attempt is made to give students individual timetables. However, as yet England is coping with much smaller numbers than Sweden (see Chapter 9 on Structure and Policy in England).

Curricula are defined by the Swedish National Board of Education, which also gives recommendations for teaching methods. There is constant revision and an organised system of experimentation, again supervised by the National Board of Education. An outline of the system for organising research projects was given by Sixten Marklund at the Karlskrona conference in 1972.[1] Despite the energy of the National Board of Education several head teachers complained of the mass of paper which swamped their offices; and many of the teachers interviewed said that they would like to have more direct practical help on the spot rather than directives. They wished for something akin to the English advisory service which operates *in* the schools. Swedish teachers are consulted about curricular matters; but this is at "union-representative" level. Some teachers felt that there was no one for them to talk to if they were in difficulties. However, it must be said that in the years since the second World War the Swedes have in many ways created a new nation, largely through the services of their education and welfare systems.

In all the Swedish schools visited, not one teacher talked about the "development of individuality", "self-expression", "development of personality", "personal fulfilment" – all current in differing degrees in replies from other countries. When this was mentioned to an official at the National Board of Education he replied that individuality was expensive and one had to get the social and economic factors right first! Perhaps because of this view, teachers tended to define their role very narrowly; a teacher teaches and a counsellor counsels. There seemed little awareness of the way in which these roles might merge into each other or enrich each other.

[1] Council of Europe, *Curriculum Planning and Development for Upper-Secondary Education*, Document No. CCC/EGT (72) 16, Strasbourg, 1973.

Germany

France, Italy and Sweden are all, to a greater or lesser extent, using their centralised systems to introduce reforms which would give more autonomy to regional authorities or to individual schools. This decentralisation is associated with chances of more participation for teachers. Germany has, for a long time, had a decentralised system of control in which the various *Länder* have had the power to organise their own education. This regional autonomy, however, has been used to maintain rigid, selective systems which therefore, as there are eleven *Länder* in Germany, make wholesale reform require eleven times as much effort as in countries which have enough to do to reform one centralised system. Furthermore, the various elements of the school system are bound tightly by different regulations.

Since 1969, however, the *Bundesministerium* has, jointly with the *Länder*, initiated several reforms and experiments under the auspices of the *Bund-Länder Kommission für Bildungsplanung*. Experimental upper-secondary schools have been set up as part of the reforms. German students elsewhere, however, have to choose a path through to a job or further studies via a range of specialist schools, each with its own curriculum, each offering qualifications of different value for further studies. Details of these have already been noted in Chapter 6: Structure and Policy in the Federal Republic of Germany.

It was not possible during the fieldwork to visit any of the experimental schools. Those which the Unit did visit seemed to be fairly typical of the types described in Chapter 6. Teachers were aware that their schools attracted different amounts of prestige and that their students were very conscious of the need to get the right qualifications. As one teacher put it, "This school is a dealer in life chances". It was clear that there was much discussion going on as to the future of vocational education, which some staff thought was too restricted to the immediate demands of industry and not broad enough to cope with the changing patterns in industrial techniques. Many of the students in schools with a technical bias were on sandwich courses or day release courses. The *Gymnasium* visited during the fieldwork had obtained permission from the city authorities to introduce a system of options in the last years at school, in which students could choose subjects and even teachers. It was thought that this would give students more motivation and lessen any difficulties of discipline which might occur. A tutor system was also being introduced for which the teachers seemed to be enthusiastic.

Some final remarks on curriculum

The different patterns of curricular provision outlined above point to various trends in education for the 16-20 age-group. It is clear from the move towards comprehensive schools, and entry into upper-secondary education as of right, that the selection systems, if they have not already done so, will become far more open. This is linked with a postponement of specialisation, together with the possibility, in some areas, to start new subjects or courses at this stage, or to change lines.

Preparation for the world of work places increasing emphasis upon general education and on the acquisition of skills and techniques rather than a particular training which quickly dates. Indeed a "general education" may, for the purposes of a job, be as important as a technical education as so many of the growing service industries depend in large measure on the ability of employees to get on with others and to adapt to conditions as yet unknown. Although, as will be seen in later chapters, a good many students complain of the vast number of facts they have to learn, there is a tendency for some of the academic courses to be pruned of superfluous content. More emphasis is placed on the ways of thinking which are associated with a particular content rather than the acquisition of large numbers of unrelated facts.

The boundaries between different types of education (i.e. general, professional and technical) seem to be less clearly defined than previously, especially as there is a trend towards a "comprehensive" upper-secondary school. Also there is a growing interest in integrated studies, or, at least, in finding some way of showing students how different styles of thinking interrelate. Perhaps the best known example of the latter is the compulsory paper in the philosophy of knowledge taken by all candidates for the International Baccalaureate.[1] A real integrated study, as opposed to a rag-bag of bits and pieces drawn from different disciplines, supposes that teachers will have had an education or preparation which enables them to present an "integrated" study.[2]

There is now a much wider acceptance of "progressive" methods such as audio-visual aids, group teaching etc.; but these of course demand much more involvement on the part of the teacher; and since these methods depend often on follow-up based on discussion, they also demand more in terms of personal skills. Training for these methods is sometimes given in a way which minimizes

[1] Details are given in Peterson, A. D. C., *The International Baccalaureate*, London: Harrap, 1972.

[2] Problems associated with this are outlined in Schools Council, *16-19: Growth and Response,* Working Paper No. 45, London: Evans/Methuen Educational, 1972, Chapter VI.

the "personal skills" aspect.

Altogether the official approaches are those which encourage more flexibility, and increasingly recognise that there are varying degrees of interest, commitment and ability within the upper-secondary student body though the degree to which these approaches are accepted *in practice* varies enormously.

Now there is an increasing demand for participation in education, both from students and from teachers. This demand varies in strength and quality, but it does exist. The curriculum is coming to be seen as a *co-operative* venture rather than the imposition of a framework of studies from above. Genuine acceptance of such a view would necessitate, for some countries, a radical re-thinking of administrative and organisational procedures. This view also emphasises the point that a curriculum, no matter how well thought out, does not really come into existence until it is perceived and accepted by the people most closely involved, students and teachers, as having some relevance to their felt needs.

On the part of some students, this acceptance is, at the moment, no more than a somewhat cynical realisation that the years in school serve only as a means to collect examination results which will take them on to a career or further studies. Such students are willing, up to a point, to come to terms with a curriculum which may not satisfy them at all in the short term, but which will at least, in their eyes, guarantee them a degree of security later on. In places where jobs of the kind sought by highly-qualified school-leavers and university graduates vary in availability and required qualifications, it is likely that students who see their future security slipping away will come to resent and question their education system, and the social set-up it is seen to represent.

Many students are in school primarily to obtain qualifications for a job or further studies; but, increasingly, they are interested in the *process* of getting those qualifications, i.e. they are interested in the experiential as well as the instrumental facets of their education. As the job situation becomes increasingly fluid and complex (and to some people more boring), and as a diploma or degree does not automatically guarantee a job which is lucrative and/or intrinsically satisfying, it becomes important that students have more intrinsic satisfaction from their time at school. This is important for their own sakes, and for the future success of any attempt at "permanent" or "recurrent" education. Those students who have, in their opinion, "suffered" an authoritarian regime at school will not readily be attracted towards any further studies, nor will they have the necessary skills to help them learn for themselves. This not to say that schools should not attempt to prepare young people for the world of work — only that the preparation could be more broadly based than it is now.

While the evidence obtained by the Comparative Research Unit was being analysed, and during the period of writing this Report, the points made above were raised by other recent studies, notably the Council of Europe symposium on *Curriculum Planning and Development for Upper-Secondary Education,*[1] the Janne/Géminard *Report on the Educational Needs of the 16-19 Age Group,*[2] and the report on the Education of Young People in Europe.[3] In his paper given to the Council of Europe symposium, Dr. W. D. Halls points out that "the recognition of the need for change has not yet been followed by the will to change"; and he then goes on to raise a number of interesting questions for the discussion of curricular development. But neither here, nor anywhere else in that report, except in token references to the importance of the participation of teachers, was there any discussion as to the implications of the *level* at which various decisions about curricular reform could be taken, nor to the role which advisory services and consultancy schemes might play.

The Janne/Géminard report gives some indications of the way in which the various groups within the education system interact,[4] and points out that, so far, little use has been made of such techniques as operational research and systems analysis to provide some insight into the workings of educational systems. Some work has already been done on this at a theoretical level by the Open University for the Education course.[5]

More work of a practical kind needs to be done which would look at the implications of introducing particular kinds of changes into particular systems. For example, it would seem to be a mistaken use of resources to work out in detail a revised curriculum for a country where there is a more urgent need for the development of advisory services for teachers and the creation of a cummunications system between teachers. A more practical "systems approach" could also look at the implications of allowing, or encouraging, particular kinds of decision to be taken at different levels. For example, to what extent can teachers become fully commited to a curriculum which is determined by a central agency? Training in management skills, and analysis of education systems according to a "systems approach" is already being done in some places in Britain.

The Janne/Géminard report, in highlighting the problem of values in

[1] Council of Europe, *Curriculum Planning and development for Upper-Secondary Education,* Document No. CCC/EGT (72) 16, Strasbourg, 1973.

[2] Janne, H., and Géminard, L., for the Council of Europe, *The Educational needs of the 16-19 Age Group,* Strasbourg, 1973.

[3] Peterson, A. D. C., and Halls, W. D., for the Council of Europe, *The Education of Young People in Europe: Developments, Problems and Trends,* Strasbourg, 1973.

education,[1] makes a distinction between "end values" and "action values", and stresses the importance of the latter in determining priorities for educational reform. The following chapters will illustrate how important many students consider the *process* of their education to be.

[1] Op. cit., pp 9-10.

CHAPTER 11

STUDENT OPINION IN ENGLAND

Stated reasons for staying on in full-time education

English students, when asked to state their reasons for staying on in full-time education, mentioned most frequently their wish for qualifications which would be of use in a job. The table below gives the frequencies with which various factors were mentioned and shows the difference between the male and female point of view. Students were asked to list all the factors which they thought influenced them.

All students %	Male %	Female %	Reason
88.9	89.5	88.6	wish for qualifications
11.6	11.8	12.2	opportunity to make new friends
21.7	21.1	22.9	could not decide what else to do
27.2	23.7	31.7	advice of teachers/counsellors
61.9	59.3	66.9	wish for higher education
50.3	49.2	52.4	influence of parents
20.3	22.5	18.1	few jobs for school leavers
7.1	9.2	7.5	did not want to start work
42.1	34.0	52.0	particular subjects interesting
5.5	6.7	4.2	stayed on to be with friends
Number of students: 1114			

English Students: Table E1
Stated reasons for staying on in full-time education

The most frequently mentioned factor was the wish for qualifications which would be of use in a job, mentioned by 88.9% of students, with hardly any difference between boys and girls. Rather more girls (66.9%) than boys (59.3%) wanted to go on to higher education. One in five students stayed on because they could not decide what else to do and the fact that there were few jobs for school leavers was mentioned by a similar number. Girls showed that they were slightly more susceptible to taking (or being given) advice than boys — more girls than boys mentioned that they were influenced by parents and teachers. These differences were very slight compared to the difference in interest in particular subjects. 34% of boys stayed on for this reason while 52% of the girls did so. Few said that they had stayed on to be with friends or to make new friends.

About one third of the students added a comment in the open-ended section where students were asked if there were any additional reasons for their staying on. Just over a third of these were concerned with jobs and the need for further studies and qualifications. Some of these were positive — a wish to qualify for a particular job or course of study. Others saw the lack of money and unpleasant conditions of jobs that, in their opinion, were available to sixteen-year-olds.

Examples of their comments follow:

"Being somewhat ambitious I wanted a different kind of job to one I could get at sixteen, i.e. more interesting. I'm not interested in pay so much as not being bored by work. If I were a dustman I could earn a bomb but I'd be dead bored".

"There's no chance of getting the job you want unless you're qualified".

"With rising unemployment I felt that higher qualifications will be needed for even the most menial of jobs".

"There are better money prospects if I can get a degree".

"I don't want to be just another labourer".

"My course is directly connected with the job I'm interested in".

> "I saw friends who left school at this age complain about underpaid boring work and having to go to night school if they wanted to improve their position at work".

> "This college is a stepping stone to university".

Some students showed a very positive interest in their education at school, and an enjoyment of the life there:

> "I wanted to exploit fully the opportunities open to me in education for my personal satisfaction, as well as for better job prospects".

> "I don't believe that you have any chance to lead an interesting life if you leave school at 16 before your education has got beyond a very basic level. I am more interested in intellectual fulfilment than money".

> "Life is always gay and exciting".

> "They say the best days of one's life are at school. (I did not want to finish them too quickly)".

Others emphasised the pressure which came from parents and from tradition either in the school or in the family which made it practically impossible to think about leaving.

> "My parents and school dominated my way of thought. My parents had the same attitude as the school only more so".

> "I come from a typically middle-class family and it was taken for granted that I would not leave school for a manual job, but stay on to qualify for a professional occupation".

> "It was generally accepted that I would. There was no question of doing anything else".

> "It was a natural progression".

English students, more than students in other countries, mentioned that they felt immature, not ready to start work. Such comments were made by a few students in all of the schools and colleges visited.

> "I did not feel that my education was complete. I suppose I wanted to adjust from being a school child to being a working person more slowly. Also I wanted to learn more about people and certain subjects".

> "I wanted more time to develop my personality before entering the rat-race and to decide what career suited me".

> "Not ready to take a job, more confidence expected by staying. (Fear of being looked down on for leaving at earliest opportunity)".

Many of these additional comments reinforce the reasons listed in the earlier question, particularly those dealing with jobs and qualifications. This was emphasised when students were asked to rank the three most important reasons which influenced them to stay on at school. (See table E2 below). Figures given are *adjusted frequencies,* after the non-replies have been subtracted from the total. The extent to which the replies fall off is shown in the bottom line of the table. Thus while 3.6% did not reply to the question, 32.0% of those who did put as their most important reason for staying on the wish for qualifications. 9.7% of students said that it was impossible to choose between the various factors involved — they were *all* important. This figure is slightly distorted as two sets of students who filled in the questionnaire were told by their respective head teachers that this was indeed the case. Over half of the students put as their main reason for staying a wish for qualifications and higher education. Higher education is a dominant factor in all three columns; but it can be seen that parental influence and interest in particular subjects support it in many cases.

Most important reason adjusted frequency	Second reason adjusted frequency	Third reason adjusted frequency	
32.0	12.9	6.4	wish for qualifications
1.5	3.2	4.3	opportunity to make new friends
4.5	6.8	9.0	could not decide what else to do
2.7	8.4	8.7	advice of teachers/counsellors
24.5	17.5	15.4	wish for higher education
5.5	17.6	20.1	influence of parents
4.1	9.8	7.4	few jobs for school leavers
1.8	4.5	5.4	did not want to start work
9.0	14.8	17.4	particular subjects interesting
.7	.8	1.7	stayed on to be with friends
4.0	3.6	4.3	other reasons (from open-ended replies)
9.7	0.2	–	impossible to make a choice
3.6	19.0	72.8	no reply

Number of students: 1114

English students: Table E2

Most important stated reasons for staying on in full-time education

Students were also asked if there was anything about their particular school or college which attracted them and encouraged them to stay on. The results are given in table E3 below. Over half thought that the standard of teaching was high. Additional factors were mentioned more frequently than in other countries, which suggests that the actual *process* of getting the qualifications and examinations necessary for careers and higher education is, for some English students, quite pleasant. 44% thought the school was a pleasant community; 30.1% mentioned easy relations with staff; freedom to organise things themselves, choice of studies, an opportunity to meet the opposite sex were all mentioned by about a third of all students. However the school's successful examination record, mentioned by 32.6% of students, reflects the English preoccupation with examinations.

%	Attraction of a particular school or college
12.5	sports facilities
30.1	easy relations with staff
12.7	extra-curricular activities
34.4	freedom for students to organise things themselves
54.3	standard of teaching high
13.0	friends came
44.0	pleasant community to work in
9.7	library facilities
13.6	training for job
38.0	possibility to choose studies
6.8	opportunity to make a new start
32.6	chance to meet opposite sex
32.6	school's successful examination record

Number of students in sample: 1114

English students: Table E3

Stated attractions of a particular school or college

In the open-ended section where it was possible to list other factors about the school one third of the students did so. Just over one third of these said that the school they were in made it almost inevitable that they stayed on. Such replies came from grammar schools, sixth form colleges, and secondary modern schools which kept their own fourth formers for a fifth and sixth year. Examples of this kind of reply were:

> "It is presumed you are going to stay on into the sixth form from the first year upwards, so nothing else seems to influence you to leave".

> "Already here, under certain obligation as school expects you to stay on". (These two from grammar school students).

> "I knew about the methods of teaching here as I've been here for six years. This school can offer the same opportunities as other schools and colleges". (Comment by a secondary modern school student in an area where there are several grammar schools).

"People took it for a fact that you would come to this college from school. You weren't asked if there was anywhere else you wanted to go — you were just given an interview here".

"I've been here since the age of 11. Would not have changed school even if there had been a choice". (These last two comments are by students from the same sixth form college).

No technical college student, of course, made this kind of comment. Some students mentioned that the school or college was near home and therefore was the most convenient place to go to. Others wanted qualifications which would get them to university or a particular course of study which they had heard about — a special technical training, a wider range of A-levels, the possibility to do an O-level course after failing examinations at sixteen. Particular departments within the schools and colleges were also known locally for their excellent teaching or equipment. Some students emphasised the pleasant atmosphere in school: "The sixth form in this school is not so regimented as in others"; "you get respect from the members of staff and that makes for a pleasant atmosphere"; "this college's lecturers treat us as adults"; "there is much more freedom than in the other school I would have gone to. At the other school students wear uniforms and were treated like kids — I didn't want to have my hair cut and conform to a lot of rules". For some, it was a case of *"faute de mieux"* — they did not see themselves as having a choice, and others were influenced by friends and family. Hardly anyone mentioned a specific training for a job at this point. Thus the open-ended answers stress the pleasantness of the school community, the possibility of choice and, above all, the inevitability of the "decision" to stay on, particularly in those schools and colleges which have their own lower school. It is to be expected, now that the school-leaving age has been raised, that far more students will find themselves in this "inevitable" position in the next few years.

When students were asked to say what, for them, were the most important attractions of their school or college, which influenced them to stay on, the largest category said that they thought that the standard of teaching was high. Results are given in table E4 below. Figures given are *adjusted frequencies*, after the non-replies have been subtracted from the total; and the bottom line of the table shows the extent to which the replies fall off. Thus 13.6% of students did not reply, but of those who did 21% said that the main attraction of the school was the high standard of teaching. The rather high figure of 19.3% who felt that it was impossible to make a choice is, once again, a reflection, to some extent of two head teachers who told their students prior to filling in the questionnaires that this was the case. The rate of response in England does not fall off so sharply as it does in other countries — 86.5% of Swedes did not list a third attraction, 77.9% of Germans did not do so. This tends to suggest that they see school in a somewhat more limited way than the English and find it a less pleasant place to be. In fact this is borne out by the open-ended questions in the next section — or perhaps it is just a sign that the English are more obliging in filling up questionnaires!

Most important attraction	Second attraction	Third attraction	
adjusted frequency	adjusted frequency	adjusted frequency	
1.7	2.0	5.2	sports facilities
3.0	7.7	9.6	easy relations with staff
1.0	2.0	2.0	extra-curricular activities
2.5	9.3	13.5	freedom for students to organise things themselves
21.0	20.1	12.2	standard of teaching high
1.8	3.5	3.5	friends came
8.8	13.9	16.4	pleasant community to work in
.1	1.0	3.2	library facilities
9.2	2.7	1.4	training for job
10.3	13.6	10.6	possibility to choose studies
.8	2.0	2.4	opportunity to make a new start
.6	1.9	3.9	chance to meet opposite sex
8.0	14.3	9.1	school's successful examination record
11.7	5.8	.9	other attraction
19.3	.1	—	choice not possible
13.6	40.0	46.9	no reply

Number of students in sample: 1114

English students: Table E4

Most important stated attractions of a particular school or college

There was hardly any difference between boys and girls in their opinion about what attracted them to a particular school or college.

English students are concerned about their future prospects but underlying this consideration there is an awareness that staying on at school, while inevitable for some, can be quite pleasant. The following pages illustrate what they expect from school once they have made the decision to stay on.

Student aims and perceived satisfactions

Students were asked to indicate from a list of items on the questionnaire what they expected from school. They were also asked to indicate whether they thought that their teachers had similar priorities or not. The histograms on the following pages illustrate student expectations and their perceptions as to whether they think their teachers share their ideas about what is important in school. Table E5 gives the frequencies of items as they occur in the questionnaire; table E6 gives the items in descending order of frequency so as to give a "profile" of student aims; tables E7 and E8 give the male and female "profiles".

The items that were listed most frequently as being important to students were the following:

87.5% — information on job/further education
87.5% — a wide choice of subjects
76.5% — examination success
75.5% — ability to work on their own.

As in other countries "information on jobs/further education" is mentioned frequently. At the time of the fieldwork, 1971-72, the unemployment situation in England was bad, and this possibly influenced a good many of the replies. Examination success is mentioned more frequently than in any other country, and comes higher up the list than in other countries. (In Italy, for example, it is eighteenth according to the frequency counts). This high frequency may be accounted for by the high marks (rather than a simple pass) which are required for university entrance in England. The frequencies given to other items in the questionnaire fall away fairly gently — seventeen of the items in the questionnaire are all mentioned by over 50% of the students as being important to them.

England

Histograms on student aims and perceived satisfactions.

Table E5 —   The right-hand line shows the frequencies of items considered to be important by students, irrespective of whether they think that teachers share their views.

—   The left-hand line shows the frequencies of items considered to be important by students where they think that teachers share their views.

Tables E6, E7, E8 —   The upper line shows the frequencies of items considered to be important by students, irrespective of whether they think that teachers share their views.

—   The lower line shows the frequencies of items considered to be important by students where they think that teachers share their views.

In all four tables, the distance between the two lines represents the gap in perceptions between students and teachers — *from the students' point of view.* Corresponding tables from the teachers' point of view are in a subsequent chapter on teachers.

*Note —*In England students in two schools were not allowed to comment on their teachers' views. A few students disregarded this and their replies have been included. If all the students in the sample from these schools had been allowed to answer these questions, then the gap between the two lines in the English table might well have been a good deal narrower.

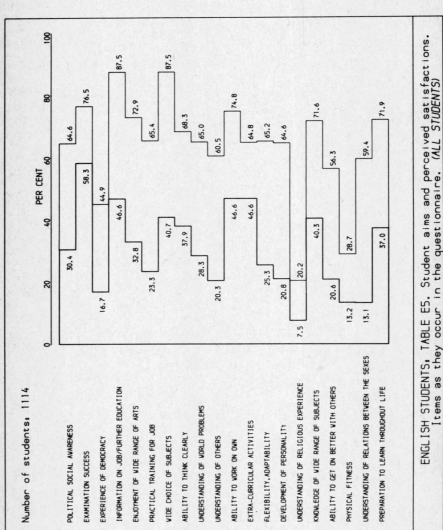

Number of students: 1114

ENGLISH STUDENTS, TABLE E5. Student aims and perceived satisfactions.
Items as they occur in the questionnaire. (ALL STUDENTS)

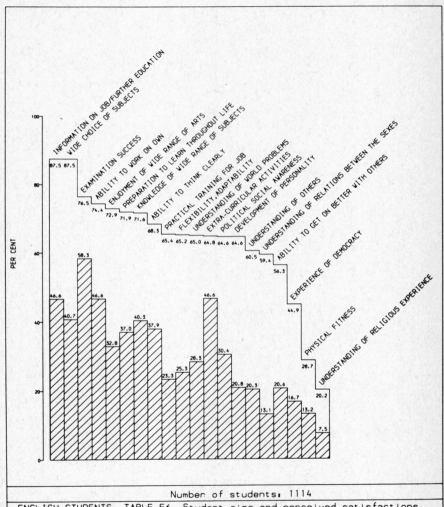

PER CENT

INFORMATION ON JOB/FURTHER EDUCATION
WIDE CHOICE OF SUBJECTS
EXAMINATION SUCCESS
ABILITY TO WORK ON OWN
ENJOYMENT OF WIDE RANGE OF ARTS
PREPARATION TO LEARN THROUGHOUT LIFE
KNOWLEDGE OF WIDE RANGE OF SUBJECTS
ABILITY TO THINK CLEARLY
PRACTICAL TRAINING FOR JOB
FLEXIBILITY, ADAPTABILITY
UNDERSTANDING OF WORLD PROBLEMS
EXTRA-CURRICULAR ACTIVITIES
POLITICAL SOCIAL AWARENESS
DEVELOPMENT OF PERSONALITY
UNDERSTANDING OF OTHERS
UNDERSTANDING OF RELATIONS BETWEEN THE SEXES
ABILITY TO GET ON BETTER WITH OTHERS
EXPERIENCE OF DEMOCRACY
PHYSICAL FITNESS
UNDERSTANDING OF RELIGIOUS EXPERIENCE

87.5 87.5 76.5 74.4 72.9 71.9 71.6 68.3 65.4 65.2 65.0 64.8 64.6 64.6 60.5 59.4 56.3 44.9 28.7 20.2

46.6 40.7 58.3 46.6 32.8 37.0 40.3 37.9 23.3 25.3 28.3 46.6 30.4 20.8 20.3 13.1 20.6 16.7 13.2 7.5

Number of students: 1114

ENGLISH STUDENTS, TABLE E6. Student aims and perceived satisfactions.
Items in descending order of frequency. (ALL STUDENTS)

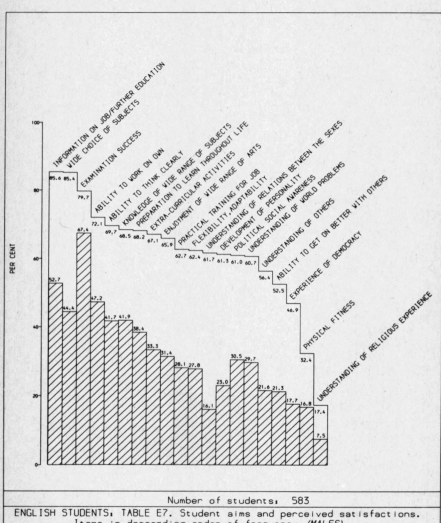

Number of students: 583

ENGLISH STUDENTS: TABLE E7. Student aims and perceived satisfactions.
Items in descending order of frequency. *(MALES)*

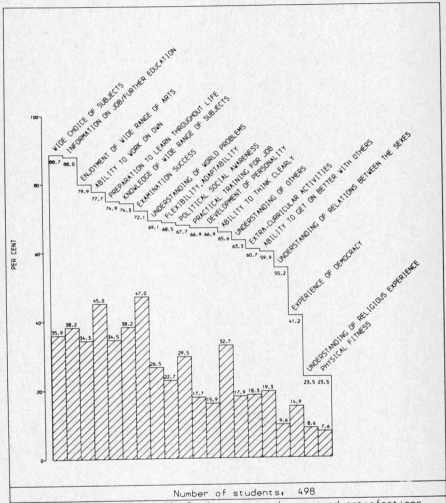

PER CENT

100

80

60

40

20

0

WIDE CHOICE OF SUBJECTS — 88.7
INFORMATION ON JOB/FURTHER EDUCATION — 88.0
ENJOYMENT OF WIDE RANGE OF ARTS — 79.9
ABILITY TO WORK ON OWN — 77.7
PREPARATION TO LEARN THROUGHOUT LIFE — 74.9
KNOWLEDGE OF WIDE RANGE OF SUBJECTS — 74.3
EXAMINATION SUCCESS — 72.1
UNDERSTANDING OF WORLD PROBLEMS — 69.1
FLEXIBILITY, ADAPTABILITY — 68.5
POLITICAL SOCIAL AWARENESS — 67.7
PRACTICAL TRAINING FOR JOB — 66.9
DEVELOPMENT OF PERSONALITY — 66.9
ABILITY TO THINK CLEARLY — 65.6
UNDERSTANDING OF OTHERS — 63.3
EXTRA-CURRICULAR ACTIVITIES — 60.7
ABILITY TO GET ON BETTER WITH OTHERS — 59.9
UNDERSTANDING OF RELATIONS BETWEEN THE SEXES — 55.2
EXPERIENCE OF DEMOCRACY — 41.2
UNDERSTANDING OF RELIGIOUS EXPERIENCE — 23.5
PHYSICAL FITNESS — 23.5

35.9 38.2 34.3 45.0 34.5 38.2 47.0 26.5 22.7 29.5 17.7 15.9 32.7 17.9 18.3 19.3 9.6 14.9 8.6 7.6

Number of students: 498

ENGLISH STUDENTS, TABLE E8. Student aims and perceived satisfactions. Items in descending order of frequency. *(FEMALES)*

Some of the items listed above which are most frequently mentioned by students as being important to them are also examples where students most often perceive that teachers have the same priorities. This is also true, for example, in Sweden; but there, at the point where there is most satisfaction, there is also the most dissatisfaction — the number of students who feel that a particular item is important to them but not to their teachers is greater than the number of those who feel that their teachers share their views. In England the reverse is the case and there is a slightly larger consensus of opinion. Thus the highest frequency counts where students perceive that the staff share their views are:

58.3% — examination success
46.6% — information on job/further education
46.6% — extra-curricular activities
46.0% — ability to work on own.

England is the only country of those visited during the course of the research which stresses the importance of extra-curricular activities and it is interesting that both students and, in their opinion, staff rate it quite highly.

The highest counts for items where students thought that teachers did not share their aims were as follows:—

46.9% — wide choice of subjects
46.3% — understanding of relationships between the sexes
43.8% — development of personality
42.1% — practical training for job.

English students often get more possibility for choosing their studies than students in other countries, yet they still feel that the options could be greater. Some schools, however, still insist that subjects should be studied according to the traditional groupings. Like other students, the English also feel that there is a great gap between their wish for a practical training for a job and what their teachers are prepared to give them in this respect. The second and third items in the list above point to a felt need for emotional and personal help in school as well as the usual academic work.

Students also felt that their teachers were, on occasion, emphasising things which they did not consider important. Highest counts here were:

28.9% — ability to work on one's own
28.4% — understanding of religious experience

20.8% —   physical fitness
13.5% —   examination success.

The element of compulsory games which still exists in some English schools probably accounts for the 20.8% above, and the 13.5% who resent the push towards examinations are part of a group of students found in all the countries visited who jib at the system.

There were no great differences between the male and female profiles: girls mentioned less frequently examination success, experience of democracy, ability to think clearly, extra-curricular activities, and understanding of relationships between the sexes, as being important to them but otherwise they mentioned items more frequently than did the boys. On the other hand the frequency with which they perceived that staff shared their views was lower — in some instances, much lower — than that of the boys. To some extent this is accounted for, as was mentioned earlier, by the fact that one school was not allowed to express an opinion of their teachers' views. Even so, whereas 67% of boys consider that their teachers think examinations are important, only 47% of girls do so; 52% of boys consider that their staff think it important to give them information on jobs and further education, but only 38.2% of girls do so; 28.1% of boys think that their teachers consider it important to give them a practical training for a job as compared to 15.9% of girls; and 33.3% of boys, compared to 18.3% of girls consider that teachers place importance on extra-curricular activities.

Apart from citing the items on the list, students were also given the opportunity of mentioning whether they thought there was anything else that the school ought to do for them, and also whether they thought there was anything else that teachers were trying to do.

About 22% of students added other things which they thought were important. On the whole these tended to emphasise the personal development of the individual; students wanted to take responsibility themselves, prepare for the "outside world", learn how to express their views, relate to other people. Only very rarely were these wishes couched in political terms. Examples of this kind of reply were:

"College should widen your interests and clear all traces of shyness and encourage you as much as possible".

"College should teach me how to think and act like an adult and not treat me like a child so that I should not miss any development in this area by not having gone out to work at an earlier age".

"There should be a greater understanding between teachers and students. Perhaps greater *equality*". (Student's emphasis).

"Give an opportunity for students to accept responsibility within the college".

"It should prepare you for the world outside your own cosy college environment".

School should "take an active part in the community life of the area in which it is situated; it should help to overcome personal shyness and provide you with a personal tutor to whom you can go for advice".

"Foster in you a desire to learn, to open your mind and develop all your potential. Try to get across how important it is to be able to change, to keep a flexible mind".

School should "be a place for working on your own and developing into what you want yourself to be".

Some students, besides mentioning the fact that they wanted more guidance as far as jobs were concerned also said that they wanted advice on practical matters: how to handle money matters; "more about what will happen when we leave school, mortgages, savings etc."; "training for the practical necessities of life — and these should be compulsory, e.g. cooking, woodwork, mending a fuse, life-insurance"; "taxes, welfare and benefits". Others wanted more time to discuss, more time for subjects not necessarily to be taken in examinations; "have more time for debates and discussions"; "opportunity to study subjects out of the ordinary". There was a fair number of students who wanted more clubs, more social activities, more chance to mix with other students. "Extra-curricular activities should become curricular, i.e. the curriculum should be more flexible"; "a wider range of sports"; "have more clubs". One grammar school student was particularly conscious of the need for mixing with others: "A selective school should attempt to ensure that it does not become a closed community and that its pupils mix with pupils of other types of school". Students at this particular school were very keen to stress their wish for more freedom and individual attention: e.g. "school could show a little more interest in me as a person rather than as a candidate for A-levels". As a rule, though, schools were not characterised by a series of "typical" student comments – there was a mixture from each.

However, the case was rather different when students were asked if there were any other things that were important to their teachers. About 20% of students added comments at this point. Although roughly one third of these saw the teachers as trying to help them in some kind of positive way, about two thirds of the comments were critical: teachers were only concerned with the rules and examinations. In most schools and colleges there was a mixture of replies. Very occasionally, though, comments on a particular institution were always critical, particularly of the pettiness of school rules; and it was as if the indignation which this aroused prevented students from seeing anything more valuable in the teaching given to them.

Examples of the positive kind of comment were: "they consider our development important"; "being able to express oneself clearly and logically"; "teach us to work on our own"; "good relationships"; "the less liberal minded (a minority) think work is all that matters. These are usually very strict. Some members (a majority) of staff consider relationships with pupils as a sort of friendship, hence respect for them is better"; "meeting students and finding out their views".

Critical comments are more explicit:

> "You have to conform to their standards for their convenience – attendance, punctuality, spelling, grammar, good appearance and polite disposition".

> "Although they profess otherwise their sole pre-occupation is really achieving good exam results for *their* (student's emphasis) class so that their personal reputation is enhanced".

> "It seems important to many teachers that all forms of innocent non-conformity should be crushed. Individual and personal development is often overlooked, and conformity is often carried to the lengths of uniformity". (These last two comments from a school where *all* comments were critical).

> "They seem to think that if you wear jewellery or nail varnish you are not learning".

Rules about appearance, length of hair, and the push towards examinations are the main grumbles, and there is a feeling that teachers should earn the respect given to them — and not insist on it as of right.

A further indication of the difference between student and teacher attitudes was shown when students were asked to rank the five items most important to them and then to rank the five items which they thought most important to their teachers. Full details of this are in Appendix III, but here it is sufficient just to compare the items which head the respective lists. Results are in table E9 below. Figures given are *adjusted frequencies* once the non-replies have been subtracted from the total. Again the high "no choice" figures are a result mainly by the intervention of two head teachers. The students' main aim, apart from the "impossible to make a choice" category, was examination success, mentioned by 26.1%; but they were outdone by their teachers, 41.1% of whom were thought to have examination success as their main aim.

There was little difference between male and female students in the above respect except on the question of examinations. 29.7% of boys put it as their own most important aim, compared to 18.7% of girls; 35% of boys thought that examination success was the most important aim of their teachers compared to 29.1% of girls.

Most important student aim	Most important teacher aim as perceived by students	
adjusted frequency	adjusted frequency	
4.7	2.0	political social awareness
26.1	41.1	examination success
.8	.7	experience of democracy
5.6	2.2	information on jobs/further education
1.9	1.3	enjoyment of wide range of arts
4.1	1.6	practical training for job
4.5	1.6	wide choice of subjects
4.0	2.2	ability to think clearly
1.5	.7	understanding of world problems
1.4	.3	understanding of others
2.9	4.1	ability to work on own
.4	.6	extra-curricular activities
1.3	.6	flexibility, adaptability
4.0	1.4	development of personality
.2	.7	understanding of religious experience
2.3	1.6	knowledge of wide range of subjects
1.0	.5	ability to get on better with others
.2	1.0	physical fitness
1.2	.2	understanding of relations between the sexes
4.0	1.6	preparation to learn throughout life
2.1	3.4	other reasons
25.8	30.6	no choice possible
4.7	21.9	no replies

Number of students: 1114

English students: Table E9

Most important student aims and most important perceived teacher aims

Some idea of the range of functions which, in the opinion of students, ought to be undertaken by a school may be seen by noting the number of items listed by individual students. In the same way, the extent to which these aims were seen to be shared by teachers can be obtained by noting the number of items where the student says that both he and his teachers share that aim. The table below shows the percentages of students who listed different numbers of items as being important to them — and the differences between male and female students in this respect.

All students %	Male %	Female %	
6.9	7.0	5.6	Between 1 and 5 items listed
23.0	24.9	21.3	Between 6 and 10 items listed
41.2	41.2	41.2	Between 11 and 15 items listed
28.8	26.9	31.9	Between 16 and 20 items listed

Number of students: 1114   Top line does not conceal any "no replies"

English students: Table E10

Percentages of students according to numbers of items considered to be important by students

From this it can be seen that English students expect quite a lot from school, girls rather more than boys. On the other hand girls do not see their teachers as sharing their aims to quite the same extent as boys, although these figures are somewhat distorted because one girls' school did not allow its students to fill in that part of the questionnaire dealing with student perception of staff values. Results are given in table E11 below.

All students %	Male %	Female %	
51.4	46.0	57.4	Between 1 and 5 items listed
32.4	37.0	26.9	Between 6 and 10 items listed
12.0	12.7	11.6	Between 11 and 15 items listed
4.1	4.3	4.0	Between 16 and 20 items listed

Number of students: 1114   Top line does not conceal any "no replies"

English students: Table E11

Percentages of students according to number of items considered to be important to them and, in the students' opinion, to their teachers

When the figures from tables E10 and E11 are cross-tabulated then it can be seen that quite a large number of students are disappointed in their expectations. Whereas 28.8% of students expect a broad range of things from school, only 4.1% see that their teachers have similar values.

	Aims important to students *and* staff			
Aims important to students	1-5 items listed	6-10 items listed	11-15 items listed	16-20 items listed
1-5 items listed	6.9			
6-10 items listed	18.0	5.0		
11-15 items listed	18.7	18.2	4.4	
16-20 items listed	7.9	9.2	7.6	4.1

Number of students: 1114

English students: Table E12

Percentages of students according to numbers of items important to them, cross-tabulated with the numbers of items where they consider that their teachers share their views

However, English students are not so disappointed in their expectations as are students in the other countries visited; and it will be seen from their opinions in the following pages just how they think that school helps them to achieve the aims which they have listed as being important to them, or hinders them.

Students' opinions as to how the subjects they study in school, the teaching methods, the school organisation and the extra-curricular activities (if any) help them or do not help them achieve their aims

English students had a fair amount to say for themselves. All the questions in this section and the next were open-ended so as not to impose categories on students or teach them the sort of replies that were expected. Their comments were the most favourable to the school system; students in the other countries visited tended to be much more critical, particularly the Italians.

Subjects

Of the 85.8% of students who commented on the helpfulness or otherwise of subjects, 86.2% made positive statements, and 13.3% made negative comments, while there were 0.5% "don't knows". The largest categories among the positive statements were:

29.3% –	subjects generally helpful
24.3% –	subjects good for examinations
13.5% –	particular subjects helpful
6.4% –	general studies helpful
4.8% –	subjects good preparation for life – social awareness, development of character, etc.
3.7% –	subjects good intellectual training.

On the negative side the largest categories were:

6.0% –	subjects useless in general
2.8% –	particular subjects useless
2.5% –	subjects good *only* for examinations/jobs.

Other criticisms were mentioned by very few students indeed, and included comments to the effect that the subjects were out of touch with reality, were a poor preparation for life in terms of character, etc., and were a poor intellectual training. Hardly anyone said that there was too much material in the syllabus.

46.9% of students made more than a single comment. Again the balance was very much in favour of the positive kind of comment, with emphasis on the same kind of factors that were mentioned above. The same applies to those students who went on to make a third comment.

Students stated their views about qualifications and examinations quite simply: "The subjects chosen are interesting and will provide me with good qualifications for when I leave school"; "the subjects I am studying will help me to obtain the job and further education I want"; "they are interesting and in the end, hopefully, will give qualifications". Other students point out the particular strengths and weaknesses of the subjects they study:

> "Geography — does not place enough emphasis on human and social geography which would help one understand about world problems. It does help you to go on learning through life as you become aware of the environment. History — also helps you to go on learning for the same reason. It can introduce you to arts and literature of various periods and can make you understand what motivates people. Religious Education — needs much work on one's own — and individual thought to understand the subject fully".

> "Political awareness is helped by studying British Constitution. Awareness of the problems of society is helped by studying Sociology. . ."

Quite often, though, the subjects are discussed in terms of the *process* that goes on in the class room, as the following replies demonstrate:

> "I would not say we "studied"; this term is too static and unchallenging. We are encouraged to open our minds and find out what we consider to be important, which is not necessarily the social norm. The things we learn about ourselves, and about life and thought, can be applied outside our studies".

> "The subjects I now study have really helped. Before I came here I was very shy and found it hard to speak for myself. Although I still have this to overcome I have improved a great deal, learnt to back up my statements and to have confidence".

Comments on general studies courses vary from school to school — the favourable ones coming from schools and colleges which try to have some kind of coherent policy on general studies, though there are always some students who jib at compulsory studies and some who are interested like the following, but worried about examinations:

> "There are a lot of general studies which broaden your outlook on relevant social issues and fields outside your A-levels. These, however, cut out some time that could be spent on examination work".

Students vary in their attitudes to qualifications for jobs, and subjects are criticised from opposite points of view:

> "They give you a range of knowledge that is sometimes helpful but not relevant to the jobs that students go to".

> "The subjects I'm studying are very limited — they are electronic systems, electrical principles, laboratory work, P.E. and liberal studies: so in fact they can't achieve much in preparing you for the other side of life, i.e. other than work".

Methods

Teaching methods were generally approved of, though it is interesting to see that students usually see these as "methods of learning" rather than methods of teaching; and their replies are often couched in terms of good relationships with staff and discussion, rather than in terms of specific techniques such as the use of audio-visual aids, etc. 81.1% of students made at least one comment on the teaching methods. Of these, 71.6% made positive comments, 14.1% made critical comments, 11.2% stated that it was not possible to separate a method from a particular subject or teacher, and there were 1.5% "don't knows". The largest categories among the positive comments were:

28.0% —	methods generally helpful
12.5% —	good staff-student relationships made it possible to benefit from the teaching methods used
8.4% —	discussion mentioned as helpful
7.7% —	working on one's own mentioned as helpful

Audio-visual aids, projects, group-work, practice, and visits, were all mentioned as helpful but by small percentages of students. 43.3% of students went on to make a second comment, usually favourable, and usually drawn from the same categories mentioned above. Those who continued with a third comment stressed, usually, that the methods were a good preparation for life in terms of social awareness, development of character etc.

On the critical side the factors included in the 14.1% total among the intial comments were that the methods were generally useless; they were "magisterial", or authoritarian, and depended too much on note-taking and parrot learning. A small number thought that there was too much cramming for examinations.

Some of the students obviously appreciated the personal interest that their teachers showed towards them:

> The teaching methods "help enormously — perhaps this is because of the personality and quality of our tutor. He is ruthlessly truthful with us about our work and our motives. He demands the best we can possibly do, and even that is not good enough".

> "The teaching methods are such that there is a good relationship between staff and pupils. Many of the former take part in extra-curricular activities and are genuinely interested in their students outside the class room; but it is equally possible for students to remain outside these relationships if they prefer".

They also appreciate time to work on their own, and discuss in class:

> "We are left to study a lot by ourselves, so you have to organise things and learn how to study. Also we are encouraged to think about things, relate them to our experience and question what we are taught and what the subjects really say".

The following criticisms imply that the kind of approach outlined above would be more welcome.

> "In science subjects you may be told that a certain relationship is true, and you might perhaps verify it. It

would certainly be better to be told to determine the relationship, or at least attempt it".

"The teachers just talk in class and tell you to write out of a book in the evening. If they treated us like adults I think they would get more response from the class".

One student was not at all sure what teaching methods were about:

"The teaching methods are inefficient because we forget what we are taught shortly after we were taught it. In fact we had one teacher tell us we could forget everything if we got our O-levels".

Thus methods are seen in terms of relationships, or else as a facet of the subject itself.

Organisation

The usual trend in the countries visited is for the students' comments to become increasingly critical: i.e., students comment most favourably on subjects, less favourably on methods, and even less favourably on organisation within the school. However, although this tendency holds true in England, the criticism is not quite so severe as in the other countries.

21% did not reply to the question about organisation; but of those who did 57.2% made positive comments, 34.5% made critical comments, 4.7% thought that the school organisation had no influence, and there were 1.6% "don't knows". The largest categories among the positive statements were:

24.4% —   the running of the school was useful for "life" —
social awareness, character development etc.
18.0% —   school organisation was generally helpful
13.9% —   *democratic* running of the school was useful for
"life" — mention of democracy or school council.

Of the negative statements the largest categories were:

16.6% —   school organisation was generally useless

6.1% —   the "democratic running of the school was a façade
5.6% —   too much discipline, too many rules.

23.8% of students went on to make a further comment. These comments were fairly evenly shared between positive and critical statements. The largest categories were:

15.8% —   the running of school was useful for life, etc.
15.0% —   too much discipline, too many rules.

Very few students indeed made more than one comment; but again these were fairly evenly divided between negative and positive.

Student comments on this subject were interesting because of the way they illuminated student response to rather different systems. The following remark, which is fairly typical, shows the importance to the students of good staff-student relations and an informal atmosphere:

> "In the sixth form the school organisation is very loose and most of the rules, etc., are common sense. If we have any troubles we can go directly to those concerned and voice any complaints or suggestions".

A more formal system of School Council also finds favour:

> "School Council helps one to express one's own opinion. It encourages you to think for yourself and provide a democratic community. Rules are minimal, and much freedom is allowed to develop a sense of self-discipline — although stricter measures can be enforced when necessary. The staff place much trust in the pupils' behaviour".

Other students in the same school, while welcoming the greater degree of freedom, are dubious about the value of the Council:

> "School Council is a good idea because it teaches how to behave at such meetings, but points are so trivial the aim is lost".

Schools tend to encourage councils and the notion of participation, but often there is a paternalist background to it. Students in technical colleges are quick to point out their greater freedoms and the fact that they have to be responsible for themselves:

> "The college organisation is very flexible and in this way you are left to get on with things by yourself. Your success depends on you, unlike school where you tend to be more spoonfed".

> "One may participate in college organisations, e.g. Students' Union. This shows, as it did for me, how much initiative one possesses and brings one in contact with a variety of characters. This experience is vital".

As yet, English schools are not politicised into extreme factions as one finds sometimes in France and Italy. Issues tend to be local and practical — more freedom as to dress and appearance, more chance to have a say in *school* and *college* matters, more opportunity to organise their own work, etc. The solution to these problems is, from the students' point of view, to have a real discussion with staff — not just a parading of opinion. The varying systems — School Council, Students Union, Head boy (or girl) and prefects, or informal meetings, seem to succeed according to the extent to which staff and students are really willing to talk on *particular* issues and *do* something to remedy them. English students have not yet been forced into the position of negotiation via slogans and demonstrations. Some students however do point out that a rigid system, imposed without thought, causes antagonism or a somewhat cynical "playing of the system". The following remarks are made by a technical college student and a grammar school student:

> "The organisation here does help because this college is run along adult lines. The normal school, however, is fighting directly against my goals by imposing false goals (money, status, etc.), and by imposing its values by means of rules which do not agree with my own values".

> "The school is almost neutral and one does one's best within the system. The rules are often petty but can be avoided. The prefect system develops a keen political sense and skill in using friends, influence and deception to gain honour and exemplary positions".

The sixth form colleges are neither grammar school nor technical college: they give more freedom to their students than many grammar schools, and they give more in terms of personal interest and care than some technical colleges. Some of the sixth form college students (as everywhere) are discontented and want complete freedom, but many do appreciate the opportunity of talking and discussing things informally with staff. The "success" of the colleges visited is, in the author's opinion, quite clearly dependent on the head or principal. These colleges had all been grammar schools — and the change of status at once meant a change of role for the head and staff. Judging the degree and pace of change as regards organisation and relationships is perhaps more difficult than agreeing on decisions about content and methods — and some of the heads showed that they had a very shrewd sense of judgement.

Extra-curricular activities

On this topic the comments are, once more, favourable on the whole. 24% of students did not reply, but of the 76% who did, 73.4% made positive comments, 19.6% made critical comments, 4.3% thought that extra-curricular activities had no influence and 1.2% said they did not know.

Amongst the positive comments the largest categories were:

22.2% —   extra-curricular activities broaden knowledge and interests
14.6% —   extra-curricular activities are useful in general
14.3% —   they help to develop character, sociability, etc.
14.0% —   they make a pleasant break from studies.

Of the negative comments the largest categories were:

12.1% —   extra-curricular activities were useless in general
2.0% —   there were not enough of them.

27.9% of students added a second comment. These tended to be favourable and were in the same categories as those mentioned above. So were the few third comments.

Some students give an idea of the range of extra-curricular activities when they answer this question, others just give a general impression:

> "Philosophy Society helps a lot in understanding yourself and others. Film Society gives a lot of information and education about the arts. There are also opportunities for a lot of sport and work in the language laboratory in our free time . . . . They also help you mix with other people in the school apart from those you have lessons with".

> "Extra-curricular activities certainly help widen your interests and help broaden your outlook on other areas of knowledge. You can meet different people and form your own opinions".

Others point out that their gain depends to some extent on staff interest and participation:

> "Extra-curricular activities broaden one's social life and I think that these activities are more likely to be followed through if linked with the school. I know many people, including a lot of our teachers, are against these activites being linked with school; but this, to me, shows that the teacher has no interest in the pupil as a person. This is probably asking too much of the average teacher but I know that some teachers show this interest and it makes a great deal of difference".

One can only feel sorry for the student in a school of some academic prestige who remarked:

> "They help you to achieve these goals very well if you have the time and can put enough effort into them. But the pressures of the examinations and the competitive spirit here, the overbearing shepherding of teachers, tend to discourage involvement . . . . The God of Work is worshipped above all else".

Students' opinions as to how the subjects they study in school, the teaching methods, the school organisation and the extra-curricular activities might be improved

The rate of reply to these questions is, for all countries visited, somewhat lower than for the questions in the previous section. In the case of English students the drop is much sharper than it would have been normally as two schools whose students comprised about 20% of the total sample specifically said that students were *not* to answer these questions and one of these schools asked for the page on which the questions were printed to be torn out of the questionnaire. It was thought that students were not in a position to be able to answer these questions.

Subjects

47% of students commented on ways in which the subjects taught in school might be improved. As was pointed out above, this low response rate would have been higher if students from certain schools had been allowed to answer these questions.

Among the students who replied, the largest category, 17.9%, were satisfied with things as they were. (This is also the largest category of *satisfied* students in all the countries visited). Specific recommendations for improvement were:

13.7% —	more possibility for choice
9.5% —	timetable to be rearranged (this usually took the form of a wish for more flexibility, longer periods, longer time for practical work)
8.6% —	additional subjects
6.9% —	some subjects to be rethought
4.2% —	less useful subjects to be dropped
4.4% —	more interdisciplinary studies
3.1% —	less emphasis on examinations

English students tend to comment on the actual content of the curriculum rather than comment on the relationships with teachers as do some students in other countries (Italy, for instance, where relationships between staff and students are more formal and distant than in England). Only 1.0% of students asked for more consultation at this point, and only 1.9% asked for subjects to be made more relevant to them. 6.9% of students said they did not know how to improve the subjects and only 1.1% said that a complete reform of the school system was needed. The same trends as those noted above were included in any second or third comments which students made.

Examples of comments were:

> "They're OK. I can think of no practicle improvement."
> (sic)

> "The subjects should be better interlinked to make a complete picture rather than individual blocks".

> "I think you should have more choice and more time on one subject instead of spreading it around".

> "Hard to say how A-level subjects could be improved. The school has little option in teaching methods; only a complete change of the examination system could help at all".

Some students did want more specialisation and emphasis on 'main' subjects; but it was interesting to see that the bulk of these came from a school where there was already more specialisation than in any of the other schools visited. Obviously the drive towards examinations so much valued by the staff had communicated itself to the students.

Methods

53.3% of students replied to this question and amongst these was once again a fair proportion of satisfied students — 13.3%. Other comments which predominated were:

14.0% —   closer staff-student relationships
14.1% —   more training and preparation of teachers

Of the improved methods which were specifically recommended discussion was mentioned most frequently:

7.9% —   more discussion
3.8% —   more audio-visual techniques
3.5% —   more visits outside school
1.5% —   more possibility to work on one's own
1.4% —   more group teaching

There were some criticisms of particular methods. The highest score here was 3.4% which went to excessive note-taking and parrot-learning. Only 1.7% mentioned more collaboration with students as being an important factor. 6.4% wanted better material facilities, and 5.2% said they did not know how teaching methods could be improved.

Second and third comments emphasised closer staff-student relationships and more training and preparation of teachers.

Examples of student comment were:

> "If the relationship between staff and students is on a mature level, without staff resorting to rules and authority to impose upon the students, then the teaching methods are all right. It is not the teaching methods which affect learning but the attitude of both staff and students".

> "Teachers could adopt a more personal relationship with students, not so detached — thus the pupils would be more willing to co-operate and ask if they do not understand. A visual teaching system or changes from time to time would prevent monotony".

One student had a point to make about teaching lower down in schools which is relevant:

> "I think lower school work should be individually styled, i.e. more working on one's own, so that sixth form work is not so much of a shock".

One recommendation for teacher training said casually:

> "Methods are quite adequate but teachers *should* (student's emphasis) have this re-training thing after so many years of teaching".

Another student called for "more facts and less padding and fiction." Perhaps he would be happier in Italy where students complain of a constant stream of facts! Another said sadly, "I am not happy with the methods, but they are effective for exams".

Organisation

46.1% of students commented on school organisation. 15.6% of these were quite satisfied with things as they were, and 7.2% said they did not know how organisation could be improved. Main recommendations were:

> 19.8% —   more real power should be given to students
> 9.1% —   more consultation with students
> 7.0% —   better staff-student relations
> 8.0% —   less rigidity in rules
> 7.0% —   better material facilities

A few students wanted either a drastic reform of school (1.9%) and even fewer a reform of school and society (0.4%). 4.3% thought that the timetable could be better arranged. Other factors were each mentioned by less than 2% of students except for the plea for more discipline by 5.1% of students. This was not general but was restricted to a couple of schools, one in particular. In both cases comments often referred to the head as being the one responsible for the lack of order. Second and third comments, of which there were few, reiterated the wish for fewer rules and closer staff-student relations.

Examples of student comment were:

> "More say for students and teachers. More joint activities between school and community. More flexible timetable. Punishment if disrupt lessons but not for such petty things as uniform, length of hair etc."

> "The sixth form should be more independent of the rest of the school, not because we want more privileges, but since we are old enough to leave school our rules should be ones appropriate for adults".

Prefect systems and sixth form hybrids or units were not so popular as sixth form colleges and technical colleges where it was felt, particularly by students who did not go to this kind of institution, that there would be a more liberal and flexible approach.

Extra-curricular activities

43.9% of students replied. Of these 24.1% said that they were satisfied with the present arrangements, and 6.1% said they did not know how to improve things. The largest categories were:

28.0% — the number should be expanded
8.8% — the situation depends on students themselves
6.7% — better facilities needed

English students are given more chance to take part in extra-curricular activities than students in other countries, so the 28.0% who want more of them obviously think them a good thing. Suggestions as to how things could be improved even more included recommendations for more flexibility in the timetable and the training of teachers specially qualified to help with such activities.

Second and third comments emphasised that it was up to students to take the initiative.

Students commented favourably on a system started by one school which had engaged a special tutor who, as part of his job, gave particular attention to extra-curricular activities. It was clear that students in other schools also thought these activities were valuable:

"They could become a more integral part of school life and be brought into school hours".

"I think more emphasis should be placed on the importance of these as they are at present, for there is a wide range of activities which are genuinely interesting and constructive".

But there are dangers in such an approach, as was pointed out by one student who said that the activities were of very little help because: "most students and tutors consider them to be part of the timetable which must be done and nothing more". The same student said that extra-curricular activities had no hope of improvement, "unless students can use the facilities to do what they decide". Another student made an interesting comment on a more extended use of extra-curricular activities than is usually accepted:

> "They could bring the school outside into the world more, with trips to industry and local government etc. They could bring in more of these activities so the pupils in the sixth form at least feel they are part of the community before they leave school".

Student perceptions of current problems

For English students the most frequently mentioned problem was an inadequate supply of books and teaching materials, followed by problems connected with assessment and of having a wide range of abilities in school.

%	Problems as seen by students
33.5	inadequate supply of books and materials
6.7	difficulty of devising an up-to-date curriculum
13.6	difficulty of implementing an up-to-date curriculum
14.6	shortage of teachers
27.1	placing of students in school according to abilities and inclinations
12.9	inadequate material facilities
31.1	conflict between what students want to learn and the realities of the job situation
6.4	inadequate initial training of teachers
16.6	placing of students in jobs/higher education according to abilities and inclinations
18.2	student apathy
13.5	devising an up to date curriculum for the less able
2.8	implementing an up to date curriculum for the less able
9.9	inadequate in-service training of teachers
15.0	maintaining of discipline
28.5	problems of assessing the standard a student has reached
9.0	difficulties of having students from a wide range of social backgrounds in school
15.4	problems stemming from students who wish to participate in planning
10.2	truancy
24.5	difficulties of having students from a wide range of ability in school

Number of students: 1114 (two schools not allowed to reply to this question)

English students: Table E13

Student perceptions of current problems

English students, compared to students in the other countries visited, are more favourably disposed towards their education system. Grumbles tend to be school-based; i.e. about rules, length of hair, teachers who want to treat them as children rather than as adults. Even these grumbles tend to be confined to particular schools rather than to the system as a whole. These trends are in contrast, for instance, to the attitudes of the French and Italians; in those countries frustrations are greater and views are more extreme.

CHAPTER 12

SUMMARY OF INFORMATION ON STUDENTS: SIMILARITIES AND DIFFERENCES

FURTHER RESULTS AND SOME CONCLUSIONS

The previous chapter gave a detailed report on student opinion in England. This chapter summarises the main findings and points to similarities which are common to all countries visited, and differences which belong to particular education systems. Before looking at the tables which draw the statistics together, readers should bear in mind that the proportions of the 15-20 age group in full-time education vary from country to country. Figures to illustrate this have been given in the section on Structure and Policy. For present purposes it is very important to remember that the different proportions enrolled introduce quite different teaching/learning problems — and also different problems of human relationships and contact with life around the schools. Indeed the recency or long-standing character of upper-secondary expansion, and the speed of growth, add further factors for consideration.

Table A1 below summarises the stated reasons for staying on in full-time education. In all countries the wish for qualifications which would be of use in a job received the highest counts. Apart from Italy, where the scores were lower, over three quarters of students in the other countries mentioned qualifications for a job, and over half again, in all countries except Italy, mentioned a wish for higher education. These proportions remain fairly constant despite the different systems and the different percentages in full-time education, and the varying levels of course. In France and Sweden, for example, the figures for the items mentioned above respectively 74.0%, 51.8% and 76.4%, 55.7%. 94.1% of the French sample were doing the long academic course leading to the *baccalauréat*; and 39.4% of the Swedish sample were doing the academic *gymnasium* course. Reasons connected with a wish to stay with friends, or make new friends, receive low scores in all countries, perhaps reinforcing the instrumental attitude towards school suggested both by the results in tables A1 and A2 (dealt with below) and the open-ended answers.

	England All Students	Male	Female	France All Students	Male	Female	Italy All Students	Male	Female	Sweden All Students	Male	Female	Germany All Students	Male	Female
wish for qualification of use in job	88.9	89.5	88.6	74.0	74.8	73.0	63.5	71.2	51.1	76.4	75.8	78.4	83.1	80.5	86.0
opportunity to make new friends	11.8	11.8	12.2	5.1	4.6	5.6	12.1	12.8	11.1	2.2	1.3	2.7	7.9	6.2	9.9
could not decide what else to do	21.7	21.1	22.9	11.9	13.5	9.7	6.9	7.4	6.2	24.5	19.2	29.7	15.8	13.8	18.1
advice of teachers/counsellors	27.2	23.7	31.7	32.5	32.4	32.6	11.3	11.4	11.3	17.8	16.2	19.5	15.6	19.2	11.7
wish for higher education	61.9	59.3	66.9	52.2	52.4	52.1	30.3	30.5	29.6	55.7	53.3	61.9	54.1	75.4	29.8
influence of parents	50.3	49.2	52.4	41.9	44.2	38.7	17.9	19.9	15.0	40.4	38.4	42.3	24.0	30.8	16.4
few jobs for school-leavers	20.3	22.5	18.1	8.4	7.9	9.1	5.3	6.9	2.9	12.4	8.8	13.8	1.4	2.1	.6
did not want to start work	7.1	9.2	7.5	24.4	24.7	23.8	13.8	16.6	9.1	9.0	6.3	11.7	34.7	37.4	31.6
particular subjects interesting	42.1	34.0	52.0	40.4	37.2	44.6	39.0	37.8	41.2	28.2	28.5	27.9	48.1	30.8	67.8
stayed to be with friends	5.5	6.7	4.2	6.5	8.6	3.9	3.1	3.3	2.9	5.0	4.5	5.1	2.7	3.1	2.3
Total number of students per country	1,114			1,534			1,628			777			366		

All students: Table A1. Stated reasons for staying on in full-time education

The figures relating to interest in particular subjects show that, despite the strong criticisms of teaching methods and poor presentation in Italy, France and Germany, there is considerable interest in the subjects offered in the curriculum. Again, all these countries have smaller percentages who stay on than Sweden, where only 27.7% of students say that they have an interest in particular subjects — despite the vast sums of money poured into curriculum development in Sweden.

The figures relating to students' indecision in England and Sweden about what else they could do, and to their feeling that there were few jobs for school-leavers, probably reflect anxiety about the unemployment which was prevalent in both countries at the time of the fieldwork. The open-ended replies, both in France and Germany, stress the unpleasantness of many of the jobs which are available to people with minimum qualifications. Students in these countries mention more often than others their wish not to start work.

Table A2 below shows the most important stated reasons for staying on in full-time education. Here the instrumental element is strong. In all countries the most important reason is the wish to obtain qualifications which will be of use in a job. This aim no doubt applies to students who want to go on to further studies anyway; as has been seen from some of the open-ended replies, further studies can be seen as the guarantee of a job, just as much as A-level or the *baccalauréat,* whether this is really true or not.

Although students in all countries show this instrumental attitude they are attracted to their particular schools for other reasons, as is shown in Table A3 below. This table reflects greater differences than tables A1 and A2 perhaps because — while the need for a job of some kind is universal — the systems in which one gains the qualifications can be very different. Both Sweden and England score fairly highly on the pleasantness of the school community; but whereas this is associated in England with easy relations with staff, that factor in Sweden is hardly mentioned at all. English students also see themselves as having far more freedom to arrange and organise things for themselves, and far more freedom when it comes to choice of studies. The competitiveness of the French and English systems is borne out by the concern for examinations. As far as standards of teaching are concerned, only 25.1% of the Swedish students thought that these were high — a low percentage considering the money and research which has been consumed; but it is only fair to remind readers again of the large numbers of students in Swedish schools. Some of the other high scores will include students who perceive that the teaching methods are "efficient" even if not pleasant. As one English student said, "I do not like the teaching methods used here, but they do get results!"

The histograms of the following pages illustrate the large gap which exists between what students consider to be important and what they consider their teachers value as important. Italian and English students expect the most from school, the Swedes the least; the Italians are the most disappointed in their expectations. The largeness of the gap even amongst the students who do not expect much, points to the lack of exploitation on the part of many teachers of the latent willingness and interest of many students. Some of the gaps suggest that there is a good deal of frustration. French and Italian students, for example, want *far more* choice in the subjects they study. There is much talk about preparing integrated humanities courses, courses of civics, etc; but many students feel that few of their teachers are keen on developing a social and political awareness. Perhaps that is why experience of democracy comes some way down the frequency counts. Either students think it is not important or not possible; or, as is the case among some students in France and Italy, they have already taken up an extreme "revolutionary" political attitude.

England	France	Italy	Sweden	Germany	
32.0	44.8	50.4	51.3	43.7	wish for qualifications
1.5	.1	.8	.5	.6	opportunity to make new friends
4.5	2.4	1.2	3.4	3.4	could not decide what else to do
2.7	4.1	1.0	1.1	.8	advice of teachers/counsellors
24.5	19.0	13.6	18.4	24.8	wish for higher education
5.5	4.0	1.3	2.1	3.1	influence of parents
4.1	1.5	1.6	2.6	–	few jobs for school leavers
1.8	2.3	1.9	.8	3.4	did not want to start work
9.0	8.7	14.8	6.6	13.5	particular subjects interesting
.7	.3	.2	.4	–	stayed on to be with friends
4.0	11.0	10.6	7.8	6.8	other reason
9.7	.1	.2	.1	–	impossible to make a choice
3.6	9.2	23.2	10.7	3.0	no reply
1,114	1,534	1,624	777	366	Total number of students per country

All students: Table A2

Most important stated reasons for staying on in full time education

England	France	Italy	Sweden	Germany	
12.5	5.7	2.9	4.2	3.3	sports facilities
30.1	10.4	5.5	2.7	6.6	easy relations with staff
12.7	9.2	6.3	.5	1.6	extra-curricular activities
34.4	6.7	11.4	5.3	4.9	freedom for students to organise things themselves
54.3	56.1	44.5	25.1	38.5	standard of teaching high
13.0	8.6	5.4	4.8	9.8	friends came
44.0	16.2	14.3	39.1	12.6	pleasant community to work in
9.7	2.0	2.3	1.0	.8	library facilities
13.6	22.9	37.0	32.6	48.1	training for job
38.0	4.0	9.4	1.1	12.6	possibility to choose studies
6.8	6.5	2.6	1.3	2.2	opportunity to make a new start
32.6	35.6	3.8	1.3	3.3	chance to meet opposite sex
32.6	36.7	3.8	1.4	3.0	school's successful examination record
1,114	1,534	1,624	777	366	Total number of students per country

All students: Table A3

Stated attractions of a particular school or college

England
France
Italy
Sweden
Germany

Histograms on student aims and perceived satisfactions

Tables E5, F5, I5, S5, G5 — the *right hand line* shows the frequencies of items considered to be important by students, irrespective of whether they think that teachers share their views.

— the *left hand line* shows the frequencies of items considered to be important by students where they think that teachers share their views.

Tables E6, E7, E8, F6, F7, F8, I6, I7, I8, S6, S7, S8, G6, G7, G8 — the *upper line* shows the frequencies of items considered to be important by students, irrespective of whether they think that teachers share their views.

— the *lower line* shows the frequencies of items considered to be important by students where they think that teachers share their views.

In all tables the distance between the two lines represents the gap in perceptions between students and teachers — *from the students' point of view*. Corresponding histograms from the teachers' point of view are in a subsequent chapter on teachers.

N.B. The lines on the English tables might well have been closer together if the heads of two schools, whose students made up 20% of the total English sample, had allowed their students to comment on their perceptions of staff.

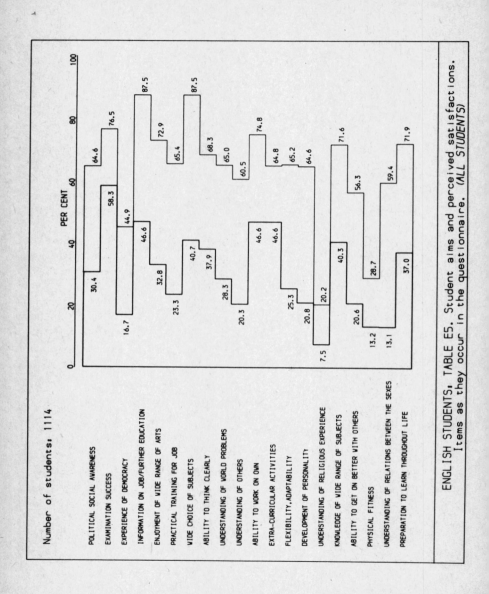

Number of students: 1114

POLITICAL SOCIAL AWARENESS — 30.4 / 64.6
EXAMINATION SUCCESS — 58.3 / 76.5
EXPERIENCE OF DEMOCRACY — 16.7 / 44.9
INFORMATION ON JOB/FURTHER EDUCATION — 46.6 / 87.5
ENJOYMENT OF WIDE RANGE OF ARTS — 32.8 / 72.9
PRACTICAL TRAINING FOR JOB — 23.3 / 65.4 / 87.5
WIDE CHOICE OF SUBJECTS — 40.7 / 68.3
ABILITY TO THINK CLEARLY — 37.9 / 65.0
UNDERSTANDING OF WORLD PROBLEMS — 28.3 / 60.5
UNDERSTANDING OF OTHERS — 20.3 / 74.8
ABILITY TO WORK ON OWN — 46.6 / 64.8
EXTRA-CURRICULAR ACTIVITIES — 46.6 / 65.2
FLEXIBILITY, ADAPTABILITY — 25.3 / 64.6
DEVELOPMENT OF PERSONALITY — 20.8
UNDERSTANDING OF RELIGIOUS EXPERIENCE — 7.5 / 20.2 / 71.6
KNOWLEDGE OF WIDE RANGE OF SUBJECTS — 40.3 / 56.3
ABILITY TO GET ON BETTER WITH OTHERS — 20.6 / 28.7
PHYSICAL FITNESS — 13.2 / 59.4
UNDERSTANDING OF RELATIONS BETWEEN THE SEXES — 13.1 / 71.9
PREPARATION TO LEARN THROUGHOUT LIFE — 37.0

PER CENT

ENGLISH STUDENTS, TABLE E5. Student aims and perceived satisfactions. Items as they occur in the questionnaire. (ALL STUDENTS)

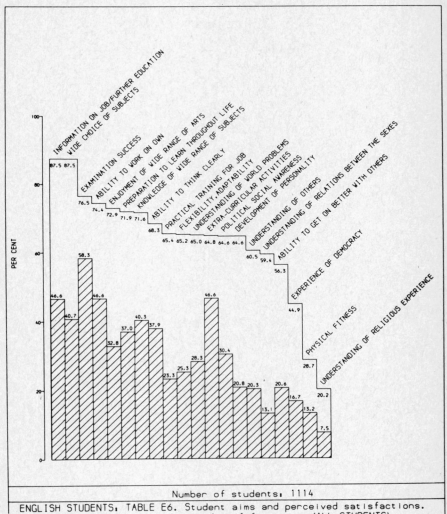

PER CENT

INFORMATION ON JOB/FURTHER EDUCATION
WIDE CHOICE OF SUBJECTS
EXAMINATION SUCCESS
ABILITY TO WORK ON OWN
ENJOYMENT OF WIDE RANGE OF ARTS
PREPARATION TO LEARN THROUGHOUT LIFE
KNOWLEDGE OF WIDE RANGE OF SUBJECTS
ABILITY TO THINK CLEARLY
PRACTICAL TRAINING FOR JOB
FLEXIBILITY ADAPTABILITY
UNDERSTANDING OF WORLD PROBLEMS
EXTRA-CURRICULAR ACTIVITIES
POLITICAL SOCIAL AWARENESS
DEVELOPMENT OF PERSONALITY
UNDERSTANDING OF OTHERS
UNDERSTANDING OF RELATIONS BETWEEN THE SEXES
ABILITY TO GET ON BETTER WITH OTHERS
EXPERIENCE OF DEMOCRACY
PHYSICAL FITNESS
UNDERSTANDING OF RELIGIOUS EXPERIENCE

87.5 87.5
76.5
74.4 72.9 71.9 71.6
68.3
65.4 65.2 65.0 64.8 64.6 64.6
60.5 59.4
56.3
44.9
28.7
58.3
46.6 40.7 46.6
32.8
37.0 40.3 37.9
23.3 25.3 28.3 30.4
20.8 20.3 20.6
13.1 16.7 13.2
20.2
7.5

Number of students: 1114

ENGLISH STUDENTS: TABLE E6. Student aims and perceived satisfactions.
Items in descending order of frequency. *(ALL STUDENTS)*

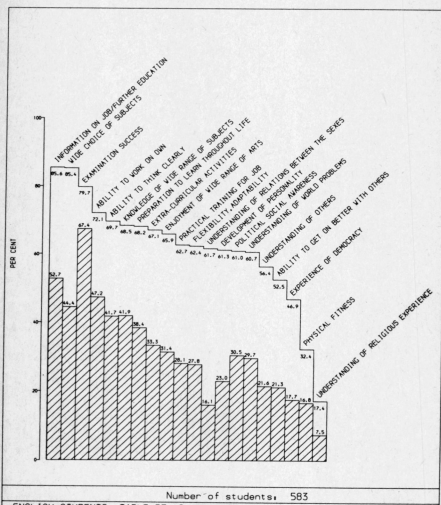

PER CENT

100

80

60

40

20

0

INFORMATION ON JOB/FURTHER EDUCATION
WIDE CHOICE OF SUBJECTS
EXAMINATION SUCCESS
ABILITY TO WORK ON OWN
ABILITY TO THINK CLEARLY
KNOWLEDGE OF WIDE RANGE OF SUBJECTS
PREPARATION TO LEARN THROUGHOUT LIFE
EXTRA-CURRICULAR ACTIVITIES
ENJOYMENT OF WIDE RANGE OF ARTS
PRACTICAL TRAINING FOR JOB
FLEXIBILITY, ADAPTABILITY
UNDERSTANDING OF PERSONALITY
DEVELOPMENT OF PERSONALITY
POLITICAL SOCIAL AWARENESS
UNDERSTANDING OF WORLD PROBLEMS
UNDERSTANDING OF RELATIONS BETWEEN THE SEXES
UNDERSTANDING OF OTHERS
ABILITY TO GET ON BETTER WITH OTHERS
EXPERIENCE OF DEMOCRACY
PHYSICAL FITNESS
UNDERSTANDING OF RELIGIOUS EXPERIENCE

85.6 85.4 79.7 72.1 69.7 68.5 68.2 67.4 67.1 65.9 62.7 62.4 61.7 61.3 61.0 60.7 56.4 52.5 46.9 32.4

52.7 44.4 47.2 41.7 41.9 38.4 33.3 31.4 28.1 27.8 23.0 30.5 29.7 21.6 21.3 17.7 16.8 17.4 16.1 7.5

Number of students: 583

ENGLISH STUDENTS, TABLE E7. Student aims and perceived satisfactions.
Items in descending order of frequency. (MALES)

PER CENT

WIDE CHOICE OF SUBJECTS 88.7
INFORMATION ON JOB/FURTHER EDUCATION 88.0
ENJOYMENT OF WIDE RANGE OF ARTS 79.9
ABILITY TO WORK ON OWN 77.7
PREPARATION TO LEARN THROUGHOUT LIFE 74.9
KNOWLEDGE OF WIDE RANGE OF SUBJECTS 74.3
EXAMINATION SUCCESS 72.1
UNDERSTANDING OF WORLD PROBLEMS 69.1
FLEXIBILITY, ADAPTABILITY 68.5
POLITICAL SOCIAL AWARENESS 67.7
PRACTICAL TRAINING FOR JOB 66.9
DEVELOPMENT OF PERSONALITY 66.9
ABILITY TO THINK CLEARLY 65.6
UNDERSTANDING OF OTHERS 63.3
EXTRA-CURRICULAR ACTIVITIES 60.7
ABILITY TO GET ON BETTER WITH OTHERS 59.9
UNDERSTANDING OF RELATIONS BETWEEN THE SEXES 55.2
EXPERIENCE OF DEMOCRACY 41.2
UNDERSTANDING OF RELIGIOUS EXPERIENCE 23.5
PHYSICAL FITNESS 23.5

35.9 38.2 34.3 45.0 34.5 38.2 47.0 26.5 22.7 29.5 17.7 15.9 32.7 17.9 18.3 19.3 9.6 14.9 8.6 7.6

Number of students: 498

ENGLISH STUDENTS, TABLE E8. Student aims and perceived satisfactions.
Items in descending order of frequency. *(FEMALES)*

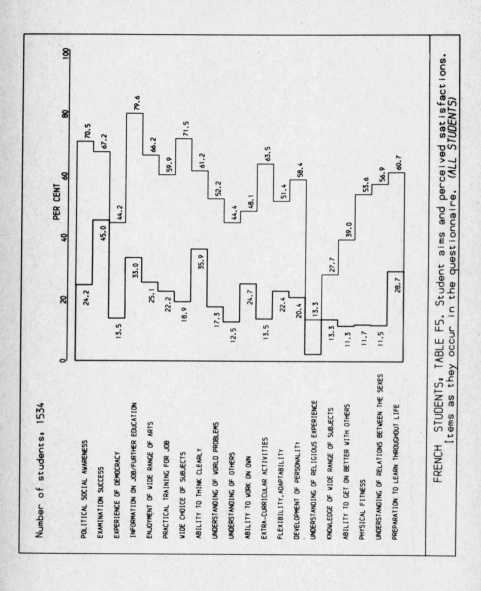

Number of students: 1534

PER CENT

POLITICAL SOCIAL AWARENESS	24.2	70.5
EXAMINATION SUCCESS	45.0	67.2
EXPERIENCE OF DEMOCRACY	13.5	44.2
INFORMATION ON JOB/FURTHER EDUCATION	33.0	79.6
ENJOYMENT OF WIDE RANGE OF ARTS	25.1	66.2
PRACTICAL TRAINING FOR JOB	22.2	59.9
WIDE CHOICE OF SUBJECTS	18.9	71.5
ABILITY TO THINK CLEARLY	35.9	61.2
UNDERSTANDING OF WORLD PROBLEMS	17.3	52.2
UNDERSTANDING OF OTHERS	12.5	44.4
ABILITY TO WORK ON OWN	24.7	48.1
EXTRA-CURRICULAR ACTIVITIES	13.5	63.5
FLEXIBILITY, ADAPTABILITY	22.4	51.4
DEVELOPMENT OF PERSONALITY	20.4	58.4
UNDERSTANDING OF RELIGIOUS EXPERIENCE	13.3	
KNOWLEDGE OF WIDE RANGE OF SUBJECTS	13.3	27.7
ABILITY TO GET ON BETTER WITH OTHERS	11.3	39.0
PHYSICAL FITNESS	11.7	53.6
UNDERSTANDING OF RELATIONS BETWEEN THE SEXES	11.5	56.9
PREPARATION TO LEARN THROUGHOUT LIFE	28.7	60.7

FRENCH STUDENTS: TABLE F5. Student aims and perceived satisfactions.
Items as they occur in the questionnaire. (ALL STUDENTS)

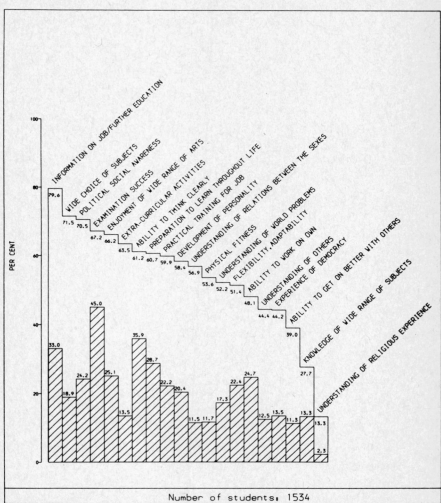

Number of students: 1534

FRENCH STUDENTS, TABLE F6. Student aims and perceived satisfactions.
Items in descending order of frequency. *(ALL STUDENTS)*

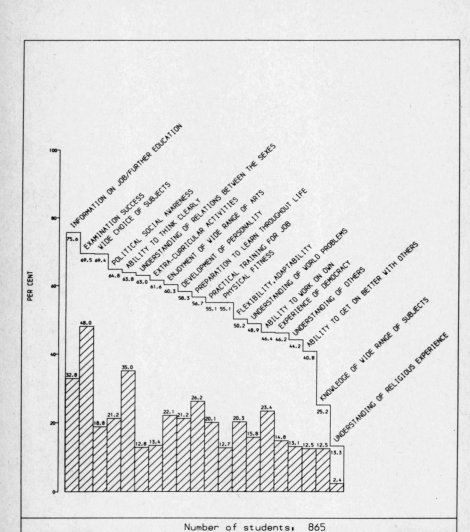

PER CENT

INFORMATION ON JOB/FURTHER EDUCATION
EXAMINATION SUCCESS
WIDE CHOICE OF SUBJECTS
POLITICAL SOCIAL AWARENESS
ABILITY TO THINK CLEARLY
UNDERSTANDING OF RELATIONS BETWEEN THE SEXES
EXTRA-CURRICULAR ACTIVITIES
ENJOYMENT OF WIDE RANGE OF ARTS
DEVELOPMENT OF PERSONALITY
PREPARATION TO LEARN THROUGHOUT LIFE
PRACTICAL TRAINING FOR JOB
PHYSICAL FITNESS
FLEXIBILITY, ADAPTABILITY
UNDERSTANDING OF WORLD PROBLEMS
ABILITY TO WORK ON OWN
EXPERIENCE OF DEMOCRACY
UNDERSTANDING OF OTHERS
ABILITY TO GET ON BETTER WITH OTHERS
KNOWLEDGE OF WIDE RANGE OF SUBJECTS
UNDERSTANDING OF RELIGIOUS EXPERIENCE

75.6 69.5 69.4 64.8 63.8 63.0 61.6 60.3 58.3 56.7 55.1 55.1 50.2 48.9 46.4 46.2 44.2 40.8 25.2

32.8 48.0 18.8 21.2 35.0 12.8 13.4 22.1 21.2 26.2 20.1 12.7 20.3 15.8 23.4 14.8 13.1 12.5 12.5 13.3 2.4

Number of students: 865

FRENCH STUDENTS, TABLE F7. Student aims and perceived satisfactions.
Items in descending order of frequency. (MALES)

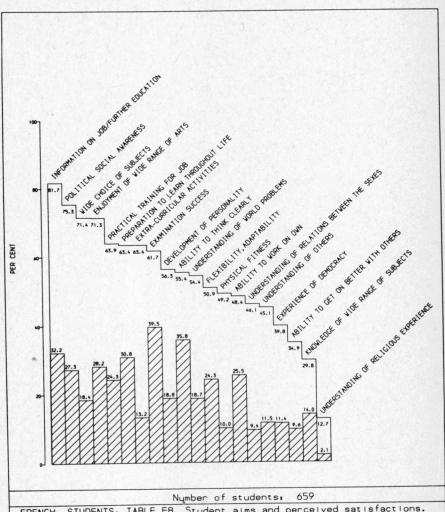

PER CENT

INFORMATION ON JOB/FURTHER EDUCATION
POLITICAL SOCIAL AWARENESS
WIDE CHOICE OF SUBJECTS
ENJOYMENT OF WIDE RANGE OF ARTS
PRACTICAL TRAINING FOR JOB
PREPARATION TO LEARN THROUGHOUT LIFE
EXTRA-CURRICULAR ACTIVITIES
EXAMINATION SUCCESS
DEVELOPMENT OF PERSONALITY
ABILITY TO THINK CLEARLY
UNDERSTANDING OF WORLD PROBLEMS
FLEXIBILITY, ADAPTABILITY
PHYSICAL FITNESS
ABILITY TO WORK ON OWN
UNDERSTANDING OF RELATIONS BETWEEN THE SEXES
UNDERSTANDING OF OTHERS
EXPERIENCE OF DEMOCRACY
ABILITY TO GET ON BETTER WITH OTHERS
KNOWLEDGE OF WIDE RANGE OF SUBJECTS
UNDERSTANDING OF RELIGIOUS EXPERIENCE

81.7 75.3 71.4 71.3 63.9 63.4 63.4 61.7 56.3 55.4 54.4 50.9 49.2 48.4 46.1 45.1 39.8 34.9 29.8

32.2 27.3 18.4 28.2 24.3 30.8 13.2 39.5 18.6 35.8 18.7 24.3 10.0 25.5 9.4 11.5 11.4 9.6 14.0 12.7 2.1

Number of students: 659

FRENCH STUDENTS, TABLE F8. Student aims and perceived satisfactions.
Items in descending order of frequency. *(FEMALES)*

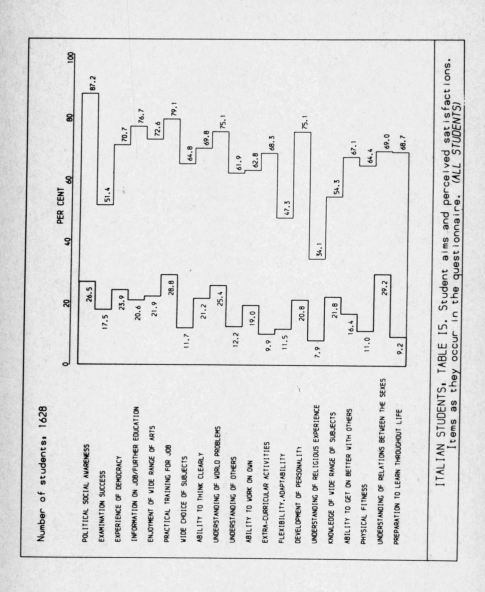

Number of students: 1628

PER CENT

POLITICAL SOCIAL AWARENESS — 26.5 / 87.2
EXAMINATION SUCCESS — 17.5 / 51.4
EXPERIENCE OF DEMOCRACY — 23.9 / 70.7
INFORMATION ON JOB/FURTHER EDUCATION — 20.6 / 76.7
ENJOYMENT OF WIDE RANGE OF ARTS — 21.9 / 72.6
PRACTICAL TRAINING FOR JOB — 28.8 / 79.1
WIDE CHOICE OF SUBJECTS — 11.7 / 64.8
ABILITY TO THINK CLEARLY — 21.2 / 69.8
UNDERSTANDING OF WORLD PROBLEMS — 25.4 / 75.1
UNDERSTANDING OF OTHERS — 12.2 / 61.9
ABILITY TO WORK ON OWN — 19.0 / 62.8
EXTRA-CURRICULAR ACTIVITIES — 9.9 / 68.3
FLEXIBILITY, ADAPTABILITY — 11.5 / 47.3
DEVELOPMENT OF PERSONALITY — 20.8 / 75.1
UNDERSTANDING OF RELIGIOUS EXPERIENCE — 7.9 / 34.1
KNOWLEDGE OF WIDE RANGE OF SUBJECTS — 21.8 / 54.3
ABILITY TO GET ON BETTER WITH OTHERS — 16.4 / 67.1
PHYSICAL FITNESS — 11.0 / 64.4
UNDERSTANDING OF RELATIONS BETWEEN THE SEXES — 29.2 / 69.0
PREPARATION TO LEARN THROUGHOUT LIFE — 9.2 / 68.7

ITALIAN STUDENTS: TABLE 15. Student aims and perceived satisfactions. Items as they occur in the questionnaire. (ALL STUDENTS)

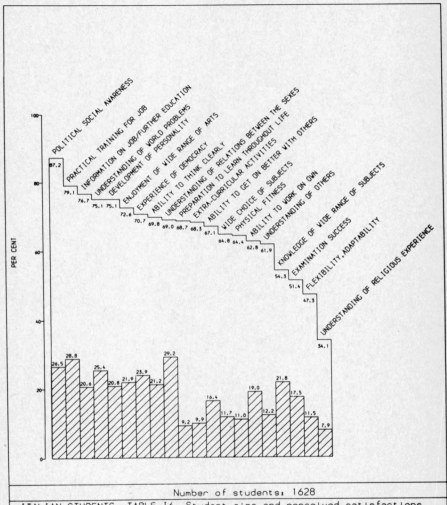

Number of students: 1628

ITALIAN STUDENTS, TABLE 16. Student aims and perceived satisfactions.
Items in descending order of frequency. (ALL STUDENTS)

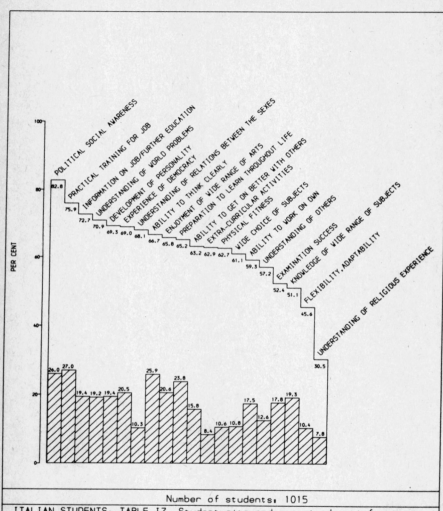

PER CENT

POLITICAL SOCIAL AWARENESS
PRACTICAL TRAINING FOR JOB
INFORMATION ON JOB/FURTHER EDUCATION
UNDERSTANDING OF WORLD PROBLEMS
DEVELOPMENT OF PERSONALITY
EXPERIENCE OF DEMOCRACY
UNDERSTANDING OF RELATIONS BETWEEN THE SEXES
ABILITY TO THINK CLEARLY
ENJOYMENT OF WIDE RANGE OF ARTS
PREPARATION TO LEARN THROUGHOUT LIFE
ABILITY TO GET ON BETTER WITH OTHERS
EXTRA-CURRICULAR ACTIVITIES
PHYSICAL FITNESS
WIDE CHOICE OF SUBJECTS
ABILITY TO WORK ON OWN
UNDERSTANDING OF OTHERS
EXAMINATION SUCCESS
KNOWLEDGE OF WIDE RANGE OF SUBJECTS
FLEXIBILITY, ADAPTABILITY
UNDERSTANDING OF RELIGIOUS EXPERIENCE

82.8
75.9
72.7
70.9
69.3 69.0 68.1
66.7 65.8 65.2
63.2 62.9 62.7
61.1
59.3
57.2
52.4 51.1
45.6
30.5

26.0 27.0
19.4 19.2 19.4 20.5
10.3
25.9
20.6
23.8
15.8
8.4
10.6 10.8
17.5
12.6
17.8 19.3
10.4
7.8

Number of students: 1015

ITALIAN STUDENTS: TABLE 17. Student aims and perceived satisfactions.
Items in descending order of frequency. (MALES)

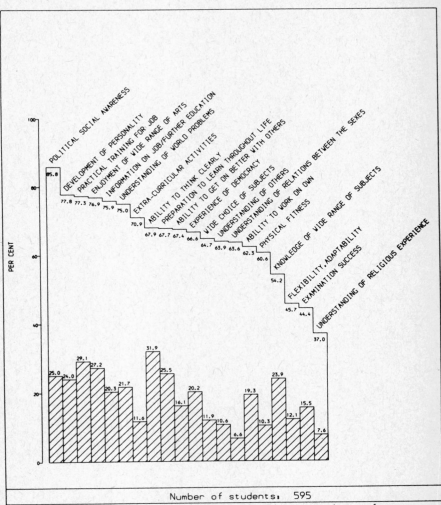

PER CENT

POLITICAL SOCIAL AWARENESS — 85.8
DEVELOPMENT OF PERSONALITY — 77.8
PRACTICAL TRAINING FOR JOB — 77.3
ENJOYMENT OF WIDE RANGE OF ARTS — 76.9
INFORMATION ON JOB/FURTHER EDUCATION — 75.9
UNDERSTANDING OF WORLD PROBLEMS — 75.0
EXTRA-CURRICULAR ACTIVITIES — 70.9
ABILITY TO THINK CLEARLY — 67.9
PREPARATION TO LEARN THROUGHOUT LIFE — 67.7
ABILITY TO GET ON BETTER WITH OTHERS — 67.4
EXPERIENCE OF DEMOCRACY — 66.6
WIDE CHOICE OF SUBJECTS — 64.7
UNDERSTANDING OF OTHERS — 63.9
UNDERSTANDING OF RELATIONS BETWEEN THE SEXES — 63.6
ABILITY TO WORK ON OWN — 62.3
PHYSICAL FITNESS — 60.6
KNOWLEDGE OF WIDE RANGE OF SUBJECTS — 54.2
FLEXIBILITY, ADAPTABILITY — 45.7
EXAMINATION SUCCESS — 44.4
UNDERSTANDING OF RELIGIOUS EXPERIENCE — 37.0

25.0 24.0 29.1 27.2 20.3 21.7 11.6 31.9 25.5 16.1 20.2 11.9 10.6 6.6 19.3 10.3 23.9 12.1 15.5 7.6

Number of students: 595

ITALIAN STUDENTS, TABLE 18. Student aims and perceived satisfactions.
Items in descending order of frequency. *(FEMALES)*

Number of students, 777

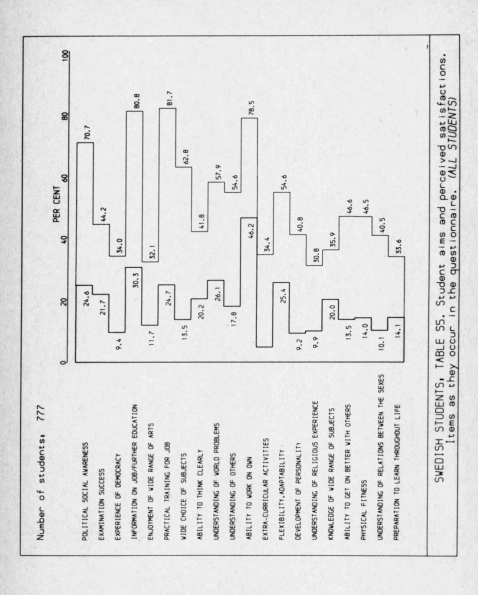

SWEDISH STUDENTS, TABLE S5. Student aims and perceived satisfactions. Items as they occur in the questionnaire. (ALL STUDENTS)

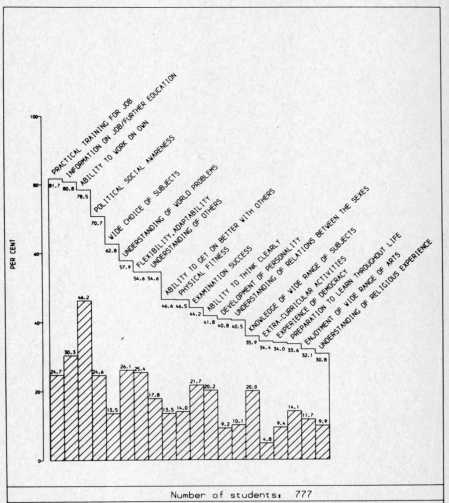

PER CENT

100 — 80 — 60 — 40 — 20 — 0

PRACTICAL TRAINING FOR JOB
INFORMATION ON JOB/FURTHER EDUCATION
ABILITY TO WORK ON OWN
POLITICAL SOCIAL AWARENESS
WIDE CHOICE OF SUBJECTS
UNDERSTANDING OF WORLD PROBLEMS
FLEXIBILITY, ADAPTABILITY
UNDERSTANDING OF OTHERS
ABILITY TO GET ON BETTER WITH OTHERS
PHYSICAL FITNESS
EXAMINATION SUCCESS
ABILITY TO THINK CLEARLY
DEVELOPMENT OF PERSONALITY
UNDERSTANDING OF RELATIONS BETWEEN THE SEXES
KNOWLEDGE OF WIDE RANGE OF SUBJECTS
EXTRA-CURRICULAR ACTIVITIES
EXPERIENCE OF DEMOCRACY
PREPARATION TO LEARN THROUGHOUT LIFE
ENJOYMENT OF WIDE RANGE OF ARTS
UNDERSTANDING OF RELIGIOUS EXPERIENCE

81.7 80.8 78.5 70.7 62.8 57.9 54.6 54.6 46.6 46.5 44.2 41.8 40.8 40.5 35.9 34.4 34.0 33.6 32.1 30.8

24.7 30.3 46.2 24.6 13.5 26.1 25.4 17.8 13.5 14.0 21.7 20.2 9.2 10.1 20.0 4.8 9.4 14.1 11.7 9.9

Number of students: 777

SWEDISH STUDENTS: TABLE S6. Student aims and perceived satisfactions.
Items in descending order of frequency. (ALL STUDENTS)

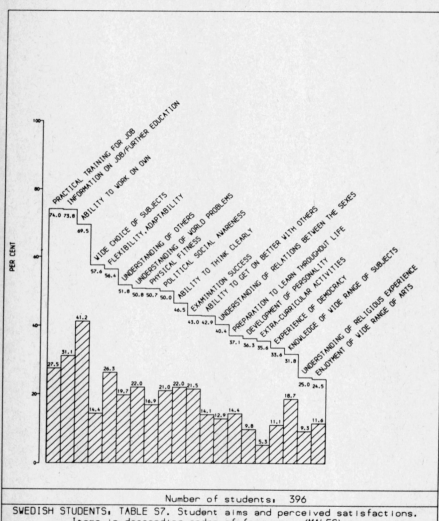

PER CENT

PRACTICAL TRAINING FOR JOB
INFORMATION ON JOB/FURTHER EDUCATION
ABILITY TO WORK ON OWN
WIDE CHOICE OF SUBJECTS
FLEXIBILITY, ADAPTABILITY
UNDERSTANDING OF OTHERS
UNDERSTANDING OF WORLD PROBLEMS
PHYSICAL FITNESS
POLITICAL SOCIAL AWARENESS
ABILITY TO THINK CLEARLY
EXAMINATION SUCCESS
ABILITY TO GET ON BETTER WITH OTHERS
UNDERSTANDING OF RELATIONS BETWEEN THE SEXES
PREPARATION TO LEARN THROUGHOUT LIFE
DEVELOPMENT OF PERSONALITY
EXTRA-CURRICULAR ACTIVITIES
EXPERIENCE OF DEMOCRACY
KNOWLEDGE OF WIDE RANGE OF SUBJECTS
UNDERSTANDING OF RELIGIOUS EXPERIENCE
ENJOYMENT OF WIDE RANGE OF ARTS

74.0 73.8
69.5
57.6 56.4
51.8 50.8 50.7 50.0
46.5
43.0 42.9
40.4
37.1 36.3 35.6
33.6
31.8
25.0 24.5

41.2
31.1
27.5
26.3
22.0   22.0 21.5
19.7
16.9
21.0
14.4   14.1 12.9 14.4
                              9.8   11.1   18.7
                                    5.3   9.3 11.6

Number of students: 396

SWEDISH STUDENTS, TABLE S7. Student aims and perceived satisfactions.
Items in descending order of frequency. (MALES)

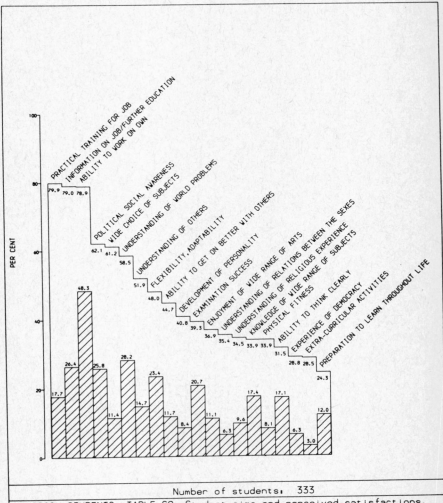

PER CENT

100—

80—

60—

40—

20—

0—

PRACTICAL TRAINING FOR JOB — 79.9
INFORMATION ON JOB/FURTHER EDUCATION — 79.0
ABILITY TO WORK ON OWN — 78.9
POLITICAL SOCIAL AWARENESS — 62.1
WIDE CHOICE OF SUBJECTS — 61.2
UNDERSTANDING OF WORLD PROBLEMS — 58.5
UNDERSTANDING OF OTHERS — 51.9
FLEXIBILITY ADAPTABILITY — 48.0
ABILITY TO GET ON BETTER WITH OTHERS — 44.7
DEVELOPMENT OF PERSONALITY — 40.8
EXAMINATION SUCCESS — 39.3
ENJOYMENT OF WIDE RANGE OF ARTS — 36.9
UNDERSTANDING OF RELATIONS BETWEEN THE SEXES — 35.4
UNDERSTANDING OF RELIGIOUS EXPERIENCE — 34.5
KNOWLEDGE OF WIDE RANGE OF SUBJECTS — 33.9
PHYSICAL FITNESS — 33.9
ABILITY TO THINK CLEARLY — 31.5
EXPERIENCE OF DEMOCRACY — 28.8
EXTRA-CURRICULAR ACTIVITIES — 28.5
PREPARATION TO LEARN THROUGHOUT LIFE — 24.3

17.7 26.4 48.3 25.8 11.4 28.2 14.7 23.4 11.7 8.4 20.7 11.1 6.3 9.6 17.4 8.1 17.1 6.3 5.0 12.0

Number of students: 333

SWEDISH STUDENTS: TABLE S8. Student aims and perceived satisfactions.
Items in descending order of frequency. *(FEMALES)*

Number of students: 366

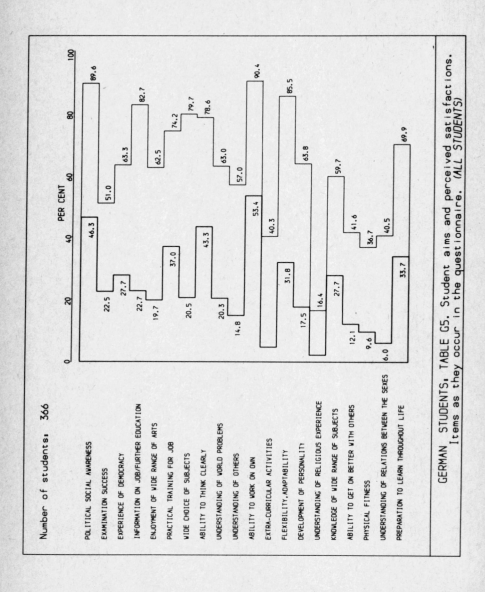

GERMAN STUDENTS, TABLE G5. Student aims and perceived satisfactions.
[Items as they occur in the questionnaire. (ALL STUDENTS)

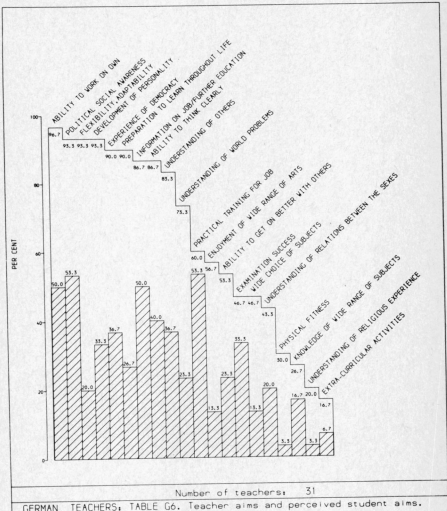

PER CENT

ABILITY TO WORK ON OWN — 96.7
POLITICAL SOCIAL AWARENESS — 93.3
FLEXIBILITY, ADAPTABILITY — 93.3
DEVELOPMENT OF PERSONALITY — 93.3
EXPERIENCE OF DEMOCRACY — 90.0
PREPARATION TO LEARN THROUGHOUT LIFE — 90.0
INFORMATION ON JOB/FURTHER EDUCATION — 86.7
ABILITY TO THINK CLEARLY — 86.7
UNDERSTANDING OF OTHERS — 83.3
UNDERSTANDING OF WORLD PROBLEMS — 73.3
PRACTICAL TRAINING FOR JOB — 60.0
ENJOYMENT OF WIDE RANGE OF ARTS — 56.7
ABILITY TO GET ON BETTER WITH OTHERS — 53.3
EXAMINATION SUCCESS — 46.7
WIDE CHOICE OF SUBJECTS — 46.7
UNDERSTANDING OF RELATIONS BETWEEN THE SEXES — 43.3
PHYSICAL FITNESS — 30.0
KNOWLEDGE OF WIDE RANGE OF SUBJECTS — 26.7
UNDERSTANDING OF RELIGIOUS EXPERIENCE — 20.0
EXTRA-CURRICULAR ACTIVITIES — 16.7

Bar values: 50.0, 53.3, 20.0, 33.3, 36.7, 26.7, 50.0, 40.0, 36.7, 23.3, 53.3, 56.7, 13.3, 53.3, 23.3, 33.3, 13.3, 20.0, 43.3, 30.0, 3.3, 26.7, 16.7, 3.3, 20.0, 16.7, 6.7

Number of teachers: 31

GERMAN TEACHERS, TABLE G6. Teacher aims and perceived student aims.
Items in descending order of frequency.

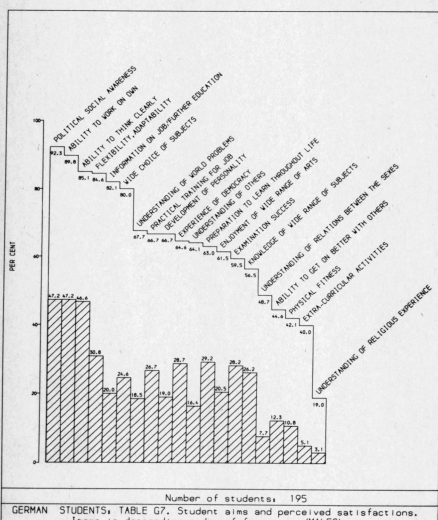

PER CENT

POLITICAL SOCIAL AWARENESS — 92.3
ABILITY TO WORK ON OWN — 89.8
ABILITY TO THINK CLEARLY — 85.1
FLEXIBILITY, ADAPTABILITY — 84.6
INFORMATION ON JOB/FURTHER EDUCATION — 82.1
WIDE CHOICE OF SUBJECTS — 80.0
UNDERSTANDING OF WORLD PROBLEMS — 67.7
PRACTICAL TRAINING FOR JOB — 66.7
DEVELOPMENT OF PERSONALITY — 66.7
EXPERIENCE OF DEMOCRACY — 64.6
UNDERSTANDING OF OTHERS — 64.1
PREPARATION TO LEARN THROUGHOUT LIFE — 63.0
ENJOYMENT OF WIDE RANGE OF ARTS — 61.5
EXAMINATION SUCCESS — 59.5
KNOWLEDGE OF WIDE RANGE OF SUBJECTS — 56.5
UNDERSTANDING OF RELATIONS BETWEEN THE SEXES — 48.7
ABILITY TO GET ON BETTER WITH OTHERS — 44.6
PHYSICAL FITNESS — 42.1
EXTRA-CURRICULAR ACTIVITIES — 40.0
UNDERSTANDING OF RELIGIOUS EXPERIENCE — 19.0

Lower bars: 47.2 47.2 46.6 30.8 20.0 24.6 18.5 26.7 19.0 28.7 16.4 29.2 20.5 28.2 26.2 7.7 12.3 10.8 5.1 3.1

Number of students: 195

GERMAN   STUDENTS, TABLE G7. Student aims and perceived satisfactions.
Items in descending order of frequency. (MALES)

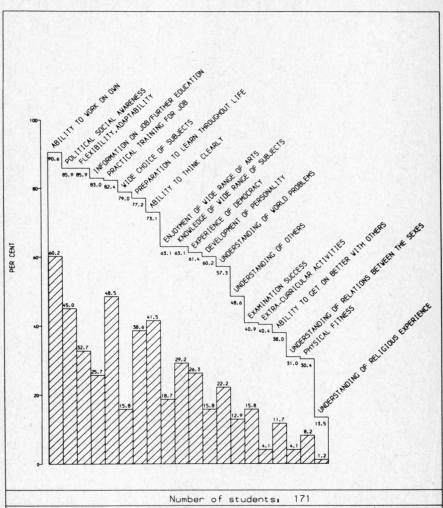

PER CENT

ABILITY TO WORK ON OWN — 90.6
POLITICAL SOCIAL AWARENESS — 85.9
FLEXIBILITY,ADAPTABILITY — 85.9
INFORMATION ON JOB/FURTHER EDUCATION — 83.0
PRACTICAL TRAINING FOR JOB — 82.4
WIDE CHOICE OF SUBJECTS — 79.0
PREPARATION TO LEARN THROUGHOUT LIFE — 77.2
ABILITY TO THINK CLEARLY — 73.1
ENJOYMENT OF WIDE RANGE OF ARTS — 63.1
KNOWLEDGE OF WIDE RANGE OF SUBJECTS — 63.1
EXPERIENCE OF DEMOCRACY — 61.4
DEVELOPMENT OF PERSONALITY — 60.2
UNDERSTANDING OF WORLD PROBLEMS — 57.3
UNDERSTANDING OF OTHERS — 48.6
EXAMINATION SUCCESS — 40.9
EXTRA-CURRICULAR ACTIVITIES — 40.4
ABILITY TO GET ON BETTER WITH OTHERS — 38.0
UNDERSTANDING OF RELATIONS BETWEEN THE SEXES — 31.0
PHYSICAL FITNESS — 30.4
UNDERSTANDING OF RELIGIOUS EXPERIENCE — 13.5

60.2 45.0 32.7 25.7 48.5 15.8 38.6 41.5 18.7 29.2 26.3 15.8 22.2 12.9 15.8 4.1 11.7 4.1 8.2 1.2

Number of students: 171

GERMAN STUDENTS, TABLE G8. Student aims and perceived satisfactions.
Items in descending order of frequency. *(FEMALES)*

Tables A4 and A5 on the following pages summarise the numbers of items listed in the questionnaire which were considered important by students, and the numbers of items considered to be important by students where they perceive that their teachers share their views. The size of the gap which the two tables represent is depressing, as are the cross-tabulations of these two tables presented in Table A6.

	England			France			Italy			Sweden			Germany		
	All Students	Male	Female	All Students	Male	Female	All Students	Male	Female	All Students	Male	Female	All Students	Male	Female
Between 1 & 5 items listed	6.9	7.0	5.6	12.8	13.1	12.0	13.4	13.7	11.8	22.8	27.5	18.3	4.9	3.6	6.4
Between 6 & 10 items listed	23.0	24.9	21.3	36.4	36.1	37.2	21.1	21.1	21.3	35.8	28.8	44.1	28.7	26.2	31.6
Between 11 & 15 items listed	41.2	41.2	41.2	33.5	33.8	33.4	26.1	27.2	24.5	29.9	28.5	30.6	41.5	41.5	41.5
Between 16 & 20 items listed	28.8	26.9	31.9	17.3	17.1	17.5	39.4	38.0	42.5	11.6	15.2	6.9	24.9	28.7	20.5
Total number of students	1,114			1,534			1,628			777			366		

All students: Table A4: Percentages of students according to numbers of items considered to be important by students

	England			France			Italy			Sweden			Germany		
	All Students	Male	Female	All Students	Male	Female	All Students	Male	Female	All Students	Male	Female	All Students	Male	Female
Between 1 & 5 items listed	51.4	46.0	57.4	71.7	72.1	71.0	75.2	75.3	74.8	77.0	74.5	79.6	66.4	67.2	65.5
Between 6 & 10 items listed	32.4	37.0	26.9	19.6	19.1	20.3	17.0	17.3	16.8	15.4	16.2	14.7	24.9	23.1	26.9
Between 11 & 15 items listed	12.0	12.7	11.6	6.3	5.9	6.8	4.9	4.6	5.4	5.8	7.1	4.2	6.8	7.2	6.4
Between 16 & 20 items listed	4.1	4.3	4.0	2.4	2.9	1.8	2.9	2.8	3.0	1.8	2.3	1.5	1.9	2.6	1.2
Total number of students	1,114			1,534			1,628			777			366		

All students: Table A5: Percentages of students according to numbers of items considered to be important by them and, in the students' opinion, by their teachers

⟶ Aims important to students *and* staff				
↓	Aims important to students	1-5 items listed	6-10 items listed	11-15 items listed	16-20 items listed
England	1-5 items listed	6.9			
France		12.8			
Italy		13.4			
Sweden		22.8			
Germany		4.9			
England	6-10 items listed	18.0	5.0		
France		32.5	3.8		
Italy		19.2	1.8		
Sweden		30.9	4.9		
Germany		24.9	11.5		
England	11-15 items listed	18.7	18.2	4.4	
France		19.9	10.6	3.0	
Italy		19.2	5.3	1.6	
Sweden		18.7	8.1	3.1	
Germany		26.0	11.5	4.1	
England	16-20 items listed	7.9	9.2	7.6	4.1
France		6.5	5.1	3.3	2.4
Italy		23.5	9.8	3.3	2.8
Sweden		4.6	2.4	2.7	1.8
Germany		10.7	9.6	2.7	1.9

All students: Table A6. Percentages of students according to numbers of items important to them, cross-tabulated with the numbers of items where they consider that their teachers share their views.

The answers to the open-ended sections, which asked students to what extent they felt that the subjects they studied, the teaching methods, the internal organisation of the school and the extra-curricular activities (if any) helped them or not to achieve those goals which were important to them, are summarised in Table A7. This was done by adding together the percentages of the first comments made by students under these headings and placing them in the simple categories listed in the table below. The "no reply" figures are relative frequencies which illustrate the extent to which students felt like replying – the English and the Germans were the most co-operative – and the other figures are adjusted frequencies, after the "no replies" have been discounted. The figures of 12.8%, 9.4%, 12% and 11.4% which are in the "Other and neutral" category under methods are, in large part, statements of the kind which say that methods cannot be separated from a particular subject or teacher. The figure of 19.6% (Italy) in the "Other and neutral" category for extra-curricular activities represents many students who were clearly talking about leisure activities which had nothing to do with school. This was because of a misunderstanding in translation.

The table shows that English students are more positive in their comments than any other country, followed by Swedish students, but Sweden had the lowest rate of reply. Swedes were among the most disappointed students on the easy-to-fill-in fixed alternative questions; so it must be assumed that the disillusioned students did not bother to answer the open-ended questions which did take quite a lot of effort!

As far as subjects, methods and organisation are concerned, the comments are always most favourable on subjects, less favourable on methods and least favourable (positively hostile in Italy!) on organisation. The pattern is always the same, although the degree of positiveness varies. The score of 57.2% in England of positive comments on school organisation reflects the care which many English teachers take in order to establish good relations with their students. The 34.5% of negative comments represents mainly comments from particular institutions rather than a cross-section from all schools and colleges visited. The low scores in other countries suggest that much more could be done in this area. The large percentage of "don't knows" in Sweden seems to reflect the mild surprise and puzzlement that one noticed, for instance, in discussions with teachers and officials that the way in which a school was run could have an educative function. The extra-curricular activities prevalent in English schools are commented on very favourably by English students – and it must be remembered that many English teachers see unpaid participation in these activities as part of their job. Changes which take into account the above remarks would obviously involve different patterns of internal organisation and very different attitudes on the part of teachers. As has been seen from the earlier chapters, comments on methods often turn on personal relationships rather than particular teaching techniques. This too would mean a different kind of training for teachers. As already pointed out, of all school elements, subjects receive the most favourable comments. The low score of 39.2% in Italy is a reflection on the encyclopaedic content of the curriculum as much as anything else.

Students were asked if they would like to study any subjects other than the ones they were already doing. Their answers, given in the table below show an interest in the field of human sciences. This was particularly strong in Italy. It was evident from some of the replies in Italy, and in other countries, that students thought that some study in this area would help them to come to terms with themselves and the world in which they lived. The most popular of the human sciences were sociology and psychology, particularly psychology. It was as if these two subjects had, between them, become a kind of modern "secular theology" for some students. Less than half of the students listed further subjects they would like to be doing. The question was open-ended and they were therefore not supplied with categories. This example, perhaps, reinforces the measure of contentment with subjects noted above, as opposed to methods and organisation. (In the table above the "no replies" are relative frequencies; the other figures adjusted frequencies).

When students were asked about ways in which the content, methods, organisation and extra-curricular activities might be improved the kind of reply given varied considerably according to the kind of system prevalent in the schools. In Italy, for example, there were always a number of students who were in such despair that their only notion of reform was an extremely drastic one which also called for a reform of society as well. This sort of comment was found hardly at all in England. Countries which had a fairly authoritarian system of teaching were more likely to want more teacher training. Where staff/student relationships were, on the whole, fairly satisfactory then it was more likely that students would comment on techniques and methods of teaching; but where the situation was bad, as in Italy for example, then discussions of method were far more likely to be conducted in terms of personal relationships and consultation.

Students were aware that school was, in some cases, artificially separated from life; and, in fact, the French references to "la vie active" which came *after* school point to this. In all countries there were students who commented that there were too many facts crammed into the programmes, that if there was less emphasis on the acquisition of facts then there could be more time for thinking, for relating the subjects to their own lives.

Many of the suggestions made by students were sensible, moderate and really constructive. The sort of comment which said such things as: "Abolish the

	ENGLAND				FRANCE				ITALY				SWEDEN				GERMANY			
	Subjects	Methods	Organisation	Extra-curricular activities	Subjects	Methods	Organisation	Extra-curricular activities	Subjects	Methods	Organisation	Extra-curricular activities	Subjects	Methods	Organisation	Extra-curricular activities	Subjects	Methods	Organisation	Extra-curricular activities
Positive	86.2	71.6	57.2	73.4	55.7	27.2	23.0	48.5	39.2	18.6	10.1	9.8	69.5	45.9	14.8	44.6	66.3	47.4	13.2	25.1
Negative	13.3	14.1	34.5	19.6	39.6	60.7	69.0	22.0	53.3	67.0	80.4	26.3	12.5	29.0	26.1	17.9	31.0	50.1	79.1	38.4
Other and neutral	—	12.8	2.0	1.5	4.3	9.4	4.0	3.4	6.3	12.0	5.8	19.6	8.7	11.4	15.0	12.1	2.1	0.9	0.4	2.9
Don't know	0.5	1.5	1.6	1.2	0.4	2.7	1.0	1.0	1.2	2.4	3.7	4.4	9.3	13.7	35.1	17.2	0.6	1.6	4.3	3.0
No influence	—	—	4.7	4.3	—	—	3.0	6.1	—	—	—	—	—	—	9.0	9.2	—	—	3.0	4.9
Non exist	—	—	—	—	—	—	—	19.0	—	—	—	39.9	—	—	—	—	—	—	—	25.7
No reply	14.2	18.9	21.0	24.0	17.3	29.2	34.6	40.5					36.4	47.7	55.5	51.3	6.0	12.8	17.2	26.8
Total number of students	1,114				1,534								777				366			

All students: Table A7. Summary of students' opinions as to whether the subjects they study in school, the teaching methods, the school organisation and the extra-curricular activities help them or do not help them to achieve their aims.

Note: The 'no replies' in the bottom line of the table are relative frequencies to illustrate the degree to which replies fall off. Other replies are adjusted frequencies. Only 1/3 of the open-ended Italian replies were coded therefore the 'no replies' are distorted.

principal for a start" and "No teachers over twenty-five", were very rare indeed. Mostly the students advocated the kind of reforms which educationists themselves have been trying to get teachers to accept and *put into practice*. Again this suggests the need for a new style of organisation and relationships, with implications for management and teacher training. It will be shown in the next chapter that many teachers also say they are in favour of such progressive methods.

Table A9 below summarises the students' perceptions of current problems. This table also illustrates some of the differences of emphasis in the various systems. However, it must be pointed out that the English figures are somewhat artificially low. Two schools were not allowed to answer this question. One school asked for the relevant page of the questionnaire to be torn out, and the other told students not to reply to this series of questions. In this latter school, quite a number of students did reply even so, and their answers are included in the totals.

Only 20.8% of Swedish students thought the supply of books and teaching materials was a problem, reflecting, perhaps the enormous amount of money spent in Sweden on these items. The choice of studies in many English schools, and the freedom for teachers to devise their own courses may be reasons why only 6.7% of English students think that it is difficult to devise an up-to-date curriculum; but, as was mentioned earlier, this figure is artificial. The difficulty of implementing an up-to-date curriculum is mentioned most frequently by German students, whose education system seems a fairly rigid one. The placing of students in school according to abilities and inclination is mentioned most frequently by students in systems where marks and competitiveness play an important part. The low English score on this point is partly a reflection of the difficulties outlined above, and partly a reflection of the fact that the system of allocating students to courses in schools is more flexible in England than elsewhere. Italy scores highest on the inadequacy of material facilities — Sweden the lowest in this respect. Italian students also mention very often the conflict between what students want to learn and the realities of the job situation afterwards. The French students also mention this frequently, and these two groups of students, French and Italian, are also the ones who see more often than other students that there are problems arising from students' wishes to participate in the planning of what goes on in school. Open-ended replies from both these countries showed that their students were more politically involved, and more politically extreme than in other countries. German students, who themselves are in a very selective system were the students who mentioned most frequently the difficulties which come from having students of a wide range of ability in school, and the problems of assessing the standard a student has reached.

England	France	Italy	Sweden	Germany	
13.4	22.4	21.9	16.3	15.4	Languages (modern)
18.9	6.2	9.9	6.7	4.8	Humanities (including classics)
4.4	.7	3.2	2.9	1.0	Mathematics and computer science
20.5	22.6	40.0	21.1	27.9	Economics and human sciences
5.1	9.3	5.6	5.1	2.9	Technical subjects
5.9	3.3	1.0	9.9	7.4	Professional subjects
14.6	14.1	7.5	15.3	14.4	Aesthetic and leisure subjects, crafts
.6	.3	.1	–	–	General studies, interdisciplinary studies
1.3	2.3	.1	0.6	13.5	Sport
15.0	15.1	6.0	10.9	12.5	Science
–	–	.1	–	–	Careers
52.8	61.4	60.0	59.7	71.6	No reply
1,114	1,534	1,628	777	366	Total number of students

All students: Table A8. Wish for other subjects

England	France	Italy	Sweden	Germany	
33.5	46.9	40.5	20.8	50.0	inadequate supply of books and materials
6.7	21.3	19.8	15.8	20.2	difficulty of devising an up-to-date curriculum
13.6	37.4	35.2	24.3	62.8	difficulty of implementing an up-to-date curriculum
14.6	27.2	14.6	9.3	26.2	shortage of teachers
27.1	51.0	28.1	39.5	45.4	placing of students in school according to abilities and inclinations
12.9	23.2	43.1	8.6	22.4	inadequate material facilities
31.1	55.1	65.8	38.7	43.2	conflict between what students want to learn and the realities of the job situation
6.4	11.3	10.6	9.7	18.0	inadequate initial training of teachers
16.6	28.7	35.8	30.2	40.2	placing of students in jobs/higher education according to abilities and inclinations
18.2	16.0	21.8	12.4	17.8	student apathy
13.5	25.5	25.1	21.8	45.9	devising an up-to-date curriculum for the less able
2.8	8.0	4.9	7.1	3.3	implementing an up-to-date curriculum for the less able
9.9	17.5	31.4	10.2	41.5	inadequate in service training for teachers
15.0	22.0	14.9	10.9	10.1	maintaining of discipline
28.5	34.4	35.9	37.1	80.1	problems of assessing the standard a student has reached
9.0	14.6	21.1	8.9	3.0	difficulties of having students from wide range of social backgrounds in school
15.4	47.4	35.9	9.4	15.6	problems stemming from students who wish to participate in planning
10.2	8.9	11.1	26.1	7.7	truancy
24.5	34.3	26.0	33.8	54.4	difficulties of having students from wide range of ability in school
1,114	1,534	1,628	777	366	Total number of students per country

All students: Table A9. Student perceptions of current problems

     Perhaps, understandably, teachers tend to see more problems than students, and their emphases are slightly different. This will be shown in the following chapter.

Preliminary examination of possible relationship between factors relating to home and school

The histograms showed that there was a difference in the expectations from school on the part of students in different systems. Of the twenty items in the questionnaire, for instance, eight were mentioned as important by over 50% of Swedish students, while eighteen were mentioned as important by over 50% of students in Italy. The highest score given to any item where it was thought that teachers shared the views of students was, in Italy, 29.2%; but in England there were nine items which each scored over 30% in this respect.

As far as numbers of items listed as important are concerned, there are, again, differences between the various systems. For example, 36.3% of students in France and 36.4% of students in Germany, listed between six and ten items from the list in the questionnaire as being important to them. Cross-tabulations showed that this 36.3% of French students was made up of 3.8% who thought that their teachers shared their views, and 32.5% who were in some measure disappointed in this respect. The corresponding figures for the German 36.4% were 11.5% and 24.9%. Again, there were 2.4% of students in France, and 2.8% of students in Italy who listed between sixteen and twenty items in the questionnaire as being important to them. These students all thought that their teachers shared their views. Also among French students there were 6.5% who listed between sixteen and twenty items as being important to them and who saw that teachers shared their views on a range of items between one and five. In Italy the corresponding figure was 23.5%.

Do such differences in expectation and satisfaction derive from the differences in the various school systems or are they in any way linked with social class and parental attitudes? Such limited tests and cross-tabulation it was possible to do in the time available were done, and it seems that the differences in expectation and satisfaction may not be linked with family background. More work needs to be done with the material available than has been done so far, but results from preliminary work are set out, briefly, below.

Crosstabulations suggested that, except for Sweden, there was no relationship between the number of items listed as important to students and their father's occupation, nor between the number of items listed as important to students on which they think that teachers share their views and father's occupation. Student aspirations and their perceptions of the parental encouragement given to them do vary (as will be seen in Section E) according to father's occupation, so these two items were correlated with student expectations and satisfactions to see if there was any relationship.

A Spearman correlation analysis showed that for the total number of students in each of the five countries there was no relationship between the number of items which students listed as important and their sex, nor between the number of items they listed as important and their further education/career aspirations, nor between the number of items listed as important and the degree of parental encouragement given to them. The same test also showed that there was no relationship between the numbers of items listed as important by students where they thought that staff shared their views and any of the three items above, i.e. sex, aspirations, parental encouragement.

Some analysis was also done of those students who expected the most from school but perceived themselves as getting the least, i.e. those students who listed between sixteen and twenty items from the questionnaire as being important to them and who thought their teachers shared their views on between one and five items only. Did these students tend to come from any one particular group? On the whole girls were represented slightly more strongly than boys but on other counts this group of students fitted in with the national pattern. In England, for example, 17.4% of the total sample had fathers whose job carried professional or higher managerial status — and students from such backgrounds made up 17% of the group of students who expected a lot but thought they received little. 53.2% of the French sample came from the two top social groups, as did 51.4% of the "highly disappointed" students. Similarly, 21.1% of all French students hoped to go on to university, or to do an equivalent course of study; so did 21.6% of the "highly disappointed" students.

Such results, at the moment, are merely an indication that students in the 16-20 age-group may be more influenced in their expectations of school by the school system itself rather than factors in their home background.

The school is, of course, in some ways, a reflection of society and its values, and so it could be said that it is not the school system which determines students' expectations and perceived satisfactions, but society in general. This might well be thought to be the case in Sweden, for example, where 80-85% of the 16-20 age group are in full-time education. Yet it was in Sweden that there was one school with students from a mixed range of social backgrounds where the range of expectations and the degree of perceived satisfactions were greater than average for that country. Also some schools in England varied in student perceptions according to the pattern of internal organisation. Such conclusions are, admittedly, tenuous. More investigation will have to be done of the variations in expectations and satisfactions in individual schools within a system, where these variations do not depend on social class.

However — whatever the reasons, influences, or associations — differences in student expectation and perceived satisfaction do exist; and as such they are a challenge to teachers. The following chapter looks at the teachers' views of their students, and once again it will be seen that the "communications gap" is fairly large.

CHAPTER 13

TEACHER OPINION IN THE COUNTRIES VISITED: CONTRASTS AND SIMILARITIES TO STUDENT OPINION; CONCLUSIONS AND IMPLICATIONS FOR POLICY

Teachers' perceptions of students' reasons for staying on in full-time education

Students mentioned the wish for qualifications of use in a job more frequently than anything else as a reason for staying on in full-time education, and their teachers, too, mentioned this reason most frequently (see table T1 on following page). With the exception of the Italians, the teachers mentioned this reason rather more often than their students. Again with the exception of the Italians, teachers thought that students' reasons for staying on were connected considerably more often with a wish for higher education than did the students themselves. Most teachers have followed the traditional path of further academic studies, without experience of jobs other than teaching, so it is perhaps understandable that they see further studies as the inevitable next step for many of their students. Also many teachers are unaware of the changes that are occurring in the job market and some schools tend to give advice which directs students to full-time further studies rather than, for example, to sandwich courses and jobs with training.

The inevitability of full-time further studies is now being questioned. The latest Swedish reforms, for example, will make it possible for work experience after school to be taken into account when an application for full-time further studies is made after some time in employment. Students themselves, as was clear from their own replies to this question, and open-ended answers to other questions, were very much concerned that they should get the right kind of job. It may be that, by their own emphasis on further studies, teachers are not exploiting as fully as they might the motivation which comes from an interest in job qualifications. This is not to say that everyone should start some kind of technical training, but that the traditional ways of presenting the humanities subjects, for example, could be made more directly relevant to students. An understanding of human relationships is just as "vocational" as many technical courses.

	ENGLAND		FRANCE		ITALY		SWEDEN		GERMANY	
	Teachers %	Students %	Teachers %	Students %	Teachers %	Students %	Teachers %	Students %	Teachers %	Students %
wish for qualifications of use in job	92.4	88.9	93.8	74.0	46.5	63.5	85.9	76.4	93.5	83.1
Opportunity to make new friends	11.7	11.8	2.5	5.1	4.7	12.1	2.8	2.2	3.2	7.9
Could not decide what else to do	66.0	21.7	43.8	11.9	10.6	6.9	60.6	24.5	35.5	15.8
Advice of teachers/counsellors	74.6	27.2	38.3	32.5	12.4	11.3	38.0	17.8	29.0	15.6
Wish for higher education	84.3	61.9	72.8	51.8	30.0	30.3	70.4	55.7	87.1	54.1
Influence of parents	84.3	50.3	73.5	41.9	37.6	17.9	76.1	40.4	51.6	24.0
Few jobs for school leavers	33.5	20.3	29.6	8.4	16.5	5.3	54.9	12.4	–	1.4
Did not want to start work	72.6	7.1	27.2	24.4	29.4	13.8	29.6	9.0	51.6	37.7
Particular subjects interesting	44.2	42.1	44.4	40.4	8.2	39.0	8.5	27.7	41.9	48.1
Stayed on to be with friends	43.1	5.5	29.6	6.5	10.6	3.1	54.9	5.0	19.4	2.7
Total numbers	197	1,114	162	1,534	170	1,628	71	777	31	366

All teachers: Table T1. Teachers' perception of students' reasons for staying on in full-time education

Again, except for the Italians, teachers thought that students were influenced more often by the advice given by teachers than did the students themselves. This was most often the case in England, less so Sweden and Germany, while in France the difference between the two figures was small. Teachers also mentioned the influence of parents more often than did students — with the usual exception of Italy. They also thought that students were influenced to stay on to be with their friends more often than the students did themselves. Thus the students, understandably perhaps, see themselves as being more autonomous than do their teachers, who see them as influenced to quite a considerable extent by parents, teachers and friends.

Teachers also see students as being influenced more often by "negative" reasons, such as indecision, a wish not to start work, and a shortage of suitable jobs, than do the students themselves, though this last factor does not apply to German teachers.

In England, France and Germany, teachers' perceptions as to how often students stayed on because they were interested in particular subjects corresponded more or less to what the students thought. However, in Italy and Sweden teachers underestimated by a considerable margin the interest of their students. (At this point it is worth pointing out that Germany's education is the most selective of the countries visited, Sweden's the least so).

Both teachers and students rank the wish for qualifications of use in jobs as being the most important reason for students deciding to stay on in full-time education. As was pointed out above, perhaps more could be done to exploit this motivation. Then teachers might come to see that their students were more autonomous and responsible, and less indecisive and negative in their outlook, than they supposed.

Teachers' perceptions of the attractions of a particular school or college to students

Teachers' perceptions of the attractions of particular schools which encourage students to continue in full-time education are more in line with students' ideas on this point than they are with students' stated reasons for staying on. (See Table T2 below). The main attractions, where the views of teachers and students most nearly correspond, are a high standard of teaching and the possibility of being trained for a particular job.

Teachers over-estimate, as was shown earlier, the influence of friends as being a reason for staying on at school. English teachers also mention, more

	ENGLAND		FRANCE		ITALY		SWEDEN		GERMANY	
	Teachers %	Students %	Teachers %	Students %	Teachers %	Students %	Teachers %	Students %	Teachers %	Students %
Sports facilities	17.3	12.5	5.6	5.7	1.8	2.9	12.7	4.2	–	3.3
Easy relations with staff	7.1	30.1	9.9	10.4	6.5	5.5	1.4	2.7	3.2	6.6
Extra-curricular activities	34.5	12.7	14.2	9.2	4.7	6.3	14.1	.5	12.9	1.6
Freedom for students to organise things themselves	42.1	34.4	10.5	6.7	7.1	11.7	2.8	5.3	9.7	4.9
Standard of teaching high	54.3	54.3	42.6	56.1	51.8	44.5	32.4	25.1	32.3	38.5
Friends came	42.1	13.0	20.4	8.6	28.2	5.4	47.9	4.8	9.7	9.8
Pleasant community to work in	39.1	44.0	8.6	16.2	8.8	14.3	40.9	39.1	16.1	12.6
Library facilities	14.7	9.7	9.3	2.0	7.1	2.3	5.6	1.0	–	.8
Training for job	33.0	13.6	23.5	22.9	32.4	37.0	43.7	32.6	51.6	48.1
Possibility to choose studies	58.9	38.0	4.9	4.0	5.9	9.4	12.7	1.1	16.1	12.6
Opportunity to make a new start	12.7	6.8	3.7	6.5	1.8	2.6	5.6	1.3	6.5	2.2
Chance to meet opposite sex	5.1	32.6	9.3	35.6	1.2	3.8	–	1.3	6.5	3.3
School's successful examination record	48.7	32.6	50.6	36.7	15.9	3.8	5.6	1.4	3.2	3.0
Total numbers	197	1,114	162	1,534	170	1,628	71	777	31	366

All teachers: Table T2.   Teachers' perceptions of the attractions of a particular school or college to students often than their students do, the influence of the possibility for choice of studies, and the provision of extra-curricular activities as attractions. French and English teachers also mention more frequently the attraction of a school's successful examination record. English teachers, however, under-estimate the value of students of the community life in school. Both English and Swedish students mention considerably more often than students in other countries the fact that they thought their school would be a pleasant community to work in, but whereas Swedish students do not seem to connect this with easy relations with staff, English students do. English teachers, however, do not seem to be aware of this as much as they might.

Teachers' aims and their assessment of students' aims

Teachers were asked to indicate from the same list that was given to students what they thought a school ought to do for its students. They were also asked whether they thought their students shared their views. The histograms on the following pages illustrate teacher aims and their perceptions of student aims. For each country there is a Table T3 and a Table T4. Table T3 gives the frequencies of items as they occur in the questionnaire, and Table T4 gives the items in descending order of frequency in order to give a "profile" of teacher aims.

In all cases there is a considerable gap between teacher aims and their perceptions of student aims. For example, flexibility and adaptability are thought to be important by 82.3% of English teachers, who think that only 16.8% of students share their views. On the other hand, 65.2% of English students say that they believe flexibility to be important, but they think that only 25.3% of their teachers have the same opinion. While 91.2% of French teachers say that preparation to learn throughout life is important, only 27.8% of French students believe that their teachers really do think this, and altogether 60.7% of French students themselves think that preparation to learn throughout life is important.[1]

English and Swedish teachers mention items listed in the questionnaire more frequently than French, Italian, or German teachers. Both in England and in Sweden, eighteen out of twenty items are listed by more than 50% of teachers as being important, though in England the frequency counts were considerably higher. These high counts on many items illustrate the wide range of functions which many English teachers think a school should fulfill.

[1] Figures for student opinion in this paragraph are taken from the histograms in Chapter 12 on student opinion.

England
France
Italy
Sweden
Germany

The histograms on the following pages illustrate teacher aims and teachers' perceptions of student aims.

In Table T3 — the right-hand line illustrates the frequency of items mentioned as important by teachers

— the left-hand line represents the frequency of items mentioned as important by teachers where they perceive that their students share their views.
(Frequencies are in questionnaire order).

In Table T4 — the upper line illustrates the frequency of items mentioned as important by teachers

— the lower line illustrates the frequencies of items mentioned as important by teachers where they consider that students share their views.
(Items given in descending order of frequency).

In all the histograms the distance between the two lines illustrates the gap in perceptions between teachers and their students, *from the teachers' point of view*. Histograms which illustrate the student point of view are in the previous chapter on students.

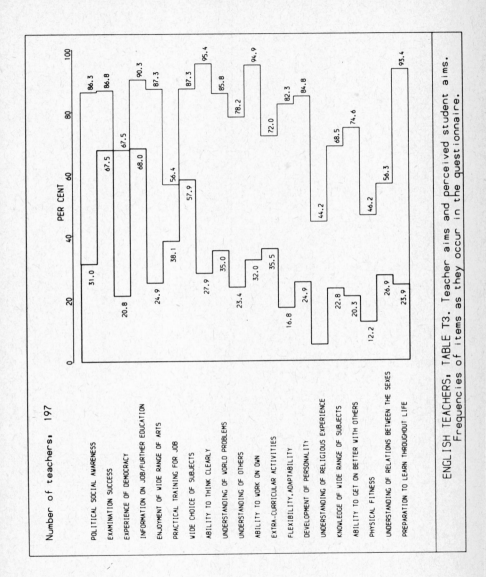

Number of teachers: 197

PER CENT

POLITICAL SOCIAL AWARENESS
EXAMINATION SUCCESS
EXPERIENCE OF DEMOCRACY
INFORMATION ON JOB/FURTHER EDUCATION
ENJOYMENT OF WIDE RANGE OF ARTS
PRACTICAL TRAINING FOR JOB
WIDE CHOICE OF SUBJECTS
ABILITY TO THINK CLEARLY
UNDERSTANDING OF WORLD PROBLEMS
UNDERSTANDING OF OTHERS
ABILITY TO WORK ON OWN
EXTRA-CURRICULAR ACTIVITIES
FLEXIBILITY, ADAPTABILITY
DEVELOPMENT OF PERSONALITY
UNDERSTANDING OF RELIGIOUS EXPERIENCE
KNOWLEDGE OF WIDE RANGE OF SUBJECTS
ABILITY TO GET ON BETTER WITH OTHERS
PHYSICAL FITNESS
UNDERSTANDING OF RELATIONS BETWEEN THE SEXES
PREPARATION TO LEARN THROUGHOUT LIFE

31.0
86.3

20.8
67.5
86.8

67.5
90.3

68.0
24.9
87.3

38.1
56.4

57.9
27.9
87.3

35.0
95.4

23.4
78.2
85.8

32.0
72.0

35.5
94.9

16.8
82.3

24.9
84.8

44.2
68.5

22.8
74.6

20.3

12.2
46.2

26.9
56.3

23.9
93.4

ENGLISH TEACHERS, TABLE T3. Teacher aims and perceived student aims.
Frequencies of items as they occur in the questionnaire.

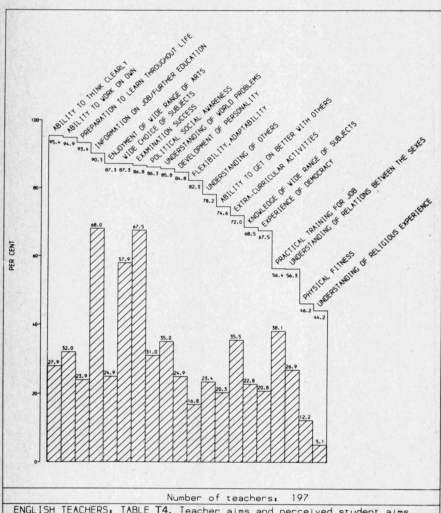

PER CENT

ABILITY TO THINK CLEARLY 95.4
ABILITY TO WORK ON OWN 94.9
PREPARATION TO LEARN THROUGHOUT LIFE 93.4
INFORMATION ON JOB/FURTHER EDUCATION 90.3
ENJOYMENT OF WIDE RANGE OF ARTS 87.3
WIDE CHOICE OF SUBJECTS 87.3
EXAMINATION SUCCESS 86.8
POLITICAL SOCIAL AWARENESS 86.3
UNDERSTANDING OF WORLD PROBLEMS 85.8
DEVELOPMENT OF PERSONALITY 84.8
FLEXIBILITY, ADAPTABILITY 82.3
UNDERSTANDING OF OTHERS 78.2
ABILITY TO GET ON BETTER WITH OTHERS 74.6
EXTRA-CURRICULAR ACTIVITIES 72.0
KNOWLEDGE OF WIDE RANGE OF SUBJECTS 68.5
EXPERIENCE OF DEMOCRACY 67.5
PRACTICAL TRAINING FOR JOB 56.4
UNDERSTANDING OF RELATIONS BETWEEN THE SEXES 56.3
PHYSICAL FITNESS 46.2
UNDERSTANDING OF RELIGIOUS EXPERIENCE 44.2

27.9 32.0 23.9 68.0 24.9 57.9 67.5 31.0 35.0 16.8 24.9 23.4 20.3 35.5 22.8 20.8 38.1 26.9 12.2 5.1

Number of teachers: 197

ENGLISH TEACHERS: TABLE T4. Teacher aims and perceived student aims.
Items in descending order of frequency.

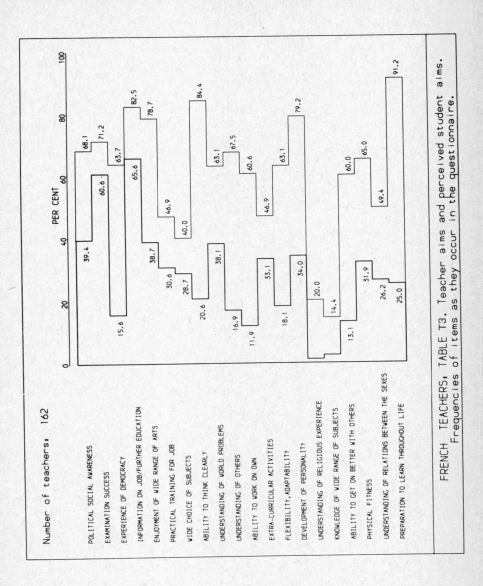

Number of teachers: 162

PER CENT

POLITICAL SOCIAL AWARENESS	39.4 / 68.1
EXAMINATION SUCCESS	60.6 / 71.2
EXPERIENCE OF DEMOCRACY	15.6 / 63.7
INFORMATION ON JOB/FURTHER EDUCATION	65.6 / 82.5
ENJOYMENT OF WIDE RANGE OF ARTS	38.7 / 78.7
PRACTICAL TRAINING FOR JOB	30.6 / 46.9
WIDE CHOICE OF SUBJECTS	28.7 / 40.0
ABILITY TO THINK CLEARLY	20.6 / 84.4
UNDERSTANDING OF WORLD PROBLEMS	38.1 / 63.1
UNDERSTANDING OF OTHERS	16.9 / 67.5
ABILITY TO WORK ON OWN	11.9 / 60.6
EXTRA-CURRICULAR ACTIVITIES	33.1 / 46.9
FLEXIBILITY, ADAPTABILITY	18.1 / 63.1
DEVELOPMENT OF PERSONALITY	34.0 / 79.2
UNDERSTANDING OF RELIGIOUS EXPERIENCE	20.0
KNOWLEDGE OF WIDE RANGE OF SUBJECTS	14.4 / 60.0
ABILITY TO GET ON BETTER WITH OTHERS	13.1 / 65.0
PHYSICAL FITNESS	31.9 / 49.4
UNDERSTANDING OF RELATIONS BETWEEN THE SEXES	26.2 / 91.2
PREPARATION TO LEARN THROUGHOUT LIFE	25.0

FRENCH TEACHERS, TABLE T3. Teacher aims and perceived student aims. Frequencies of items as they occur in the questionnaire.

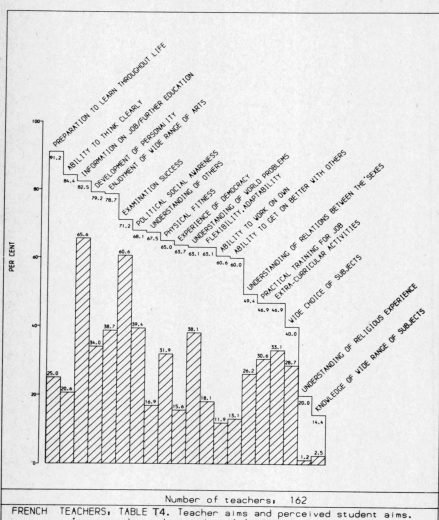

PER CENT

PREPARATION TO LEARN THROUGHOUT LIFE
ABILITY TO THINK CLEARLY
INFORMATION ON JOB/FURTHER EDUCATION
DEVELOPMENT OF PERSONALITY
ENJOYMENT OF WIDE RANGE OF ARTS
EXAMINATION SUCCESS
POLITICAL SOCIAL AWARENESS
UNDERSTANDING OF OTHERS
PHYSICAL FITNESS
EXPERIENCE OF DEMOCRACY
UNDERSTANDING OF WORLD PROBLEMS
FLEXIBILITY, ADAPTABILITY
ABILITY TO WORK ON OWN
ABILITY TO GET ON BETTER WITH OTHERS
UNDERSTANDING OF RELATIONS BETWEEN THE SEXES
PRACTICAL TRAINING FOR JOB
EXTRA-CURRICULAR ACTIVITIES
WIDE CHOICE OF SUBJECTS
UNDERSTANDING OF RELIGIOUS EXPERIENCE
KNOWLEDGE OF WIDE RANGE OF SUBJECTS

91.2 84.4 82.5 79.2 78.7 71.2 68.1 67.5 65.0 63.7 63.1 63.1 60.6 60.0 49.4 46.9 46.9 40.0 20.0 14.4 2.5

65.6 60.6 39.4 38.7 34.0 31.9 38.1 33.1 30.6 28.7 26.2 25.0 20.6 18.1 16.9 15.6 13.1 11.9 1.2

Number of teachers: 162

FRENCH TEACHERS, TABLE T4. Teacher aims and perceived student aims.
Items in descending order of frequency.

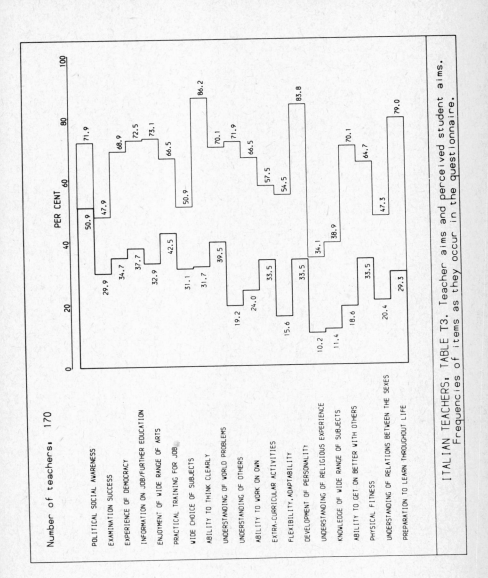

Number of teachers: 170

PER CENT

POLITICAL SOCIAL AWARENESS — 71.9 / 50.9 / 29.9

EXAMINATION SUCCESS — 47.9 / 34.7

EXPERIENCE OF DEMOCRACY — 68.9 / 37.7

INFORMATION ON JOB/FURTHER EDUCATION — 72.5 / 32.9

ENJOYMENT OF WIDE RANGE OF ARTS — 73.1 / 42.5

PRACTICAL TRAINING FOR JOB — 66.5 / 31.1

WIDE CHOICE OF SUBJECTS — 50.9 / 31.7

ABILITY TO THINK CLEARLY — 86.2 / 39.5

UNDERSTANDING OF WORLD PROBLEMS — 70.1 / 19.2

UNDERSTANDING OF OTHERS — 71.9 / 24.0

ABILITY TO WORK ON OWN — 66.5 / 33.5

EXTRA-CURRICULAR ACTIVITIES — 57.5 / 15.6

FLEXIBILITY, ADAPTABILITY — 54.5 / 33.5

DEVELOPMENT OF PERSONALITY — 83.8 / 34.1

UNDERSTANDING OF RELIGIOUS EXPERIENCE — 10.2

KNOWLEDGE OF WIDE RANGE OF SUBJECTS — 38.9 / 11.4

ABILITY TO GET ON BETTER WITH OTHERS — 70.1 / 18.6

PHYSICAL FITNESS — 64.7 / 33.5

UNDERSTANDING OF RELATIONS BETWEEN THE SEXES — 47.3 / 20.4

PREPARATION TO LEARN THROUGHOUT LIFE — 79.0 / 29.3

ITALIAN TEACHERS; TABLE T3. Teacher aims and perceived student aims.
Frequencies of items as they occur in the questionnaire.

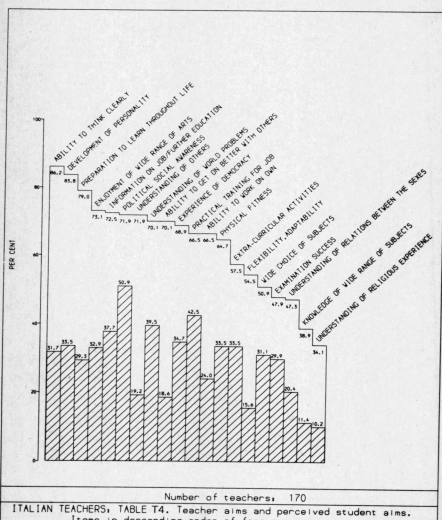

Number of teachers: 170

ITALIAN TEACHERS, TABLE T4. Teacher aims and perceived student aims.
Items in descending order of frequency.

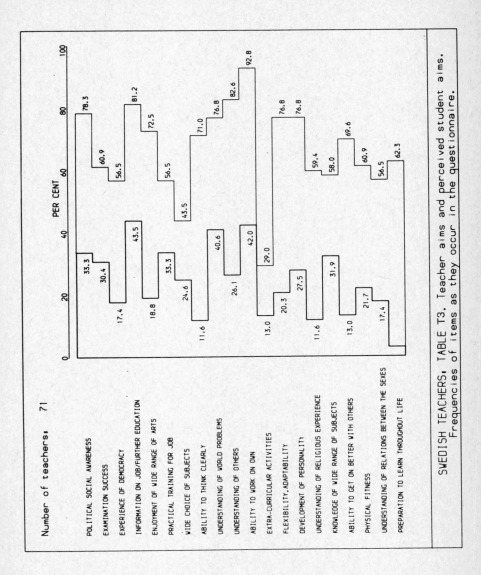

Number of teachers: 71

	PER CENT	
POLITICAL SOCIAL AWARENESS — 33.3, 78.3
EXAMINATION SUCCESS — 30.4, 60.9
EXPERIENCE OF DEMOCRACY — 17.4, 56.5
INFORMATION ON JOB/FURTHER EDUCATION — 43.5, 81.2
ENJOYMENT OF WIDE RANGE OF ARTS — 18.8, 72.5
PRACTICAL TRAINING FOR JOB — 33.3, 56.5
WIDE CHOICE OF SUBJECTS — 24.6, 43.5
ABILITY TO THINK CLEARLY — 11.6, 71.0
UNDERSTANDING OF WORLD PROBLEMS — 40.6, 76.8
UNDERSTANDING OF OTHERS — 26.1, 82.6
ABILITY TO WORK ON OWN — 42.0, 92.8
EXTRA-CURRICULAR ACTIVITIES — 29.0, 76.8
FLEXIBILITY, ADAPTABILITY — 13.0, 76.8
DEVELOPMENT OF PERSONALITY — 20.3
— 27.5, 59.4
UNDERSTANDING OF RELIGIOUS EXPERIENCE — 11.6, 58.0
KNOWLEDGE OF WIDE RANGE OF SUBJECTS — 31.9, 69.6
ABILITY TO GET ON BETTER WITH OTHERS — 13.0, 60.9
PHYSICAL FITNESS — 21.7, 56.5
UNDERSTANDING OF RELATIONS BETWEEN THE SEXES — 17.4, 62.3
PREPARATION TO LEARN THROUGHOUT LIFE

SWEDISH TEACHERS: TABLE T3. Teacher aims and perceived student aims.
Frequencies of items as they occur in the questionnaire.

PER CENT

100

ABILITY TO WORK ON OWN — 92.8

UNDERSTANDING OF OTHERS — 82.6
INFORMATION ON JOB/FURTHER EDUCATION — 81.2
POLITICAL SOCIAL AWARENESS — 78.3
UNDERSTANDING OF WORLD PROBLEMS — 76.8
FLEXIBILITY, ADAPTABILITY — 76.8
DEVELOPMENT OF PERSONALITY — 76.8

ENJOYMENT OF WIDE RANGE OF ARTS — 72.5
ABILITY TO THINK CLEARLY — 71.0
ABILITY TO GET ON BETTER WITH OTHERS — 69.6

PREPARATION TO LEARN THROUGHOUT LIFE — 62.3
EXAMINATION SUCCESS — 60.9
PHYSICAL FITNESS — 60.9
UNDERSTANDING OF RELIGIOUS EXPERIENCE — 59.4
KNOWLEDGE OF WIDE RANGE OF SUBJECTS — 58.0
EXPERIENCE OF DEMOCRACY — 56.5
PRACTICAL TRAINING FOR JOB — 56.5
UNDERSTANDING OF RELATIONS BETWEEN THE SEXES — 56.5

WIDE CHOICE OF SUBJECTS — 43.5

EXTRA-CURRICULAR ACTIVITIES

42.0   26.1   43.5   33.3   40.6   20.3   27.5   18.8   11.6   13.0   2.9   30.4   21.7   11.6   31.9   17.4   33.3   17.4   24.6   29.0   13.0

Number of teachers: 71

SWEDISH TEACHERS: TABLE T4   Teacher aims and perceived student aims.
Items in descending order of frequency.

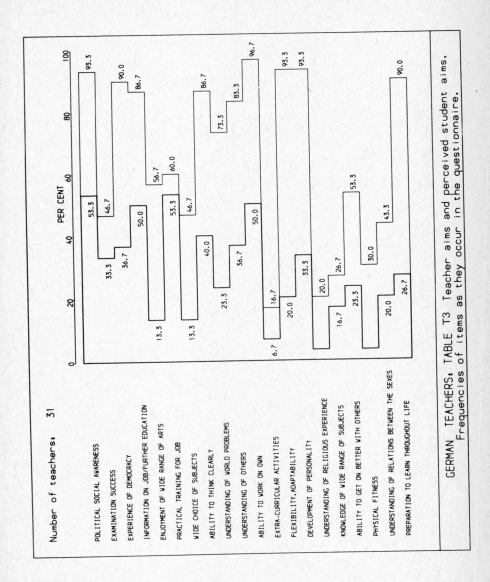

Number of teachers: 31

GERMAN TEACHERS: TABLE T3 Teacher aims and perceived student aims. Frequencies of items as they occur in the questionnaire.

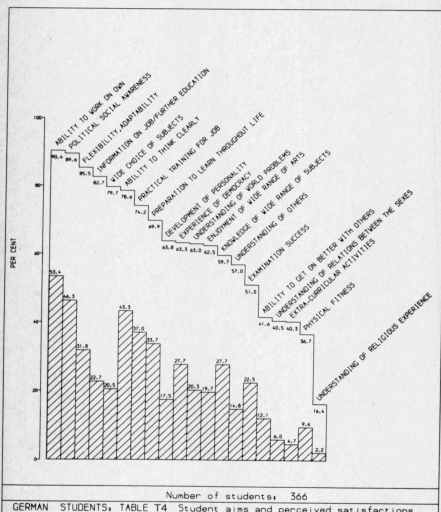

PER CENT

ABILITY TO WORK ON OWN — 90.4
POLITICAL SOCIAL AWARENESS — 89.6
FLEXIBILITY, ADAPTABILITY — 85.5
INFORMATION ON JOB/FURTHER EDUCATION — 82.7
WIDE CHOICE OF SUBJECTS — 79.7
ABILITY TO THINK CLEARLY — 78.6
PRACTICAL TRAINING FOR JOB — 74.2
PREPARATION TO LEARN THROUGHOUT LIFE — 69.9
DEVELOPMENT OF PERSONALITY — 63.8
EXPERIENCE OF DEMOCRACY — 63.3
UNDERSTANDING OF WORLD PROBLEMS — 63.0
ENJOYMENT OF WIDE RANGE OF ARTS — 62.5
KNOWLEDGE OF WIDE RANGE OF SUBJECTS — 59.7
UNDERSTANDING OF OTHERS — 57.0
EXAMINATION SUCCESS — 51.0
ABILITY TO GET ON BETTER WITH OTHERS — 41.6
UNDERSTANDING OF RELATIONS BETWEEN THE SEXES — 40.5
EXTRA-CURRICULAR ACTIVITIES — 40.3
PHYSICAL FITNESS — 36.7
UNDERSTANDING OF RELIGIOUS EXPERIENCE — 16.4

Lower bars: 53.4 46.3 31.8 22.7 20.5 43.3 37.0 33.7 17.5 27.7 20.3 19.7 27.7 14.8 22.5 12.1 6.0 4.7 9.6 2.2

Number of students: 366

GERMAN   STUDENTS, TABLE T4   Student aims and perceived satisfactions.
Items in descending order of frequency. (ALL STUDENTS)

The teachers tend to mention most frequently, as being important, such items as ability to think clearly, ability to work on one's own, preparation to learn throughout life, information on jobs and further education, ability to enjoy a wide range of arts, and political and social awareness. The students mention most frequently information on jobs and further education, a wide choice of subjects, political and social awareness (*except* in England), ability to work on one's own (Germany), and examination success (France and England).

The items where there is the largest amount of common ground between teachers and students, are, *from the teachers' point of view*, such items as: information on jobs and further education (England, France, Sweden), examination success (England and France), practical training of use in a job (Germany and Italy), and political and social awareness (Italy). Items where there is the largest amount of common ground, *from the students' point of view*, are an ability to work on one's own (England, Sweden and Germany), examination success (England and France) and, rather surprisingly, an understanding of relationships between the sexes (Italy).

Thus, there is some common understanding between teachers and students as to what should, and does, happen in school, and some agreement as to what should happen, even if neither side appreciates fully that the other has the same aims in mind. However, as we noted earlier, the gap in perceptions between teachers and students is what is most noticeable. One has only to refer back, for example, to the histograms for Italy in the previous chapter to see how wide that gap can be: eighteen of the items listed in the questionnaire were listed as important by over 50% of students; but the highest frequency given to items thought important by teachers was 29.2%. Swedish students expect less than Italian students, but they are disappointed almost as often as the Italians. The German teachers and their students have almost similar lists of items which are important to them, yet there is still a large "communications gap".

The size of this gap seems to be more important than the fact that expectations may be higher in one country than in another. Students have been shown to want far more than their teachers know how to give. If this motivation could be exploited more fully by teachers, then some of the problems in upper-secondary education could be eased considerably. Some teachers are aware of ways in which this is being done, and could be developed further, as is shown in the following sections.

Ways in which teachers think that subjects, teaching methods, organisation and extra-curricular activities help, or do not help, their students to achieve the aims which teachers believe to be important

It was not possible to code the open-ended replies to these questions and the following remarks are based on impressions from reading replies. The table which summarised the student replies in the last chapter showed that students commented most favourably on subjects, less favourably on methods, and least favourably on school organisation. Comments on extra-curricular activities were mixed. English students' comments were generally the most favourable, Swedish students' somewhat less so (but their rate of reply was the lowest), and Italian students were the most critical. Many of the student comments on methods and organisation were based on a wish for an improvement in staff-student relationships. Teachers, of course, were not likely to say that they were inadequate in this respect, nor that their teaching methods were unhelpful. Their criticisms tended to be directed towards, for instance, the administrative system, lack of material facilities, the pressure of examinations, the mass of material in official syllabuses, the shortage of teachers, and the insufficiency of the training and qualifications of teachers (other than themselves, of course).

For the most part, however, teachers' comments were constructive, and tended to reflect the same concerns voiced by students. Their rate of reply seemed broadly similar to that of the students.

As far as subjects were concerned staff thought that the subjects they taught were helpful in a general way in encouraging clear thinking and a sense of judgement. Teachers of humanities subjects also stressed that these subjects developed an aesthetic, moral, and emotional sensibility. Understanding of such subjects as history and economics gave an insight into world problems. English teachers particularly commented on the value of some kind of general studies course.

Teaching methods were seen to be helpful where they emphasised individual work, the use of discussion, a practical approach — in fact, anything which demanded involvement from the students was seen to be beneficial. Just as students saw teaching methods as "methods of learning" when they made constructive comments, so teachers tended to see themselves as developing thinking skills in students, and acting as "educational counsellors". English teachers sometimes stressed the value of working in depth within a particular field of study.

Comments on school organisation were more mixed. English teachers thought that the relaxed atmosphere which seemed, they thought, to prevail in most sixth forms and colleges enabled students to get to know staff, to establish some kind of independence and responsibility for themselves. Where there was a School Council this was seen as framework within which the students could learn to express themselves and learn something of the way in which society organises itself. French teachers tended to see the organisation in more bureaucratic terms. They commented on the supply of libraries and teaching materials, and said that the schools tried to give adequate information to students. They complained of the lack of space for students to do their own work in school, and of the very large classes they had to teach. Many French teachers made no comment at all, and some were quite mystified at the thought that school organisation might have an educational as well as an administrative function. Italian and Swedish teachers did not offer much at all in the way of comment on organisation, and German teachers also offered little comment, but thought that the School Council did offer some opportunity for contact between staff and students.

As far as extra-curricular activities were concerned, the replies from English teachers were the most detailed. England is the only country of those surveyed where schools have an extensive range of extra-curricular activities, and where teachers are expected to take an active interest in these as part of their job. English teachers see the main functions of such activities as the development of a range of interests, abilities, and personal initiative. Other teachers reply rarely, and, as with the students' replies, it is not always clear whether teachers are referring to activities based on school or outside school altogether. Those who do comment see them as encouraging a wider range of interests, and developing personality.

Ways in which teachers think that subjects, teaching methods, organisation and extra-curricular activities might be improved

Recommendations as to the way in which subjects might be improved echo the replies on the helpfulness of subjects. English teachers particularly also add that some kind of integrated studies would be useful, and other teachers do comment on the value of establishing some sort of links between subjects. A number of teachers complain of the mass of facts contained in official syllabuses and say that this makes it difficult for them to have adequate time for discussion.

An improvement in teaching methods again reflected the concern outlined in teachers' perceptions as to the helpfulness of particular methods. A number of teachers did add that they thought that more teacher training was necessary, both initially and at the in-service stage.

School organisation received fewer comments than other factors. Some comments were administrative — but implied a change in educational values. For example, some teachers wanted the timetable to be made more flexible, to allow for longer blocks of time for teaching particular subjects, to allow time for visits outside school, and to allow more "free" time in the afternoons for extra-curricular activities. Some English teachers wanted to be relieved of the burden of administrative paper work to do with examinations etc., so that they could get on with their "real" job. Teachers also saw the need for more contact with students, expressed formally in the need for greater democratisation and more participation by students, and informally in such terms as:

> "It is necessary to create an atmosphere where it is a
> pleasant and normal thing to do for students and staff to
> stay behind after the last lesson, if only for a coffee and
> a natter".

That was said by an Englishman, but one or two of the Italian comments were looking towards the same degree of informality.

Extra-curricular activities were seen to need more time, more money, more commitment and interest from teachers.

It was shown in the chapters on student opinion that many of the comments made by students were sensible and constructive. The teachers who chose to answer the open-ended replies also made the same kind of comment. The "communications gap" illustrated by the histograms and the open-ended critical comments from students suggest that a radical reform of means is needed rather more than a drastic revision of content. Changes which teachers notice, and expect, in the intake of students into upper-secondary education emphasise this.

Teachers' perceptions of changes in the student intake

Teachers in selective systems, i.e. in all the countries visited except Sweden, saw that in future there would be students coming into the upper-secondary sector who would be less academic, less able than the traditional student. Some teachers thought they would be not so well prepared in basic skills, less amenable to discipline, less interested in the academic approach.

In all countries included in the survey teachers thought that students were much more influenced than they used to be by the mass media. This meant, in some cases that they had some knowledge (though sometimes in a superficial way) about a wider range of subjects than previously. Also students were seen to be more open and frank, less likely to hold the teacher in awe (some teachers felt threatened by this), more likely to want to discuss all manner of topics.

In all countries it was thought that students would become more critical of the education offered to them and that they would want to have more say in the planning of it. Except in England, and, to a lesser extent in Sweden, this was seen as coming from an increasing political awareness which was sometimes very strong but lacking in depth.

Changes which were thought necessary to cope with these developments involved even more emphasis on individual work, a practical approach, more discussion, more participation from students, more flexible timetabling, more flexible examining — in fact more response to individual needs, and more training of teachers.

Teachers' perceptions of current problems

Table T5 below illustrates teachers' views of current problems. Teachers' perceptions, like those of students, reflect in some measure the system of the country concerned.

In Sweden, where a great deal of money is spent on education, figures are comparatively low for such problems as an inadequate supply of books, poor facilities and shortage of teachers. On the other hand, Swedish teachers mention, more frequently than other factors, problems of truancy, and the difficulty of having students from a wide range of ability in school. These problems, of course, are more likely to occur in a system which caters for 80-85% of the 16-19 age-group. Similarly, in Italy, where there is very little initial training of a practical kind for secondary school teachers, 56.5% of teachers thought that this lack of training was a problem.

The perceptions of those most closely involved in the educational process, teachers and students, give some indication for those who make decisions about new developments, as to where changes might be encouraged. The following pages outline some suggestions.

Problems as seen by teachers	Germany %	Sweden %	Italy %	France %	England %
inadequate supply of books and teaching materials	35.5	23.9	24.1	29.0	28.4
difficulty of devising an up-to-date curriculum	51.6	19.7	32.4	58.0	18.3
difficuly of implementing an up-to-date curriculum	51.6	45.1	39.4	43.8	29.4
shortage of teachers	67.7	4.2	24.1	40.7	10.7
placing of students in school according to abilities and inclinations	38.7	49.3	31.2	48.4	36.5
inadequate material facilities	35.5	19.7	38.8	49.4	40.1
conflict between what students want to learn and the realities of the job situation	25.8	31.0	60.0	62.3	35.0
inadequate initial training of teachers	38.7	16.9	56.5	32.1	21.3
placing of students in jobs/higher education according to abilities and inclinations	22.6	28.2	35.9	46.3	27.9
student apathy	25.8	32.4	46.5	54.9	41.6
devising an up-to-date curriculum for the less able	32.3	45.1	29.4	38.3	37.1
implementing an up-to-date curriculum for the less able	22.6	49.3	26.5	32.7	37.1
inadequate in-service training of teachers	61.3	25.4	47.6	20.4	25.4
maintaining of discipline	6.5	11.3	21.8	27.2	8.6
problems of assessing the standard a student has reached	54.8	31.0	17.1	19.1	11.7
difficulties of having students from a wide range of social backgrounds in school	16.1	22.5	32.9	49.4	15.2
problems stemming from students who wish to participate in planning	22.6	2.8	22.4	21.0	10.2
truancy	19.4	38.0	32.4	20.4	8.6
difficulties of having students from a wide range of ability in school	41.9	60.6	68.2	21.6	42.1
Total numbers	31	71	170	162	197

All teachers: Table T5. Teachers' perceptions of current problems

Recommendations and implications for policy

At the beginning of this section of the Report it was said that describing a curriculum was like describing a dynamic process. More simply it was a description of a game of "Chinese Whispers". The previous chapters have tried to illustrate: first, the trends in curricular provision within the areas visited from an "official" point of view; secondly, the way in which the curriculum is "received" by students, together with their ideas as to how the curriculum might be improved; and thirdly, the way in which teachers see themselves as "giving" the curriculum. Outlines of findings in these three areas have already been given.

It is clear that changes in the curricular provision for the 16-20 age-group are occurring at different rates, and with different emphases, in the countries visited. These countries have different cultural and historical backgrounds but the *kinds* of change are similar, though the strength of tradition, and the assumptions made about education by those who have the power to take decisions, influence the pace and degree of change.

This difference in tradition helps or hinders particular kinds of reform in varying degrees. An efficient centralised system, for example, can bring the physics syllabus up-to-date "at a stroke"; an advisory service of the English kind, rather than a series of official directives, might be more successful at changing the attitudes of teachers. Two quotations, the first from the headmistress of a mixed sixth form college in England, and the second from a teacher in Italy, illustrate some aspects of different systems:

> "I feel that the most important thing is the quality of personal relationships within the community: if these are right then many of the other important things follow. But it is impossible to pinpoint in a few words an aspect of teaching method, organisation etc., which helps to build up respect and concern for one's neighbour, a sense of the value of each as an individual, and an acceptance of responsibility (not necessarily organisational) within a community. Everyone's daily behaviour affects this".

> "No rethinking of subjects or the curriculum generally, no changes in any school activity, can be initiated by anyone who works in schools — everything is done through circulars and laws coming from the Ministry".

Differences in administrative and organisational procedures of the kind suggested by these two quotations will obviously affect the way in which reforms are initiated and implemented. The following recommendations for experiment and development are curricular but they often imply changes in organisation, and in teacher training.

The experience of the English sixth form colleges in offering subjects to beginners is so far limited, but some of their results are interesting. Many staff emphasised the importance of motivation and did not think that results in O-Level examinations were always a trustworthy indication of potential ability. More experiments could be carried out to look at the possibilities of beginning subjects at various levels, and capitalising on motivation. This implies a system in which there is possibility for choice, and a good counselling service.

Teachers and students commented sometimes that the time-table was inflexible and did not allow for large enough blocks of time to do experiments, or to go on visits outside school, for example. Some schools allowed members of staff to "accumulate" blocks of time during the school year so that there could be a period of concentrated study of a particular subject. One school timetabled an "accelerated" course concurrently with a more leisurely paced one so that it would be possible to transfer students from one group to another. Often timetabling is no more than fitting staff and students to rooms (difficult enough anyway); but perhaps more could be done to increase flexibility.

Although subjects received more favourable comments from students than either methods or organisation there were, all the same, criticisms. Some of the content in various programmes could be cut down, more opportunities for choice could be encouraged in some of the systems. Increasing areas of knowledge and growth of new knowledge mean that, more than ever, selection of content and development of accompanying skills are important. Students sometimes mentioned that they were not able to relate the disciplines they learnt in school to their own lives, nor to see the relationship between various areas of subject matter. More could be done to develop a series of options which could be studied at different levels, together with some kind of integrated or interdisciplinary study. The International Bacclaureate is already working along these lines in terms of academic curricula.

More could be done to bring together general, technical and professional aspects of education. (This would imply some common ground in teacher training). Already in England some universities offer mixed courses, engineering plus a foreign language for example, or courses in "new" subjects which involve a grounding in several different disciplines. This is not just a matter of broadening the range and scope of subject matter offered but widening the scope of the teaching. Traditional subjects have been regarded as "noble" because of the intellectual and "spiritual" qualities they are thought to foster in students. However, the acquisition of such qualities by students is often a result of the teaching/learning process itself. Several teachers of technical subjects remarked that they would have appreciated a more broadly based training.

More could be done to open up schools, to allow the outside community to come in and to encourage students to see more of what happens outside. Community colleges in England are already developing a whole range of activities for the whole community.

Students were critical of magisterial, authoritarian methods of teaching and some staff showed that they appreciated the need for a more varied approach. Comments from students showed that they wanted to be able to discuss, to learn from solving problems. This means that more support will have to be given to teachers as they modify their traditional role, and more done in initial and in-service training to help them capitalise on the use of discussion. Development of such personal skills in teaching are as important as development of the "progressive" techniques of programmed learning, use of audio-visual aids etc.

In making use of such discussion techniques more could be done to break down the unit of the lesson as a means of teaching. One physics department in England, for example, used lectures, tutorials, small group discussions, and laboratory experiments in a very flexible manner according to the needs of the student and the content that was being learnt. This meant that there could be short periods of intensive tutorial work with individuals or small groups of students when this was needed.

The most severe criticism from students was made on the subject of school organisation. Any reform here depends, in large measure, on changes in attitudes. The head teacher quoted earlier remarked, "Everyone's daily behaviour affects this". Changes in attitude, in this respect, would depend on staff working together rather than as isolated individuals as often happens at the moment.

Together with a more flexible timetable, and a more open school, more provision for extra-curricular activities could be offered. Many schools are building a block of time into the official time-table now because it is recognised that students learn when they enjoy something, and do it of their own free choice.

Such developments as those outlined above are easy to recommend. But who is to implement them, and how? Much of the literature on education at the moment emphasises the importance of teacher participation, just as much pedagogy now recommends teachers to get the students involved in their own work. Students should, so we are told, be encouraged to take responsibility for their own work, they should learn by solving problems. Suppose these recommendations were applied to teachers? A recent OECD document[1] pointed out, "Change is suspect when it is imposed on teachers who have played no part in promoting it". At what level can teachers play a significant role in taking decisions?

Chapter 10 illustrated the kinds of change that were taking place in curriculum. Often these changes depend on changes in attitude. Development of such attitudes needs the support of a sympathetic advisory and administrative system. More experiments are needed to look at the ways in which various kinds of change can be successfully implemented.

[1] O.E.C.D., *The Changing Role of the Teacher and its Implications*, Document No. ED(72)12, Paris: 1972.

SECTION E

SOCIOLOGICAL ASPECTS

CHAPTER 14

INTRODUCTION: NATURE AND AIMS OF THE SOCIOLOGICAL ASPECTS OF THE RESEARCH

The sociological part of the research was based on questionnaires and interviews in 54 schools. 5,419 students took part, together with — wherever possible — the principal or head teacher of each institution, and teachers concerned with counselling and/or guidance. The proportions of male and female students, and the total number from each country, are shown in Table 1.

Country	Male Students		Female Students		Sex Not Stated	Total Number
	Number	%	Number	%		
ENGLAND	583	53.9	498	46.1	33	1,114
FRANCE	865	56.8	659	43.2	10	1,534
ITALY	1,015	63.0	595	37.0	18	1,628
SWEDEN	396	54.3	333	45.7	48	777
FEDERAL REPUBLIC OF GERMANY	195	53.3	171	46.7	–	366

Table 1: Number of Students from Each Country who Took Part in the Research

(Note on percentages: Throughout Section E, unless otherwise stated, percentages have been adjusted to exclude those students who did not reply to the question concerned. These are known as *adjusted percentages*, as opposed to *relative percentages* which include no-replies).

But questionnaires and interviews in schools were not the only source of information. Officials in the various countries, such as representatives of the Careers Service in England, the National Board of Education in Sweden, and the Ministry of National Education in France, provided a considerable amount of additional information and insights. These helped the researchers to interpret the replies obtained from students and teachers, and to put them in their wider context.

However, the sociological study described in this section of the report was essentially school-based. In this respect it differed from the structure and policy studies. The sociological part of the research did not aim to describe the *national* situation in each of the countries visited, but rather to examine *local* circumstances in a range of upper-secondary schools and colleges. These institutions did not necessarily represent outstanding centres of innovation. Instead, many were characteristic or typical institutions. In them, the researchers hoped more to discover indications of change and innovation that could be applied at a general level, than to witness spectacular experimental work restricted to a few selected schools or colleges.

The Questionnaires

A copy of the three questionnaires used in the sociological part of the research can be found in Appendix (1).

The *students' questionnaire* included questions on family background, such as parents' level of education and the extent to which parents had encouraged their son or daughter to continue into upper-secondary school. It also dealt with students' ambitions, and the extent to which they felt confident of achieving these. The questionnaire also investigated students' perceptions of educational and employment opportunities, and their regrets (if any) concerning upper-secondary education. Lastly, students were asked about the counselling and guidance that they had received, and the type of such information and advice that they would find most helpful.

The *principals' or head teachers' questionnaire* included questions on the range of social backgrounds represented by upper-secondary students in the school. It also dealt with the types of educational and employment opportunities taken up by students after leaving the school or college. In addition, the principal or head teacher was asked to describe the structure of counselling and guidance provision within the school, as well as his or her perceptions of likely and of desirable developments with regard to:

(i)   the range of social backgrounds catered for by the school or college

(ii)   educational and employment opportunities for upper-secondary school leavers.

The *questionnaire for teachers or others concerned with the provision of counselling and guidance* dealt with the nature of the counselling/guidance work undertaken, including the range of students involved, and special provision such as work experience schemes. It also asked for details of any liaison with other counselling and guidance workers within the school or college and with external social, psychological or employment services. Lastly, the teachers or others were asked to describe developments in counselling and guidance which they thought were (i) likely to emerge in the foreseeable future, (ii) desirable.

Except in the case of students, these questionnaires were — whenever possible — supplemented by information and insights obtained from interviews. Indeed, sometimes the head teachers' or counsellors' questionnaire was used as the framework for a structured and wide-ranging interview, instead of simply being filled in by the individual concerned. In this way, the researcher was able to obtain far more information and insights than would otherwise have been possible.

The Broader Context

Clearly, the sociological perspective in a research project such as this ranges over factors which lie outside the school system itself. Traditionally, sociologists working in the field of education have studied problems such as the relationship between home background and educational achievement. We know, for example, that factors such as linguistic skills and parental attitudes can affect a child's attainment level. We know too that school systems tend to operate in favour of children from more privileged home backgrounds. Pupils who are socially and culturally disadvantaged also tend to be at a disadvantage within the school system. They sometimes lack the linguistic skills and the motivation and attitudes familiar to their teachers. Consequently, these childrens' measured attainment level often does not match their potential ability. Not surprisingly, many of these boys and girls leave school without realising their full potential. And the greatest "wastage of ability" is found among those from the lower social groups.

So the conventional image of those who remain in school beyond the compulsory stage has been of a minority group which represents to some extent a social and academic élite.

But recent developments in upper-secondary education have resulted in a broader and more flexible concept. These developments are discussed in detail in earlier sections of the Report, so will be mentioned only briefly here. They include: the relaxation of minimum entry standards; the broadening of curricular choices; the introduction of new teaching-learning methods; the increase in studies not leading to examinations; the development of new institutions catering solely for the upper-secondary age-group; and the relaxation of traditional patterns of school organisation.

The researchers were particularly interested in the possible relationship between such developments and the emergence of a new concept of the upper-secondary student. He or she would no longer represent an academic and social élite minority group, but rather a wide range of home backgrounds, abilities, interests and ambitions.

The Sociological Research Objectives

Hence, one of the major aims of the sociological part of the research was to investigate upper-secondary students' home background and ambitions, and the relationship between them.

There were two other major sociological objectives, and they were closely related. Both are discussed at greater length later in this section of the Report, so will be mentioned only briefly here. The first concerns the educational and employment opportunities available to upper-secondary students, and the second the provision of information, advice and guidance on these.

Upper-secondary students to-day are faced with the prospect of an increasingly complex employment structure and choice of educational options. Often — as in Sweden — employers demand not only formal qualifications but also practical work experience. Overall, the level of education required in almost every sphere of employment is rising, and future prospects for those without formal qualifications seem to be coming increasingly limited. Furthermore, rapid shifts in the employment structure lead to swift growth and decline in the demand for particular types of skills. Job opportunities in some sectors wane or change dramatically, while in other fields whole new areas of employment emerge and grow.

In this situation it is vital that upper-secondary students receive adequate information, advice and guidance about educational and employment opportunities. Schools clearly have an important role to play here. Fluctuations in the employment structure, and uncertainties about links between educational and occupational attainments make the transition from school to work and/or further studies an increasingly complex process for the upper-secondary student. And the fact that he is rapidly coming to represent a majority rather than a minority of young people is almost certain to aggravate rather than to ease the problem.

For these reasons it was decided that particular attention should be paid to students' perceptions of educational and employment opportunities, and to the provision of information, advice and guidance on these in upper-secondary schools and colleges.

CHAPTER 15

THE SOCIAL AND FAMILY BACKGROUND OF THE STUDENTS WHO TOOK PART IN THE RESEARCH

(a) Father's Occupation

Father's occupation is often the only indication of social background that is given in research reports. Admittedly, it is a convenient 'social class label', and one that is used in the compilation of many official statistics. But it obviously cannot convey anything like a complete impression of social and family background. It should, therefore, be examined in conjunction with other variables, such as parental attitudes and level of education.

Because occupational classifications vary from country to country, comparisons are problematic. The categories themselves differ, and so do the social connotations which particular occupations carry. For these reasons, each country is considered separately.

Let us first look at the English students, whose fathers' occupation is shown in table 2. The father of one out of every eight English students was in the top occupational category, or social class I. One father in every three was in the second group, corresponding to social class II.

This means that almost half of all the English students came from the two highest social groups. If those whose father had a skilled non-manual job are added to this total, we see that in all more than 60% of English students were from non-manual backgrounds. At the other end of the social scale, less than 8% of fathers were in semi- or un-skilled occupations.

What impression of English students' social background do these figures convey? Since the majority of students came from non-manual workers' families, they might be thought of — in a general sense — as being 'middle class' rather than 'working class'. But two points should be borne in mind. Firstly, roughly a quarter of these students' fathers were in 'white collar' jobs, rather than in professional, managerial or senior technical employment. So they could be described as 'lower middle class', as opposed to 'middle ·class'. Secondly, although semi- and un-skilled workers' families were scarcely represented at all, one English student in every five was the son or daughter of a skilled manual worker. So students from backgrounds traditionally thought of as being solidly 'middle class' (i.e. social class I and — to a lesser extent — II) did not have a complete monopoly of upper-secondary education in the schools and colleges visited by the researchers.

But the fact that these students were more 'middle class' than the population as a whole is illustrated by table 3, which shows the social class distribution of the total working population of Great Britain in 1966.

Table 2: Fathers' Occupation — English Students		
Father's Occupation	Number	%
Professional or higher managerial (I)	134	12.2
Lower managerial or senior technical (II)	372	34.0
Other non-manual (skilled) (III)	182	16.6
Skilled manual (III)	211	19.3
Semi- and un-skilled (IV) and (V)	83	7.6
Services (i.e. Armed Forces)	3	0.3
Inadequately described occupations	13	1.2
Dead; retired	69	6.3
Do not know	28	2.6
No reply	19	—

Note: In table 2, the figures in brackets refer to the social class to which these occupational categories broadly correspond. (Ref. Classification of Occupations. Registrar General for England and Wales).

Table 3: Economically Active Population of Great Britain — Analysis by Social Class, 1966	
Social class	Percentage of the total economically active population:
I	2.9
II	14.6
III	49.1
IV	22.3
V	8.0
Not classified	3.0

(Ref: 'Social Trends' Number 3. 1972. Central Statistical
Office. HMSO 1972)

The contrast between the social class distribution of the total working population and the students is striking.

For example, social class I accounted for only 2.9% of the former, but four times that proportion of the latter. And although one sixth of the total working population came from social class II, this group provided one third of the upper-secondary students. But social classes IV and V, which made up 30.3% of the total working population, accounted for only 7.6% of the English students.

Clearly, not too much emphasis should be placed on comparisons drawn from statistics relating to two different populations at different points in time. Nor can one generalise from 1114 students in twelve institutions to English upper-secondary pupils as a whole. Nevertheless, one is left with the impression that the process of democratising English upper-secondary education is not yet complete.

Let us now turn to an examination of the French students' social background, shown in table 4:

Table 4: Father's Occupation — French Students:		
Father's occupation:	Number	%
Cadre supérieur: profession libérale	411	27.1
Cadre moyen	396	26.1
Employé de bureau; commerçant	129	8.5
Artisan; petit commerçant	87	5.7
Fermier	30	2.0
Ouvrier manuel	260	17.1
Autres professions	92	6.1
Dead; retired	99	6.5
Do not know	13	0.9
No reply	17	—

The largest single group of fathers, 27%, were in the highest occupational category. Almost as many, 26%, had 'middle class' jobs. So these two groups together accounted for more than half of all the French students. Only one student in six came from a manual worker's family. These figures indicate that the majority of French students who took part in the research were from relatively provileged social backgrounds, and that the higher occupational groups dominated upper-secondary education to an even greater extent than in England. But once again, one must remember that the schools chosen were not necessarily representative or typical of the country as a whole.

We shall now turn to the Italian students, whose fathers' occupation is shown in table 5.

Table 5: Father's Occupation — Italian Students		
Father's occupation:	Number	%
Dirigente; professionista	342	21.4
Personale executivo, amministrativo	251	15.7
Commerciante; artigiano; coltivatore dirretto	250	15.7
Lavoratore salariato	441	27.6
Domestico	3	0.2
Other occupations	125	7.8
Dead; retired	176	11.0
Do not know	8	0.5
No reply	32	—

More than one in five Italian students came from professional or managerial backgrounds, and another one in every six were from administrative or executive workers' families. But a sizeable proportion of fathers were in the lower occupational categories; the largest single group, representing more than a quarter of the total, were *'lavoratore salariato'*.

Let us now look at the Swedish students. Their fathers' occupation is described in table 6.

Table 6: Father's Occupation — Swedish Students		
Father's occupation:	Number	%
'Highest occupational group' (class I)	50	8.7
'Higher middle class' (IIA)	116	20.1
'Lower middle class' (IIB)	107	18.6
Class IIIA	149	25.9
Class IIIB	109	18.9
Class IIIC — diverse occupations	35	6.1
Dead; retired	10	1.7
No reply	201	—

The figures relating to Sweden should be interpreted with some care, because more than a quarter of the students failed to state their father's occupation. This was partly due to the fact that many students came from one parent families. In Sweden, perhaps more than in some other countries, it is socially acceptable for a woman to have a child and act as the head of the family, rather than to marry the child's father and set up a conventional nuclear family.

However, those Swedish students who did state their father's occupation appeared to be fairly evenly distributed among the 'middle' and 'lower' occupational groups. Less than 10% of fathers were in the highest group, or class I.

Lastly, let us look at German students' social background. The classification of their fathers' occupations was problematic, because no officially or generally recognised categories could be obtained. Faced with this situation, the researcher decided to adopt the Registrar General's classification used in England. This was obviously an imperfect solution, but it did have the advantage of permitting closer comparisons of English and German data than would have otherwise been possible.

Table 7: Father's Occupation — German Students		
Father's occupation:	Number	%
Professional or higher managerial	36	10.9
Lower managerial or senior technical	87	26.4
Other non-manual (skilled)	92	27.9
Skilled manual	74	22.4
Semi- or un-skilled	2	0.6
Dead; retired	37	11.2
Do not know	2	0.6
No reply	36	—

Just over one third (37%) of German fathers were in the top two occupational groups. (The corresponding proportion of English fathers was 46%). But when those in other non-manual jobs is added to this total, the percentage of students from all non-manual backgrounds is almost indentical in the two countries. However, there was a striking contrast in the proportion of students from semi- and un-skilled workers' families: 7.6% in England, but only 0.6% in the Federal Republic of Germany.

But again it must be stressed that such comparisons should be interpreted with care, partly because of lack of representativeness of the schools concerned, and partly because of the small number of German students, resulting from the fact that only one area in the Federal Republic of Germany was visited.

To summarise:

In England, France and the Federal Republic of Germany, the majority of upper-secondary students came from the higher social groups. But in Sweden, and — to a lesser extent — in Italy, students represented a more even spread of social backgrounds.

(b) Parents' level of Education

As we have seen, comparisons between occupational groups in different countries can present problems. Similar difficulties arise in comparisons of educational levels. For this reason, statistics relating to parents' education in the various countries are presented separately. But first, a summary covering all five countries:

Educational level:	England		France		Italy		Sweden		Federal Republic of Germany	
	Number	%	Number	%	Number	%	Number	%	Number	%
Both parents had upper-secondary or higher education	92	8.3	332	21.6	440	27.0	41	5.3	35	9.6
Father only had upper-secondary or higher education	172	15.4	268	17.5	273	16.8	77	9.9	67	18.3
Mother only had upper-secondary or higher education	44	3.9	258	16.8	78	4.8	20	2.6	11	3.0
Other replies	806	72.4	676	44.1	837	51.4	639	82.2	253	69.1

Table 8: Parents' Level of Education – a Summary

Note: Percentages quoted in table 8 are relative percentages – i.e. they include those students who did not reply to the question

The following definitions of 'upper-secondary or higher education' were used:

England   –   Higher School Certificate (superseded by the General Certificate of Education, Advanced level)
       –   University or equivalent

France   –   Lycée
       –   Autre établissement avec diplôme
       –   Université ou équivalent
       –   Autre forme d'education post-secondaire

Italy   —   Liceo
              —   Scuola magistrale; istituto magistrale
              —   Altre scuole medie superiori
              —   University or equivalent

Sweden   —   Studentexamen
              —   University or equivalent

Federal
Republic of
Germany   —   Abitur
              —   University or equivalent

Bearing in mind the caveat about making international comparisons, we see that the proportion of students who came from homes where both parents had received an upper-secondary or higher education was highest in Italy, and lowest in Sweden. But the broad contrasts that exist are partly due to the differences in definition of 'upper-secondary or higher education'. So let us now look at each country in more detail; first England:

Table 9: Parents' Level of Education — England				
Level of Education	Fathers Number	%	Mothers Number	%
Elementary school only, or with some short further education or training	463	42.2	532	48.3
School Certificate (superseded by the General Certificate of Education, Ordinary level)	155	14.1	232	21.1
Higher School Certificate (superseded by the General Certificate of Education, Advanced level)	105	9.6	74	6.7
University or equivalent	159	14.5	62	5.6
Do not know	216	19.7	202	18.3
No reply	16	—	12	—

Generally speaking, fathers of English students were rather better educated than mothers. More than twice as many fathers (14.5%) had received a University or equivalent education, and a larger proportion had reached Higher School Certificate level (9.6% compared with 6.7%).

Let us now look at French parents' level of education:

Table 10: Parents' Level of Education — France

Level of Education	Fathers Number	%	Mothers Number	%
Ecole primaire	526	35.3	615	42.2
Lycée	149	10.0	213	14.6
Autre établissement secondaire avec diplôme	216	14.5	194	13.3
Autre établissement secondaire sans diplôme	86	5.8	125	8.6
Université ou équivalent (sauf les grandes écoles)	162	10.9	120	8.2
Autre forme d'éducation post-secondaire	73	4.9	63	4.3
Une des grandes écoles*	158	10.6	16	1.1
Do not know	120	8.1	113	7.7
No reply	44	—	75	—

*   *Note on table 10*
     This particular percentage is unreliable, because in colloquial usage, *"grande école"* can mean simply post-primary school. It would appear that this was in fact how it was interpreted, in the case of many fathers' education

The contrast between fathers' and mothers' levels of education was less marked in France than in England. In fact, an equal proportion (40%) of fathers and mothers had received an upper-secondary or higher education (as defined in table 9).

Let us now turn to Italian students' parents' level of education, shown in table 11.

As in England, mothers in Italy were less well educated, on average, than fathers. But a far higher proportion had attended a *scuola — or istituto — magistrale*. One other point is worth noting: that the percentage of fathers who had been to a University or equivalent institution was higher in Italy (20%) than in either France (11%) or England (14.5%):

Table 11: Parents' Level of Education — Italy				
Level of Education:	Fathers Number	%	Mothers Number	%
Primary school	507	32.4	688	43.4
Scuola media inferiore	303	19.4	333	21.0
Liceo	76	4.9	68	4.3
Scuola magistrale; istituto magistrale	36	2.3	188	11.8
Altre scuole medie superiori	291	18.6	138	8.7
University or equivalent	310	19.8	124	7.8
Do not know	42	2.7	48	3.0
No reply	63	–	41	–

Next, Sweden:

Table 12: Parents' Level of Education — Sweden				
Level of Education:	Fathers Number	%	Mothers Number	%
Folkskola	332	55.2	378	62.4
Realskola	57	9.5	85	14.0
Studentexamen	59	9.8	40	6.6
University or equivalent	59	9.8	21	3.5
Do not know	91	15.1	77	12.7
No reply	176	–	171	–

Once again, the Swedish figures should be treated with particular care, because of the high proportion of students (22% or 23% of the total) who failed to answer the question. But even so, the Swedish replies do convey the impression that parents' level of education was low compared with those in other countries. More than half of all the Swedish fathers, and almost two thirds of mothers, had received only an elementary education. And only 10% of fathers had been to a University or equivalent institution (compared with 14.5% in England, and 20% in Italy). But — and this point has already been stressed — this type of cross-cultural comparison is hazardous, because of the national differences it masks. So it should be thought of, at best, as a rough guideline.

Lastly: The Federal Republic of Germany:

Table 13: Parents' Level of Education — Federal Republic of Germany				
Level of Education:	Fathers Number	%	Mothers Number	%
Folk- oder Hauptschule	124	37.2	174	52.1
Mittlere Reife	95	28.5	107	32.0
Abitur	56	16.8	35	10.5
University or equivalent	46	13.8	11	3.3
Do not know	12	3.6	7	2.1
No reply	33	—	32	—

German parents' level of education was broadly similar to the English. The proportion of fathers who had attended a University or equivalent institution was almost identical, and in both countries around 40% of fathers and 50% of mothers had received only an elementary education. But one must remember that the number of parents represented by the German percentages is very small compared with those in the other countries.

To summarise:

With the exception of France, fathers' level of education was noticeably higher than mothers' in all the countries. Despite the pitfalls involved in making this type of international comparison, one is left with the impression that a higher proportion of parents in France and Italy had received an upper-secondary or higher education than in England, Germany or Sweden. The largest percentage of 'first generation' upper-secondary students was found in Sweden.

(c) Parents' attitudes towards their child's upper-secondary education

The first two sections of this chapter on students' social and family background were concerned with father's occupation and parents' education. While it has become almost a research orthodoxy to include these two variables, another dimension — namely, parental attitudes — is more frequently omitted. Reasons for this may be pragmatic: attitudinal research is notoriously hazardous, because of the difficulties of obtaining reliable and valid measurements. Or they may be conceptual, in the sense that attitudes fall outside the researcher's schema.

However, we felt that it was important to obtain *some* indication of parental attitudes. Partly because so much previous research in education has revealed the significance of parents' attitudes for children's performance in school. Partly because father's occupation and parents' level of education alone provide such an incomplete picture of a student's social and family background. And also because it was felt that parental attitudes — as reflected by the degree of encouragement to stay on at school — might be particularly significant at the upper-secondary level, i.e. at the post-compulsory stage of education.

So we decided to look at two aspects of parental attitudes. The first one — degree of encouragement to stay on at school — has already been mentioned. The second was the amount and helpfulness of information and advice about education and employment given to students by their parents. It should be stressed that what we obtained were *students' perceptions* of their parents' attitudes; parents themselves did not take part in the research.

Let us first look at *parental encouragement*. Table 14 is a summary of all the countries. This is followed by more detailed figures for England, France, Italy, Sweden and Germany separately.

Table 14: Parental Encouragement to Stay On Into Upper-secondary Education – a summary

Parental Encouragement	England		France		Italy		Sweden		Germany	
	Number	Relative %	Number	Relative %	Number	Relative %	Number	Relative %	Number	Relative %
Both parents: encouraged/ greatly encouraged	692	62.1	944	61.5	863	53.0	360	46.3	166	45.4
Father only: encouraged/ greatly encouraged	75	6.7	68	4.4	97	6.0	30	3.9	24	6.6
Mother only: encouraged/ greatly encouraged	122	11.0	154	10.0	191	11.7	73	9.4	55	15.0
All other replies	225	20.2	368	24.0	477	29.3	314	40.4	121	33.1

In both England and France, 62% of students had been encouraged by both parents to stay on into upper-secondary education. In Italy, this proportion dropped to 53% and in Sweden and Germany to around 45%.

Before we examine possible reasons for these differences, let us first look at each country in more detail.

Table 15: Father's Encouragement To Stay On Into Upper-secondary Education In the Five Countries

Degree of Encouragement	England		France		Italy		Sweden		Germany	
	Number	%	Number	%	Number	%	Number	%	Number	%
Greatly encouraged	364	33.3	597	40.6	407	26.4	156	26.0	76	24.0
Encouraged	403	36.8	415	28.2	553	35.8	234	38.9	114	36.0
Neutral: neither encouraged nor discouraged	264	24.1	354	24.0	466	30.2	192	31.9	105	33.1
Discouraged	9	0.8	10	0.7	5	0.3	4	0.7	3	0.9
Greatly discouraged	4	0.4	1	0.1	2	0.1			2	0.6
Do not know	50	4.6	95	6.5	110	7.1	15	2.5	17	5.4
No reply	20	–	62	–	85	–	176	–	49	–

Table 16: Mother's Encouragement To Stay On Into Upper-secondary Education In The Five Countries

Degree of Encouragement:	England		France		Italy		Sweden		Germany	
	Number	%	Number	%	Number	%	Number	%	Number	%
Greatly encouraged	400	36.3	664	44.7	453	28.7	169	27.4	84	25.2
Encouraged	414	37.6	434	29.2	601	38.1	264	42.8	137	41.1
Neutral: neither encouraged nor discouraged	252	22.9	309	20.8	412	26.1	176	28.5	98	29.4
Discouraged	9	0.8	2	0.1	11	0.7	2	0.3	2	0.6
Greatly discouraged	1	0.1	2	0.1	1	0.1			4	1.2
Do not know	26	2.4	73	4.9	99	6.3	6	1.0	8	2.4
No reply	12	–	50	–	51	–	160	–	33	–

In every country, mothers provided a greater degree of encouragement than fathers. Some interesting national differences also emerged. Looking at the proportion of students who felt that they had been 'greatly encouraged', this was highest in France and lowest in Germany. In fact, there is a clear split between France and England on the one hand, and Italy, Sweden and Germany on the other.

Let us now consider some of the factors which might be linked with variations in parental encouragement. These could include parents' own level of education and social background, as well as their ambitions for their child, and perceptions of current opportunities for young people. Some of these factors — namely, parents' ambitions and perceptions — lay outside the scope of this research project. But we can look at parents' educational level and social background.

Firstly, educational level:

We have already seen that the majority of parents in each country had not received an upper-secondary education. This might lead parents to encourage their children to take advantage of opportunities which they themselves had missed. Alternatively, it could mean that parents do not perceive any advantages in extended education, and for this reason do not encourage their son or daughter to stay on at school. Let us see which of these alternatives appears to be the more feasible, by looking at a cross-tabulation of English parents' educational level and degree of encouragement.

Table 17: The Relationship Between Parents' Level of Education and Degree of Encouragement — ENGLISH STUDENTS

Degree of Encouragement	Parents' Level of Education:							
	Both parents had upper-secondary or higher education		Father only had upper-secondary or higher education		Mother only had upper-secondary or higher education		Neither parent had/ all other replies	
	Number	Col. %	Number	Col. %	Number	Col. %	Number	Col. %
Both parents encouraged	66	71.7	128	74.4	28	63.6	470	58.3
Father only encouraged	2	2.2	15	8.7	2	4.5	56	6.9
Mother only encouraged	6	6.5	9	5.2	8	18.2	99	12.3
Neither parent encouraged/ all other replies	18	19.6	20	11.6	6	13.6	181	22.5

Table 17 shows that 72% of fathers and mothers who had both received an upper-secondary or higher education had both encouraged their son or daughter to continue their studies. But, perhaps surprisingly, this proportion was slightly higher — 74% — among families where only the father had received an upper-secondary or higher education. However, as one would expect, the percentage fell sharply — to 58% — in families where neither parent appeared to have experienced upper-secondary or higher education. So overall, there did seem to be a relationship between parents' level of education and degree of encouragement.

Secondly, social background:

Research in the past had indicated that parents from different social groups vary in their attitudes towards their children's education. It appears, for example, that "middle class" parents are more likely to encourage their children to continue their education beyond the compulsory stage. 'Working class' families, on the other hand, are less likely to perceive any value in extended education.

Generalised findings of this kind obviously mask many individual differences, so should be interpreted with caution. But is a similar broad pattern evident in our own research? In order to see whether this was so, parental encouragement was cross-tabulated with father's occupation in England.

**Table 18: The Relationship Between Parental Encouragement
and Father's Occupation — England**

Father's occupation	Degree of Parental Encouragement							
	Both parents encouraged		Father only encouraged		Mother only encouraged		All other replies	
	Number	Row %	Number	Row %	Number	Row %	Number	Row %
I Professional or higher managerial	107	79.9	6	4.5	7	5.2	14	10.4
II Lower managerial or senior technical	241	64.8	23	6.2	33	8.9	75	20.2
III Other non manual	122	67.0	13	7.1	9	4.9	38	20.9
III Skilled manual	125	59.2	18	8.5	24	11.4	44	20.9
IV & V Semi/un-skilled manual	42	50.6	9	10.8	14	16.9	18	21.7
Services (i.e. Armed Forces)	2	66.7	–	–	1	33.3	–	–
Not classifiable	12	92.3	–	–	–	–	1	7.7
Dead; retired	30	43.5	2	2.9	24	34.8	13	18.8
Do not know	5	17.9	3	10.7	7	25.0	13	46.4

Note: Throughout the report:
  Row % refers to the percentage of the row (i.e. horizontal) total.
  Column % refers to the percentage of the column (i.e. vertical) total.

From Table 18, there would appear to be some relationship between parental encouragement and social class. For example, 80% of students from professional or higher managerial families were encouraged by both parents to stay on at school. But only 65% of those from lower managerial or senior technical homes, and 51% from semi- or un-skilled backgrounds, had been.

To summarise:

In each country, mothers have provided a greater degree of encouragement to stay on at school than fathers. But there were also marked national differences. French and English parents had been noticeably more encouraging than their Italian, Swedish and German counterparts. Social class appeared to be related to the degree of parental encouragement: in England, the proportion of students who had been encouraged by both parents was highest among those from professional or higher managerial families. Parents' level of education also appeared to be a relevant factor.

Turning now to the second dimension of parental attitudes, *the amount of information and advice about education and employment that parents provided*, let us first look at a summary table showing every country:

Table 19: Parental Information and Advice Concerning Education and Employment — a summary										
Amount of information and advice	ENGLAND		FRANCE		ITALY		SWEDEN		GERMANY	
	Number	%	Number	%	Number	%	Number	%	Number	%
'A lot' or 'some'										
.... from both parents	564	50.6	570	37.2	558	34.3	186	23.9	102	27.9
.... from father only	186	16.7	208	13.6	283	17.4	88	11.3	59	16.1
.... from mother only	114	10.2	190	12.4	136	8.4	71	9.1	48	13.1
All other replies	250	22.4	566	36.9	651	40.0	432	55.6	157	42.9

This time, English parents stood out clearly from those in other countries. Half of the English students had received 'a lot' or 'some' information and advice from both their father and mother. Only a third of French and Italian students, and about one quarter of the Swedes and Germans, had done so.

Let us now look at each country in a little more detail:

Table 20: Fathers' Information and Advice About Education and Employment In The Five Countries

Amount:	ENGLAND		FRANCE		ITALY		SWEDEN		GERMANY	
	Number	%	Number	%	Number	%	Number	%	Number	%
A lot	257	23.6	262	17.8	195	12.7	27	4.5	42	13.0
Some	493	45.3	516	35.1	646	42.1	247	41.2	119	36.8
Hardly any	194	17.8	294	20.0	309	20.1	202	33.7	55	17.0
None at all	100	9.2	322	21.9	331	21.5	102	17.0	91	28.2
Not applicable	45	4.1	74	5.0	55	3.6	22	3.7	16	5.0
No reply	25	–	66	–	92	–	177	–	43	–

Table 21: Mothers' Information and Advice About Education and Employment In The Five Countries

Amount:	ENGLAND		FRANCE		ITALY		SWEDEN		GERMANY	
	Number	%	Number	%	Number	%	Number	%	Number	%
A lot	204	18.6	261	17.6	119	7.5	30	4.8	37	11.1
Some	474	43.2	499	33.6	575	36.3	227	36.5	113	34.0
Hardly any	274	25.0	298	20.1	409	25.9	229	36.8	74	22.3
None at all	121	11.0	367	24.7	431	27.2	126	20.3	100	30.1
Not applicable	23	2.1	59	4.0	48	3.0	10	1.6	8	2.4
No reply	18	–	50	–	46	–	155	–	34	–

Figures relating to individual countries tend to reinforce the impression given by the summary table on page 482. The proportion of students who had received 'a lot' of information and advice from their father and mother was highest in England. French parents ranked second, while Swedes provided the least information and advice. In each country, fathers provided rather more than mothers.

The very last section of this chapter deals with the *extent to which students found their parents' information and advice helpful.*

Table 22: Students' Assessment of Their Parents' Information and Advice - a summary										
Assessment:	ENGLAND		FRANCE		ITALY		SWEDEN		GERMANY	
	Number	%	Number	%	Number	%	Number	%	Number	%
Both parents helpful	544	48.8	536	34.9	537	33.0	191	24.6	88	24.0
Father only helpful	144	12.9	173	11.3	183	11.2	56	7.2	33	9.0
Mother only helpful	97	8.7	152	9.9	115	7.1	53	6.8	31	8.5
All other replies	329	29.5	673	43.9	793	48.7	477	61.4	214	58.5

Once again, English parents came out "on top": almost half of all the students rated their information and advice as helpful. This proportion dropped to one third in France and Italy, and a quarter in Sweden and Germany.

Looking at each country in rather more detail, we see that everywhere fathers' information and advice was rated more highly than mothers':

Table 23: Students' Assessment of Their Father's Information and Advice In The Five Countries										
Assessment:	ENGLAND		FRANCE		ITALY		SWEDEN		GERMANY	
	Number	%	Number	%	Number	%	Number	%	Number	%
Very helpful	221	20.5	237	17.4	176	11.7	48	8.5	35	11.1
Fairly helpful	467	43.2	472	34.6	544	36.2	199	35.4	86	27.2
Not really helpful	229	21.2	304	22.3	313	20.8	184	32.7	67	21.2
Not at all helpful	44	4.1	81	5.9	289	19.2	58	10.3	18	5.7
Not applicable	119	11.0	271	19.9	180	12.0	73	13.0	110	34.8
No reply	34	–	169	–	126	–	215	–	50	–

Assessment:	ENGLAND		FRANCE		ITALY		SWEDEN		GERMANY	
	Number	%	Number	%	Number	%	Number	%	Number	%
Very helpful	180	16.5	232	16.8	138	9.0	48	8.2	30	9.2
Fairly helpful	461	42.4	456	33.1	514	33.4	196	33.4	89	27.2
Not really helpful	266	24.4	314	22.8	349	22.7	204	34.8	82	25.1
Not at all helpful	78	7.2	91	6.6	345	22.4	70	11.9	18	5.5
Not applicable	103	9.5	286	20.7	193	12.5	68	11.6	108	33.0
No reply	26	–	155	–	89	–	191	–	39	–

Table 24: Students' Assessment of Their Mother's Information and Advice In The Five Countries

To summarise:

English students stood out clearly from those in the other countries, both in the amount of information and advice they felt they had received from their parents, and in the degree to which they had found it helpful. For example, 50% of English students felt they had been given 'a lot' or 'some' information and advice by both their parents, compared with 34% in Italy and 24% in Sweden. In all countries, students felt that fathers had provided rather more information and advice than mothers, and that it had been more helpful.

This concludes the section on students' family and social background. Considerable attention has been paid to parental encouragement and help, as well as to the more conventional indices, namely educational level and father's occupation.

The reasons for this emphasis were three-fold. Firstly, to add a dimension of students' family background sometimes omitted in research of this kind, and present a broader picture than father's occupation and parents' education alone could ever provide.

Secondly, to illustrate some of the differences that appear to exist between the various countries. Although social class and parents' education present problems of international comparison, it is possible to compare variables such as parental encouragement. Even so, difficulties of interpretation remain.

For example, did the fact that English students rated their parents' information and advice more highly than those in other countries simply mean that their perceptions of their parents were less critical, or did English fathers and mothers really provide more helpful information and advice?

Thirdly, to enable comparisons to be made between the role of parents and the school, with regard to the provision of information and advice about education and employment.

It is hoped that readers will find this section of the report a useful background to the other chapters concerned more specifically with upper-secondary educational provision. As we have said before, education takes place within a social context: the student's family is one important part of that context.

CHAPTER 16

STUDENTS' ASPIRATIONS, EXPECTATIONS AND PERCEPTIONS CONCERNING EDUCATIONAL AND EMPLOYMENT OPPORTUNITIES

One of the most important aims of the sociological part of the research project was to investigate upper-secondary students' hopes, expectations and perceptions concerning educational and employment opportunities after completing their course of studies.

(a) Students' Aspirations

This section deals with students' aspirations; that is to say, what students *hoped* to do after completing their upper-secondary course. Clearly, these aspirations vary in their significance from one country to another. For example, to go to university does not have the same implications in France as it does in England. University applicants in England have to undergo a rigorous selection process, and usually are admitted only partially on the basis of their G.C.E. Advanced Level examination results. Candidates often have to attend an interview, during which their aptitude and suitability are assessed subjectively by members of the University Department concerned. The validity of such selection methods has frequently been questioned; indeed, a recent National Foundation for Educational Research publication cast new doubts on the predictive value of G.C.E. Advanced Level results for university performance. In France, of course, the system is very different. There, every student who has passed the *baccalauréat* examination has an automatic right of entry to university.

Contrasts such as this make international comparisons difficult. For this reason, findings from each country are presented separately.

Let us first see what English upper-secondary students hoped to do after completing their course of studies.

Table 25: Students' Aspirations — ENGLAND		
Aspiration	Number	%
University or equivalent	399	36.4
Employment involving some form of studies or training	190	17.3
Full-time studies (other than university or equivalent, or College of Education)	152	13.9
Employment involving training/studies leading to a professional qualification (e.g. in accountancy, law, or nursing)	127	11.6
College of Education (i.e. teacher training)	121	11.0
Employment involving no studies or training	32	2.9
Services (i.e. Army; Navy; Air Force)	24	2.2
Do not know	43	3.9
Other replies	8	0.7
No reply	18	—

Just over one third of all English students hoped to go on to university or equivalent studies. A further 25% aimed to enrol at a College of Education or in some other form of full-time studies. Together, these groups account for more than 6 out of 10 English students.

Of the remainder, almost all intended if possible to enter employment involving some form of studies or training (including that leading to professional qualifications). Only 3% of students were aiming to enter jobs where no training or studies would take place. Very few students — les than 4% — did not know what they hoped to do at the end of their upper-secondary course.

The comments made by English students about their aspirations were wide-ranging and varied. But replies from individual schools and colleges differed in this respect. For example, students from a girls' grammar school with a sixth form unit tended to have fairly conventional aspirations: many of them hoped to read subjects such as history, modern languages or medicine at university.

By way of contrast, students from a co-educational sixth form college named options such as polytechnic sandwich courses, degrees in Polymer Chemistry or Plastics Technology, and the Ordinary National Diploma course in Hotel Management. But few students regarded polytechnics as being equivalent to universities. Comments such as "apply to polytechnics as second choice" were frequent. One student summed up the situation as follows; "A university degree is still the shortest route to betta employment"!

What might be called the "social mobility" factor in aspirations was evident in replies from several English schools and colleges. For example, one student at a co-educational sixth form college, whose father was a retired bricklayer, hoped to read architecture at university. Another, the son of a chargehand in an engineering firm wanted to study medicine.

What picture of English students' aspirations emerges from these figures? As we have seen, 60% of ambitions involved full-time education, and another 30% included some form of studies or training. So nine out of every ten embodied a perspective of "continuing education", in the sense that the completion of upper-secondary education did not signify the end of all studies or training.*

How do English students' aspirations compare with those of French students?

Table 26: Students' Aspirations — FRANCE

Aspiration	Number	%
University or equivalent	646	42.7
Other studies or professional training	328	21.7
Preparatory classes for "*les grandes écoles*"	319	21.1
Employment involving no studies or training	146	9.6
Other replies	68	4.5
Do not know	7	0.5
No reply	20	–

* Details of students' aspirations in individual schools and colleges can be found in Appendix III.

More than 4 out of every 10 French students hoped to embark on a university or equivalent course of studies. Another 2 aimed to begin some other form of studies or professional training, and an equal proportion — a fifth of all the students — were planning to enter the preparatory classes for the *grandes écoles*. In this specific context, it seems safe to assume that the term *"grandes écoles"* was not misinterpreted, as it appeared to be in the case of father's education.

Although many French students stated fairly conventional educational or employment ambitions, some others expressed views similar to those of Swedish students.

For instance, one student wanted to be himself and do what he wanted, when he wanted: *"Etre moi et faire ce qu'il me plait au moment ou je veux et quand je veux"*. Another wished to live and travel; studies were a purely secondary consideration: *"Vivre. Voyager. La question des études reste purement secondaire"*.

But perhaps the most unusual reply came from the following student, whose membership of a socialist zionist movement would lead him to spend one year in Israel, followed by two years in France studying psychology, and then a return to Israel:

> *"Je veux partir au kibbutz, en Israël, après mon bac, je*
> *pars pour 1 an, reviens en France 2 ans, où je ferai des*
> *études de psychologie, puis je repars définitivement. Je*
> *suis ce cycle car j'appartiens à un mouvement sioniste*
> *socialiste qui nous destine à ça"!*

What picture do these figures present? As in England, many students had strongly academic, educationally oriented ambitions. But one must remember that the schools selected by the French authorities to take part in our research did not reflect the whole spectrum of upper-secondary education in France. Several of the schools chosen embodied a strong academic tradition which was — not surprisingly — reflected in students' aspirations.

Let us now turn to the Italian students.

Table 27: Students' Aspirations — ITALY		
Aspiration	Number	%
University or equivalent	1000	62.2
Some other type of studies or training	151	9.4
Employment involving no form of studies or training	330	20.5
None of these	114	7.1
Do not know	13	0.8
No reply	20	—

How did Italian students' ambitions compare with those of their English and French counterparts? Table 26 shows that a much higher proportion of Italians — over 60% — were aiming to go to a university or equivalent institution. Yet one student in five hoped to enter employment involving no form of studies or training. The corresponding proportions in France and England were one in ten and one in thirty three. So Italian students' aspirations were more strongly polarised than in either of the other two countries. But these differences should be interpreted with caution, because of variations in the types of opportunities available to students, which were reflected in the options presented in the questionnaire.

Contrasts between countries in this respect arguably account for part of the difference. But the predominance of academically oriented institutions that occurred in the French fieldwork did not happen in Italy to anything like the same extent. So it is unlikely that this factor could offer a total explanation for the strikingly high proportion of Italian students whose aspirations lay in the sphere of university or equivalent education.

Turning now to the Swedish students, we see that their aspirations were strikingly different from those of their contemporaries in England, France and Italy.

Table 28: Students' Aspirations — SWEDEN		
Aspiration	Number	%
Employment involving no form of studies or training	197	27.6
Full-time studies (not university or equivalent)	169	23.7
University or equivalent	116	16.2
None of these	83	11.6
Employment involving some studies or training	59	8.3
Do not know	51	7.1
Services (i.e. Armed Forces)	23	3.2
Employment involving training leading to professional qualifications	16	2.2
No reply	63	—

More than a quarter of all the Swedish students aimed to enter jobs that involved no studies or training. In Italy, the corresponding proportion had been similarly high — 20%; but in France it was only 10%, and in England 3%.

Altogether four out of every ten Swedes were hoping to continue in full-time education, but less than half of this group were thinking in terms of a university or equivalent institution.

A strikingly high proportion of Swedish students did not know what they wanted to do after completing their upper-secondary education: 7%, compared with 0.8% in Italy, 0.5% in France, and 4% in England.

Another 12% knew what they hoped to do, but their ambitions were not concerned with further studies, or with employment — at least for a while. These students were aiming to go abroad for a year or so, or to do nothing at all, as an antidote to the pressures of their upper-secondary studies.

Some of their comments, and those of other students, help to illustrate their views. Remarks such as, "Have a year off, save some money and go to the USA to study", and "I want to go abroad and work at something I like. Money isn't too important — I want to meet people", were fairly typical.

Other students wanted to "leave school as soon as possible, and start something different: practical studies that lead to a job", or to take up "some occupation in which you feel you're doing something — perhaps nursing or nursery school teaching".

In fact, most students were more concerned with the quality of their life than with financial considerations. Comments such as the following were very rare: "I want a job — anything as long as it is quite well paid".

It would appear that Swedish students' ambitions were less concerned with specifically educational objectives than those of English, French or Italian students were. Whereas nine out of every ten English students' aspirations embodied a perspective of "continuing education", the corresponding proportion in Sweden was only five out of ten.

Finally, we come to German students' aspirations. Only five institutions in one area of the Federal Republic were visited, so the numbers concerned are much smaller than in any of the other countries. Furthermore, two of the schools were vocationally oriented. In one, students were being prepared for jobs involving the use of modern languages — although many of these jobs would have required further studies or training first. The other school was a *Fachschule für Sozialpädagogik*: for this reason, teaching was included as a separate option in the German questionnaires.

Table 29: Students' Aspirations — FEDERAL REPUBLIC OF GERMANY		
Aspiration	Number	%
Full-time studies (other than university or equivalent)	115	31.8
University or equivalent	96	26.5
Employment involving no studies or training	34	9.4
Teaching	34	9.4
Employment involving some form of studies or training	25	6.9
Employment with training leading to professional qualifications	22	6.1
None of these	17	4.7
Do not know	14	3.9
Services (i.e. Armed Forces)	5	1.4
No reply	4	—

More than a quarter of the German students were hoping to attend a university or equivalent institution. Another 32% aimed to go on to some other form of full-time studies. Together these two groups accounted for almost six out of every ten German students. The proportion of English students who hoped to continue in full-time education was almost exactly similar. 13% planned to take up employment involving studies or training (and this excludes the 9% who hoped to teach). So once again, the picture that emerges is one of educationally oriented ambitions. Only a small minority of students did not envisage continuing their formal education in one way or another after the end of upper-secondary school.

Our examination of students' aspirations in the five countries has revealed some similarities and differences. In some cases, we need to look at specific national situations in order to explain them; but sometimes the reasons for these variations may lie elsewhere.

To take one example: we have seen that the proportion of students aiming to go on to a university or equivalent institution varied considerably from one country to another. It was highest in Italy, followed by France and England, then Germany, and lastly Sweden.

A number of factors have already been cited as possible and partial explanations for these differences. The system of university admission was one: rigorous selection process in England restricts the number of students. The "final marks" system in Sweden, and a *numerus clausus* policy in Germany, produce similar effects. But in France and Italy, all those who are successful in the *baccalauréat* and *maturità* level examinations have an automatic right of entry to university.

Two other groups of factors concerned the choice of schools which participated in the research, and national differences in the types of opportunities available to upper-secondary school leavers. But there are other factors which transcend national frontiers. One of these relates to what might be termed a student's "self image", which is reflected in his or her ambitions.

This self image develops in the context of the family, the school, and the wider society. Parents, teachers, friends and the mass media convey certain norms regarding a young person's future.

For example, in some families, a strong university tradition might exist. This may take the form of a particular institution or subject, or a general assumption and expectation that every member of the family will receive a university education.

Similarly, many schools' curriculum and pattern of teaching-learning relationships foster a climate of expectations in which a student's transition to tertiary education becomes almost an automatic process.

Such conventions, particularly if they are reinforced by a student's peer group, can be powerful influences. Hence, some students come to regard themselves as university material, while others do not. Furthermore, we know from previous research[1] that social class is a relevant factor here. The untapped "pool of ability" referred to by the Robbins Committee contained many children from "working class" homes whose potential attainment level equalled that of many "middle class" pupils. But a striking contrast existed between the expectations surrounding these two groups — early leaving and employment for one, upper-secondary and perhaps tertiary education for the other. J.W.B. Douglas's work makes this point strongly[2].

Apart from his "self-image", a student's perceptions of opportunities available to him with and without a university degree might also affect his aspirations. For example, a number of English students appeared to believe that opportunities for graduates were diminishing rather than increasing in scope, and that the spectre of graduate unemployment was growing. This might lead students to select an option promising more tangible rewards than a university degree seemed to do. For instance, they might choose a job providing opportunities to gain professional qualifications in law, accountancy or nursing.

These points are discussed in greater detail in the section on students' opportunity perceptions. But first let us see whether two variables often alleged to account for differences in aspirations, namely sex and social class, appear to do so in our research findings. For this purpose, we shall look only at English students' aspirations.

Firstly, the relationship between aspirations and sex:

Table 30: The Relationship between Aspirations and Sex — ENGLISH STUDENTS				
Aspiration	Male students Number	Row %	Female students Number	Row %
University or equivalent	230	57.6	162	40.6
College of Education (i.e. teacher training)	36	29.8	83	68.6
Other full-time studies	77	50.7	72	47.4
Employment involving studies or training leading to professional qualifications	71	55.9	48	37.8
Employment involving some other form of studies or training	97	51.1	87	45.8
Employment involving no studies or training	16	50.0	16	50.0
Services (i.e. Armed Forces)	16	66.7	8	33.3
None of these	4	50.0	4	50.0
Do not know	24	55.8	16	37.2

[1] See, for example, the Report on Higher Education published by the Robbins Committee, 1964.

[2] J.W.B. Douglas, J.M. Ross & H.R. Simpson: "All Our Future", 1968.

Note: Row percentages do not always add up to exactly 100
per cent, because students who did not state their sex
have been excluded from the table.

The main contrasts between male and female students' aspirations lay in the proportions aiming at university or equivalent level courses, at employment leading to professional qualifications, and at College of Education. In the first two cases, male students were predominant, whereas female students accounted for more than two thirds of the College of Education aspirants.

These findings will cause little surprise. Large-scale research such as the Schools Council's[1] has already shown that differences between male and female students' ambitions persist. But why do they? Explanations have been sought in parents' and teachers' expectations (see page 319) and the subsequent channelling of boys and girls into so-called appropriate paths. Whereas a "bright" boy might have been urged to aim for university, his female counterpart would be directed towards a College of Education.

Arguably these differences have disappeared to some extent in recent years, as traditional views of male and female roles in society have increasingly been questioned. But contrasts are still evident, reflecting, perhaps, persistent assumptions which are implicit — if not explicit — in school curricula, and parents' and teachers' expectations.

Let us now examine the relationship between aspirations and students' social background as indicated by their father's occupation. Once again, we shall look at figures relating only to England, rather than all five countries.

[1] Sixth Form Survey. Schools Council. 1970.

Table 31: The Relationship between Aspirations and Social Background
— ENGLISH MALE STUDENTS

Aspiration   Father's occupation

	Professional or higher managerial		Lower managerial or senior		Other non -manual (skilled)		Skilled manual		Semi- and unskilled	
	No.	Col. %	No.	Col. %	No.	Col. %	No.	Col. %	No.	Col. %
University or equivalent	38	73.1	80	43.0	40	37.4	40	32.0	10	25.0
College of Education	3	5.8	15	8.1	6	5.6	7	5.6	1	2.5
Other full-time studies	2	3.8	29	15.6	14	13.1	14	11.2	6	15.0
Employment leading to professional qualifications	2	3.8	21	11.3	16	15.0	22	17.6	4	10.0
Employment involving some other form of studies or training	5	9.6	22	11.8	19	17.8	24	19.2	13	32.5
Employment involving no studies or training	–	–	2	1.1	4	3.7	3	2.4	3	7.5
Services (i.e. Armed Forces)	1	1.9	5	2.7	2	1.9	6	4.8	1	2.5
None of these	–	–	2	1.1	–	–	–	–	1	2.5
Do not know	1	1.9	7	3.8	5	4.7	9	7.2	–	–

Table 32: The Relationship between Aspirations and Social Background
— ENGLISH FEMALE STUDENTS

Aspiration   Father's occupation

	Professional or higher managerial		Lower managerial or senior		Other non -manual (skilled)		Skilled manual		Semi- and unskilled	
	No.	Col. %	No.	Col. %	No.	Col. %	No.	Col. %	No.	Col. %
University or equivalent	38	47.5	62	35.0	23	31.5	16	20.0	9	23.7
College of Education	12	15.0	30	16.9	12	16.4	12	15.0	11	28.9
Other full-time studies	13	16.3	30	16.9	6	8.2	12	15.0	3	7.9
Employment leading to professional qualifications	4	5.0	20	11.3	7	9.6	9	11.3	2	5.3
Employment involving some other form of studies or training	7	8.8	23	13.0	13	17.8	20	25.0	11	28.9
Employment involving no studies or training	3	3.8	1	0.6	2	2.7	5	6.3	2	5.3
Services (i.e. Armed Forces)	–	–	2	1.1	3	4.1	3	3.8	–	–
None of these	1	1.3	–	–	3	4.1	–	–	–	–
Do not know	2	2.5	7	4.0	4	5.5	3	3.8	–	–

Amongst male students, those from professional or higher managerial families stood out clearly from the rest. 73% were aiming at university or equivalent courses of study, compared with 43% from lower managerial or senior technical homes. This proportion dropped to 32% in the case of students from skilled manual backgrounds, and 25% of those whose father was a semi- or un-skilled worker.

On the other hand, one third of male students from this last group hoped to enter employment involving non-professional training or studies. Only 10% from higher managerial or professional backgrounds aimed to do so.

So there would appear to be a general relationship between social class and aspirations. But it is worthwhile noting that the main contrasts were between those from professional or higher managerial (class I) families and those from semi- and un-skilled (classes IV and V) backgrounds. Between these extremes, differences between the other occupational groups, representing classes II and III, were barely discernible.

The pattern of female students' aspirations was broadly similar. However, contrasts in the proportions aiming for university were less marked, even though the highest percentage was still found among students from professional or higher managerial homes.

To summarise

In all the countries except Sweden, the aspirations of most students involved some form of studies or training. The proportion who hoped to go on to university or an equivalent course of studies varied from 60% in Italy, 43% in France, and 36% in England, to 26% in Germany and 16% in Sweden.

Only a minority of students in each country aimed to enter employment involving no further studies or training after completing their upper-secondary education. In Sweden, this group accounted for 28% of all students. 20% of Italian students fell into this category, but only 9% or 10% of French and German, and 3% of English students did so.

Cross-tabulations based on the English figures suggested that there was a general relationship between aspirations and sex and social background. To take one example, students from professional or higher managerial homes were more likely to have university aspirations than those from other social groups. And male students more frequently hoped to go to university, and less often aimed to attend a College of Education, than female students.

(b) Students' Expectations

We have seen what students in the various countries hoped to do after completing their upper-secondary course. But did they think that they would actually be able to achieve these aims? This distinction between aspirations and expectations is often not made, although it is an important one. Consequently, students in each country were asked whether or not they expected to achieve their ambitions. Their replies are shown in Table 33.

Table 33: Students' Expectations of Achieving Their Aspirations — A Summary										
Expectation	ENGLAND		FRANCE		ITALY		SWEDEN		GERMANY	
	No.	%	No.	%	No.	%	No.	%	No.	%
Expect to achieve aspiration	787	73.4	1306	88.0	1497	94.2	552	81.7	312	90.7
Do not expect to achieve aspiration	28	2.6	106	7.1	61	3.8	105	15.5	29	8.4
Unsure/Do not know	257	24.0	72	4.9	32	2.0	19	2.8	3	0.9
No reply	42	–	50	–	38	–	101	–	22	–

Italian students emerged as the most confident, with 94% of them expecting to achieve their aspirations. German and French students were close behind: 91% and 88% respectively thought that they would be successful. Only in England did this proportion fall below the 75% mark.

In the circumstances, it is worth looking at the English figures in more detail. First of all, let us see whether male students were more confident than female students, or vice versa.

Table 34: The Relationship between Expectations and Sex — ENGLISH STUDENTS				
Expectation	Male Students		Female Students	
	No.	Col. %	No.	Col. %
Expect to achieve aspiration	409	70.2	363	72.9
Do not expect to achieve aspiration	17	2.9	8	1.6
Unsure/Do not know	134	23.0	113	22.7

The difference between male and female students in this respect was marginal. Girls were slightly more confident of achieving their aspirations than boys were.

So what about the *type* of aspiration that students had? For instance, were those who hoped to go to university less confident of achieving this goal than students whose ambitions concerned employment involving professional training? Table 35 suggests that this was so.

Table 35: The Relationship between Expectations and Aspirations — ENGLISH MALE STUDENTS

Aspiration	Expectation					
	Expect to achieve aspiration		Do not expect to achieve aspiration		Unsure/Do not know	
	No.	Row %	No.	Row %	No.	Row %
University or equivalent	165	71.7	6	2.6	58	25.2
College of Education	29	80.6	2	5.6	5	13.9
Other full-time studies	51	66.2	1	1.3	22	28.6
Employment involving professional training/studies	58	81.7	1	1.4	12	16.9
Employment with some other form of training/studies	75	77.3	6	6.2	15	15.5
Employment with no training/studies	13	81.3	–	–	3	18.7
Services (i.e. Armed Forces)	13	81.3	1	6.3	2	12.5

Table 36: The Relationship between Expectations and Aspirations
— ENGLISH FEMALE STUDENTS

Aspiration	Expectation					
	Expect to achieve aspiration		Do not expect to achieve aspiration		Unsure/Do not know	
	No.	Row %	No.	Row %	No.	Row %
University or equivalent	120	74.1	3	1.9	39	24.1
College of Education	73	88.0	–	–	8	9.6
Other full-time studies	49	68.1	1	1.4	18	25.0
Employment involving professional training/studies	36	75.0	–	–	12	25.0
Employment with some other form of training/studies	64	73.6	3	3.4	18	20.7
Employment with no training/studies	12	75.0	–	–	4	25.0
Services (i.e. Armed Forces)	6	75.0	–	–	2	25.0

NOTE: Because the "no reply" category has been excluded, row percentages do not always total exactly one hundred per cent

Table 35 shows that the male students most confident of achieving their aspiration were those who hoped to enter employment involving professional training or studies. Students who were aiming at university or other full-time education were most pessimistic about their chances of success.

Among female students (Table 36), College of Education aspirants were the most optimistic. Girls hoping to begin other full-time studies — but not at university — were least confident of achieving their aspirations.

To summarise

In each country, the vast majority of students were confident of achieving their aspirations. In Italy, 94% of students fell into this category; only in England did the percentage fall below the 75% mark.

A further examination of the English figures revealed that students with educational ambitions were least optimistic about their chances of success (although this was not true in the case of girls who hoped to attend a College of Education). But sex did not appear to be a relevant factor: boys were not significantly more or less confident than girls.

One could speculate at length about the reasons for differences between countries in this respect. Inevitably, individual differences in personality make some people more confident of achieving their ambitions than others. But students' perceptions of the availability of particular options could also be relevant. Information and advice from parents, teachers, friends and the mass media would colour these perceptions.

In addition, real differences in systems of university admission mean that students in England would have justifiable anxieties about their chances of success with university applications. French and Italian students would not have the same worry, provided they passed the *baccalauréat* or *maturità* level examinations.

In fact, the reason given by students themselves tended to confirm this. 124 English and 63 Swedish students thought that required levels of attainment would prevent them from achieving their aspirations. They were possibly referring to "final marks" in Sweden, and G.C.E. "A" level examination grades in England. The degree of competition for places was the reason given by a further 75 English students.

The number of students to whom this question applied in the other three countries was comparatively small. This meant that replies represented too tiny a proportion of students to justify analysis. For instance, 16 German students gave the degree of competition for places as their reason for expecting not to achieve their aspirations.

(c) Students' Perceptions Concerning Educational and Employment Opportunities

Students in each country were asked to describe the types of opportunities that existed for young people like themselves at the end of their upper-secondary course, and after further studies. They were also asked to assess their job prospects at these two points in time.

(i) Opportunities and Prospects after Upper-secondary Studies

Table 37 shows the extent to which students in each country thought that their job prospects would be better or worse after upper-secondary education.

Table 37: Students' Assessment of Their Job Prospects After Upper-secondary Studies										
	ENGLAND		FRANCE		ITALY		SWEDEN		GERMANY	
Prospects will be	No.	%	No.	%	No.	%	No.	%	No.	%
Much better after	844	77.1	744	50.2	374	23.4	233	32.0	263	73.3
A little better after	222	20.3	397	26.8	823	51.6	351	48.1	64	17.8
About the same	21	1.9	190	12.8	319	20.0	102	14.0	19	5.3
A little worse	6	0.5	62	4.2	45	2.8	28	3.8	8	2.2
Much worse	2	0.2	71	4.8	33	2.1	14	1.9	5	1.4
Do not know	–	–	19	1.3	2	0.1	–	–	–	–
No reply	19	–	51	–	32	–	48	–	7	–

Replies to this question revealed some striking differences between students from the various countries. In England and Germany, roughly three out of every four students felt that their job prospects would be "much better". But in France only half of the students shared this view, while in Sweden this proportion dropped to one third, and in Italy to one quarter.

A rather different picture emerges when one looks at the proportion of students who thought that job prospects would be worse after upper-secondary studies. Once again, English and German students were the most optimistic: in England less than 1% felt that prospects would be worse; and in Germany 3.6% did so. But this proportion rose to 4.9% in Italy, 5.7% in Sweden, and 9% in France.

These figures become more meaningful if one knows more about the type of opportunities that students had in mind — both after upper-secondary education and before. So students were asked to describe both of these. Their replies revealed another interesting fact — that many of them had never considered leaving school at the end of the compulsory stage. For these students, the transition from lower- to upper-secondary education had been a more or less automatic process. But for the majority, some weighing-up of the pro's and con's had been involved.

England

The largest single group of English students, representing 27% of the total, had considered no alternatives to upper-secondary education, because they had never thought of leaving school at the end of the compulsory stage. A further 23% mentioned employment involving some form of training or studies (such as an apprenticeship) as a possible alternative. 14% of students referred to jobs providing opportunities to obtain professional qualifications. Less than one student in ten mentioned employment involving no studies or training at all, and only two students in every hundred felt that opportunities for 15-16 year olds were limited.

English students' opinions of the types of opportunities that existed after upper-secondary studies varied considerably. These variations seemed to be related to the school or college they were at. For instance, some boys from a "secondary modern" type institution claimed that, "Many opportunities would be available if I gained 'O' levels" and "Virtually any employment opportunities would be open if I gained 'A' levels or higher". On occasions, their degree of optimism was undoubtedly misplaced. One student alleged that after his present course of studies, he would be able to go to "a collage for the training of becoming a doctor". Another envisaged becoming an "arcetect, cartoonist or comershal artist"% One must remember that the academic attainment level of these students was lower than in some of the other English schools or colleges. Many of the boys were engaged in G.C.E. 'O' level or C.S.E. work — and in this sense were truly "new" upper-secondary students in the Schools Council's definition[1].

The contrast with replies from a boys' grammar school with a strong academic tradition was marked. One student commented, "With only 'A' levels I feel that more exams must be passed or hard work undertaken to get anywhere". The range of opportunities mentioned by boys from this school was somewhat traditional and rigid. After upper-secondary studies, many envisaged options

[1] Schools Council Working Paper 45: 16-19: Growth and Response (i) Curricular bases (1972).

such as university, including medical school; law; the armed services; research work of various types; and the Civil Service.

It is interesting to note that these students' perceptions of opportunities were barely distinguishable from their own aspirations. A few boys had stated ambitions involving "sandwich courses", including the newer "thick sandwich courses" (consisting of three years of higher education preceded and followed by a year in industry). But university aspirations predominated, particularly those concerning Oxbridge and subjects such as law, accountancy, engineering, natural sciences and medicine. And social background influences seemed of little consequence compared with the impact of this school's educational traditions: for instance, the son of a bus driver planned to take the Oxbridge scholarship examinations.

A similar picture emerges from the replies of students at a girls' grammar school with a sixth form unit, again with a strong academic tradition. Their perceptions of opportunities after upper-secondary studies were closely linked with their own aspirations, and centred around: university, College of Education, Polytechnics, the executive level of the Civil Service, banking and the social services.

Perhaps the most detailed and interesting comments about opportunities came from students at a co-educational sixth form college. Many of the remarks were optimistic, and emphasised the pay and prospects angle.

For example, one student felt that "employment with better salaries and possibly better prospects will be available having passed 'A' levels than would have been available with only 'O' level qualifications". Another, taking four subjects at G.C.E. 'A' level, jubilantly predicted that there would be "an abundant supply of jobs".

One student described at length the improvement in opportunities that accompanied 'A' level qualifications: "'A' levels can be the passport to university if the grades are high enough. They also improve one's chances of being accepted in a Polytechnic or College of Education. There is more chance of promotion in Civil Service/local government for candidates with the required number of 'A' level passes".

And another felt that 'A' level qualifications were almost essential at the present time: "Most jobs now stipulate employees to have studied *up to* 'A' level or to have gained 1 or 2 'A' levels. I feel 'O' levels no longer hold the importance they did, say, 5 years ago. The standard is higher".

But perhaps one should leave the last word to the student who paid the following tribute to his upper-secondary education: "I know that I can enter into employment at a higher level. I think I have learnt more about people as well as academic subjects . . .".

Finally, some comments from students at a technical college. In general they too were optimistic about the pay-off of upper-secondary studies in terms of job prospects. One student remarked, "I think it is easier to get any sort of job after 'A' levels. Especially clerical jobs where 'A' levels can give more opportunities". But another was less confident: "(Maybe) I won't get a job because of the unemployment in the country. At least I will be able to think clearer queuing for the dole".

France

Just over a quarter of the French students, when asked to describe the opportunities that existed as alternatives to upper-secondary education, mentioned jobs involving professional or other training or studies. Less than half that proportion referred to employment opportunities in which no training or studies took place. 18% of all French students said that they did not know what opportunities existed at that stage. One student in ten had never considered leaving school, and less than 1% thought that 15-16 year olds would find opportunities limited.

When asked about the opportunities that would be available at the end of upper-secondary education, many French students replied that they thought the *baccalauréat* qualification had very limited value. One student remarked, *"Avec le bac on ne peut pas faire beaucoup de choses. Sans le bac on ne peut rien faire"*. "You can't do much with the *baccalauréat*. Without it you can't do anything".

The consensus seemed to be that without qualifications it would be difficult to get a job, particularly an attractive one. Two students were especially gloomy about their prospects, describing them in terms of, *"Un métier bureaucratique détestable"*, and jobs that were, *"sans avenir, sans gloire, et très peu attrayante"*!

But on the whole, students in France made fewer comments about opportunities before and after upper-secondary education than English students did.

Italy

60% of Italian students thought that employment involving no training or studies was the major alternative to staying on into upper-secondary education. As in France, 10% had never considered leaving school at that stage, so had not considered the alternatives. Another 10% of Italian students said that they did not know what the opportunities for young school leavers were, but only 1.5% thought that prospects were limited.

When asked to describe the types of opportunities that would be available at the end of upper-secondary education, more than half of the Italian students named specific employment or educational opportunities. But one in every six students claimed that with the *maturità* qualification they could go to university, but that was all. This echoes the views of some French students, and possibly helps to explain why such a high proportion of Italians had university aspirations. Only 5% felt that they faced the prospect of unemployment at the end of their upper-secondary course.

Sweden

In general, Swedish students' perceptions of alternatives to upper-secondary education were very vague. 50% mentioned "a job" or "working" or "travelling", but no specific types of opportunities. Another 22% thought that employment involving no training or studies was the major alternative. One student in ten did not know what opportunities existed for those who left school at the end of the compulsory period. But interestingly enough, in a country where 80% or more do stay on — a far higher proportion than in England, France, Italy or Germany — no students said that they had not considered any alternatives because they had never thought of leaving school.

One student's alternative to upper-secondary school was particularly gloomy: "I would probably have been in the underground world; I think that if you're working when you're very young and there's nothing to do in the evenings, the possibility that I would use drugs and alcohol is great".

Several students referred to the possibility of unemployment; "I'd have been without a job in this horrible society" was a fairly typical comment.

When asked to describe the types of opportunities that would exist *after* upper-secondary school, about a third of the Swedish students mentioned specific employment or educational opportunities. 6% of students envisaged that there would be no possibility of obtaining a job, while 20% did not know what opportunities existed, either in general or in relation to their own specific course of studies. Furthermore, one should point out that 145 students (18.7% of the total) failed to answer the question at all. We can only speculate about the reason for this, but it is possible that at least some of these students were unable to think of any opportunities for upper-secondary school leavers.

Federal Republic of Germany

More than 40% of the German students saw employment involving training or studies as the major alternative to upper-secondary education. Another 18% did not know what opportunities existed, and half that proportion had not considered any alternatives because they had never thought of leaving school. A further 9% put forward employment without training or studies as an alternative.

Compared with the Swedes, German students were highly specific about the types of opportunities available to upper-secondary school leavers. 60% of them named particular employment and educational prospects. The possibility of unemployment or of very limited opportunities was mentioned by less than 1% of German students.

(ii) Opportunities and Prospects after Further Studies

Table 38 shows the extent to which students in each country thought their job prospects would be better or worse after further studies following their upper-secondary course:

Table 38: Students' Assessment of Their Job Prospects After Further Studies										
	ENGLAND		FRANCE		ITALY		SWEDEN		GERMANY	
Prospects will be	No.	%	No.	%	No.	%	No.	%	No.	%
Much better after	682	62.6	743	51.8	661	41.5	274	37.8	199	55.4
A little better	276	25.3	421	29.3	651	40.8	317	43.7	122	34.0
About the same	114	10.5	154	10.7	252	15.8	99	13.7	33	9.2
A little worse	11	1.0	59	4.1	15	0.9	19	2.6	4	1.1
Much worse	7	0.6	41	2.9	11	0.7	16	2.2	1	0.3
Do not know	–	–	17	1.2	4	0.3	–	–	–	–
No reply	24	–	99	–	34	–	52	–	7	–

Once again, English students were more optimistic about the improvement in their job prospects than students in the other countries. 63% of them thought that prospects would be "much better" after further studies, compared with 55% in Germany, and 52% in France. Swedish students were the most pessimistic — only 38% felt that prospects would be "much better", and this proportion was only marginally higher in Italy (41.5%).

But in one respect, there was far more consensus than there had been in assessments of job prospects after upper-secondary studies. Then, the proportion of students who thought that prospects would remain "about the same" had ranged from 2% in England to 20% in Italy. But now, approximately 10% of students in England, France and Germany felt that further studies would leave job prospects relatively unchanged. This proportion was only slightly higher in Sweden (14%) and Italy (16%).

Let us now look at each country in a little more detail.

England

When asked about the type of opportunities that would be open to them after a further course of studies, more than half of the English students named specific jobs or types of jobs. But many were dubious about the value of further studies. The views of three students at a co-educational sixth form college illustrate this point:

> "Employment opportunities would for me be no better, I feel. A further 3-4 years' training at university or colleges of further education would not be beneficial to me as I find it a waste of time when graduates leaving these places spend *months* looking for suitable jobs to fit their qualifications. Often they never do".

> "No more (opportunities) than after my present training. Industry is not willing to employ 'over-qualified' people".

> "With a degree in modern languages as I hope to obtain, there is not much option to careers except teaching. Very few translators or interpreters are needed. I think the opportunities are much the same after a university

course in arts as they are for having completed 'A'
levels . . . ."

Students at a technical college were obviously concerned about the link
between further studies and the type of job they led to. One student remarked:

"I'm not too sure because a lot of people I know here
have taken degrees and ended up doing a job totally
different to what they expected".

Another student — this time from a secondary modern type school —
commented:

"University entrance may not necessarily lead to a better
job (more security, more money) nowadays. A college of
further education might well do if the training is
specialised. There can be no guarantee that further
education will secure a better job".

Specialisation was also mentioned by students from a grammar school with
a strong academic tradition. One boy remarked that opportunities after further
studies: " . . . would tend to be of a far more specialised nature in a profession.
Too much specialised education can however lead to difficulties with changing
demands of economy and society".

Clearly, much depended on the type of studies concerned. One student
from another co-educational sixth form college made this point:

"It depends on the course. If I studied a pure science
course it would be difficult to get a job, but if I went
studying applied science it would not be so bad".

But the problem was probably felt most acutely by students at a School of
Art. This was partly due to the fact that — rightly or wrongly — these students
were reluctant to broaden their perspective of opportunities. Comments such as
the following were fairly typical:

"Work is a low form of Art, probably not even real Art".

"After university — work not connected with the degree
taken, which is absurd. I would have to be trained again

for the commercial world, or teach".

However, one student's visions were broader than this, even though his or her spelling was weak:

"Personally I am looking for a vocation on a team of Ecologests or Naturrelests . . ."!

Let us end on that note, and move on to the French students!

France

When asked to describe the types of opportunities that would exist for them after further studies, four out of ten French students named specific jobs. Very few mentioned unemployment (3%) or the prospect of limited opportunities (2%).

Only a small minority made comments about the pro's and con's of tertiary education, as English students had done. But one girl did strike a humorous note, saying that one should be optimistic: she wanted to study languages at university in order to become a teacher, so the possibilities open to her would be: in the teaching profession! *("Soyons optimiste. Etant normalienne et désirant suivre les cours en faculté de langues pour devenir professeur, les possibilités seront: le professorat")*.

Italy

A large number of Italian students (322 = 19.8% of the total) did not reply at all to the question about opportunities after further studies. Of those who did reply, only one student in five named specific jobs or types of employment. 14% did not know what opportunities would exist, either in general or in relation to particular courses of study, and 9% mentioned the possibility of unemployment or limited prospects.

As in France, relatively few Italian students made detailed comments. But the following remarks are worth noting:

". . . I have come to realise that the devaluation in

university qualifications will inevitably lead to a shortage of jobs for the less highly educated. . . . . . And unfortunately, many university graduates — as is happening today — will remain out of work, or will be employed at a lower level than their qualifications merit"

". . . in a few years' time we shall have university graduates working in little offices — not because they can't find work but because they don't really know anything".

". . . we are told that by continuing our studies we'll have a better chance of entering the world of work. All this is just an illusion: all students in upper-secondary education are already destined — apart from a very few — to be unemployed. The years they then spend at university only serve to postpone the time when they will become unemployed . . . .".

'. . . Even if the universities have a range of faculties with a large number of specialised courses, many students can't find jobs corresponding to their particular specialism when they come out of university, so there is an increase in the number of people unemployed".

So graduate unemployment was very much in the thoughts of some Italian students. This is particularly significant when one remembers the high proportion of students whose ambition was to go to university.

Sweden

The proportion of students who failed to answer this question was even higher in Sweden than in Italy (216 students = 27.8%), and of those who did reply, almost one third said that they did not know what opportunities would exist after further studies. Only 20% were able to name specific jobs or types of employment. No students made detailed comments of the kind already quoted from England, France and Italy.

Federal Republic of Germany

Almost half of the German students (46%) were able to name specific employment opportunities that would exist after further studies. Virtually no students mentioned the possibility of unemployment or limited prospects. But as in Sweden, no one made detailed comments of any sort.

CHAPTER 17

STUDENTS' REGRETS CONCERNING UPPER-SECONDARY EDUCATION

Students in each country were asked whether or not they ever regretted staying on into upper-secondary education, and if so, their reasons for this.

First of all, let us look at Table 39, which shows the frequency with which students in the various countries regretted continuing into upper-secondary education:

Table 39: Frequency of Students' Regrets Concerning Upper-secondary Education										
Frequency	ENGLAND		FRANCE		ITALY		SWEDEN		GERMANY	
	No.	%	No.	%	No.	%	No.	%	No.	%
Often	26	2.3	37	2.5	74	4.6	8	1.1	6	1.7
Sometimes	153	13.8	92	6.3	196	12.2	102	14.3	13	3.6
Very occasionally	312	28.1	250	17.1	202	12.5	166	23.2	57	15.7
Never	619	55.8	1,081	74.0	1,141	70.7	439	61.4	286	79.0
No reply	4	—	74	—	15	—	62	—	4	—

The majority of students in every country claimed that they never regretted staying on into upper-secondary education. But the size of that majority varied considerably from one country to another. In Germany, it represented four-fifths of all students, and in France, three quarters. Yet only 61% of Swedish students, and 56% of English students, never had any regrets about their upper-secondary education.

Since English students emerge as the most regretful, let us take a closer look at this group, and see, for example, whether their frequency of regret is related to either their social background or to their main reason for staying on at school.

Firstly, their main reason for staying on at school: (*Note*: This variable comes from the curriculum and teaching/learning questionnaire, not from the sociological one. Three reasons only were selected for the purposes of this cross-tabulation: "I wanted qualifications which would lead to a better job"; "I wanted to go on to some form of higher education"; and "I could not decide what else to do.")

Table 40: The Relationship Between Frequency of Regret and Main Reason for Staying On Into Upper-Secondary Education – ENGLISH STUDENTS

Frequency of Regret	Main Reason for staying on:					
	I wanted qualifications which would lead to a better job		I could not decide what elso to do		I wanted to go on to some form of higher education	
	No.	Col. %	No.	Col. %	No.	Col. %
Often	5	1.5	4	8.3	2	0.8
Sometimes	43	12.6	15	31.3	25	9.5
Very occasionally	104	30.4	17	35.4	67	25.6
Never	188	55.0	12	25.0	168	64.1

The largest proportion of students who never had any regrets was found amongst those whose main reason for staying on into upper-secondary school was connected with higher education. This pattern is repeated throughout: these students consistently expressed less regret than those whose main reason for staying on concerned qualifications for a job. And students who had been unable to decide what else to do were more regretful than either of these two groups.

Let us now turn to the relationship between frequency of regret and students' social background:

Table 41: The Relationship Between Frequency of Regret and Social Background — ENGLISH MALE STUDENTS

Frequency of Regret:	Social Background (Father's Occupation):									
	Professional or higher managerial		Managerial or senior technical		Other non-manual		Skilled manual		Semi- or unskilled manual	
	No.	Col. %	No.	Col. %	No.	Col. %	No.	Col. %	No.	Col. %
Often	1	1.9	4	2.2	2	1.9	6	4.8	1	2.5
Sometimes	8	15.4	26	14.0	17	15.9	17	13.6	11	27.5
Very occasionally	7	13.5	50	26.9	37	34.6	41	32.8	8	20.0
Never	36	69.2	106	57.0	51	47.7	61	48.8	19	47.5

Table 42: The Relationship Between Frequency of Regret and Social Background — ENGLISH FEMALE STUDENTS

Frequency of Regret:	Social Background (Father's Occupation):									
	Professional or higher managerial		Managerial or senior technical		Other non-manual		Skilled manual		Semi- or unskilled manual	
	No.	Col. %	No.	Col. %	No.	Col. %	No.	Col. %	No.	Col. %
Often	—	—	2	1.1	1	1.4	2	2.5	—	—
Sometimes	3	3.8	27	15.3	4	5.5	8	10.0	6	15.8
Very occasionally	30	37.5	46	26.0	22	30.1	27	33.8	10	26.3
Never	47	58.8	101	57.1	46	63.0	42	52.5	22	57.9

Tables 41 and 42 show that contrasts between students from different social backgrounds were greater amongst male than female students. Amongst the former, the proportion of students who never regretted staying on into upper-secondary education fell from 69% of those from professional or higher managerial backgrounds to 48% of boys from "other non-manual" or "semi- or un-skilled manual" families. But there were no such differences between female students. In fact, the highest proportion of girls who never had any regrets concerning their upper-secondary education was found amongst those from "other non-manual" backgrounds.

We have seen how often students in the various countries claimed to have regrets concerning their upper-secondary education; let us now look at their reasons for regret. This question obviously applied to only a minority of students, so the numbers shown in Table 43 are often small.

Table 43: Students' Reasons for Regret Concerning Upper-Secondary Education.

Reason for Regret:	ENGLAND		FRANCE		ITALY		SWEDEN		GERMANY	
	No.	%	No.	%	No.	%	No.	%	No.	%
Lack of financial independence	120	11.0	–	–	17	1.1	33	5.0	29	8.2
Work load; exam pressure	117	10.7	40	2.8	27	1.7	62	9.5	16	4.5
Uncertainty or anxiety about links with employment or further studies	73	6.7	52	3.7	76	4.8	20	3.1	2	0.6
Curriculum; organisation or pattern of studies	45	4.1	131	9.3	207	13.2	43	6.6	10	2.8
Lack of freedom, adult status or independence – in school	37	3.4	4	0.3	5	0.3	–	–	–	–
Lack of freedom, adult status or independence – in general	40	3.7	53	3.8	1	0.1	–	–	6	1.7
Boredom	21	1.9	–	–	–	–	–	–	–	–
Other reasons	24	2.2	10	0.7	94	6.0	45	6.9	3	0.8
Question does not apply	616	56.4	1,081	76.9	1,142	72.7	439	68.9	287	81.1
No reply	21	–	128	–	58	–	123	–	12	–

Table 43 reveals some striking differences between countries. For example, 13% of Italian students, and 9% of French students, gave as their reason for regret the upper-secondary curriculum or pattern of studies. Only 3% of German, and 4% of English students did so.

By way of contrast, just under 11% of English students, and 10% of Swedish students, cited work load or examination pressure as a reason for regret. In the other three countries, only between 2% and 5% did so.

A further 11% of English students complained of a lack of financial independence. This was in fact the reason for regret most frequently mentioned by English students.

Apart from these contrasts, Table 43 also reveals some surprising omissions. One might, for instance, have expected a lack of freedom, adult status or independence in school to have been mentioned by more students. Similarly, relatively few students cited uncertainty or anxiety about links between upper-secondary education and employment or further studies as a reason for regret.

So — to summarise — it would appear that English students' main regrets concerned work load or examination pressure, and their lack of financial independence. In the case of French and Italian students, the curriculum or pattern of studies represented the most common reason for regret. In Germany, lack of financial independence, and in Sweden, work load or examination pressure, were most frequently mentioned.

However, another part of the questionnaire revealed deeper and wider ranging areas of concern, particularly among French and Italian students. At the end of the sociological questionnaire, a space had been left blank for students' comments. In Germany and Sweden, this was often not used, but in France and Germany, and — to a lesser extent — England, students did take advantage of this opportunity to air their views.

Many of the comments concerned the link between upper-secondary education and further studies or employment, or the provision of counselling and guidance. These will be dealt with in the following chapter. Others dealt with the research project itself; and a relatively small number of students made specific comments — generally adverse in nature — about their particular school and/or teaching staff.

But a sizeable minority of students made comments on wider issues, such as the whole relationship between education and the rest of society. Let us look at some of these comments in a little more detail:

France

Some French students expressed concern about the function of upper-secondary education. One student claimed that:

> "School does not help us to know ourselves, but only to alienate us, to condition us into becoming, 'a good little blind capitalist policeman'...... Everything must change! Especially the *lycée* which is nothing but a prison, an asylum, a direct route to the Army and Fascism".

A similar comment was made by another French student:

> "Not all young people want to enter society as it is at present, and contribute to the continuity of a capitalist system of which they are the victims. They don't want to be directed towards materialistic goals".

In complete contrast came the following, surprisingly right-wing, remark:

> "This questionnaire is nothing but the reflection of a left-wing society. Students in school shouldn't have the right to express their views: they are there to learn".

Other students were more concerned about the nature and quality of educational goals:

> "Education's *actual* goal is to turn us into workers who can increase the country's rate of economic growth. It's not concerned about the lives (in every sense of the word of the individuals for whom it's responsible .... Education's goal *should* be to encourage the growth of harmonious personal relationships, to develop our personality, to tell us about all the problems we face .... It should also develop in us a taste for Art .... and enable us to feel at ease in any social group".

It is worth noting that comments criticising education and society were made most frequently by students from strikingly "middle class" schools (in terms of the catchment area, and the social background of the students themselves). This phenomenon of rebellion against the existing social system has been described by writers and journalists so often that it has become almost a cliché. But it is none-the-less interesting to see that a research project such as this has unearthed a similar dissatisfaction with society as a whole.

Unfortunately — but not surprisingly — solutions were conspicuous by their absence. The only remedies suggested by these students tended to be a total reform of the school system and the destruction of capitalist society. But the alternatives envisaged, the means involved, and the implications of such actions, were never discussed.

However, one French student *did* put forward some specific suggestions, albeit extreme and alarming ones (particularly to English ears)! One only hopes that his intentions were not serious; may be he simply disliked questionnaires:

> "When I am grown up and have a lot of money, I shall buy a lot of dynamite, and then there won't be any more *lycées*, and even fewer questionnaires on this subject, and no more English courses, because I am an Anglophobe. (And to be one you don't need to be grown up, to have a lot of money or a large amount of dynamite).
>
> But while I'm waiting, ... as I don't like *lycées*, I'm amusing myself by making holes in the desks, breaking the chairs, making the teachers tremble with fright, and filling in questionnaires in a facile way".

Italy

A large number of Italian students made comments emphasising the need for complete social and education reform, and criticising the remoteness of schools from the rest of society. A few quotations may help to illustrate their views:

> "The problems of the school must be tackled at the base by radically changing the present structure, without bothering about small or partial reforms. Only in this way can the school progress at the same rate as social change".

"(Reforms are needed) from the institutions right through to the curricula and the behaviour of teachers. Curricula should be able to adapt themselves to the political and economic situation in industry".

But a contrasting view was held by the following student:

"School is subordinated to industry and consequently embodies a capitalist system that I deplore. If you really want to improve it, you have to change the whole system. Reforms within the school aren't valid for me, since those will simply serve industry's interests . . . ."

"Schools isolate the student from the problems of a worker of the same age; . . . . they try to create a gulf between us and the political life of the country".

"The school system is wrong for our way of life. By considering the school as a world apart they don't give us a chance to widen our horizons . . . . Students change their way of life when they enter a classroom. True friendship doesn't exist — you have to look for this outside school. And this is a very important problem for me from the human point of view".

There is a striking similarity between these comments and those of French students. Both groups, like English students, were concerned about the transition between upper-secondary school and employment or further studies, and the school's provision of information and guidance about this process. This will be discussed in the following chapter.

But unlike English students, the French and Italians also expressed considerable concern about wider issues, and so broadened the concept of regrets about upper-secondary education. This degree of social and political awareness and interest was not evident amongst English, German and Swedish students. This is not to say that it did not exist, but simply that it failed to come to light in students' replies. The contrast between French and Italian students on the one hand, and English, German and Swedish students on the others, in this respect, is clear and striking.

CHAPTER 18

COUNSELLING AND GUIDANCE: THE SITUATION IN THE SCHOOLS, AND STUDENTS' VIEWS CONCERNING IT.

The final section of the sociological questionnaire for students dealt with their views concerning the counselling and guidance that they had received at school or college, and would like to receive. In this chapter, students' replies are compared with those of teachers and others concerned with providing counselling and guidance. It should perhaps be pointed out here that the term "counselling and guidance" is used merely as a convenient piece of shorthand referring to the provision of various forms of information, advice and guidance concerning educational, employment and also personal matters.

a) Students' Views of Counselling and Guidance

Students in each country were asked to say how much information, advice and guidance they felt they had received at school or college concerning education and employment. Their replies are shown in Tables 44 and 45.

Table 44: The Amount of Information, Advice and Guidance Provided By The School or College About *Employment* Matters.

Amount:	ENGLAND		FRANCE		ITALY		SWEDEN		GERMANY	
	No.	%	No.	%	No.	%	No.	%	No.	%
A lot	204	19.4	151	10.7	79	5.1	17	2.4	20	5.5
Some	430	40.9	498	35.4	423	27.3	177	24.7	104	28.7
Hardly any	288	27.4	460	32.7	393	25.4	334	46.6	109	30.0
None at all	129	12.3	298	21.2	653	42.2	189	26.4	130	35.8
No reply	63	—	127	—	80	—	60	—	3	—

Table 45: The Amount of Information, Advice and Guidance Provided By The School or College About *Educational* Matters.

Amount:	ENGLAND		FRANCE		ITALY		SWEDEN		GERMANY	
	No.	%	No.	%	No.	%	No.	%	No.	%
A lot	388	35.9	388	26.1	161	10.6	109	15.1	18	5.0
Some	468	43.3	644	43.4	558	36.9	381	52.8	123	34.5
Hardly any	162	15.0	313	21.1	383	25.3	176	24.4	102	28.6
None at all	63	5.8	139	9.4	411	27.2	56	7.8	114	31.9
No reply	33	–	50	–	115	–	55	–	9	–

Tables 44 and 45 reveal some striking similarities — and also contrasts — between students from the various countries. With the exception of Germany, students everywhere felt that they had received considerably more information, advice and guidance about education than about employment. In Sweden, for example, only 2% of students considered that their school had provided them with "a lot" of information, advice and guidance about employment, but 15% of students thought so in the case of education.

Generally speaking, English students felt that they had received more information, advice and guidance than those in other countries. One in five considered that they had received "a lot" about employment, compared with 5% of German and Italian, and 2% of Swedish students. And whereas only 12% of English students claimed that they had received "none at all" 26% of Swedish, 36% of German, and 42% of Italian students did so.

These contrasts were equally, if not more, striking in the case of educational information, advice and guidance. More than one third of English students felt that they had received "a lot". Only 5% of German, 11% of Italian, and 15% of Swedish students shared this view.

Obviously, these figures need to be interpreted with some caution. Partly because of the subjective (and intentionally so) nature of the questions, partly because some students' replies referred to the institution in which they had spent their lower- as well as upper-secondary years, while others referred to an exclusively upper-secondary school or college.

Furthermore, these replies do not necessarily represent a value judgement in the sense that students who felt that they had received only a little counselling and guidance were dissatisfied with this situation. In order to get an indication of students' degree of satisfaction with existing counselling and guidance provision, we need to examine their views concerning (i) the helpfulness of that information and guidance, (ii) the amount and type of counselling and guidance that they would like to receive.

Firstly, how helpful had students found the information, advice and guidance that they had received? The answer is given in Tables 46 and 47:

Table 46: Students' Assessment of the Employment Information, Advice and Guidance Provided by the School or College.

Assessment:	ENGLAND		FRANCE		ITALY		SWEDEN		GERMANY	
	No.	%	No.	%	No.	%	No.	%	No.	%
Very helpful	149	14.8	76	11.8	64	7.1	15	3.1	9	4.2
Fairly helpful	359	35.7	259	40.3	324	36.0	109	22.8	47	22.2
Not really helpful	307	30.5	231	36.0	388	43.1	259	54.1	108	50.9
Not at all helpful	98	9.7	76	11.8	125	13.9	96	20.0	48	22.6
Question does not apply	94	9.3	–	–	–	–	–	–	–	–
No reply	107	–	892	–	727	–	298	–	154	–
	(= 9.6% total)		(= 58% total)		(=45% total)		(=38% total)		(=42% total)	

Table 47: Students' Assessment of the Education Information, Advice and Guidance Provided by the School or College.

Assessment:	ENGLAND		FRANCE		ITALY		SWEDEN		GERMANY	
	No.	%	No.	%	No.	%	No.	%	No.	%
Very helpful	289	27.2	141	17.4	115	10.8	69	11.8	11	5.0
Fairly helpful	482	45.4	366	45.2	460	43.2	278	47.4	72	33.0
Not really helpful	175	16.5	236	29.1	404	38.0	210	35.8	111	50.9
Not at all helpful	65	6.1	67	8.3	85	8.0	30	5.1	24	11.0
Question does not apply	51	4.8	–	–	–	–	–	–	–	–
No reply	52	–	724	–	564	–	190	–	148	–
	(=4.8% total)		(=47% total)		(=35% total)		(=25% total)		(=40.4% total)	

Tables 46 and 47 need to be interpreted with caution, because in every country except England, a sizeable proportion of students failed to answer the questions at all. Bearing this in mind, and also remembering the two "caveats" given earlier (about the subjective nature of students' replies, and the fact that not all replies referred to exclusively upper-secondary institutions), we are nevertheless left with the impression that English students were more satisfied than those in any of the other countries. For example, more than a quarter of the English students claimed to have found the school's information, advice and guidance about education "very helpful". The corresponding proportion in Italy and Sweden was 11% and 12%.

Let us now see how much information, advice and guidance students felt they would like to receive, compared with the amount currently provided by their school or college.

Table 48:
The Amount of Information, Advice and Guidance Wanted by Students.

Amount:	ENGLAND		FRANCE		ITALY		SWEDEN		GERMANY	
	No.	%	No.	%	No.	%	No.	%	No.	%
Much more	554	50.4	1,065	70.9	1,156	73.2	515	70.5	285	79.2
A little more	342	31.1	316	21.0	351	22.2	175	24.0	60	16.7
About the same amount as now	198	18.0	108	7.2	68	4.3	36	4.9	13	3.6
A little less	5	0.5	2	0.1	1	0.1	2	0.3	–	–
Much less	1	0.1	12	0.8	3	0.2	2	0.3	2	0.6
No reply	14	–	31	–	49	–	47	–	6	–

In every country except England, at least seven out of ten students wanted "much more" information, advice and guidance than they currently received. Everywhere, under 1% of students asked for "less". Using this criterion, English students again appeared to be more satisfied with existing provision than those in other countries. Only 50% wanted "much more" information, advice and guidance, and 18% asked for "about the same amount as now", compared with between 4% and 7% in the other countries.

Let us take a closer look at the English figures, and see whether or not this degree of satisfaction varied with students' aspirations.

Table 49: The Relationship Between Aspirations and the Amount of Information, Advice and Guidance Asked for by English Male Students.

Amount:	Aspiration: University or equivalent %	College of Education %	Other full-time studies %	Employment with professional training %	Employment with non-professional training %	Employment without training %	Services %	None of these %	Do not know %
Much more	55.2 (127)	58.3 (21)	66.2 (51)	60.6 (43)	42.3 (41)	56.3 (9)	31.3 (5)	50.0 (2)	66.7 (16)
A little more	32.2 (74)	25.0 (9)	28.6 (22)	21.1 (15)	39.2 (38)	37.5 (6)	43.8 (7)	25.0 (1)	20.8 (5)
About the same amount as now	12.2 (28)	16.7 (6)	2.6 (2)	18.3 (13)	17.5 (17)	6.3 (1)	25.0 (4)	25.0 (1)	8.3 (2)
A little less	0.4 (1)	–	–	–	1.0 (1)	–	–	–	4.2 (1)
Much less	–	–	1.3 (1)	–	–	–	–	–	–

Note: The number of replies to which each percentage refers is given in brackets below the percentage.

Table 50: The Relationship Between Aspirations and the Amount of Information, Advice and Guidance Asked For by English Female Students.

Amount:	Aspiration: University or equivalent %	College of Education %	Other full-time studies %	Employment with professional training %	Employment with non-professional training %	Employment without training %	Services %	None of these %	Do not know %
Much more	42.0 (68)	26.5 (22)	54.2 (39)	43.8 (21)	37.9 (33)	81.3 (13)	50.0 (4)	25.0 (1)	62.5 (10)
A little more	34.0 (55)	38.6 (32)	27.8 (20)	25.0 (12)	31.0 (27)	12.5 (2)	25.0 (2)	25.0 (1)	18.7 (3)
About the same amount as now	21.6 (35)	32.5 (27)	16.7 (12)	29.2 (14)	25.3 (22)	6.3 (1)	25.0 (2)	50.0 (2)	12.5 (2)
A little less	0.6 (1)	–	1.4 (1)	–	–	–	–	–	–
Much less	–	–	–	–	–	–	–	–	–

Note: The number of replies to which each percentage refers is given in brackets below the percentage.

Some of the numbers in Tables 49 and 50 are small, but they do suggest that students' aspirations *were* related to their request for more counselling and guidance. For instance, among the girls, only 26% of those who hoped to attend a College of Education asked for "much more" information, advice and guidance. This proportion rose to a staggering 81% of those who aimed to enter a job involving no further studies or training.

Among the boys, the contrasts were less extreme. The highest proportion who requested "much more" information, advice and guidance was found amongst those who either hoped to continue their full-time studies (but not at University or College of Education), or who did not know what they wanted to do. The lowest proportion was found amongst the small number of boys who aimed to enter one of the Armed Services.

These figures serve to reinforce the impression that students with more traditional or conventional aspirations (such as the Services in the case of boys, College of Education in the case of girls, and University or equivalent studies in the case of both sexes) tend to receive more information, advice and guidance than those whose aims are less familiar to counselling and guidance staff.

Before we move on to examine the work of these staff, let us look at one final and important aspect of students' views: their ideas concerning the type of information, advice and guidance that they would like to receive. Table 51 provides a summary:

Table 51: The Types of Information, Advice and Guidance wanted (a) by Students in ENGLAND.

Type:	Number	Relative %
Personalised guidance about employment opportunities	220	19.7
General information about the range of employment opportunities	174	15.6
General information about the nature of employment opportunities	146	13.1
Visits to places of work/educational institutions	133	11.9
Personalised guidance about educational opportunities	118	10.6
Talks by people working in various occupations	116	10.4
General advice about University/College entrance; examination requirements	72	6.5
Information about job entry requirements	60	5.4

Note:

In England, many students gave more than one reply to this question. Consequently, the *total* number of mentions of various types of information, advice and guidance is shown, and the percentages quoted are relative percentages (i.e. calculated as a percentage of the *total* number of students). Very small numbers and percentages have been omitted both in this and in the other sub-tables.

Table 51: The Types of Information, Advice and Guidance Wanted (b) by Students in FRANCE.

Type:	Number	Adjusted %
Talks by people working in various occupations	225	19.0
Information/advice about the range and nature of employment opportunities in general	205	17.4
General pleas for more detailed information/advice about every aspect of education and employment	96	8.1
Information/advice about the range and nature of educational opportunities following the *baccalauréat*	74	6.2
Information/advice about the range and nature of educational opportunities in general	68	5.7
Literature	59	5.0
Visits to places of work/educational institutions	43	3.6
(No reply)	347	—

Table 51: The Types of Information, Advice and Guidance Wanted (c) by Students in ITALY.

Type:	Number	Adjusted %
Information/advice about the range and nature of educational opportunities following the *maturità*	169	14.6
General plea for more detailed information/advice about every aspect of education and employment	144	12.5
Work experience schemes	84	7.3
Talks by people working in various occupations	77	6.7
Personalised guidance in general	73	6.3
Information/advice about the range and nature of employment opportunities in general	55	4.8
Personalised guidance about employment opportunities	53	4.6
Information/advice about the range and nature of employment opportunities following the *maturità*	47	4.1
(No reply)	472	—

Table 51: The Types of Information, Advice and Guidance Wanted (d) by Students in SWEDEN.

Type:	Number	Adjusted %
Information/advice about examination requirements	84	15.5
Information/advice about employment opportunities in general	65	12.0
Personalised guidance in general	54	9.9
Talks by people working in various occupations	43	7.9
Work experience schemes	24	4.4
Information/advice about the range of employment opportunities	24	4.4
Advice about the difficulties of entry to various professions	22	4.1
(No reply)	234	–

Table 51: The Types of Information, Advice and Guidance Wanted (e) by Students in GERMANY.

Type:	Number	Adjusted %
Personalised guidance in general	52	16.0
Talks by people working in various occupations	47	14.5
Information/advice about the range and nature of educational opportunities after present studies	34	10.4
Personalised guidance about employment opportunities	20	6.2
Information/advice about the range of educational opportunities in general	20	6.2
Work experience schemes	16	4.9
Lessons/courses	15	4.6
Literature	15	4.6
Specialised careers staff	14	4.3
Visits to places of work/educational institutions	13	4.0
General plea for more detailed information/advice about every aspect of education/employment	13	4.0
(No reply)	41	–

Before we discuss these five tables, it should perhaps be emphasised that the question asking students to describe the types of counselling and guidance they wanted was an open-ended one. In other words, the students were free to write whatever they wished, rather than being asked to choose from a list of pre-selected alternatives. By avoiding the risk of directing students' replies either by suggesting examples or by providing a list of alternatives, the researcher hoped to obtain a picture of what the students themselves really wanted in the way of counselling and guidance. The headings which appear in the tables, such as "Personalised guidance about educational opportunities", or "Work experience schemes", are merely convenient pieces of shorthand devised after detailed analysis of students' replies.

England

The most frequent request made by English students was for guidance on an individual and personal basis about employment opportunities. Clearly, the question of employment opportunities represented their greatest cause for concern; requests for information about the range and nature of these exceeded even those for personalised guidance. Visits to places of work, and talks by people employed in various occupations, were also mentioned by a large number of students.

By comparison, requests for information, advice or guidance about educational opportunities were rare, although a sizeable minority of English students felt that there was a need for personalised guidance on these matters, and a smaller number asked for advice about University or College entrance or about examination requirements.

Let us illustrate these points with some examples of students' replies from various schools and colleges. Many of them reveal an underlying source of concern, namely the adequacy of counselling and guidance staffing within schools and colleges.

From a mixed sixth form college:

Personal contact/staffing:

> "Perhaps the greatest stumbling block is that our careers staff consists of two members . . . . who cannot afford to spend a great deal of time with individuals".

> "A more personal contact is necessary between staff and

students . . . . It is very difficult in a Sixth Form College of this type where Staff cannot possibly be expected to know what type of person you are and advise you as to the most advantageous subjects to take. How can they possibly be expected to guide people whom they have never met before?"

"More interest taken, not having to seek advice but to have it offered when necessary. Here if one doesn't seek advice he/she never gets it. . . . . More interest should be taken in the individual so that the staff are able to help more in advice on the suitability of a student for a certain job. Students should each have a regular time to visit such a teacher and discuss progress in work in the college and changing attitudes towards future plans for jobs or courses in Colleges, etc. . . . . This would help communications within College tremendously".

"Informal assessment of capabilities and aptitudes for certain subjects and certain types of work . . . . staff do not seem to have sufficient experience to give this kind of advice or maybe they are unwilling to commit themselves or just aren't interested".

More and different information and advice about employment rather than education:

"There is sufficient information concerning further education, but a definite lack of information concerning employment".

"This college concentrates almost exclusively on higher education in universities and colleges of education . . . ."

"First hand information as if from the horse's mouth . . . . Sometimes teachers don't even know what the job entails, they only learn from books, and I am sure I'm not going to take a job on their advice. It would be helpful if there were more trips to various firms and hear about the likes and dislikes from the workers themselves".

"The necessary qualifications required for jobs should be considered before choosing further studies, instead of the other way round, i.e. Encouraged into studies which have no link with the future job or training concerned".

". . . . The different ways of entering a business or industry. Whether it is better to be more qualified (University) or experienced, for example".

From a technical college:

More and different information about the nature of various types of employment:

"Not just a list of possible . . . . jobs but a breakdown of what they entail and cover".

"More information on employment, excursions into industry, etc. to find out what it is really like and what professions would suit you most".

"I find the classification of jobs rather annoying, the attitude of "Well, you're good enough to go into one of the professions so that's what you should do", as if Banking and other commercial concerns were the only organisations in the world".

"The practical help from persons in the type of job or profession you are considering. This is because the time spent doing this . . . . is more profitable than a lot of booklets which become outdated, and teachers' knowledge is so very limited in specific fields of careers".

From a girls' sixth form college:

Personal contact/staffing:

> "It is not so much the type of guidance, but who guides. The arrangement of one careers mistress, who is also a full-time teacher, is not very satisfactory".

> "Careers advisors tend to look at your subject, results, etc. and give you stock answers without taking personality and temperament into account".

Wide-ranging information and advice:

> ". . . . break down the boundaries and find out as much as possible about as many careers as we can".

> "I think we should be made more aware of the range of careers we could choose from at an earlier age . . . . otherwise to a very large extent we are limited to a choice which accepts the qualifications we have achieved".

> "It has always been assumed by all concerned that I would go to University, no-one has ever bothered to explain or suggest alternatives."

From a boys' grammar school:

More and different information about employment:

> "Information concerning availability of certain types of occupations with required academic standard and also popularity of different occupations. More general information about each course of employment. Education information sufficient".

Personalised guidance:

> "I worked out my own career with little or no help from the school . . . . This should not have been the case!"

> "At the present, the school does not take enough interest in one's future career. One receives one's U.C.C.A. form, fills it in and that is it. Compulsory or semi-compulsory interviews for dicussion, personally, of the job opportunities, etc. is not provided, and should be".

> "A more realistic and concerned attitude towards after-school prospects is required in the school (from the staff side). There should be less presuming: "He'll get to University", and more individual attention concerning other contingencies".

Staffing:

> "This school requires someone, not necessarily working here, who is fully aware of university and employment opportunities. But he, or she, must be concerned with this, and this alone. The existing system here where the job of careers master seems to be reluctantly taken on by a teacher who for some reason has a less full timetable than others is absolutely useless".

From a mixed secondary modern school:

Personalised guidance:

> "More individual attention and help in choosing a career, rather than being given large piles of leaflets to read".

> ". . . . a better effort to find out the needs of the people he deals with. When I was doing 'O' levels, the only choice I was offered was the Army; the Army; the

Army; and if I passed a few 'O' levels, the R.A.F."

Literature:

"Going to places of employment only gives an insight into their workings, ... I think it would be far more profitable if there were more leaflets on the subject that could be obtained from school".

Yet other students felt that literature "tends to look through everything with "rosy coloured spectacles"."

Preparation for employment:

"mock interviews"

"meeting prospective employers"

"advice on what impression I should make and what I should say to my prospective employer".

To summarise:

As we have seen, many English students waxed eloquent about the shortcomings of counselling and guidance provision in their school or college. This was clearly a major pre-occupation with them, for English students often filled the space at the end of the questionnaire, marked "For Your Comments", with additional remarks on this subject. In France and Italy — as we saw in an earlier chapter — students' comments were concerned with wider-ranging social and political issues.

English students' comments dealt mainly with the lack of individual attention and advice concerning education and/or employment opportunities, and the need to provide information and guidance about a wider range of fields. Their remarks often carried either an explicit or implicit criticism of existing counselling and guidance staff, and pointed to the need for more generous allocation of resources to provide specialist personnel with first-hand experience over a wide variety of fields, capable of providing up-to-date advice and guidance to individual students. Comments also provided an interesting reflection of the changing composition and outlook of upper-secondary schools and colleges. There were frequent complaints about over-emphasis of opportunities in tertiary education (particularly at University) and traditional fields such as the Civil Service, Armed Forces, and Banking.

Instead, students asked for coverage of a wider and more imaginative range of opportunities, particularly in the field of employment, without the built-in assumption that students would pursue further full-time studies immediately. This suggests that in some cases a gulf or time-lag exists between students' perceptions and those of counselling and guidance staff, whose values and outlook are more traditional in nature.

Let us now turn our attention to the French students:

France

Table 51(b) showed that French students' most frequent requests were for talks by people working in various occupations, and information and advice concerning employment opportunities. As in England, requests for information, advice or guidance about educational opportunities were, by comparison, rare.

Many students were clearly concerned about the links between their present studies and employment, and felt that their upper-secondary education provided them with a totally inadequate preparation for working life.

"Orientation"

There were several complaints about the system of *"orientation"* at the *"classe de troisième"* stage, when decisions are taken as to the branch of upper-secondary education that individual pupils should enter. Some students felt that this guidance process tended to be somewhat arbitrary, and was carried out at a stage when individual personalities and aptitudes were still developing. Several students thought that they should have an opportunity to voice their own opinions and preferences. On the occasions when these were sought, they were then ignored. One French student went so far as to claim that the *"orientation"* process was one of "total incompetence".

Lack of information and advice

But the most common grievance was simply that students were provided with insufficient information and advice about education and employment opportunities. Remarks such as the following were typical:

> "There is an enormous gap in the teaching about opportunities open to pupils; the staff and principal seem to concern themselves with these problems hardly at all".

> "Information provided by the school is too imprecise, and above all, it reaches us much too late. At the beginning of the *"terminale"* class, we should be given details of all the opportunities that exist: we would then have a whole year to make up our mind (and that's a minimum, because the rest of our life depends on that choice)".

> "Many students are deceived as a result of a lack of information and advice. For example, they dream of being an electronics engineer, only to realise later on that it wasn't at all as they expected".

Work experience schemes

Several students favoured the introduction of work experience schemes, either to provide them with some insights into the particular occupation they had chosen, or to give them some experience of a variety of jobs:

> "It isn't enough to choose a career and consequently a whole future simply by saying, 'I should like to be a mechanic'. There should be a period of work experience in the field of mechanics at the beginning of the year, so that one can see exactly what a mechanic's job involves. Otherwise, ... one enters a job one doesn't really like".

Many students suggested *visits to places of work*, and *contact with people in various types of jobs* — two recommendations echoed by many English students. One student put forward the idea of a *placement organisation at 'lycée' level* to arrange employment in firms suited to pupils' specialist aptitudes and training.

There were some differences of opinion about the value of *literature*. Some students thought that this type of information about the types of employment that one could enter, and the opportunities associated with various courses of study was useful. Others felt that the lack of information and advice concerning opportunities after the *baccalauréat*, and their future studies or career, could be better solved by *personal discussions*.

Finally, although the vast majority of French students' comments revealed a considerable amount of dissatisfaction with existing counselling and guidance provision, at least one student took a very different view:

> "I always work on the principle that nothing is handed to you on a plate. Whether it's a matter of guidance about educational or employment opportunities, it's up to you to obtain information and advice, and find out what you would most like to do. Many pupils are in the same boat. There isn't much time for individual attention. It's up to you to find out for yourself, and decide".

To Summarise:

In general French students made far fewer comments about counselling and guidance than those in England had done. But the underlying message was the same: one of almost unanimous dissatisfaction.

There were frequent complaints that insufficient information and advice was available, and that what was provided tended to be unrealistic, subjective and out of date. As in England, many students felt that there should be more contact with people able to offer first-hand insights and experience. Several French students clearly thought that the important task of counselling and guidance should not be left to inadequately trained and informed teachers, but that more emphasis should be placed on external sources. Specific suggestions included: visits to schools by experts; meetings with representatives of various fields of employment; and the further development of existing bodies such as the Ministry of National Education's *O.N.I.S.E.P.* (*"Office National d'Information Sur les Enseignements et les Professions"*).

Many French students felt that information and advice both about education and employment opportunities should be provided at an earlier stage in their school career, and should take more into account the current employment situation. Some thought that it should be based on personality tests designed to discover individual aptitudes and interests.

Lastly, several students suggested the setting-up of job placement agencies within schools, and advocated more co-operation between schools and firms in finding employment for pupils.

Italy

Table 51(c) showed that the most frequent requests made by Italian students were for information and advice concerning educational opportunities following the *maturità*, and a general plea for more details about all aspects of education and employment. Talks by people working in various occupations received less emphasis than in England or France, but Italian students placed a higher priority on work experience schemes.

Compared with either French or English students, very few Italians made detailed comments about the type of counselling and guidance they would like. Specific suggestions were few and far between, and remarks such as the following were typical:

> ".... we have been told very little about what the world of work is really like or about further studies (University).... we are entering a world in which we are completely lost, one that we don't know anything about".

> "We should have clearer information about future prospects; as it is, we arrive at University without any information or clearly-defined ambitions".

> "I don't think that this type of school (a *'liceo scientifico'*) is sufficiently adapted to providing information or advice about future employment".

> ".... it would be very useful to be able to turn to school and vocational advice offices.... There are some

of these offices in Italy (I remember having gone to one at the end of the '*scuola media*'), but I don't think that they are publicised enough, or that there are enough of them".

"Schools should do their best to help prepare pupils for a job or further studies through discussions that allow the teacher to understand and get to know the pupil, and vice versa".

"Schools in Italy should be more practical, that is to say, they should give us a more accurate idea of what awaits us both if we continue with our studies and if we don't".

Comments such as these are mild in comparison with those of many French and English students. Why should this be so? Perhaps the answer lies partly in the pre-occupation with wide social and political issues that distinguished Italian students from those in other countries (see Chapter 21). This might possibly go hand in hand with what appears to be a relative lack of concern with counselling and guidance *per se,* particularly when Italian students saw few links between upper-secondary schools and the rest of society. Furthermore, the proportion of students who aimed to go on to University was higher in Italy than in any of the other countries. Perhaps in these circumstances, students in Italy were less immediately concerned with information, advice and guidance about employment opportunities, although they felt strongly that more attention should be given to education opportunities following the *maturità*.

Sweden

Table 51(d) shows that the most frequent requests made by Swedish students were for information and advice about examination requirements and employment opportunities. Many students were clearly concerned about the levels of 'final marks' from upper-secondary school required for admission to various sectors of higher education, and their anxiety about this was reflected in their requests for information and advice on examination requirements.

However, most of their comments concerning counselling and guidance provision referred to employment rather than educational opportunities. This is not altogether surprising when one remembers that in all more than a third of Swedish students were aiming to begin work after completing their upper-secondary studies.

Comments tended to be brief, and less detailed than those made by students in the other countries, but one or two examples might help to illustrate Swedish students' main concerns:

Work experience

This was mentioned by a large number of students. Remarks such as the following were typical:

> "I should like the school to let students try different sorts of jobs".

> "Information about work experience opportunities during the summer holidays".

> "Short courses to see which job is suitable for me".

Future employment prospects

Many Swedish students were keenly aware of the rapidly changing employment structure, and felt that schools should provide more information about future trends:

> "What occupations are safe in the future?"

> "Range of employment in ten years' time?"

> "Information about which jobs need employees; jobs with a future".

Aptitude testing/personal guidance

Some Swedish students asked for job aptitude tests, or for a more individual and personalised approach to counselling and guidance, although the proportion doing so was small in comparison with England:

> "Personalised advice, and the opportunity to ask about my own future".

> "What sorts of jobs *I* have a chance of getting".

Nature of employment opportunities/job placement

A number of Swedish students specifically asked for information concerning the characteristics of various jobs, while others felt that schools should help students to obtain jobs at the end of their studies.

> "Advantages and disadvantages of the occupation: salary; promotion prospects; length of training".

Lastly, some Swedish students asked for information or advice about *opportunities linked with their particular course* of studies:

> "We've got too little information about our future and about further studies. I don't know what job I'll get by studying these subjects".

To summarise:

Swedish students in general made fewer requests for additional or different types of information and guidance than students in England or France, and their main concern was with employment rather than educational opportunities. It is interesting to note that Swedish students' comments omitted any reference to *sources* of information or advice, either within or external to upper-secondary schools. In contrast, English and French students' replies had emphasised the need to improve the staffing aspect of counselling and guidance. It would be unwise to conclude from this that Swedish students were completely satisfied with existing staffing arrangements. Rather their comments suggest that they were simply concerned with one half of the question: i.e. the *content* of counselling and guidance, but not the *providers*. These two aspects are obviously closely related, and it is therefore somewhat surprising that Swedish students' replies reflected so great a concern with one, but not the other.

Germany

German students' most frequent requests were similar to those of many English students: namely, a personalised approach to counselling and guidance; and information and advice from people with first-hand experience of particular occupations. Information and advice about educational opportunities after their present course of studies was also mentioned by a sizeable proportion of German students.

The small number of students who took part in the German fieldwork makes it difficult to draw inferences or conclusions. Let us first look at their requests in more detail:

Students at a language school (*'Fremdsprachenschule'*) emphasised the need for: more detailed information and advice at an earlier stage, i.e. before upper-secondary studies were begun; objective information (i.e. listing negative as well as positive aspects) about different types of employment and their prospects; careers advisors who cared about students' futures, and who really knew their job; and talks by former students and by both young and old employees in various occupations. Students at a *'Fachoberschule'* stressed the need for similar innovations, namely: the provision of information and advice at an earlier stage; closer communication with teachers, who should be concerned with individual abilities; and information about job promotion prospects. But they also mentioned the need for encouragement to continue one's studies, and for more help with career choices linked to one's own course of studies.

Replies from a *'Fachschule für Sozialpägogik'* emphasised the need for objective information and advice about jobs and their prospects that had been mentioned by students at the other schools' But they also requested: literature; lectures; information about further educational opportunities; and individual advice from a psychologist and sociologist. Several students complained that the only means of obtaining advice at present available was to ask a teacher during a lesson.

These complaints or requests were largely echoed by students at a

'*Wirtschaftsgymnasium*', who also asked for talks about the range of employment opportunities. Finally, students from a traditional '*Gymnasium*' stressed the need for *young* careers advisors; information on the educational requirements, and prospects of certain jobs; details of a wider range of educational opportunities after their present studies; and more information about the '*numerus clausus*' concept, which limits the number of admissions to some University departments.

To summarise:

These requests are strikingly similar to those of many English students in their concern with personalised and objective information and advice, and with the long-term implications of educational decisions taken during lower- and upper-secondary studies. Unlike Swedish students, many Germans referred to the *providers* of counselling and guidance, particularly their level of expertise, age, and range of concern.

b) Counselling and Guidance Provision for Upper-secondary Students

This section does not aim to present a comprehensive survey of current counselling and guidance provision in the five countries visited by the researchers. Rather, its objective is to show how the expansion of the upper-secondary population and recent changes in their future prospects have highlighted the need for fundamental reform of the present structure and content of counselling and guidance. Unfortunately, it proved extremely difficult to obtain insights into counselling and guidance provision in Italy and the Federal Republic of Germany, because in many of the schools visited by the researchers there appeared to be no such provision. Hence, the emphasis in the following pages is inevitably on England, France and Sweden.

(I)   Problems

Expansion of the upper-secondary population

The point was made earlier in the Report that the fact alone that more young people are staying on into upper-secondary education has necessitated a re-thinking of present arrangements. Furthermore, as we have seen, this expansion is being accompanied by a fundamental change in the traditional concept of upper-secondary education. No longer can we think of it as catering for a minority, for an academic and to some extent a social elite.

As the range of interests, aspirations and abilities represented by upper-secondary students broadens, so too must the scope of counselling and guidance work. It was clear from interviews and discussions with those concerned with providing information and advice to students that a wide gulf often existed between their perceptions and those of the students concerned. Counselling and guidance staff were generally able to provide at least some information and advice in areas with which they were familiar. But they tended to be at a loss when faced with students who did not have the inclination and/or the ability to follow traditional paths in tertiary education or employment. Furthermore, staff who were concerned with students' personal problems often had to deal with situations and values far removed from their own realm of experience. Rapid social change, and the emergence of what is often described as a "youth culture" have meant that the world of young people today – their values, attitudes and life style – presents complex and often bewildering contrasts with the world familiar to many older people, including teachers and counselling and guidance staff. In this sense, all upper-secondary students are "new", and their growing numbers make the task of counselling and guidance staff all the more complex.

Staffing

These difficulties were sometimes particularly apparent where counselling and guidance was the responsibility of upper-secondary teachers themselves. Their realm of experience was inevitably limited, especially with regard to employment matters. So too was their time, since counselling and guidance functions often had to be fitted into a teaching timetable, sometimes leaving them with only a few hours per week in which to see students and keep abreast of new developments. This inevitably meant that the time available for seeing students individually was very limited, if not non-existent. So in France, for example, teachers with special *O.N.I.S.E.P.* (*'Office National d'Information sur les Enseignements et les Professions'*) responsibilities sometimes could do little more than distribute literature, display posters, and suggest other sources of information and guidance.

In England, it sometimes appeared that counselling and guidance duties were allocated simply on the basis of work load; in other words, those with the lightest teaching timetable were given responsibility for providing information and advice about education, employment, and so on. Hardly the best qualifications for counselling and guidance work! But it was more usual for the various counselling and guidance functions to be distributed amongst a number of teachers all of whom were allocated time for their work. Sometimes these members of staff would have only half a normal teaching load. Time is clearly an important factor. Without it, no counselling or guidance worker — no matter how competent — can be expected to perform their duties effectively, given that those duties include seeing students on an individual basis.

Training is also vital. The well-meaning amateur is an outdated and hazardous concept as far as counselling and guidance is concerned. This is not to suggest by any means that only professional social workers or careers experts should be involved. Far from it. Indeed, these 'external' experts often present problems of their own. In Sweden, for example, the 'Kurator', (a counsellor and advisor with a social work training, serving one or a number of schools) sometimes faced difficulties in integrating himself or herself into the life of the school. Students, who did not come across the 'Kurator' during the course of their normal school life, were reluctant to approach these counsellors. In one of the schools visited by the researchers, the 'Kurator' expressed surprise and dismay that students were backward in coming forward to see him in his office. He decided to overcome this by making sallies forth into the various other parts of the school, and chatting informally to students over a cup of coffee. Unfortunately, his good intentions apparently back-fired, and he was regarded with the utmost suspicion by many students!

This raises a serious question, namely whether counselling and guidance functions should be the responsibility of those who actually teach the students, other teachers in the school or college who do *not* teach them, or non-teachers. In Sweden — despite problems of the type described above — a system of non-teachers seemed to be favoured. In England, the reverse was generally true. For example, in some of the sixth form colleges visited by the researchers, a 'tutorial' system was in operation; A small number of students, usually between fifteen and twenty, were allocated to a teacher who was then responsible for their well-being. Allocation was sometimes on the basis of a shared subject interest; in other colleges, it was done on an alphabetical basis. Generally the tutors dealt with personal matters themselves, and joined forces with other members of staff with special careers or education advisory functions when necessary. Most of the tutors interviewed believed strongly that it was mutually advantageous for tutors and students to have a teaching-learning relationship as well. They argued that this enabled each side to get to know the other, and for the tutor to give information and advice on a truly individual basis, because he or she knew the student's interests, ambitions, college performance and — in some cases — home background. This knowledge made for a far more personal approach than would otherwise be possible.

In fact, many English 'tutors' laid particular stress on the importance of getting to know their students as individual personalities. Some went to considerable lengths to do so: by inviting students informally to their home; by organising 'extra-curricular' activities at weekends or in the evenings; or by establishing contact with students' own families. These teachers felt that such informal meetings in out-of-college situations were invaluable in helping to create a 'rapport' between tutors and students.

Yet ironically, this personalised approach — requested by so many students, and emphasised by a large number of English teachers concerned with counselling and guidance — raised several fundamental problems. In certain situations, the last thing that students wanted to do was to talk to someone whom they knew and who knew them. This seemed to be the case particularly with personal problems concerned, for example, with family circumstances or with sexual relationships. The question of confidentiality and anonymity was often a crucial one.

Many of the staff involved were keenly aware of this, and expressed concern about ensuring that students were not deterred from discussing problems by fears that their confidences would be betrayed. This could be difficult if — as was the case in one particular English sixth form college — the head teacher insisted on being involved in such matters and indeed on taking over all responsibility. Many of the tutors concerned felt that their work was severely limited as a result of this attitude, which they perceived as interference and a negation of their counselling and guidance role.

Yet teachers who took on these personal counselling responsibilities generally realised their own limitations, and expressed anxiety about being confronted with problems that were really 'too big to handle'. In such situations, close liaison with external specialists, such as psychologists and social workers, was desirable. Some tutors were also aware of the problems of personal involvement and possible loss of 'objectivity' as a result of knowing the student concerned.

Co-ordination between lower- and upper-secondary institutions

But whoever is responsible for providing counselling and guidance — whether it is teachers or others with specialist knowledge and training — additional problems arise where educational structure and organisation involve a break-off point in secondary studies. That is to say, when students receive their lower-secondary education in one institution, but must switch to another, upper-secondary one if they wish to continue their studies.

Such a system has many undoubted advantages — including organisational, curricular and social ones — but it does present special counselling and guidance problems.

Counselling and guidance — particularly the aspects concerned with educational and employment choices — is essentially a long-term process, and not something which begins at the stage of upper-secondary education. The reason for this is obvious: many crucial decisions, for example concerning choice of courses, may be taken before this stage. In England, for example, specialisation in the form of subject choices for the General Certificate of Education (G.C.E.) or Certificate of Secondary Education (C.S.E.) often takes place at the age of thirteen or thereabouts, i.e. long before the end of compulsory secondary education. Yet students sometimes discover the implications of those choices only years later when they come to apply for admission to tertiary education or certain types of employment. Similarly in France, the *'orientation'* process referred to earlier in this chapter takes place during the *'classe de 3^e'*. Decisions regarding choice of upper-secondary courses taken at this stage have long-term implications.

It is clear that those responsible for counselling and guidance at lower-secondary level must be fully aware of the range of educational and employment paths open to their students later on. Above all, they must ensure that options are kept open as long as possible, so that decisions taken at lower-secondary level do not impose undesirable and unforeseen limitations on students' choices later on.

This clearly calls for close co-ordination between lower- and upper-secondary institutions. The long-term process of counselling and guidance — if it is to be really effective — demands a considerable amount of knowledge of individual students on the part of those responsible for this work.

But when students switch institutions at the point of beginning their upper-secondary education, the knowledge which has been accumulated in the preceding years must somehow be transferred with them in order that counselling and guidance at upper-secondary level can be personalised and effective. Easier said than done, for although 'objective' information about school performance and so on can be transferred without too much difficulty, more 'subjective' insights into a student's interests and ambitions pose far greater problems.

Indeed, in all the English sixth form colleges visited by the researchers, and several of the French upper-secondary institutions, the difficulties of getting to know students in a relatively short space of time were continually stressed. Yet it should also be pointed out that some counselling and guidance staff held the view that it was better if students entered upper-secondary education with a 'clean slate', in other words, without any assessment of their previous performance or of their personality. This enabled the students to make a fresh start, and meant that at least the counselling and guidance staff could work without the handicap of preconceptions or prejudices.

The changing employment and educational scene

It has become a cliché to say that we live in a rapidly changing world, but it is nevertheless true, and makes the role of counselling and guidance in upper-secondary education all the more vital.

The range of employment and educational opportunities open to young people to-day is bewilderingly complex. Shifts in the employment structure mean that demands for certain skills — particularly in some of the traditional industries — have declined or even disappeared completely. In their place have grown whole new areas of employment in the tertiary sector which call for a relatively high level of general education that enables workers to be flexible, and learn new skills as and when necessary. But even in these new fields, demands may alter rapidly. Computer programming is one example. Some years ago, there was an enormous growth in opportunities in this field. But more recently, supply has outstripped demand, and the job prospects for programmers have often failed to live up to their earlier promise. Those with higher levels of skills — such as systems analysts — have been less affected in this way.

Besides the growth of completely new areas of employment, many existing job opportunities have changed in nature, and have demanded new skills on the part of workers. The clerical field is an obvious example. Accounts clerks now often have to contend with computer print-out rather than ledgers, and the growth of 'reprographic' units, with an array of complex equipment, are a far cry from the old-style duplicating machinery.

Furthermore, the range of employment opportunities open to people with particular levels of qualifications has also changed. In general, there has been a 'down-grading' of the value of qualifications. In England, for example, a post-graduate degree is now often demanded where in the past a first degree would have been sufficient. At the other end of the scale, General Certificate of Education Ordinary Level or Certificate of Secondary Education passes are asked for, where before no formal qualifications would have been needed.

Employers are no doubt sometimes at fault in this respect, and the situation becomes even more complex for young people when − as in Sweden − employers also demand practical work experience, or in England show reluctance to employ 17 or 18 year old leavers with limited formal qualifications. Instead employers sometimes prefer to take on a younger school leaver with similar qualifications.

Although the *potential* range of employment opportunities has no doubt expanded, the *actual* scope for upper-secondary leavers can be limited, partly because of this down-grading of qualifications referred to earlier. Upper-secondary students in France, Italy and Sweden were particularly concerned about this problem, and tended to react in one of two ways. In France and Italy, they often chose to continue their studies further, thus delaying the transition from education to employment. In Sweden, students were more likely to attempt to secure a job as soon as possible. Either way, they needed a good deal of imaginative and realistic counselling and guidance, which was often conspicuous by its absence.

The responsibility of upper-secondary education to include the provision of expert information and advice is enormous, especially at a time when the whole spectrum of opportunities is changing so rapidly. Clearly, students' friends and family lack the detailed up-to-date knowledge required, and may in fact act as a negative force, conveying outdated and unrealistic ideas to students. So the burden inevitably falls largely on the educational structure.

There is a particular need to alert students to *new* types of opportunities, to dispel the myth that the only alternatives are the ones referred to earlier i.e. full-time tertiary education or employment. Possibilities of combining studies and a job need to be explored and publicised far more, especially when the employment structure is changing so rapidly.

Above, all, it seems vital to keep options open as long as possible. It is likely that in the climate of growing criticism of early specialisation, the period of upper-secondary education will increasingly become a flexible and fluid one, during which choices can crystallise to *some* extent, but need not be finalised. Again, the implications of this for counselling and guidance are enormous.

(II)   Recommendations

The preceding pages have outlined some of the major problems involved in counselling and guidance work at upper-secondary level to-day. Some remedies have also been touched on. Let us now look at these in a little more detail.

Personal counselling

Although this was seldom if ever referred to by the students themselves, there would seem to be a very real need for personal counselling (i.e. advice and guidance on personal matters). There are two major reasons for this. One of them concerns the structure of secondary education, and has already been discussed. That is to say, when students have to — or choose to — switch institutions at the point of beginning their upper-secondary education, a considerable degree of adjustment on their part is called for. For instance, the upper-secondary school or college may have a social and educational organisation quite different from students' previous school. The whole climate of expectations may be totally new. Students may, for example, be expected to organise their work themselves, and to exercise a degree of self-discipline unheard of in lower-secondary institutions. Many students welcome these changes, and appreciate the more 'adult' climate, but find that the transition is now without its strains and tensions, particularly if they do not know any other students. Superficial self-confidence might hide anxieties and uncertainties beneath the surface.

A tutorial system of the type outlined earlier in this chapter could do much to ease the transition. But it requires sensitive and perceptive teaching staff, *and* trained and expert counsellors, attached to schools and colleges, to whom problems can be referred by tutors if they exceed the boundaries of the tutors' capabilities. In most cases, specialist social or psychological help will not be needed, but only the friendly ear of someone "with no axes to grind" and the time to ensure that contact consists of more than a weekly ten-minute meeting or a five-minute chat in the corridor.

The second reason is that upper-secondary students, whether or not they have transferred to a new institution, are faced with the problems of emotional adjustment that characterise the period of late adolescence/early adulthood. This is a time when family relationships are sometimes strained, and peer group influences are strong, although the latter can produce their own problems and conflicts. The combination of personal tutors and trained counsellors already referred to could be invaluable in dealing with students' difficulties. Clearly, the question of confidentiality and anonymity would need to be resolved, particularly with regard to referral to specialist social or psychological workers, or — if applicable — to the student's family.

Education and employment information, advice and guidance

A pragmatic distinction has been made between personal counselling, and advice and guidance concerned with education and employment. There are obviously links between the two, but it nevertheless seems possible and desirable to make this distinction.

The need for specialists with up-to-date knowledge of the whole spectrum of educational — and particularly employment — opportunities has already been stressed. It is clear that present systems of information and guidance operating in upper-secondary institutions are inadequate. Particularly in the field of employment, students are not provided with sufficiently wide-ranging, accurate and recent information and advice linked with their own course of study, aptitudes and interests. Very few students are given any insights into the real world of employment or further studies, or made aware at a sufficiently early stage of the long-term implications of decisions taken during the course of their upper-secondary education or even earlier.

Despite the organisational and other difficulties involved, it seems essential that upper-secondary students should be given insights into the world of employment in particular. This could be achieved in three ways. Firstly, by allowing a greater degree of contact between upper-secondary students and those working in various occupations. Something more than 'work visits' is required here. The possibility could be explored of specially selected and trained employees from a range of employment fields being given the equivalent of a sabbatical year, during which they would visit schools or colleges, and discuss their field of employment with students. In certain spheres, it might even be feasible for them to participate in the teaching process itself.

Secondly, by achieving a greater degree of interplay between the worlds of education and employment allowing teachers to gain experience of various occupations (i.e. an extended period of 'in-service' training with a difference, or a version of the 'sabbatical year' concept). Also those who have worked in other fields could be encouraged to enter the teaching profession. Their insights and experience would be invaluable to students.

Thirdly, by giving upper-secondary students themselves some practical work experience. Admittedly, many of the schemes arranged for secondary pupils in England and Sweden have raised vast organisational and other problems, but this does not mean that the whole concept is necessarily invalid or unworkable. One possible development might involve abandoning the idea that 'work experience schemes' last only a few days or weeks at the most, and are squeezed into an already full timetable. If more opportunities for part-time upper-secondary studies could be explored and made available, longer and more meaningful periods of work experience would be feasible. Other countries can show examples.

As in the case of personal counselling, there is a strong need for co-ordination between teachers and tutors on the one hand, and specialist careers and educational advisors on the other. Both have an important part to play. The former are familiar with individual students' abilities, interests and aptitudes, and can acquaint the specialist advisors with these. The latter then have the task of providing information, advice and guidance that is both linked with the individual student's abilities, interests and aptitudes, and is up-to-date, wide-ranging and accurate. Such specialist advisors would represent a new breed: they would be attached to a school or college, and work from it; they would be full-time, with no teaching duties but preferably with some teaching experience and they would be specially trained to carry out the tasks of advising individual students, liaising with teachers and with employers and others, and of keeping abreast of new developments.

This proposal is in no way intended to imply any criticism of − for example − the excellent work done by the Careers Service in England. But, given its already enormous work load, and staff shortage, the author feels that any expansion of its duties on the lines suggested would − at least under present circumstances − probably not be feasible.

Underlying all is the assumption that a greater degree of contact between upper-secondary institutions and the world of employment is both desirable and necessary. Furthermore, that present systems of counselling and guidance in upper-secondary schools and colleges are no longer equipped − if indeed they ever were − to cope with the demands made upon them by the expansion of upper-secondary education and by the rapidly changing social and economic context in which that education is taking place.

The responsibilities of counselling and guidance are too great for them to remain with teachers and others with insufficient time, resources and expertise. All the good intentions and motivation in the world cannot compensate for a shortage of these. Only specially trained, full-time expert advisors, backed up by those who know and teach the students concerned, can hope to provide a truly effective counselling and guidance system. We owe it to the upper-secondary students, and to ourselves, to ensure that such expert information and advice is made available. Otherwise the majority of students will continue to receive inadequate counselling and guidance, and eventually both they and the rest of society will pay the cost.

Author's Note:

This chapter was written *before* the publication of a report prepared for the Department of Education and Science by the Inspectorate of Schools. (Careers Education in Secondary Schools. Education Survey 18. H.M.S.O. October 1973). The degree of similarity between its findings and recommendations, and those of the author, is striking.

SECTION F:

CONCLUSIONS

CHAPTER 19

SOME CONCLUSIONS FROM THE RESEARCH

(A) Structural Aspects and Policy Implications

The research programme has attempted to discover and present fresh aspects of post-compulsory education in Western Europe, with special reference to the perceptions and aspirations of the 16-20 age-group and of those providing for them within the context of today's schools and colleges.

Of course, that context is changing rapidly; and all formal educational activity in any kind of institution or setting shows the strains of response to a situation without precedent — unprecedented in the size and rapid increase of enrolments; in the composition, expectations, and motivation of students; in the devising of new institutions and curricula; in different instrumentation and relationships within the process of education; and, above all, in the prospect of recurrent education through a multiplicity of contacts and agencies.

Therefore, there are continuously unfamiliar tasks to be faced within and around the schools or colleges: there are new responsibilities for counselling, guidance, and information services; there are implications for the reorientation of teachers — both initially and throughout professional life; at the same time, the manifold diffusion of educational services requires both greater devolvement of initiative or responsibility and more systematic support from all official agencies. It has been a major intention of the research to point to these new tasks, to analyse their elements in terms of the ideas, institutions, and methods currently accepted for the 16-20 age-group, and to suggest critical points for decision and further enquiry.

In previous chapters many critical factors or decision-points were presented in the individual contexts of particular educational systems, or in particular social and curricular settings, even though comparability and international relevance were main considerations throughout the investigation and analysis. The present chapter draws together some indications presented earlier — not to summarise them, but to make their interdependence clearer and to show their relevance in a wider perspective. The researchers have more opportunity here to take account of collateral enquiries in fields adjacent to their own; they can relate their observations to current recommendations or experiments in the wider context; and they can spell out some conclusions of their own.

The importance of case-studies for effective innovation

No matter what conclusions are reached by the present research team, and no matter what recommendations are internationally made for any educational improvement, each country's representatives always take those observations back to their own national context. If they did not, no educational change would ever happen, since general propositions could never become practice. Indeed, there is a far more important reason why educational advice or research findings — though "objectively" presented, and conceived with "detachment" — must always be referred back to the local and topical context: the fact that countries or regional authorities own or manage their formal education systems in a way in which they do not possess or control other enterprises.

School systems (and all their ramifications in colleges, higher education, and technological training) are in some countries the property of the government, whose civil servants the teachers, inspectors, and professors are. In other countries the ownership is less absolute, but the controls are massive: legislation and finance determine the outer limits of scholastic obligation, and the inner minima; the status of schools, and examinations, subject-matter and teachers are likewise prescribed. Even in those countries where contextual possibilities are not officially determined in this way, nevertheless special subventions and administrative priorities (including the priority given to certain kinds of research and development finance) strongly influence the dimensions and proportions of any educational development, public or private. The provision, distribution, training and in-service refreshment of teachers depend on political priorities, as does the status of higher and technological education.

Indeed, unprecedented commitment to education (for manpower, political or social reasons) makes governments and voters see every single educational recommendation in some sort of "generally political" perspective — even where no party-political line is evident, and no administrative-financial shift of priorities is envisaged. All highly urbanised countries and regions are experiencing the tension between those deep cultural traditions and habits which have invested the citizens' minds like language or religion, and those contradictory challenges which arise from an altered life-style developing in a plurality of new possibilities. Fluid though this situation seems to be, it nevertheless is experienced in each country (and by each person judging) as one of delicate balance of judgement between the "best of the old" and the "best of the new". Such a truism is justified here simply because it is so often overlooked in international conferences and research reviews. Pluralism and ostensible "openness" in France, Germany, Sweden and Britain are as nationally idiomatic — as topical in expression — as in Japan or the U.S.A.

Therefore members assembled for international conferences can always be observed "understanding" general recommendations (even when they agree with them) in terms of consequences back home. Desirable innovations usually have to find their "point of penetration" at some specific crack in a well established structure; or else they depend upon some new but acceptable change in structure, such as a "college" for the over-16s, or a "middle school". Hence, both communication and implementation depend upon a national or regional frame or reference. That is why so many important studies of educational innovation have been presented (for example, by OECD) in the framework of national case-studies, where the repercussions can be appreciated in all their variety. There is another aspect of communication which, at the risk of cynicism, may be underlined in this connection. The people who pay most attention to *general* statements about educational reform and reorientation are professors and students in "Education" courses; those who pay attention to country case-studies, or to case-studies of particular institutional crossroads, are the people who make or implement decisions. The latter are also, in most cases, the best contact-points for possible innovation in *new or evolving institutions and programmes.*

That is why, in this Report, all the material in Section C on Structure and Policy, and much in Section D on Curriculum and Teaching-Learning Relationships, was presented as evidence from country case-studies. The people most likely to take effective notice will read about themselves or their neighbours in process of confrontation with actuality — at least, "actuality as perceived within the schools and colleges. Among the active and responsible people nowadays we count the teachers and their students, especially in the post-compulsory years which bring such different kinds of adults together for unprecedented but vital decisions. One indication of imperfect communication is the reply: "It doesn't quite apply to me (or us)". Therefore, in the hope of communicating sympathetically and effectively, case-studies have been presented which it is hoped may facilitate decisions and implementation, in addition to offering outsiders a truer picture of "inside perceptions".

In some contrast, Section E on Sociological Aspects was presented more as an analysis of themes; yet even here the English example was realistically prominent throughout. England was the researchers' operational base; it was also the country in which sociological and occupational data were most reliably gathered (or understood). Of course, scrupulous attention was paid to all available national and international evidence; but varying patterns of classification and understanding raised a few doubts about students' or teachers' responses on some matters. On the other hand, economic, occupational, and social change is not so closely tied to school structure and organisation as are such things as variations in enrolment or teacher-student relationships. Though socio-economic changes surround and penetrate the school's system of habits and preferences, they neither "identify" very obviously nor are so readily controllable by official decisions. They certainly do not "belong" to public authorities as schools and colleges in large measure do. Therefore a more independent international analysis is justified.

Overall too, research into the 16-20 age-range does generally offer at least the possibility of examining, in a sort of "no man's land", the strategic possibilities of a whole range of educational changes which do not necessarily come into confrontation with national preferences or preconceptions developed in connection with other types and levels of school. There is no exact precedent, no handy model of a plan. Because, for the reasons already given, the whole complex of problems is in some sense new, the local case-studies and local chain-reactions of response are at this level variations on a general theme. The researchers feel strongly that the general theme of post-compulsory education as revealed in the survey is one without precedent — one whose dimensions and implications are as yet largely unmeasured by those professionally or politically responsible for it. Thus they are emboldened to present some general conclusions, beginning with observations on the changed context of discussion, enquiry, and decision.

Changes in the context of discussion, enquiry and decision

It seems important to begin the summary of general conclusions with an emphasis on the changed context of discussion. The problems of educating the 16-20 age-group now are not the same (perhaps not nearly the same) as ten or twenty years ago — not only because of numbers, curricular change, institutional development, different instrumentation, and what might generally be called circumstantial factors in education, but because different questions of principle are being asked with different intent. These questions, taken together now instead of being severally analysed by specialists, mark a further stage in educational and social evolution. The present stage calls for synthesis and sympathy in researchers and in those who use their findings, instead of isolation or piecemeal treatment. This chapter provides an occasion for showing how that general change in attitude bears upon decisions for the education of young adults in the earliest post-compulsory years.

The 1950s were the era of national replanning and postwar reconstruction, and also of educational reorganisation or consolidation. For example, in France the large national plans increasingly included an educational element as an instrument of economic and social reorganisation; and in any case demographic growth and popular demand for more schooling necessitated provision for it in plans for material development. The German "economic miracle" resulted in part from international investment, in part from systematic programming. England took the deliberate decision to double its supply of science and technological skill through new educational foundations and through elaboration of existing establishments. Spontaneous developments (like the "sixth form" explosion) also called for official analysis in policy reports such as the 1959 Crowther Report, called simply *15 to 18*. At the international level, a growing awareness that education and the economy were interdependent in a two-way relationship sponsored such developments as the establishment of OECD in 1960 and the International Institute for Educational Planning in 1963.

Yet in all this dedication to economic, social, and educational renaissance the planners (so to speak) stood outside education. During the 1950s many of them were motivated by political theories, by attempts to establish social justice, and sometimes by theories about the aims of education-in-society which were based on *a priori* presuppositions. Indeed, that attitude was reinforced in some countries by dreams of national resurgence or of overtaking prosperous neighbours. Sometimes, too, the vision of a "new Europe" or of pacific coexistence added a further theoretical ingredient; but as a rule this level of discussion still regarded education as an object or instrument rather than as a social and personal process, almost as though from outside.

Within education itself, structural and operational considerations became paramount in the 1960s. During that decade the development of education was dominated by considerations of management – at least in the rapidly expanding upper-secondary and tertiary ranges. Postwar demographic increase in highly industrialised countries, combined with an increasing tendency to stay on in school and college, understandably faced governments and their accountants with problems of accommodating, sorting, efficiently instructing and rationally using new resources of educated manpower.

It was as though the "second stage" of technological and social development described in Chapter 4 was being belatedly applied in education to the special needs of the post-compulsory period, so as to assimilate the newcomers within a "convergent" or "managed" control over technology and society, with an eye on cost-effectiveness and without waste of human potential. Likewise, better use was made of existing institutions (provincial or technical establishments), or of diploma and certificate courses capable of being upgraded, or of higherto neglected people (girls, pupils from inferior schools, and so forth). This attitude was hardly surprising, since participation in post-secondary education alone doubled in North America and Western Europe within the decade, while education — in the post-compulsory range especially — was generally regarded as the prime means of developing social and economic policy.

On the other hand, trends in the social field and requirements inherent in modern industries and commerce already implied a different expectation — those of a "third stage" of technological and social development, a stage characterised by "polyvalent" adaptability, initiative in continuous enterprise and learning, with feedback and interchange in a "communications society". In the social field proper, the claims of "democratisation" expanded beyond numerical extension of schooling opportunities to that "qualitative democratisation" recognising the need for varieties of style in learning and living. Furthermore, such claims were advanced not simply as a matter of permissiveness or protest but more positively as the basis for a more humane society more effectively served by continuously re-adapted industries and communications.

Slowly, in the 1970s, public discussion of these altered circumstances affecting everyone's life-style has borne in upon discussions of education at the highest levels — more in international than national discussions. (These tend to be bogged down in ways-and-means and the here-and-now clutter inherited from previous administration). In universities and technological education we increasingly hear talk of a "sophistication factor" introduced by subtler expectations, better background acquaintance with the possibilities of education in a world of expanding horizons, an elaborate array of instrumentation and services, more intelligent and better trained management (in social as well as technical respects). In all of this, at least some of the over-16s — an increasing proportion of them — are already thinking and learning within that realm of discourse where the most advanced discussions of planners are being formulated. Of course, young adults lack knowledge and experience; but they are beginning to *perceive* knowledge and experience in ways comparable to those of their most sophisticated mentors.

Some of the research findings revealed in answers to the questionnaires show, in rather disorderly fashion, that this is the case. Clearer evidence of the temper of discussion came in some interviews. Yet it should be remembered that the sample available to the researchers tended perhaps to be more conventional than otherwise, if only because of being enrolled (as already "selected" or persevering students) within mainly well-managed systems, and also because administrators assisting the researchers in their visits understandably guided them to characteristic or "respectable" institutions. For that reason, the researchers were at pains to acquire in other ways some of the information which supports conclusions offered in this chapter.

Changes in the institutional framework

Sufficient has been said in previous chapters to preclude the giving of structural details here; but the huge impact of structural reorganisation in many countries' secondary systems must affect any thoughts about upper-secondary and lower-tertiary education. Such reorganisation is in response to, and itself a main cause of, staying on in post-compulsory education. It retains more boys and girls until they are young men and women; it keeps the sexes together in most countries; it gradually draws in students from different kinds of family and social background. Primary and lower-secondary (or "middle") schools meet end-on without formal selection in many countries, and in some cases merge into a continuum. Common middle schools or comprehensive secondary schools are established or recommended in perhaps a majority of systems (at least to the end of compulsory attendance — itself usually 16 in advanced countries).

Thus reorganisation manages to introduce diversity without rigidly "selecting" or "predicting" boys or girls for particular futures, though we must not underestimate the amount of differentiation which goes on because of class-repeating, choice of subjects, or advice on careers. However, options are increasingly kept open until the age of about 14 or later; selection in any proper sense is more often postponed until about the age of 16; selection even then is mitigated by increasing "polyvalence" of studies and by opportunities to return later; new institutions in the upper-secondary/lower-tertiary range provide comprehensive opportunities for study and socialisation for a varied range of students, and with various access-points to higher learning; and the prospect of "recurrent" or lifelong learning through a multiplicity of agencies is now official policy in all advanced European countries.

Paradoxically, governments are readier to envisage such radical changes in their higher education than at lower levels of secondary or technical education; but the turmoil in higher education which some fear heralds the "twilight of the universities" undoubtedly carries special implications for the immediately post-compulsory age-range. There, of necessity, enrolments and expectations without precedent require new provision. That includes: separate or special accommodation, often in adapted buildings; a wider range of courses and teaching/learning methods; a different supply of teachers – both conventionally specialised, and specialised in a new adaptation to the learning needs of the over-16s; more self-management and more external contacts; different patterns of association with further learning and training; and – perhaps most important of all – abandonment of school-to-school, subject-to-subject progression in an unbroken sequence determined by previous prescription.

Instead, learning-experience-learning interplay and life-work-learning feedback are accepted not only in principle but in institutional and curricular organisation, implicitly at least. It will not be long before pressure of current changes and problems of teacher supply and readiness encourage still greater alterations in post-compulsory education. Perhaps the strongest justification for that belief is the now universal insistence on building the perspective of "recurrent" learning into all education at every level of secondary school, as well as in those higher ranges which follow the critical post-compulsory phase.

A supporting corollary is the belief that an individual student may have a "profile" of different levels of attainment – and those in a wider range of interests than was traditional – instead of a specific level of simultaneous marks in required subjects. (This innovation is already recognised in "units" and "modules"). Moreover, returners to "recurrent" education from work or life-experience transform the structure, composition, relationships and orientation of upper-secondary/lower-tertiary short-cycle institutions.

For all these reasons, many countries have already found (and others are discovering by experimental programmes) that the post-compulsory phase of education is pivotal not only for decisions about secondary education and training at normal age-levels but about the structures of higher education and "recurrent education" afterwards. Obviously, there are repercussions right down the school system too; but even if attention is focussed on the post-compulsory phase, it is clear that innovation and re-training in in-service education for teachers are imperative for its new needs. Educational technology, the supply of resource material, development of educational programmes individualised or in groups to meet the need for interdisciplinary studies, links with vocational or social experience, co-operation between institutions (including overlap between secondary and higher education in some cases) – all these prerequisites for more effective and more varied education come into sharp focus in the immediately post-compulsory phase.

Evidently, therefore, the "fresh look" needed for a realistic look at post-compulsory education in Western Europe is bound to throw light on some wider-ranging problems of education at lower and higher levels of atainment. On that ground alone — in addition to its being a topic of common concern across all national boundaries — it is a *point d'appui* for further enquiries. But what still remains to be undertaken within the over-16 range itself is a sustained programme of researches (with feedback) into *new and evolving educational provision* specially made for studies and training now normally undertaken between the ages of about 16 and 20.

(B) Curriculum and Teaching/Learning Aspects

I.   Despite different historical, cultural, and educational backgrounds, the different countries visited acknowledge the importance of the following curricular trends — *at least, in official policy* — towards:

1)   less rigid selection systems;
2)   postponement of specialisation;
3)   a more realistic preparation for the world of work, with emphasis on the acquisition of skills and techniques rather than on a particular training which quickly dates;
4)   a similar trend in the "academic" curriculum, towards a less encyclopaedic content, with emphasis on the different modes of thinking rather than the acquisition of facts;
5)   a less distinct division between general, professional and technical education, less categorising into "academic" and "non-academic";
6)   an interest in developing some kind of integrated study;
7)   an acceptance of "progressive" methods; e.g. audio-visual aids, group teaching etc., which demand more involvement from student and teacher, and an altogether more "open" school;
8)   a concern in many areas for *individual* development which acknowledges the varying degrees of interest, commitment, ability etc., in different students, and their need for a more "tailor-made" education. (This assumes a good counselling service).

II.   Whereas all systems acknowledge the above trends, the degree to which these trends are *actually* implemented varies considerably from country to country. Main trends in the implementation of such policies are:

1)   some form of decentralisation;
2)   more consultation with teachers — which assumes an efficient administrative and advisory service;
3)   an acknowledgement that the role of the teacher should change though no common pattern of *how* this is to be done emerges.

III.   The importance of finding satisfactory ways of implementing curricular reforms in such a way that they are recognised by students as being of some interest and use to them is shown by the large gap which exists between what students would like from school, and what they perceive themselves as getting. Main findings here are:

1)   students expect more from school than they think their teachers suppose;
2)   students are often disappointed in their expectations — often by a very large margin;
3)   students' expectations and perceived satisfactions from *school* seem to be a function of the school system itself and do not appear to be related to social class;
4)   students comment most favourably on subjects of study, less favourably on teaching methods, and least favourably on the organisation of their schools. (Political comments are strongest in authoritarian systems);
5)   many of their comments are couched in terms of *relationships* with teachers, rather than in terms of specific teaching methods;
6)   the findings outlined above point to a "communications gap" between students and teachers, which, if it derives from the school system as it appears to, could be lessened by appropriate implementation of curricular reform through more sophisticated management skills.

IV.   The importance of finding satisfactory ways of implementing curricular reforms is further emphasised by the gaps which exist in teachers' understanding of their students. Main findings here are:

1)   teachers in the sample are more idealistic than they think their students are;

2) their comments show that they are aware of some changes in the types of students in upper-secondary education, and that curricula and teaching methods need to be developed along the lines outlined in I, above;

3) a comparison of their opinions with those of the students again emphasises the "communications gap".

V. *Theoretical* considerations as to suitable curricula and learning styles for this age group are developing rapidly; but the *implementation* of such curricula is, in some areas, slow. Successful implementation of new reforms is urgent because of the disappointment voiced by so many students. Those administrators and teachers responsible for implementation need to understand how the characteristics of a particular kind of curriculum affect decisions about the appropriateness of alternative methods of implementation. To put it bluntly — is there any point in *telling* an authoritarian teacher not to be authoritarian?

C) Sociological Aspects

The social background of upper-secondary students

Our research has indicated that certain sectors of the population, namely those in manual occupations, sometimes appear to be under-represented in upper-secondary education, while others, such as those in the professions and higher levels of management, are over-represented.

In part, this situation is a reflection of the relationship between home background and educational attainment. But it also reflects the traditional concept of upper-secondary education's serving an academic and social elite, to some extent. The notorious wastage of ability amongst pupils from certain social backgrounds can be effectively reduced only if the concept of upper-secondary education continues to be broadened. The removal of attitudinal as well as physical barriers is essential. In other words, the abolition of minimum entry requirements, and the development of open-access institutions is to be welcomed. But it must be accompanied by moves aimed at encouraging pupils from backgrounds previously unfamiliar with upper-secondary education — and their parents — to think that upper-secondary education is for "us, as well as them". New curricula and teaching-learning methods, and the development of courses to suit the whole range of abilities and interests are obviously important in this respect. So too is the provision of counselling and guidance *before* the transition to upper-secondary education. This will be discussed more fully later in this chapter. Finally, if upper-secondary education is to attract pupils from a whole range of social backgrounds it must surely be seen to have real links with later life, and not to be taking place in a vacuum. This too will be discussed more fully later in this chapter.

Upper-secondary students' prospects, and the links between education and employment

Trends in the employment structure indicate that opportunities for unskilled and unqualified workers are diminishing. A longer period of formal education is fast becoming a necessity rather than a luxury; and despite gloomy predictions concerning a flood of over-qualified individuals on to the labour market, such fears may yet prove to be somewhat exaggerated. For example, at the time of writing, job prospects for university graduates look brighter than they have done for some years.

It seems likely that this situation will contribute to a continued growth in upper-secondary enrolments for some time to come. This seems particularly likely in England, where the proportion of the age-group currently enrolled remains lower than in some other countries. But at what point saturation will be reached is difficult to predict. We have already witnessed a dropping-off of enrolments in Sweden. Young people there are faced with a particularly difficult situation. The prospects for those who leave school at the age of sixteen are very limited; those who, after completing their upper-secondary education, wish to start work rather than continuing their studies, are faced with demands from employers for practical experience in addition to formal qualifications. Easier said than done. It may well be that in future, Swedish employers will be asked to contribute both financially and with ideas and action to the education and training of young people.

Certainly this remains a thorny problem. It may be that the only solution − albeit a drastic one − lies in the re-structuring of secondary and tertiary education to take account of changes in the employment and social structures. At present, the lag between educational provision and movements in the employment structure is serious. This is not to say that educational decisions should be governed by economic criteria. But the former cannot afford to ignore the latter.

An example may help to illustrate this dilemma. At one English sixth form college, the researchers found that the "open-access" policy had attracted many pupils with limited intellectual ability. From several points of view, their enrolment in upper-secondary education was encouraging and praiseworthy. But it did present problems for the students themselves, because what they had gained from upper-secondary education in personal and broad educational terms had to be set against increased job finding difficulties. Local employers were reluctant to take on eighteen year olds with one or two C.S.E. passes: they preferred to recruit sixteen year old school leavers and train them over a period of two years or so.

It seems inevitable that we shall need to think more carefully about the links between education and employment, and adopt a more flexible system of transition between one and the other. Perhaps, for example, a break between lower- and upper-secondary and upper-secondary and tertiary education, will become the rule rather than the exception. Certainly, we shall need to shed our "railway track" mentality, whereby we channel individuals along rigid lines, making a switch between education and employment difficult if not impossible. The plea here is a familiar one and perhaps even a cliché: for greater flexibility, both in concepts and in their implementation, including a fresh look at the potential of existing systems, such as part-time and "sandwich" courses.

Counselling and guidance

All this underlines the need to improve counselling and guidance facilities in schools, both before and during the upper-secondary stage. Our research has revealed a clear dissatisfaction on the part of many students with existing provision. Chief among their complaints were a lack of personalised information and advice, and a shortage of up-to-date, wide-ranging guidance over the whole spectrum of opportunities, which took account of current and foreseeable trends in the employment structure.

Clearly, counselling and guidance work needs to be developed and expanded. It needs more resources, particularly in the form of trained personnel. Above all, it needs to be thought of as a continuing process, beginning in the lower-secondary school, aimed at developing individuals' consciousness of their own abilities and interests, and of the whole range of opportunities open to them.

It also needs to provide pupils with deeper insights into the world outside school, including the world of employment. Admittedly, this is easier said than done. Previous experiments with work-experience schemes have been restricted to only a tiny minority of pupils, and have met with only limited success. Certainly, the administrative problems involved are enormous, and for this reason, perhaps — as was suggested earlier — we should take a fresh look at the possibilities of part-time or "sandwich" style upper-secondary education with regard to providing pupils with this type of experience.

One final issue, related to all of this, concerns the recruitment of teachers for this age-group. Clearly, many upper-secondary students feel that their teachers are out of touch, unworldly, or too limited in their range of experiences. Arguably, we shall need to think in terms of dramatically expanding our present concepts of in-service training and/or of allowing a greater flow of individuals between the teaching profession and other sectors of employment. One obvious field is counselling and guidance; the students who took part in our research have not been alone in criticising the frequent "monopoly" of teachers, and in calling for an inflow of people with first-hand experience of a range of employment and educational fields. This is one way in which links between education and industry might be strengthened.

The need for information, research and collaboration

Every research report begs for more information and still further enquiry. This one is no exception. Point is, however, added to the present plea by the very fact that the Schools Council Working Party on the over-16s in England emphasised the extreme difficulty of obtaining (let alone co-ordinating) information about who the enrolled post-compulsory students are in Britain, how many they are likely to be outside the conventional "sixth form" categories, and what happens to them. Likewise a recent report published by the National Union of Teachers was hampered by lack of statistical information, especially where it was necessary to come down to details and diagnose evolving trends.

Lack of reliable facts is most likely to occur in connection with new sectors of the population, or in the case of new types of institution or programme, since many of these fall outside the categories about which previous enquiries were made. Hence the over-16s, themselves unprecedented in dimensions and interests, and differently considered by those catering for them in schools or employment or advertising, now have a different range of educational questions asked about them from anything found in previous enquiries conducted with different intentions. So the need for a stronger information service, with factual answers to questions previously unasked, is plain enough.

Objective information therefore needs to be continuously compiled, co-ordinated, and disseminated – not merely nationally but internationally. No clearing-house of information can ever reach completeness in compilation or evaluation, since this is the most changing area of rapidly changing educational systems. Likewise, the social, economic, and personal uses to which information is put complicate the collecting and dissemination of data – at this level more than most; while changing patterns of international interdependence add a further dimension of uncertainty.

Perhaps even more cogent arguments for continuing research and exchange of experience arise from the *subjective* aspects of learning, teaching, and otherwise facilitating the development of young adults' education. What new institutions, programmes, methods, and relationships appear *to the participants* to work out best? What does this mean in terms of structure, organisation, and perhaps enhanced demand? The serious study of new and evolving provision for the over-16s – constantly creating new conditions, with new implications at levels above and below – calls for the exchange of insights and information not easily reducible to statistics. About many of the most important things in life the most significant "facts" are learned and used in experience and interchange.

Rigorous analysis is needed, of course; and hard data are needed too, wherever possible; but by the very nature of education as now understood the process of enquiry in future demands participant and subjective gathering and exchange of information. Some team research, and some in-service programmes of research-and-review, come near to this desideratum; but many initiatives do not get very far for lack of overall systematisation or co-ordination, or because it is not seen that new problems and new solutions are emerging, instead of appendages to the old. For that reason, research must be based on form recognition that the education of young adults in the post-compulsory phase today gives rise to *new* perceptions and concerns. These need special working-over by unprecedented means – in research and information supply, as in all else.

It is easy to see areas of special unawareness: in counselling and guidance; in the transition from school to work and back again; in the setting up and management of new kinds of provision for the over-16s; in reconciling personal satisfactions or needs with those of employment or of educational programmes; in training, supporting, and reinforcing teachers – especially for the 16-20 age-range, but also with an eye to the return of older students to resume education at that kind of attainment level.

In comparable countries, like those of Western Europe and perhaps regions of sophisticated urbanisation elsewhere, the continuous prompting of research and conversation about findings can be conducted through the great international agencies of scholarship and development. But intermittent congresses can never do much good. The gearing-in of research to programming, and the interlocking of programming with evidence from feedback, are examples of problem areas where new, co-operative enquiries and action-research must become (so to speak) endemic in each country but pandemic in purview.

At the same time, what develops a thriving situation in one place or time may be quite unsuited to another. Therefore the particular needs of unusual cultures, or of situations where economic and/or scholastic development is not served by equipment and presuppositions acceptable in Europe and North America, call for local research on the ground — not copying. The "folkways" and indigenous institutions may be a firmer foundation for education than the school patterns which have proliferated in the West, themselves often by-products of the industrialising process but already outmoded by the approach of a new technological era.

It becomes all the more necessary to call for new, sensitive research-in-action because much enquiry conducted "objectively" by the firm disciplines surrounding education has long missed the essence of education by being content with easily assessable categories, or with data which in the matter of education are really only constituent parts of a much bigger thing. That is why the programme of research reported on here was motivated by desire to obtain and present the "inside view" of the over-16s and their mentors. By the same token, present and future action taken on their behalf demands meticulous documentation, wide publicity and discussion, and continuous action-research.

ACKNOWLEDGEMENTS

The Comparative Research Unit owes its existence to funding by the Social Science Research Council, and acknowledges this support with gratitude.

The Comparative Research Unit is also very grateful to research organisations, individual researchers, and educational administrators in all the countries concerned for the help they have given — particularly in facilitating contact with schools. The Unit greatly appreciates help given by other officials, including representatives of the Careers Service and its equivalents. Many unofficial colleagues have also helped with advice and introductions.

The researchers thank the Swedish National Board of Education and the City School Board of Hamburg for the translation, printing, and distribution of questionnaires.

They also thank head teachers, teachers, and students for their very generous co-operation, not only in completing the questionnaires but also giving freely of their time for interviews and discussion.

The researchers gratefully acknowledge the financial contribution of the Council of Europe to travel expenses, and help received in other ways from embassies.

Particular thanks are due to University of London King's College for many services, including those generously given by Mr. J. Tandy and other colleagues in the Computer Unit.

Finally, the authors are very grateful to Mrs. Barbara Grice for unfailing patience and meticulous care in typing this Report and all preparatory documents, with complicated tables and many passages in foreign languages.

APPENDIX I

QUESTIONNAIRES USED FOR THE SURVEY

UNIVERSITY OF LONDON KING'S COLLEGE
COMPARATIVE RESEARCH UNIT

Enquiry into the educational and social implications of the expansion of upper-secondary education in England and Western Europe

RESEARCH REQUIREMENTS IN
SCHOOLS/COLLEGES
ENGLAND

For the attention of the
Head Teacher or Principal

The Research Programme in Schools

In order that schools and colleges may be as little disturbed as possible by the visits of Research Staff, the following notes may be found useful. If head teachers or principals would like further details, enquiries will be welcomed by the Research Director.

The research work is based on a series of questionnaires and interviews. While an attempt has been made to make these questionnaires as 'universal' as possible, the researchers realise that the wide variety of organisation found in English schools means that they may not suit any one school or college. Head teachers and principals are therefore invited to comment if they feel that the questionnaires do not give an adequate picture of the school or college structure, curriculum, teaching, and careers guidance and counselling systems.

Sample copies of all questionnaires are sent in advance to the head teacher or principal. Questionnaires for staff and head teacher or principal are also usually sent in advance; these may then be completed at convenient times, and queries may be raised when the researchers visit the school. All teachers who take part in the enquiry will receive a printed explanation of the research. Student questionnaires are brought to the school by the research staff.

All information given to the Unit is confidential and anonymous.

The research programme in any one school takes approximately one day to complete. It is hoped that the following information will enable head teachers or principals to arrange a timetable which will cause minimal interruption to the life of the school or college.

Questionnaires and Interviews

A.   The head teacher or principal

Questionnaires. There are three questionnaires for the head teacher or principal.

(a)   K   This questionnaire is concerned with admissions, transfers and staffing. It is possible for some of the detail to be filled in by secretarial staff. The questionnaire takes approximately one hour to complete.

(b)   CM1   The second questionnaire is concerned with the school catchment area, the social background of students and the patterns of higher education and occupations followed by students after they leave school. It takes approximately one hour to complete.

(c)   JM3   This is a list of subjects as they may appear on the school timetable. It is completed by ticking off those subjects which are taught in the school and marking in in the appropriate column the level to which they are taught. This questionnaire, which takes about fifteen minutes to answer, may be completed by the head teacher or principal, or by the member of staff responsible for the timetable. Head teachers and principals are also asked to fill in the general sections of the teachers' questionnaire JM1 Questions 17 – 37.

Interviews. The researchers hope it will be possible for them to have an interview with the head teacher or principal.

B. The school/college staff

Questionnaires. There are two questionnaires for staff:

(a) CM2 This questionnaire is for those staff who are especially concerned with careers guidance and counselling.

(b) JM1 This is concerned with teachers' perceptions of students' reasons for staying on in full-time education, perception of students' educational needs and the ways in which these needs are met by the school or college. There are also questions on the development of curricula and teaching methods. It is hoped that as many as possible of the staff who teach the student sample, and as many heads of department as possible, will complete this questionnaire.

Interviews

(a) Careers, guidance and counselling. Because of the difficulties already mentioned, arising from the variety of structure in schools and colleges Mrs. Moor would appreciate an opportunity to meet (either individually or in small groups) those members of staff who are particularly concerned with guidance and counselling.

(b) Curriculum and teaching/learning relationships. Miss Mundy would appreciate an interview with the Director of Studies, if one exists, or a member of staff or small group of staff familiar with curricular trends within the school or college.

C. The students

Questionnaires. There are two questionnaires for students, which together take approximately between one hour and one and three-quarter hours.

(a) CM3 This is concerned with the students' social background, their perceptions of counselling and guidance in school/college, and their educational/career aspirations and expectations.

(b) JM2 A questionnaire concerning reasons for staying on in full-time education, subjects studied, students' perception of their educational needs, and the ways in which these needs are met in school/college.

It is desirable that 100-150 students in each school/college complete the

questionnaires, selected in such a way as to ensure a representative balance of the range of pupils' intellectual abilities and social background and of the subjects offered in the timetable. (Students participating in any new curriculum developments should be represented). These students will be selected by the head teacher or principal, or someone appointed by him, and not by the Research Staff.

It is not necessary for all students to complete the questionnaires at the same time; nor do the researchers need to be present. Students are not asked to put their names on the questionnaires. However, the questionnaires are numbered, and it is important that each student be given a CM3 and a JM2 questionnaire with identical numbers, so that the data obtained can be correctly processed. Students should be supervised while they are completing the questionnaires – a copy of the information sheet for staff is on the following page. There are further copies of this in the boxes of questionnaires, and in the head's folder.

COMPARATIVE RESEARCH UNIT

UNIVERSITY OF LONDON KING'S COLLEGE

For the attention of staff who administer the student questionnaires

There are two questionnaires for each student: a CM3 and a JM2 (the latter is in two sections, A and B). Students are not asked to write their names on the questionnaires as their replies are confidential and anonymous. The questionnaires are numbered and it is important to give to each student a CM3 and a JM2, each with the *same* number, so that the data obtained can be processed correctly. The CM3 questionnaire is filled in first, followed by the JM2.

Experience has shown that students take between one hour and one and three-quarter hours to complete the two questionnaires. They should be supervised while they are doing this. It is not necessary for students to stay in the room after they have finished but this, obviously, is at the discretion of the head or principal.

If, by any chance, students do not understand particular questions then staff may explain the question, but without suggesting an answer.

When the questionnaires are collected it is important that:

1. Students are reminded that the two parts of the JM2 questionnaire should each have the school number and student number written on them (pages JM2/2 and JM2/12) and that both parts should be fastened together with a paperclip.

2. The CM3 and JM2 questionnaires are collected in separate piles and that these piles are in numerical order.

* * *

The researchers would like to apologise to staff for any inconvenience which this supervision may have caused them, and to thank them most gratefully for the help they have given.

UNIVERSITY OF LONDON KING'S COLLEGE   K/1

COMPARATIVE RESEARCH UNIT

Questionnaire for Heads of Upper-secondary Schools and/or Administrators Responsible

Admissions, Staffing, and Transfers

(Your kind co-operation is requested in answering the following questions. Not all of them will apply to your type of institution, though the questions have been designed to suit as many institutions as possible and a wide range of patterns of administration. For that reason the questions have been simplified and standardised so that reasonably comparable data can be gathered in all the countries surveyed, and the main trends examined.

We hope that it will be easy for you to move quickly past the questions which do not apply directly to yourself. In many cases it will be sufficient to mark with a pencil the part of the question which really applies to you.)

1. Do you accept all applicants who have completed the requisite number of years of previous education?   Yes/No

2. If not, are there special entry requirements for the entire school?   Yes/No
part of the school or curriculum? (Please specify):

3. Does this school/college run parallel to other upper-secondary schools requiring different levels of attainment before admission?   Yes/No
Or does this school/college run parallel to institutions offering higher and/or lower qualifications in the upper-secondary age-range?   Yes/No

4. If a certificate of competence in a lower school (as mentioned above) is not required for all or part of the admissions to this school/college do you still sometimes reject applicants on other grounds? (Please specify):

5. Do all your applicants come from one type of lower school?   Yes/No
If from one kind of school only, please name that kind:

6. Are certificates or marks obtained in the lower school used to allocate students to particular courses in the upper school?   Yes/No

7. If not, how are students allocated to the various courses which you offer?

8. Is there a quota or numerus clausus for the various "lines" or courses offered in the upper-secondary school?   Yes/No

9. If there is a restriction on numbers allowed to enter certain courses, what criteria do you use? Please tick all the following items which seem appropriate:
   (i) attainment shown in the lower school ....
   (ii) report about working habits from the previous school ....
   (iii) reports about behaviour from the previous school ....
   (iv) performance at an interview .....
   (v) previous experience of a relevant kind outside the school ....
   (vi) other reasons (please specify):

10. Do more boys than girls seek to enter particular courses?   Yes/No
If your answer is "yes", please list the courses or "lines" most sought by:
boys.....
girls....

11. Please list the courses or "lines" which you offer in *descending* order of popularity with students and/or parents (i.e. with the most popular listed as number (i)).
   (i)
   (ii)
   (iii)
   (iv)

12. Which courses are generally considered by yourself and your teachers to be most important for admission to higher education and the more "educated" careers?
   (i)
   (ii)

(iii)

(iv)

(v)

(Please put the most important as number (i)).

13. Has there been a change in this order of importance in about the last 10 years? If so, which subjects have become more important in terms of career prediction, and which less important?

More important ....

Less important ....

14. If only some courses or "lines" lead to a full certificate of maturity admitting to the university, please name those courses:

(i)

(ii)

(iii)

(iv)

(v)

15. Are all the courses in the usual curriculum offered within this school/college, or are some courses given in other places?

If some are given outside or in co-operation with other institutions, please name the courses and institutions below:

(i)

(ii)

(iii)

(iv)

(v)

16. If all the courses of the usual curriculum are offered *here* but specialist teachers are brought in from outside for particular parts of the curriculum, please name the subjects for which such teachers are introduced:

(i)

(ii)

(iii)

(iv)

(v)

17. Is it possible for students who begin their work in this upper-secondary school to transfer to another type of school if they prove unsuitable for the studies they have begun, or for some good reason find the work uncongenial?   Yes/No

18. If your answer to the previous question is "yes", is the transfer named at the student's request, or at the teacher's recommendation?

19. If students are not very successful, can they take a shortened course in this institution, and gain a qualification lower than the usual one given on full completion?   Yes/No

20. If students are not very successful but wish to continue here, can they take a longer period than usual to prepare for the examination admitting to higher education?   Yes/No

21. At the end of the upper-secondary school course, do students take *one* type of examination (for example, as a combined school-leaving and university admission certificate)?   Yes/No

22. If your answer to the previous question is "yes", are higher and lower levels required for admission to various types of full-time post-secondary institution (for example, university and non-university institutions)? Please give details briefly:

23. Do the teachers who give courses here leading to university admission examination also teach part-time in post-secondary colleges or universities?   Yes/No

24. If your answer to the previous question is "yes", does that apply only to academic study or also to practical studies and vocationally-linked training?   Yes/No

25. Please list any advantages which you think the present school structure has for the maintenance and development of the curriculum associated with this school/college:

26. Please list any disadvantages which you think the present school structure has for the maintenance and development of the curriculum associated with this school/college:

27. Do some teachers and/or department(s) have distinct responsibility under your direction for particular "lines" or courses?   Yes/No

28. If your answer to the previous question is "yes", are such departments or lines self-contained, or are parts of a common curriculum shared by all or most of the students in the school? (Please specify briefly):

29. Are teachers with distinguishable qualifications (for example, degrees or lower certificates) engaged exclusively for work in one particular department and/or "line" (or closely related subject interest)?

30. If teachers are so differentiated according to their qualifications and/or types of teaching they do, do they receive lower rates of pay and/or inferior working conditions? (Please give brief details):

31. Is there a Council or similar body representing the students?   Yes/No

32. If your answer to the previous question is "yes", in what areas of school life does such a school Council have powers of:

    recommendations or comment:

    effective decision:

33. If there is such a school Council, which members of staff (if any) sit on it?

34. Do ordinary teachers have an opportunity of making their views on the curriculum and/or school organisation felt?   Yes/No

35. Is there a Parent-Teacher Association?   Yes/No

36. If your answer to the previous question is "yes", does such a Parents' Association influence the school curriculum and/or administration? (Please give details):

37. Are there other ways in which local citizens or the local administration can influence or encourage parts of the school's life? (Please give brief details):

UNIVERSITY OF LONDON KING'S COLLEGE

COMPARATIVE RESEARCH UNIT

Confidential

This questionnaire forms part of our research, sponsored by the Social Science Research Council. The project is concerned with the implications for schools and for society as a whole of the fact that increasingly large numbers of young people are now staying on in full-time education beyond the age of 15/16.

Our research covers England, France, West Germany, Italy and Sweden. Its aim is to investigate new trends in upper-secondary education, and the attitudes and opinions of teachers and students involved. In this way we hope to indicate directions for educational policy in the future.

We should be most grateful for your co-operation in completing the following questionnaire.

All replies will be anonymous and completely confidential. There is no question of judging any school or college, teacher or student.

Thank you for your co-operation.

PLEASE TURN TO PAGE TWO.

1. From which geographical area do your upper-secondary students (i.e. those aged 16 or over, doing full-time courses) come? (Please indicate the boundaries of the area, and if possible briefly describe its main social and economic characteristics).

2. From which social groups (as indicated by their father's occupation) do these students come?
(Please tick all that apply, and indicate with a figure 1 the group from which *most* students come)

...... Professional or higher managerial

...... Intermediate managerial, technical or "white collar" occupation

...... Lower technical, clerical or other non-manual occupation

...... Skilled manual

...... Semi- or un-skilled manual

IF YOUR SCHOOL OR COLLEGE HAS *LOWER-* AS WELL AS UPPER-SECONDARY PUPILS, PLEASE ANSWER *QUESTIONS 3 & 4. IF NOT, PLEASE PROCEED TO QUESTION 5.*

3. Do your lower-secondary pupils come from:

...... the same geographical area as your upper-secondary students?

...... a larger area?

...... a smaller area?

(Please tick whichever applies, *and, if your reply is "a larger area" or "a smaller area"*, please indicate the boundaries of that area and if possible briefly describe its main social and economic characteristics).

4. From which social groups (as indicated by their father's occupation) do your *lower-secondary* pupils come? (Please tick all that apply, and indicate with a figure 1 the group from which most pupils come).

...... Professional or higher managerial

...... Intermediate managerial, technical or "white collar" occupation

...... Lower technical, clerical or other non-manual occupation

...... Skilled manual

...... Semi- or un-skilled manual

5. On average, what percentage of *upper-secondary* students leaving this school or college each year proceed to;

	BOYS %	GIRLS %
...... University or equivalent courses of study?		
...... College of Education?		
...... Other full-time studies (including Art School)?		
...... Jobs with training leading to a professional qualification (e.g. accountancy or nursing)		
...... Other jobs with training		
...... Jobs involving no training (or no further training after upper-secondary studies)		
...... Services (Army; Navy; Air Force)		
...... None of those mentioned above		
IF no details known, TICK HERE		

6. We should be most grateful if, in addition, you could supply details of the *types of* studies or employment chosen most frequently by students leaving this school or college. If possible, please indicate by a figure (1) the type chosen by *most* students, by a figure (2) the *next most* frequently chosen, and so on:

	BOYS	GIRLS
...... University or equivalent courses of study		
...... College of Education		
...... Other full-time studies		
...... Jobs with training leading to a professional qualification		
...... Other jobs with training		
...... Jobs involving no training (or no further training)		
...... Services (Army; Navy; Air Force)		
...... None of these mentioned above		

Page CM1/5

7. Do upper-secondary students from this school or college ever leave before completing their course of studies?

..... Yes *(If so, please answer question 8)*

..... No *(If so, please disregard question 8 and go straight to question 9)*

8. (a) On average, how many boys and girls leave each year before completing their course of studies?

.... *boys?*

.... *girls?*

(b) For what reasons do they leave?
(If these are known, please list them in the spaces below. 1 represents the most common reason, 2 the next most common reason, and so on)

.... *boys*	.... *girls*
1.	1.
2.	2.
3.	3.
4.	4.

(c) Do boys and girls who leave before completing their course of studies tend to represent any particular (e.g.) types of home background? attainment level? course of studies?

..... Yes, please give details)

.... No

9. Research has suggested that children's performance in school, and hence their educational and occupational attainments, are to some extent related to their home background.

In this school or college, are their any discernible differences *between upper-secondary students from different home backgrounds* with regard to:

a) THE PROPORTIONS ENTERING VARIOUS TYPES OF EDUCATION, TRAINING OR EMPLOYMENT?

b) THE *KINDS* OF COURSES OR JOBS CHOSEN BY STUDENTS *WITHIN* THESE TYPES OF EDUCATION, TRAINING OR EMPLOYMENT?

For a) and b), please answer *"Yes"* if there *are* differences according to home background, and *"No"* if there *are no* such differences, and give details in the space provided for your comments.

(1) *UNIVERSITY OR EQUIVALENT STUDIES*

a) Are there differences according to home background in the *proportions* of students entering?

	BOYS	GIRLS
	...... Yes	...... Yes
	...... No	...... No
For your comments		

b) Are there differences in the *courses and institutions chosen by students* from different home backgrounds?

	BOYS	GIRLS
	...... Yes	...... Yes
	...... No	...... No
For your comments		

(II) *OTHER TYPES OF FULL-TIME STUDIES*

a) Are there differences according to home background in the *proportions of students entering?*

	BOYS	GIRLS
Yes	......	
No	......	

Yes
No

For your comments

b) Are there differences in the *courses and institutions chosen by students* from different home backgrounds?

	BOYS	GIRLS
Yes	......	
No	......	

Yes
No

For your comments

(III) *EMPLOYMENT WITH TRAINING (PROFESSIONAL OR OTHER)*

a) Are there differences according to home background in the *proportions of students entering?*

	BOYS	GIRLS
Yes	......	
No	......	

Yes
No

For your comments

b) Are there any differences in the *types of employment with training* chosen by students from different home backgrounds?

	BOYS	GIRLS
Yes	......	
No	......	

Yes
No

(IV) *EMPLOYMENT INVOLVING NO TRAINING (OR NO FURTHER TRAINING AFTER UPPER-SECONDARY COURSE)*

a) Are there differences according to home background in the *proportions of students entering?*

	BOYS	GIRLS
Yes	......	
No	......	

Yes
No

For your comments

b) Are there differences in the *types of employment* chosen by students from different home backgrounds?

	BOYS	GIRLS
Yes	......	
No	......	

Yes
No

For your comments

10. Do any staff in this school or college have special responsibilities for providing upper-secondary students with information, advice or guidance concerning:

a) *Students' work in school or college?* (choice of courses; progress, etc.)

...... Yes

...... No

IF "YES", PLEASE ANSWER QUESTION 11

b) *Educational opportunities after upper-secondary studies?* (University; Colleges of Education; Further Education; other courses of study or training, etc.)

...... Yes

...... No

IF "YES", PLEASE ANSWER QUESTION 12

c) *Careers?*

...... Yes

...... No

IF "YES", PLEASE ANSWER QUESTION 13

d) *Personal matters?*

...... Yes

...... No

IF "YES", PLEASE ANSWER QUESTION 14

N.B. We realise that counselling and guidance work may cover two or more of these areas simultaneously, and hence not fit neatly into any one category.

11. *Students' work in school or college*

a) Who is responsible for providing this type of information, advice or guidance?

b) How are they selected to do this work?

c) Are they required to have any special training or qualifications?

...... Yes

...... No

If "yes"

what type of training or qualifications?

12. *Educational opportunities after upper-secondary studies*

a) Who is responsible for providing this type of information, advice or guidance?

b) How are they selected to do this work?

c) Are they required to have any special training or qualifications?

...... Yes

...... No

If "yes"

What type of training or qualifications?

13. *Careers*

a) Who is responsible for providing this type of information, advice or guidance?

b) How are they selected to do this work?

c) Are they required to have any special training or qualifications?

...... Yes

...... No

If "yes"

What type of training or qualifications?

14. *Personal Matters*

a) Who is responsible for providing this type of information, advice or guidance?

b) How are they selected to do this work?

c) Are they required to have any special training or qualifications?

...... Yes

...... No

If "yes"

What type of training or qualifications?

15. Are any other sources of information, advice or guidance available to upper-secondary students in this school or college concerning:

a) *Their work in school or college?*

...... Yes

...... No

If "yes" – please give details:

b) *Educational opportunities after upper-secondary studies?*

...... Yes

...... No

If "yes" – please give details:

c) *Careers?*

...... Yes

...... No

If "yes" – please give details:

d) *Personal matters?*

...... Yes

...... No

If "yes" – please give details:

16. What trends

(i) *have you seen in recent years*

(ii) *do you expect to see in the next few years*

(iii) *would you like to see in the next few years*

in:

a) *The range of students catered for by a school or college like this one?*

(i)

(ii)

(iii)

b) *Students' expectations concerning employment and educational opportunities after upper-secondary studies?*

(i)

(ii)

(iii)

Page CM1/13

16. c) *The actual range of employment and educational opportunities open to upper-secondary students leaving a school or college like this one?*

(i)

(ii)

(iii)

FOR YOUR COMMENTS

UNIVERSITY OF LONDON KING'S COLLEGE

COMPARATIVE RESEARCH UNIT

CONFIDENTIAL

This questionnaire forms part of our research, sponsored by the Social Science Research Council. The project is concerned with the implications for schools and for society as a whole of the fact that increasingly large numbers of young people are now staying on in full-time education beyond the age of 15/16.

Our research covers England, France, West Germany, Italy and Sweden. Its aim is to investigate new trends in upper-secondary education, and the attitudes and opinions of teachers and students involved. In this way we hope to indicate directions for educational policy in the future.

We should be most grateful for your co-operation in completing the following questionnaire.

All replies will be anonymous and completely confidential. There is no question of judging any school or college, teacher or student.

Thank you for your co-operation.

PLEASE TURN TO PAGE TWO.

Does your counselling or guidance work cover:

a) STUDENTS' WORK IN SCHOOL OR COLLEGE? (choice of courses, progress; etc.)

...... Yes *(If "Yes", please turn to section A on page 3)*

...... No

b) EDUCATIONAL OPPORTUNITIES AFTER UPPER-SECONDARY STUDIES? (University; Colleges of Education; Further Education; other courses of study or training, etc.)

...... Yes *(If "Yes", please turn to section B on page 5)*

...... No

c) CAREERS?

...... Yes *(If "Yes", please turn to section C on page 7)*

...... No

d) PERSONAL MATTERS?

...... Yes *(If "Yes", please turn to section D on page 11)*

...... No

PLEASE DISREGARD ALL SECTIONS WHICH DO NOT APPLY TO YOU

N.B. We realise that counselling or guidance work may cover two or more of these areas simultaneously, and hence not fit neatly into any one category. There is a space at the end of the questionnaire for your comments on this or any other points.

SECTION A: STUDENTS' WORK ON SCHOOL OR COLLEGE

1. (a) Does your counselling or guidance work take up:

       ...... All your time in school or college?

       ...... Part of your time in school or college?

    (b) How many hours per week, on average, does this represent?

2. Do you deal with:

       ...... All students? – *IF SO, GO STRAIGHT TO QUESTION 4*

       ...... Only some students? – *IF SO, PLEASE ANSWER QUESTION 3*

3. (a) How many students does this mean?

    (b) Please indicate with which students you deal (e.g. do they tend to be from: particular home backgrounds? courses of study? Age groups? etc.)

4. What exactly does your counselling or guidance work involve? (Please give as detailed a picture as possible)

5. Does anyone else besides yourself, either in this school or college or outside it, have responsibilities for providing students with this type of counselling or guidance?

       ...... Yes – IF SO, PLEASE ANSWER QUESTION 6

       ...... No – IF SO, PLEASE GO STRAIGHT TO QUESTION 7

6. (a) Who else has responsibilities for this form of counselling or guidance?

    (b) Please give details of their work with students in this school or college.

    (c) What liaison, if any, is there between your work and theirs?

7. What developments, if any, in the provision of this form of counselling and guidance work would you like to see?

414   Post-Compulsory Education in Western Europe

Page CM2/5

SECTION B: EDUCATIONAL OPPORTUNITIES AFTER UPPER-SECONDARY STUDIES

1. (a)   Does your counselling or guidance work take up:

...... All your time in school or college?

...... Part of your time in school or college?

(b)   How many hours per week, on average, does this represent?

2. Do you deal with:

...... All students? *IF SO, GO STRAIGHT TO QUESTION 4*

...... Only some students? – *IF SO, PLEASE ANSWER QUESTION 3*

3. (a)   How many students does this mean?

(b)   Please indicate with which students you deal (e.g. do they tend to be from: particular home backgrounds? courses of study? age groups? etc.)

4. What exactly does your counselling or guidance work involve? (Please give as detailed a picture as possible)

Page CM2/6

5. Does anyone else besides yourself, either in this school or college or outside it, have responsibilities for providing students with this type of counselling or guidance?

...... Yes – IF SO, PLEASE ANSWER QUESTION 6

...... No – IF SO, PLEASE GO STRAIGHT TO QUESTION 7

6. (a)   Who else has responsibilities for this form of counselling or guidance?

(b)   Please give details of their work with students in this school or college.

(c)   What liaison, if any, is there between your work and theirs?

7. What developments, if any, in the provision of this form of counselling and guidance work would you like to see?

SECTION C: CAREERS

1. (a) Does your counselling or guidance work take up:

...... All your time in school or college?

...... Part of your time in school or college?

(b) How many hours per week, on average, does this represent?

2. Do you deal with:

...... All students? – *IF SO, GO STRAIGHT TO QUESTION 4*

...... Only some students? – *IF SO, PLEASE ANSWER QUESTION 3*

3. (a) How many students does this mean?

(b) Please indicate with which students you deal (e.g. do they tend to be from: particular home backgrounds? courses of study? age groups? etc.)

4. What exactly does your counselling or guidance work involve? (Please give as detailed a picture as possible)

(N.B: Replies to questions 5-10 may have been included in your answer to question 4. If you have already given all necessary details of work visits and work experience schemes, please disregard questions 5-10 and proceed to question 11).

5. Does this school or college arrange visits to places of work (e.g. offices; factories; industrial plants)?

...... Yes – for all students – IF SO, PLEASE ANSWER QUESTION 6, BUT NOT 7.

...... Yes – for some students – IF SO, PLEASE ANSWER QUESTIONS 6 AND 7.

...... No – IF SO, GO STRAIGHT TO QUESTION 8.

6. (a) Please give details of the types of places of work visited by students.

(b) How are these places chosen?

(c) How are the visits arranged?

(d) How long do these visits usually last?

...... Half a school or college day, or less

...... More than half, or one whole day

...... More than one whole day.

(e) How many visits to places of work does each student make, on average?

7. (a) How many students does this mean?

    (b) Which students go on these visits? (e.g.) does it depend on their: course of studies? interests? age? attainment level?

8. Does this school or college arrange for students to gain practical experience of employment by working in (e.g.) a factory, office or shop for a period of time during the course of their studies?

    ...... Yes – for all students – IF SO, PLEASE ANSWER QUESTION 9, BUT NOT 10.

    ...... Yes – for some students – IF SO, PLEASE ANSWER QUESTIONS 9 AND 10.

    ...... No – IF SO, GO STRAIGHT TO QUESTION 11

9. (a) In which types of employment do students gain practical experience?

    (b) How are the firms or organisation which take part chosen?

    (c) How are these periods of practical work experience arranged?

    (d) How long do these periods of work experience usually last?

    (e) How many periods of work experience does each student have, on average?

10. (a) How many students does this mean?

     (b) Which students participate in these work experience schemes? (e.g. does it depend on their: course of studies? interests? age? attainment level?

11. Does anyone else besides yourself, either in this school or college or outside it, have responsibilities for providing students with this type of counselling or guidance?

     ...... Yes – IF SO, PLEASE ANSWER QUESTION 12

     ...... No – IF SO, PLEASE GO STRAIGHT TO QUESTION 13

12. (a) Who else has responsibilities for this form of counselling or guidance?

     (b) Please give details of their work with students in this school or college.

     (c) What liaison, if any, is there between your work and theirs?

13. What developments, if any, in the provision of this form of counselling and guidance work would you like to see?

Page CM2/11

SECTION D: PERSONAL MATTERS

1. (a) Does your counselling or guidance work take up:

   ...... All your time in school or college?

   ...... Part of your time in school or college?

   (b) How many hours per week, on average, does this represent?

2. Do you deal with:

   ...... All students? – IF SO, GO STRAIGHT TO QUESTION 4.

   ...... Only some students? – IF SO, PLEASE ANSWER QUESTION 3

3. (a) How many students does this mean?

   (b) Please indicate with which students you deal (e.g. do they tend to be from: particular home backgrounds? courses of study? age groups? etc.)

4. What exactly does your counselling or guidance work involve? (Please give as detailed a picture as possible)

Page CM2/12

5. Does anyone else besides yourself, either in this school or college or outside it, have responsibilities for providing students with this type of counselling or guidance?

   ...... Yes – IF SO, PLEASE ANSWER QUESTION 6

   ...... No – IF SO, PLEASE GO STRAIGHT TO QUESTION 7

6. (a) Who else has responsibilities for this form of counselling or guidance?

   (b) Please give details of their work with students in this school or college

   (c) What liaison, if any, is there between your work and theirs?

7. What developments, if any, in the provision of this form of counselling and guidance work would you like to see?

THE FOLLOWING PAGE IS LEFT BLANK FOR ANY COMMENTS YOU WISH TO MAKE

Page CM2/13

FOR YOUR COMMENTS

Page CM3/1

UNIVERSITY OF LONDON KING'S COLLEGE

COMPARATIVE RESEARCH UNIT

CONFIDENTIAL

This questionnaire forms part of our research, sponsored by the Social Science Research Council. The project is concerned with the implications for schools and for society as a whole of the fact that increasingly large numbers of young people are now staying on in full-time education beyond the age of 15/16.

Our research covers England, France, West Germany, Italy and Sweden. Its aim is to investigate new trends in upper-secondary education, and the attitudes and opinions of teachers and students involved. In this way, we hope to indicate directions for educational policy in the future.

Please help us by taking part in this research project and answering the following questions.

All replies will be anonymous and completely confidential. There is no question of judging any school, teacher or student.

Thank you for your co-operation.

PLEASE TURN TO PAGE TWO

Page CM3/2

REFERENCE

	School	Student
Male		1
Female		2

Please answer as many questions as you can. If you want to add comments which might explain some of your answers, please do so.

Most questions can be answered simply by putting a ring around the number opposite the appropriate answer. For example, in the box above, you ring 1 if you are a male, and 2 if you are female.

If, on second thoughts, you wish to change an answer then put *a large cross* through that answer and then ring the number you want to give as your answer.

PLEASE DO NOT WRITE IN THIS MARGIN

1. What type of job does your father have?
(Please write in the space below as precise a description as possible).

If any of the following circumstances apply in your case, please ring the relevant number instead

Father dead, retired or not working	8
Father's job not known	9

2. What type of education have your father and mother had?
(Please ring the relevant number in each column)

	Father	Mother
Elementary school only, or with some shorter further education or training	1	1
School certificate (now called G.C.E. 'O' level)	2	2
Higher School Certificate (now called G.C.E. 'A' level)	3	3
University or equivalent	4	4
I do not know	9	9

3. To what extent did your father and mother encourage you to stay on in full-time education beyond the age of 15/16?

	Father	Mother
Greatly encouraged me	1	1
Encouraged me	2	2
Neither encouraged nor discouraged me	3	3
Discouraged me	4	4
Greatly discouraged me	5	5
I do not know/ question does not apply	9	9

4. How much information or guidance on employment and/or education opportunities would you say you have received from your father and mother?

	Father	Mother
A lot	1	1
Some	2	2
Hardly any	3	3
None at all	4	4
Question does not apply	9	9

5. How helpful have you found the information or guidance you received from your father and mother?

	Father	Mother
Very helpful	1	1
Fairly helpful	2	2
Not really helpful	3	3
Not at all helpful	4	4
Question does not apply (i.e. received no information or guidance)	9	9

PLEASE TURN TO PAGE 4 FOR QUESTION 6

PLEASE DO NOT WRITE IN THIS MARGIN

6. When you finish your present course of studies, what do you hope to do?
(Please ring only one answer in each column, and write details in the space provided below each answer)

	1st choice	2nd choice
University, or equivalent course of studies or training	1	1
College of Education	2	2
Other course of full-time studies (including Art School)	3	3
Job with training leading to professional qualification (e.g. nursing)	4	4
Other job with training	5	5
Job involving no training (or no further training)	6	6
None of these	7	7
Services (Army; Navy; Air Force)	8	8
I do not know	9	9

7. Do you think that you will in fact achieve your first choice, as stated in question 6.

Yes	1
No	2
Unsure; don't know	3

PLEASE DO NOT WRITE IN THIS MARGIN

Page CM3/5

PLEASE DO NOT WRITE IN THIS MARGIN

8. If your reply to question 7 was "No" or "Unsure; don't know," why do you think this? (Please ring one of the following reasons):

Standard or qualifications required — 1
Degree of competition for places — 2
Not sure that I shall complete my present course of studies — 3
All other reasons — 4
Question does not apply (i.e. reply to question 7 was "Yes") — 8
Do not know — 9

9. If your reply to question 7 was "No" or "Unsure, don't know," what do you think you will do instead of your first choice, when you finish your present course of studies?

Second choice as stated in question 6 — 1
Something else (please give details) — 2

Question does not apply (i.e. reply to question 7 was "Yes") — 8
Do not know — 9

10. If you had not continued in full-time education beyond the age of 15/16, what do you think you would have done instead? (If you wish, you may ring two answers, but no more than two)

Another type of studies or training (e.g. a secretarial course) — 1
Job with training leading to professional qualification (e.g. nursing) — 2
Other job with training (e.g. apprenticeship) — 3
Job involving no training (or no further training) — 4
Services (Army; Navy; Air Force) — 5
Very few or limited opportunities available at 15/16 — 6
I never considered leaving school at 15/16 — 7
None of these — 8
Do not know — 9

Page CM3/6

PLEASE DO NOT WRITE IN THIS MARGIN

11. Do you ever regret having continued in full-time education beyond the age of 15/16?

Yes, often — 1
Yes, sometimes — 2
Yes, very occasionally — 3
No, never — 4

12. Why do you regret having continued in full-time education beyond the age of 15/16? (If you wish, you may ring two answers, but no more than two. If your reply to question 11 was "No, never", please ring number 8).

The curriculum itself/way in which courses of study are organised or presented — 1
Uncertain/anxious about links between present studies and future employment/education — 2
Work load/pressure of examinations — 3
Want more freedom/independence/adult treatment in school or college — 4
Want more freedom/independence/adult treatment in general — 5
Want more financial independence — 6
Other reasons — 7
Question does not apply (i.e. reply to question 11 was "No, never") — 8
Boredom with upper-secondary studies — 9

13. After you complete your present course of studies, will your job prospects be:

Much better — 1
a little better — 2
about the same — 3
a little worse — 4
much worse — 5

..... than they would have been if you had left school at the age of 15/16?

PLEASE
DO NOT
WRITE
IN THIS
MARGIN

14. If you were to go on to another course of studies or training after completing your present studies, would your job prospects then be:

much better   1
a little better   2
about the same   3
a little worse   4
much worse   5

..... than they would be at the end of your present course of studies?

15. What kinds of employment and educational opportunities do you think will be open to you *at the end of your present course of studies?* (Please give details below).

16. What kinds of employment opportunities would be open to you *after a further course of studies or training?* (Please give details below).

17. How much information or guidance on employment and education opportunities have you received at *school/college?*

	Employment	Education
a lot	1	1
some	2	2
hardly any	3	3
none at all	4	4

PLEASE
DO NOT
WRITE
IN THIS
MARGIN

18. How helpful have you found the information or guidance you have received at school/college?

	Employment	Education
Very helpful	1	1
Fairly helpful	2	2
Not really helpful	3	3
Not at all helpful	4	4
Question does not apply (i.e. received no information or guidance)	9	9

19. *How much* information and guidance on employment and education would you *like* to receive at *school/college?*

much more   1
a little more   2
neither more nor less 3
a little less   4
much less   5

..... than you have received?

20. What type of information and guidance would you find most helpful? (Please give details).

FOR YOUR COMMENTS

EXPLANATION FOR TEACHERS

UNIVERSITY OF LONDON KING'S COLLEGE

COMPARATIVE RESEARCH UNIT

Enquiry into the educational and social implications of the expansion of upper-secondary education in England and Western Europe.

The comparative Research Unit has received a grant from the Social Science Research Council to conduct a 3-year enquiry into the educational and social implications of the expansion of upper-secondary education in England and four other Western European countries (France, German Federal Republic, Italy, and Sweden).

Background of the enquiry

The number of students staying on into the upper-secondary level of education, between the ages of 15-16 and 19 or 20, has grown rapidly in recent years, and in some countries has doubled or trebled since 1945.

In order to cater effectively for the needs of such a student population, representing a wider range of social and educational backgrounds, attainment levels, interests, aspirations and expectations than did previous generations of upper-secondary students, the traditional structure and content of education for this age-group are being widely reviewed. New curricula, teaching-learning relationships, and institutions are currently being designed in some places with this aim in mind.

Purpose of the enquiry

Your co-operation is earnestly invited in helping the researchers to obtain answers to some important questions. Your replies will be treated as anonymous and in the utmost confidence. There is no question of judging any school, teacher or student.

The researchers have designed a set of simple questionnaires, with separate lists of questions for Heads of schools, teachers and students. The questionnaires have been carefully co-ordinated so that the researchers can obtain inter-related information on institutional arrangements, curricular developments, teaching-learning arrangements, and student aspirations and expectations. The researchers wish to discover emerging trends, solutions which seem most helpful to those most directly concerned with upper-secondary education (i.e. teachers and students), and indications for future policy.

The central themes of the enquiry

1. What new institutions, curricula and teaching-learning arrangements have been, or are being, devised for the expanded upper-secondary school population?

2. What student needs have been recognised by teachers and the students themselves?

3. What arrangements so far (e.g. with regard to institutions, curricula and teaching-learning relationships) seem to teachers and students most helpful in meeting these needs?

4. What alternative arrangements are recommended by teachers and students?

5. What are the implications of these answers for other forms of educational provision?

The Researchers

Dr. Edmund J. King, Research Director, is concerned with the comparative study of institutional change and educational policy, and with the co-ordination of the research programme.

Mrs. Christine H. Moor, Research Associate, is concerned with social and economic changes as they affect the needs and occupational and educational aspirations and expectations of the expanding upper-secondary school population, and with the provision of counselling and careers guidance in schools.

Miss Jennifer A. Mundy, Research Associate, is concerned with curricular change, and with evolving arrangements for teaching and learning, with particular reference to the new needs of the expanding upper-secondary school population.

UNIVERSITY OF LONDON KING'S COLLEGE

COMPARATIVE RESEARCH UNIT

CONFIDENTIAL

This questionnaire forms part of our research, sponsored by the Social Science Research Council. The project is concerned with the implications for schools and for society as a whole of the fact that increasingly large numbers of young people are now staying on in full-time education beyond the age of 15/16.

Our research covers England, France, West Germany, Italy and Sweden. Its aim is to investigate new trends in upper-secondary education, and the attitudes and opinions of teachers and students involved. In this way, we hope to indicate directions for educational policy in the future.

We would be most grateful if you would help us in this research by completing the following questionnaire.

All replies will be anonymous and completely confidential. There is no question of judging any school, teacher or student.

Thank you for your co-operation

PLEASE TURN TO PAGE TWO.

PLEASE
DO NOT
WRITE
IN THIS
MARGIN

*Card A
and Card B*
Col.

1,2
3,4

SECTION A

School number: 50
Staff number: 25

Many questions can be answered simply by putting a ring round the number, or letter, opposite the appropriate answer, or by writing numbers or letters in the circles provided. If you wish to add comments which might explain some of your answers, please do so. If, on second thoughts, you wish to change an answer, then put a large cross through that answer and then give the answer you wish to give.

The questionnaire has been put together in two sections, A and B, because several people will have to work on the two sections afterwards. When you have finished we would be grateful if you would make sure that both sections are fastened together with one paper clip.

Page JM1/3

PLEASE
DO NOT
WRITE
IN THIS
MARGIN

Card A
Col.

1. For how many years have you been teaching?
Please ring the relevant number

0- 5 years	1
6-10 years	2
11-15 years	3
16-20 years	4
20 years plus	5

5

2. For how many years have you taught in this school/college? Please ring the relevant number

0- 5 years	1
6-10 years	2
11-15 years	3
16-20 years	4
20 years plus	5

6

3. Have you had experience of working in other types of career? Please ring the relevant number

Yes	1
No	2

7

4. a) If so what was the duration of that work?
Please ring the relevant number.

0- 5 years	1
6-10 years	2
11-15 years	3
16-20 years	4
20 years plus	5
Question does not apply to me	6

8

b) What was the nature of your work? Please explain briefly

9

5. Why did you decide to leave that work and come into teaching? Please explain briefly.

10
11

Page JM1/4

PLEASE
DO NOT
WRITE
IN THIS
MARGIN

Card A
Code Col
12
13

6. Would you please list below the subjects which you teach here?

SUBJECT	LEVEL	HOURS PER WEEK
i)		
ii)		
iii)		
iv)		

7. Would you please list below any extra-curricular activities in which you take part or for which you are responsible?

i)
ii)
iii)
iv)

14
15

8. Would you please list below any special responsibilities or duties you have in school or college other than your teaching and the extra-curricular activities mentioned above?

i)
ii)
iii)
iv)

9. Are you satisfied with the syllabus for your subject(s) for students who stay on beyond the official school-leaving age? Please ring the relevant number

Yes	1
To some extent	2
No	3

If 'Yes', please go to Question 11.

16

10. If you are not satisfied, in what ways do you think the syllabus for your subject(s) could be improved?

17
18
19
20

Page JM1/5

PLEASE DO NOT WRITE IN THIS MARGIN
Card A Code Col.

11. Do you think there will be any changes in the foreseeable future in the kind of student who will want to study your subjects? Please ring the relevant number.

   Yes   1
   No   2

   21

   If not, please go on to Question 15

12. If so, in what ways will the students be different?

   22
   23
   24

13. Will the syllabus and/or teaching methods for your subject(s) have to be adapted to suit these students? Please ring the relevant number

   Yes   1
   No   2

   25

   If not, please continue to Question 15

14. In what ways will the syllabus and/or teaching methods have to be adapted to suit these students?

   26
   27
   28
   29

Page JM1/6

PLEASE DO NOT WRITE IN THIS MARGIN
Card A Code Col

15. Quite apart from adapting the syllabus and/or teaching methods to suit new types of student do you foresee, or hope for, any fairly immediate changes in syllabus and/or teaching method for your subject(s)?

   Please ring the relevant number

   Yes   1
   No   2

   30

   If not, please go on to Question 17.

16. If so, what changes in syllabus and/or teaching method do you foresee, or hope for?

   31
   32
   33
   34

17. We would like to know why you think students decide to continue in full-time education. In the list below, please ring the number or letter opposite all the reasons which you think apply to students in this school/college:

	Code Col.
	0 35
They want qualifications which would help them to get a better job	1 36
They think it will be a good opportunity to make new friends	2 37
They cannot really decide what else to do	3 38
Teachers and/or counsellors advised them to do so	4 39
They want to go on to some form of higher education	5 40
Their parents think it is a sensible thing for them to do	6 41
They may well think about leaving at the official school-leaving age, but as there are few jobs available, opt to stay on instead	7 42
They want to study particular subjects which are of real interest to them	8 43
They are reluctant to start work	9 44
Most of their friends stay on in full-time education so they decide to do so as well	A 45

PLEASE DO NOT WRITE IN THIS MARGIN

Card A

18. If there are any other *general* reasons why students stay on, please list them in the spaces below, each separate reason opposite a letter B.

B

B

B

PLEASE DO NOT WRITE IN THIS MARGIN

Card A   Col.

19. From the list in questions 17 and 18 will you please write down in order of importance the number or letter of the *three* factors which you think most strongly influenced the students in your school/college. Put the most important first. Enter the number or letter in the circles provided.

i   46

ii   47

iii   48

If you find it difficult to make a list or think that a lot of things are equally important, leave the first three circles blank and enter a letter C in circle iv.

iv   49

20. Are there several schools and/or colleges in this area for students to choose from? (at the level immediately following the official school-leaving age)

Please ring the relevant number

Yes   1

No   2

If not, please go on to Question 25.   50

21. If there are several institutions in this area, do you have any students here for whom this school/college is a second, rather than a first choice?

Please ring the relevant number

Yes   1

No   2   51

22. Why, as a rule, are these students unable to go to the school/college of their first choice?

Please explain briefly.

23. When these students have been here for some time does it continue to matter to them that they are not in the school/college of their first choice?

Please ring the relevant number

Yes   1

No   2   52

24. Why do you think that it does continue to matter to them?

Please explain briefly.

25. Quite apart from *general* reasons for wanting to stay on, are there any *particular* factors which influence students to come here? Please ring the number or letter opposite all the reasons which apply to students in this school/college.
(N.B. We want to know those factors which influenced them to come rather than which they learn about after being here for some time.)

		PLEASE DO NOT WRITE IN THIS COLUMN
		Card A
		Code Col.
		0 53
The sports facilities are good here	1	54
They want the opportunity to take part in the extra-curricular activities	2	55
Students think that relations with staff will be easy here	3	56
There is freedom for students to organise things for themselves here	4	57
Students think that the standard of teaching here is high	5	58
Their friends decide to come here, so they come too	6	59
This school is a pleasant community to work in	7	60
The library facilities here are good	8	61
Students can be trained for particular jobs here	9	62
Students here can choose their own pattern of courses	A	63
They come here to get away from their old acquaintances and to make a new start	B	64
They want the chance to meet members of the opposite sex	C	65
This school/college is very successful at getting students through examinations	D	66

26. If there are any other reasons which influence the students to stay on in this school/college, please list them in the spaces below, each separate reason opposite a letter E

.... E

.... E

.... E

27. From the list in Question 25 and 26 will you please write down, in order of importance, the number or letter of the *three* factors which most strongly influence students to come here. Put the most important first. Enter the number or letter in the circles provided.

If you find it difficult to make a list or think that a lot of things are equally important, leave the first three circles blank and enter a letter F in circle iv.

	PLEASE DO NOT WRITE IN THIS SECTION
	Card A
	Col.
i ◯	67
ii ◯	68
iii ◯	69
iv ◯	70

		A	B	Card B Code Col 1,2 3,4
28 (contd.)				
School/college should help you to understand what is going on politically and socially in your own country		1	1	5
It should try to make sure that students pass their examinations		2	2	6
School/college should give you some experience of what it is like to live in a democracy		3	3	7
Staff should give you information which would help you to decide on a job or further course of education		4	4	8
School/college should give you the opportunity of learning to enjoy a wide range of arts like literature, films, music etc.		5	5	9
School/college should give you some kind of practical training which would be useful in a job after leaving school		6	6	10
An ideal school/college would give you a wide range of subjects from which to choose		7	7	11
School/college should teach you to think clearly		8	8	12
School/college should help you to have some understanding of important world problems, e.g. hunger, poverty, pollution		9	9	13
School/college should give you some understanding of what other people are like		A	A	14
School/college should teach you to work on your own		B	B	15
There ought to be plenty of extra-curricular activities in school/college so that people can find out what they like to do in their spare time		C	C	16
School/college should teach you to be flexible and adapt what you have learned to changing circumstances		D	D	17
School/college should help you to understand the sort of person that you are and develop your personality		E	E	18
School/college should give you some understanding of religious experience		F	F	19
School/college should make sure that you have some knowledge of a wide range of subjects		G	G	20
School/college should teach you how to get on better with other people		H	H	21
School/college should make sure that you are physically fit		J	J	22
School/college should give you some understanding of relationships between the sexes		K	K	23
School/college should prepare you to go on learning throughout life		L	L	24

School number 50
Staff number 25

SECTION B

PLEASE
DO NOT
WRITE
IN THIS
COLUMN

28. Students continue in full-time education for a variety of reasons and expect different things. What do you think a school or college, of the type in which you teach, should do for its students?

Over the page you will find a list of things which a school or college might try to do for students who stay on beyond the official school-leaving age.

In Column A please ring the numbers or letters opposite all those items which *you* think a school or college should do for its students. (You may think that most of the things should be included in your list, or just a few.)

In Column B please ring the number or letters opposite all those items which *your students* consider to be valuable and important. (Again you may think that most of the items should be included in your list, or just a few).

PLEASE
DO NOT
WRITE
IN THIS
MARGIN
Card B

	Col
i	31
ii	32
iii	33
iv	34
v	35
vi	36

32. Please list the numbers or letters of those items which you think *your* students consider to be *most* important, putting the most important one first. (You may think that only one or two are important, in which case just list those). Enter the numbers or letters in the circles provided.

If you find it difficult to make
a list or consider a lot of items
to be equally important then leave
the first five circles blank and
enter N in circle vi.

Please turn over for Question 33.

PLEASE
DO NOT
WRITE
IN THIS
MARGIN
Card B

	Col

29. Please list below any other things that *you* think a school or college should do for its students. Place each item opposite a letter M.

M

M

M

i	25
ii	26
iii	27
iv	28
v	29
vi	30

30. Now, from the lists in Questions 28 and 29 please list the numbers or letters of those items which *you* consider to be *most* important, putting the most important one first. (You may think that only one or two are important, in which case just list those). Enter the numbers or letters in the circles provided.

If you find it difficult to make a
list or consider a lot of items to
be equally important then leave the
first five circles blank and enter
N in circle vi

31. Please list below any other things which *your students* seem to consider important. Place each item opposite a letter M.

M

M

M

Page JM1/15

33. At the beginning of this Section you listed certain factors with which you thought school/college should be especially concerned. We would like to know in which ways you think this school/college helps its students, or does not help its students to achieve these goals.

PLEASE DO NOT WRITE IN THIS MARGIN
Card B
Code Col
0   37

i) How do you think the *subject(s)* you teach help students to achieve these goals?

38
39
40

ii) How do you think the *teaching methods* you use help students to achieve these goals?

41
42
43

iii) How do you think the *school organisation* (rules, School Council etc.) help students to achieve these goals?

44
45
46

v) How do you think the *extra-curricular activities* help students to achieve these goals?

47
48
49

Page JM1/16

34. Are there any ways in which you think that the present arrangements in this school/college could be improved?

PLEASE DO NOT WRITE IN THIS MARGIN
Card B
Code Col
0   50

i) How could the subjects, individually, or the curriculum as a whole, be improved?

51
52
53

ii) How could the teaching methods be improved?

54
55
56

iii) How could the school organisation be improved?

57
58
59

iv) How could the extra-curricular activities be improved?

60
61
62

Page JM1/17

PLEASE DO NOT WRITE IN THIS MARGIN
Card B
Code Col
0   63

35. Many developed countries are becoming concerned about the provision of education for those students who stay on in full-time education after the official school-leaving age. We would like to know which problems you consider to be of immediate concern for your type of school. Please circle the number or letter opposite all those items you consider significant.

Item	Code	Col
Inadequate supply of books and teaching materials	1	64
Difficulty of devising an up-to-date curriculum	2	
Difficulty of implementing an up-to-date curriculum	3	65
Shortage of teachers	4	
Problems connected with the satisfactory placing of students on courses in school according to their abilities and inclinations	5	66
Inadequate provision of facilities, e.g. libraries and laboratories	6	
Conflict between what students want to learn and the realities of the employment situation after school	7	67
Inadequacy of initial training for teachers	8	
Problems connected with the satisfactory placing of students in jobs or in institutions of higher education according to their abilities and inclinations	9	68
Student apathy	A	
Difficulty of devising an up-to-date curriculum for the less able	B	69
Difficulty of implementing an up-to-date curriculum for the less able	C	
Inadequacy of in-service training for teachers	D	70
Difficulty of maintaining discipline	E	
Difficulty of assessing the standard which a student has reached	F	71
Problems connected with adapting the school to cope with pupils from a wide range of social backgrounds	G	
Problems with students who want to take a large part in deciding on the curriculum and organisation	H	72
Truancy	J	
Problems connected with adapting the school to cope with pupils from a wide ability range	K	73

Page JM1/18

PLEASE DO NOT WRITE IN THIS MARGIN
Card B
Col

36. Are there any other problems which you could specify? Please list them in the spaces below, each separate item opposite a letter L.

L

L

L

37. From the lists in Questions 35 and 36 please write down in order of importance the number or letter of the three items which you think are cause for the most concern. Put the most important first. Enter the number or letter in the circles provided.

i)   74

ii)   75

iii)   76

Page JM1/18

PLEASE
DO NOT
WRITE
IN THIS
MARGIN

Card B   *Col*

77

FOR YOUR COMMENTS

Page JM2/1

UNIVERSITY OF LONDON KING'S COLLEGE

COMPARATIVE RESEARCH UNIT

CONFIDENTIAL

This questionnaire forms part of our research, sponsored by the Social Science Research Council. The project is concerned with the implications for schools and for society as a whole of the fact that increasingly large numbers of young people are now staying on in full-time education beyond the age of 15/16.

Our research covers England, France, West Germany, Italy and Sweden. Its aim is to investigate new trends in upper-secondary education, and the attitudes and opinions of teachers and students involved. In this way we hope to indicate directions for educational policy in the future. Please help us by taking part in this research project and answering the following questions.

All replies will be anonymous and completely confidential. There is no question of judging any school, teacher or student.

Thank you for your co-operation.

PLEASE TURN TO PAGE TWO.

Page JM2/2

	PLEASE DO NOT WRITE IN THIS MARGIN
	Col
Card A & Card B	1, 2
	3, 4, 5

SECTION A

School number . . . .

Student number . . . .

Please answer as many questions as you can. If you wish to add comments which might explain some of your answers, please do so.

Most questions can be answered simply by putting a ring round the number, or letter, opposite the appropriate answer, or by writing numbers or letters in the circles provided.

If, on second thoughts, you wish to change an answer, then put a large cross through that answer and then give the answer you wish to give clearly.

The questionnaire has been put together in two sections, because several people will have to work on the different sections afterwards. When you have finished please make sure that:

1. The sections are in order, A and B;

2. Both the school number and student number which you will find at the top of this page are entered at the top of Section B, page JM2/10;

3. Both sections are fastened together in one paperclip.

Please turn to page 3.

Page JM2/3

1. Why did you decide to stay on in full-time education? In the list below please ring the number or letter opposite *all the reasons which applied to you:*

PLEASE DO NOT WRITE IN THIS MARGIN
Card A
Code Col
0   40

	Code	Col
I wanted qualifications which would help me to get a better job	1	
I thought it would be a good opportunity to make new friends	2	41
I could not really decide what else to do	3	42
My teachers and/or counsellor advised me to stay on	4	43
I wanted to go on to some form of higher education	5	
My parents thought it was a sensible thing to do	6	
I thought about leaving but there are very few jobs for people who leave school as soon as they can	7	
I just did not want to start work	8	44
I wanted to study particular subjects because they are interesting	9	
Most of my friends were staying on so I thought I would too	A	45

2. If there were any other *general* reasons for staying, please list them in the spaces below, each separate reason opposite a letter B.

B

B

B

Page JM2/4

PLEASE DO NOT WRITE IN THIS MARGIN
Card A
Col

3. From the list in questions 1 and 2, will you please write down in order of importance the number or letter of the three factors which most strongly influenced your decision. Put the most important first. Enter the number or letter in the circles provided.

i   ○   46

ii   ○   47

iii   ○   48

iv   ○   49

If you find it difficult to make a list or think that a lot of things are equally important, leave the first three circles blank and enter a letter C in circle iv.

4. When you decided to stay on in full-time education were there a number of institutions for you to choose from? Please ring the relevant number

Yes   1
No   2   50

5. If there were a number of institutions for you to choose from are you now in the one you most wanted to go to? Please ring the relevant number

Yes   1
No   2
This question does not apply to me   3   51

6. If you are not in the institution of your first choice why were you not able to go there? If this question applies to you, please explain briefly.

PLEASE DO NOT WRITE IN THIS MARGIN

7. Now that you have been in this institution for some time does it still matter to you that you are not in the institution you originally wanted to go to?

Please ring the relevant number

Card A

		Col.
Yes	1	
No	2	
This question does not apply to me	3	52

8. Why does it still matter to you that you are not at the institution you originally wanted to go to? If this question applies to you, please explain briefly.

9. Quite apart from general reasons for wanting to stay on in full-time education was there anything about this particular institution which influenced you to come here? Please ring the number or letter opposite *all the reasons which applied to you*

	Code	*Col*
I knew the sports facilities were good here	1	
I thought that relations with staff would be easy here	2	53
I wanted the opportunity to take part in the extra-curricular activities	3	
I thought there would be freedom for students to organise things for themselves here	4	54
I thought the standard of teaching would be high	5	55
Most of my friends decided that they were going to come here so I did too	6	
I thought this school/college would be a pleasant community to work in	7	
I knew that the library facilities here were very good	8	56
I wanted to be trained for a particular job (please state which)	9	57
I knew that students here could choose their own pattern of courses to study	A	
Not many of my friends came here and I thought it would be a good place to make a new start	B	
I wanted the chance to meet members of the opposite sex	C	58
This school/college is very successful at getting students through examinations	D	59

0   60

PLEASE DO NOT WRITE IN THIS MARGIN

10. If there were any other *particular* reasons for staying on in this particular institution, please list them in the spaces below, each separate reason opposite a letter E.

E   61

E   62

E   63

11. From the list in questions 9 and 10 will you please write down in order of importance the number or letter of the *three* factors which most strongly influenced your decision. Put the most important first. Enter the number or letter in the circles provided.

i ◯

ii ◯

iii ◯

If you find it difficult to make a list or think that a lot of things were equally important, leave the first three circles blank and enter a letter F in circle iv

iv ◯   64

12. Please list below the subjects you are studying here

SUBJECT	*LEVEL* *'A' or 'O' or CSE etc.*	*Class hours per week*
1.		
2.		
3.		
4.		
5.		
6.		
7.		
8.		
9.		
10.		

0

65

66, 67

Page JM2/7

13. Please list below any extra-curricular activities in which you regularly take part.
    1.
    2.
    3.
    4.
    5.
    6.

14. Are you studying the subjects you wanted to study when you decided you wanted to stay on here?
    Please ring the relevant number

Yes	1
No	2

    [68]

15. If you are not studying the subjects you originally wanted to study, does this still matter to you?
    Please ring the relevant number

Yes	1
No	2
This question does not apply to me	3

    [69]

16. If it still matters to you that you are not studying the subjects you originally wanted to study, why does it still matter to you? If this question does *not* apply to you, ring number 3; if it does apply, ring the number or letter opposite the *one* reason which best corresponds to your feelings.

Not applicable	3
Subjects not the right ones for my *career*	4
Subjects not the right ones for further studies	5
Subjects not right for further studies and career	6
I just like the subjects I originally wanted *more* than the ones I do now	7
I am just not happy with the subjects I do now	8
Some other reason: please ring A, and then explain briefly	A

    [70]

Page JM2/8

17. How was it decided that you study the subjects you are now doing? Please explain briefly.

    [71]

18. Are there any other subjects you would now like to be doing, and if so, what are they?

    [72]
    [73]

19. a) How many hours private study do you do in school in an average school week? Please ring the appropriate number (and reply in hours *not* periods)

0- 2 hours	1
3- 4 hours	2
5- 6 hours	3
7- 8 hours	4
9-10 hours	5
11-12 hours	6
12 hours plus	7

    [74]

19. b) How many hours private study do you do *outside school* in an average week? Please ring appropriate number.

0- 4 hours	1
5- 8 hours	2
9-12 hours	3
13-16 hours	4
17-20 hours	5
21-24 hours	6
25 hours plus	7

    [75]

20. Do you have a job in the evenings or at week-ends? Please ring appropriate number

Yes	1
No	2

    [76]

SECTION B

21. What do you expect from school/college? People stay on in full-time education for various reasons and expect different things. Ideally, what should a school or college do for you?

Over the page you will find a list of things which a school or college might try to do for someone of your age.

At the side of the list are two columns of numbers headed A and B.

In column A please ring all the numbers or letters opposite those items which, ideally, a school or college should do *for you*. (You may think that most of the things should be included in your list, or just a few.)

In column B please ring all the numbers or letters opposite those items which *your teachers* seem to consider as valuable and important. (Again you may think that most of the items should be included, or just a few.)

PLEASE DO NOT WRITE IN THIS MARGIN

Card B
Code Col
1, 2
3, 4, 5

21. cont.

School number
Student number

Item	A	B	Col
School/college should help you to understand what is going on politically and socially in your own country	1	1	6
It should try to make sure that students pass their examinations	2	2	7
School/college should give you some experience of what it is like to live in a democracy	3	3	8
Staff should give you information which would help you to decide on a job or further course of education	4	4	9
School/college should give you the opportunity of learning to enjoy a wide range of arts like literature, films, music	5	5	10
School/college should give you some kind of practical training which would be useful in a job after leaving school	6	6	11
An ideal school/college would give you a wide range of subjects from which to choose	7	7	12
School/college should teach you to think clearly	8	8	13
School/college should help you to have some understanding of important world problems, e.g. hunger, poverty, pollution	9	9	14
School/college should give you some understanding of what other people are like	A	A	15
School/college should teach you to work on your own	B	B	16
There ought to be plenty of extra-curricular activities in school/college so that people can find out what they like to do in their spare time	C	C	17
School/college should teach you to be flexible and adapt what you have learned to changing circumstances	D	D	18
School/college should help you to understand the sort of person that you are and develop your personality	E	E	19
School/college should give you some understanding of religious experience	F	F	20
School/college should make sure that you have some knowledge of a wide range of subjects	G	G	21
School/college should teach you how to get on better with other people	H	H	22
School/college should make sure that you are physically fit	J	J	23
School/college should give you some understanding of relationship between the sexes	K	K	24
School/college should prepare you to go on learning throughout life	L	L	25

Page JM2/11

22. Please list below any other things that *you* think a school or college should do for you. Place each item opposite a letter M.

   M

   M

   M

Card B

23. Now from your list in questions 21 and 22 please list the numbers or letter of those items which are *most* important *to you*, putting the most important one first. (You may think that only one or two are important, in which case just list those). Enter your numbers or letters in the circles provided.

Col.

i   ◯   26

ii   ◯   27

iii   ◯   28

iv   ◯   29

v   ◯   30

vi   ◯   31

If you find it difficult to make a list or consider a lot of items to be equally important, then leave the first five circles blank and enter N in circle vi.

24. Please list below any other things which *your teachers* seem to consider important. Place each item opposite a letter M.

   M

   M

   M

Page JM2/12

Card B   Col

25. From the items you have listed in questions 21 and 24, what do *your teachers* consider to be most important? (Again you may think that only one or two are important, in which case just list those). Enter your numbers or letters in the circles provided, putting the most important first.

i   ◯   32

ii   ◯   33

iii   ◯   34

iv   ◯   35

v   ◯   36

vi   ◯   37

If you find it difficult to make a list, or consider a lot of items to be equally important, then leave the first five circles blank and enter N in circle vi.

Please turn over to question 26.

(The next few questions may be a little difficult, but they are probably the most important).

26. In the last section you listed certain items with which you thought that school/college should be especially concerned and we would like to know the ways in which this school/college helps you, or does not help you to achieve these goals.

i. How do you think the *subjects* you now study really help you or do not help you to achieve these goals

ii. How do you think the *teaching methods* help you or do not help you to achieve these goals?

iii. How do you think the *school organisation* (rules, School Council etc.) helps you or does not help you to achieve these goals?

iv. How do you think the *extra-curricular activities* help you, or do not help you, to achieve these goals?

PLEASE DO NOT WRITE IN THIS MARGIN

Card B
Code Col
0   38

39
40
41

42
43
44

45
46
47

48
49
50

27. How do you think that the present arrangements in your school/college could be improved (under the following headings)?

i. How could the *subjects individually or the curriculum as a whole* be improved?

ii. How could teaching methods be improved?

iii. How could the school organisation be improved?

iv. How could the extra-curricular activities be improved?

PLEASE DO NOT WRITE IN THIS MARGIN

Card B
Code Col

51
52
53

54
55
56

57
58
59

60
61
62

Page JM2/15

28. Many developed countries are becoming concerned about the provision of education for those students who stay on in full-time education after the official school-leaving age. We would like to know which problems you consider to be of immediate concern for your type of school. Please circle the number or letter opposite all those items you consider significant

PLEASE DO NOT WRITE IN THIS MARGIN

Card B

	Code	Col
	0	63
Inadequate supply of books and teaching materials	1	
Difficulty of devising an up-to-date curriculum	2	
Difficulty of implementing an up-to-date curriculum	3	64
Shortage of teachers	4	65
Problems connected with the satisfactory placing of students on courses in school according to their abilities and inclinations	5	
Inadequate provision of facilities, e.g. libraries and laboratories	6	66
Conflict between what students want to learn and the realities of the employment situation after school	7	67
Inadequacy of initial training for teachers	8	
Problems connected with the satisfactory placing of students in jobs or in institutions of higher education according to their abilities and inclinations	9	68
Student apathy	A	
Difficulty of devising an up-to-date curriculum for the less able	B	
Difficulty of implementing an up-to-date curriculum for the less able	C	69
Inadequacy of in-service training for teachers	D	
Difficulty of maintaining discipline	E	70
Difficulty of assessing the standard which a student has reached	F	
Problems connected with adapting the school to cope with pupils from a wide range of social backgrounds	G	71
Problems with students who want to take a large part in deciding on the curriculum and organisation	H	72
Truancy	J	73
Problems connected with adapting the school to cope with pupils from a wide ability range	K	

29. Are there any other problems which you could specify? Please list them in the spaces below, each separate item opposite a letter L.

L _____

L _____

L _____

30. From the lists in questions 28 and 29 please write down in order of importance the number or letter of the *three* items which you think are cause for the most concern. Put the most important first. Enter the number or letter in the circles provided.

PLEASE DO NOT WRITE IN THIS MARGIN

Card B

	Col
i	74
ii	75
iii	76

FOR YOUR COMMENTS   77

APPENDIX II

DETAILS OF CURRICULA IN THE ENGLISH SCHOOLS VISITED

Head teachers were invited to complete a form which listed fifty subjects which might be studied in schools. Details of the rubric are on the following page. Lists of subjects follow. Additional subjects, comments, notes etc. were made by the head teachers and have been reproduced.

SUBJECTS STUDIED IN SCHOOL/COLLEGE

1. This form may be filled in by the Head Teacher or Principal, or by the member of staff responsible for the time-table.

2. Please complete the form by ticking the appropriate columns.

3. *'Beginners'* 'A' Level', etc., means that subjects under this heading may be *started* at 16+, without previous qualification or course of study.

Grammar School A (Girls) — Page 2

Subject	'A' Level	Beginners' 'A' Level	'O' Level	Beginners' 'O' Level	C.S.E.	Beginners' C.S.E.	Examination other than G.C.E. or C.S.E. (specify)	Non-examination course	Compulsory for all students	Compulsory for some students	Studied by some students at local F.E. or another school	Studied by some students from local F.E. or another school
Geology								x				
German	x			x				x				
Greek	x			x								
Greek literature in translation												
History	x											
Home Economics	x							x				
Human Biology		x		x								
Italian		x		x								
Latin	x											
Latin literature in translation												
Law	x											
Mathematics (Applied)	x											
Mathematics (Pure)	x											
Mathematics (Pure and Applied)									(General)			
Mathematics with statistics												
Metalwork												
Music	x			x					(General)			
Physics	x			x								
Political Studies									(General)			

Grammar School A (Girls) — Page 1

Subject	'A' Level	Beginners' 'A' Level	'O' Level	Beginners' 'O' Level	C.S.E.	Beginners' C.S.E.	Examination other than G.C.E. or C.S.E. (specify)	Non-examination course	Compulsory for all students	Compulsory for some students	Studied by some students at local F.E. or another school	Studied by some students from local F.E. or another school
Accounting												
Applied Mechanics												
Archaeology												
Art	x							(General)				
Biology	x											
Botany	x											
British Constitution	x	x		x								
Chemistry	x		x									
Commerce												
Computer Science												
Chemistry w. Physics												
Dressmaking and Needlework		x		x				x				
Economics	x	x		x								
Engineering Science									(General)			
English	x							x	(General)			
French	x							x	(General)			
General Science									(General)			
General Studies								x	x			
Geography	x							x				

Grammar School
A (Girls)
Page 3

Subject	'A' Level	Beginners' 'A' Level	'O' Level	Beginners' 'O' Level	C.S.E.	Beginners' C.S.E.	Examination other than G.C.E. or C.S.E. (specify)	Non-examination course	Compulsory for all students	Compulsory for some students	Studied by some students at local F.E. or another school	Studied by some students from local F.E. or another school
Psychology								×				
Philosophy	×							(General)				
Religious Knowledge								(General)				
Rural Studies												
Russian	×	×		×				×				
Sociology	×											
Spanish	×	×		×				×				
Statistics												
Technical Drawing												
Use of English	×											
Woodwork												
Zoology	×											
Other: please specify												

Grammar School B (Boys) — Page 2

Subject	'A' Level	Beginners' 'A' Level	'O' Level	Beginners 'O' Level	C.S.E.	Beginners' C.S.E.	Examination other than G.C.E. or C.S.E. (specify)	Non-examination course	Compulsory for all students	Compulsory for some students	Studied by some students at local F.E. or another school	Studied by some students from local F.E. or another school
Geology		x										
German	x							x				
Greek	x											
Greek literature in translation	x	*x										
History	x											
Home Economics												
Human Biology												
Italian	x			x								
Latin	x			x								
Latin literature in translation												
Law												
Mathematics (Applied)	x +	x +										
Mathematics (Pure)	x							x				
Mathematics (Pure and Applied)	x									x		
Mathematics with statistics												
Metalwork												
Music	x							x				
Physics	x							x				
Political Studies												

Grammar School B (Boys) — Page 1

Subject	'A' Level	Beginners' 'A' Level	'O' Level	Beginners 'O' Level	C.S.E.	Beginners' C.S.E.	Examination other than G.C.E. or C.S.E. (specify)	Non-examination course	Compulsory for all students	Compulsory for some students	Studied by some students at local F.E. or another school	Studied by some students from local F.E. or another school
Accounting												
Applied Mechanics												
Archaeology	x							x				
Art	x	*x						x				
Biology	x											
Botany												
British Constitution												
Chemistry	x	x						x				
Commerce												
Computer Science												
Chemistry w. Physics												
Dressmaking and Needlework												
Economics	x	x										
Engineering Science												
English	x							x	x[1]			
French	x							x				
General Science												
General Studies								x				
Geography	*x	*x						x	x[1]			

Grammar School B (Boys) — Page 4

Subject	'A' Level	Beginners' 'A' Level	'O' Level	Beginners' 'O' Level	C.S.E.	Beginners' C.S.E.	Examination other than G.C.E. or C.S.E. (specify)	Non-examination course	Compulsory for all students	Compulsory for some students	Studied by some students at local F.E. or another school	Studied by some students from local F.E. or another school
History of Science								x				
Physical Education								x				

Grammar School B (Boys) — Page 3

Subject	'A' Level	Beginners' 'A' Level	'O' Level	Beginners' 'O' Level	C.S.E.	Beginners' C.S.E.	Examination other than G.C.E. or C.S.E. (specify)	Non-examination course	Compulsory for all students	Compulsory for some students	Studied by some students at local F.E. or another school	Studied by some students from local F.E. or another school
Psychology								x				
Philosophy								x				
Religious Knowledge				x					x			
Rural Studies												
Russian												
Sociology												
Spanish												
Statistics				x			x	x		x		
Technical Drawing	x											
Use of English								x		x		
Woodwork												
Zoology								x				
Other: please specify												
Ancient History								x				
Current Affairs								x				
Environmental Studies		x										
Classical Drama								x				
Astronomy								x				

*Would allow though unusual
‡These are not the exam subject but studies in general see elsewhere.
§Begins in the VIth but must be in combination with A-level pure mathematics.

Sixth Form College — A (Boys) — Page 2

Subject	'A' Level	Beginners' 'A' Level	'O' Level	Beginners' 'O' Level	C.S.E.	Beginners' C.S.E.	Examination other than G.C.E. or C.S.E. (specify)	Non-examination course	Compulsory for all students	Compulsory for some students	Studied by some students at local F.E. or another school	Studied by some students from local F.E. or another school
Geology	×		×	×								
German	×		×	×				×				
Greek											×	
Greek literature in translation	×		×	×				×				
History	×		×	×				×				
Home Economics								×				
Human Biology	×		×	×				×				
Italian	×		×	×								
Latin	×		×	×								
Latin literature in translation	×							×				
Law	×							×				
Mathematics (Applied)	×							×				
Mathematics (Pure)	×							×				
Mathematics (Pure and Applied)	×		×	×				×				
Mathematics with statistics	×		×	×				×				
Metalwork	×		×					×				
Music	×		×	×				×				
Physics Nuffield / Traditional	×		× ×	× ×				×				
Political Studies								×				

Sixth Form College — A (Boys) — Page 1

Subject	'A' Level	Beginners' 'A' Level	'O' Level	Beginners' 'O' Level	C.S.E.	Beginners' C.S.E.	Examination other than G.C.E. or C.S.E. (specify)	Non-examination course	Compulsory for all students	Compulsory for some students	Studied by some students at local F.E. or another school	Studied by some students from local F.E. or another school
Accounting			×					×				
Applied Mechanics			×					×				
Archaeology	×							×			×	
Art	×		×	×				×				
Biology	×		×					×				
Botany	×		×									
British Constitution	×		×	×				×				
Chemistry	×		×					×				
Commerce								×				
Computer Science								×				
Chemistry w. Physics			×									
Dressmaking and Needlework								×				
Economics	×		×									
Engineering Science	×							×		×		
English Language Literature	× ×		× ×	× ×				×				
French	×		×	×				×				
General Science								×				
General Studies								×				
Geography	×		×	×				×				

Sixth Form College — A (Boys) — Page 4

Subject	'A' Level	Beginners' 'A' Level	'O' Level	Beginners' 'O' Level	C.S.E.	Beginners' C.S.E.	Examination other than G.C.E. or C.S.E. (specify)	Non-examination course	Compulsory for all students	Compulsory for some students	Studied by some students at local F.E. or another school	Studied by some students from local F.E. or another school
Spoken English			X									
Certificate of Proficiency in English							X		•			
Boat/Canoe Building								X				
Design in Plastics								X				
Jewellery Making								X				
Photography								X				

Sixth Form College — A (Boys) — Page 3

Subject	'A' Level	Beginners' 'A' Level	'O' Level	Beginners' 'O' Level	C.S.E.	Beginners' C.S.E.	Examination other than G.C.E. or C.S.E. (specify)	Non-examination course	Compulsory for all students	Compulsory for some students	Studied by some students at local F.E. or another school	Studied by some students from local F.E. or another school
Psychology								X				
Philosophy	X		X					X				
Religious Knowledge	X							X				
Rural Studies												
Russian												
Sociology	X		X					X				
Spanish	X		X	X				X				
Statistics												
Technical Drawing	X		X	X			X					
Use of English			X									
Woodwork	X		X									
Zoology	X											
Other: please specify												
Physical Science	X		X									
Economic History			X									
Computer Appreciation							X					
Computer Programming							X					
Drama							X					

Sixth Form College — B (Girls) — Page 2

Subject	'A' Level	Beginners' 'A' Level	'O' Level	Beginners' 'O' Level	C.S.E.	Beginners' C.S.E.	Examination other than G.C.E. or C.S.E. (specify)	Non-examination course	Compulsory for all students	Compulsory for some students	Studied by some students at local F.E. or another school	Studied by some students from local F.E. or another school
Geology	x	x	x	x								
German	x	x[1]	x	x				x				
Greek	x	x[1]	x	x				x				
Greek literature in translation			Occasionally x				x (I.B)	x				
History	x	x	x	x			x	x				
Home Economics	x	x	x	x				x				x
Human Biology			x		Mode 3 x			x				
Italian	when req. x	x	x	x				x				
Latin	x	x[1]	x	x[1]				x				
Latin literature in translation								x				
Law	\- May be introduced in 1972, at least as part of Common Studies, now that we have a member of staff qualified to teach this subject.											
Mathematics (Applied)	**x**	**x**	x	x				x				
Mathematics (Pure)	x	x	x	x[2]	x			x				
Mathematics (Pure & Applied)	x	x	x	x[3]				x				
Mathematics with statistics			x	x				x				
Metalwork								x				
Music	x	x	x	x			x	x				
Physics	x	x	x	x								
Political Studies								x				

Sixth Form College — B (Girls) — Page 1

Subject	'A' Level	Beginners' 'A' Level	'O' Level	Beginners' 'O' Level	C.S.E.	Beginners' C.S.E.	Examination other than G.C.E. or C.S.E. (specify)	Non-examination course	Compulsory for all students	Compulsory for some students	Studied by some students at local F.E. or another school	Studied by some students from local F.E. or another school
Accounting	x			x								
Applied Mechanics	(part of mathematics course only)											
Archaeology								x				
Art	x	x	x	x				x			x	x
Biology	x	x	x	x	x	x		x				
Botany	x		x		x							
British Constitution			x		x							
Chemistry	*	*	*	Mode 3 x	x							
Commerce			x	x	Mode 3 x	x	x	x				
Computer Science			x	x	x			x				
Chemistry w. Physics			x					x				
Dressmaking and Needlework	x	x	x	x	x		Fashion Mode 3 x	x				
Economics	x		x	x	x			x				
Engineering Science	+	+	x	x			x					
English	xq	x	x	x	x		x		x			
French	x	x[1]	x	x	x		x	x				
General Science												
Common General Studies	Taken by all Sixth Formers											
Geography	x		x	x	x		x	x				

Sixth Form College B (Girls) — Page 4

Subject	'A' Level	Beginners' 'A' Level	'O' Level	Beginners' 'O' Level	C.S.E.	Beginners' C.S.E.	Examination other than G.C.E. or C.S.E. (specify)	Non-examination course	Compulsory for all students	Compulsory for some students	Studied by some students at local F.E. or another school	Studied by some students from local F.E. or another school
Shorthand							x					
Secretarial Duties							x					
Embroidery												
Physical Education	x		x	x	x (Mode 3, 1972–3)							
Child Care (Child health, development and education)			x	x	x (Mode 3) = 2 subjects			x			x	x
Photography (Taken partly here and partly at the College of Art)				x				x			x	x
Drama (Some activities shared with nearby College)												

Legend:
* occasionally when required
+ A-level only if required
1 after short introductory course
2 not required but could be available
3 Additional *pure* or *pure & applied*
4 Some take a reading course

Sixth Form College B (Girls) — Page 3

Subject	'A' Level	Beginners' 'A' Level	'O' Level	Beginners' 'O' Level	C.S.E.	Beginners' C.S.E.	Examination other than G.C.E. or C.S.E. (specify)	Non-examination course	Compulsory for all students	Compulsory for some students	Studied by some students at local F.E. or another school	Studied by some students from local F.E. or another school
Psychology	x	x	x	x				x				
Philosophy								x				
Religious Knowledge	x	x	x	x (From 1972)				x				
Rural Studies			x (From 1972)	x				x	x[4]			
Russian	x	x[1]	x	x								
Sociology	(as part of Common Studies)											
Spanish	x	x[1]	x	x	x			x				
Statistics								x				
Technical Drawing	x[1]	x[1]	x[1]	x	x (Mode 3)		x					
Use of English	x	x					GCE (not O or A) x	x				
Woodwork								x			x	
Zoology	x	x										
Other: please specify												
First Aid							x					
Ancient History	x	x										
Arithmetic							x	x				
Physical Science	x	x					x					
Typewriting							x	x				

Sixth Form College C (Mixed) — Page 2

Subject	'A' Level	Beginners' 'A' Level	'O' Level	Beginners' 'O' Level	C.S.E.	Beginners' C.S.E.	Examination other than G.C.E. or C.S.E. (specify)	Non-examination course	Compulsory for all students	Compulsory for some students	Studied by some students at local F.E. or another school	Studied by some students from local F.E. or another school
Geology		x		x		x		x				
German	x	x	x	x	x	x			(Fr) (Ge)			
Greek		x		x								
Greek literature in translation	x1											
History	x		x	x	x	x		x	x			
Home Economics			x	x	x	x		x	x			
Human Biology	x	x	x	x	x	x		x	x	i.e. sex education & human relationships	x	
Italian		x	x	x								
Latin	x	x										
Latin literature in translation	x											
Law												
Logic												
Mathematics (Applied)	x	x										
Mathematics (Pure)	x	x										
Mathematics (Pure & Applied)	x	x										
Mathematics with statistics (SMP)	x	x		x				x	x			
Metalwork	x	x	x	x	x	x		x	x			
Music	x	x	x	x	x	x	x	x	x			
Physics	x	x	x	x	x	x		Electronics x x	x	Electronics		
Political Studies	See British Constitution and Civics											

Sixth Form College C (Mixed) — Page 1

Subject	'A' Level	Beginners' 'A' Level	'O' Level	Beginners' 'O' Level	C.S.E.	Beginners' C.S.E.	Examination other than G.C.E. or C.S.E. (specify)	Non-examination course	Compulsory for all students	Compulsory for some students	Studied by some students at local F.E. or another school	Studied by some students from local F.E. or another school
Accounting	x	x										
Applied Mechanics	x	x	x	x								
Archaeology		x										
Art	x	x	x	x	x	x		x	x			
Biology	x	x	x	x	x	x		x	x			
Botany		x										
British Constitution	x	x			Civics x			x	x			
Chemistry	x	x	x	x	x	x		x	x			
Commerce		x					x					
Computer Science												
Chemistry w. Physics	x	x	x	x	x	x		x	x			
Dressmaking and Needlework		x	x		x							
Economics	x	x	x	x	x	x		x	x			
Engineering Science	x	x	x		x	x		x	x			
English Language Literature	x x	x	x x	x	x	x	x1	x	x			
French	x	x	x	x	x	x	x1	x	x2			
General Science												
General Studies	x		x					x				
Geography		x	x					x	x			

Sixth Form College C (Mixed) — Page 4

Subject	'A' Level	Beginners' 'A' Level	'O' Level	Beginners' 'O' Level	C.S.E.	Beginners' C.S.E.	Examination other than G.C.E. or C.S.E. (specify)	Non-examination course	Compulsory for all students	Compulsory for some students	Studied by some students at local F.E. or another school	Studied by some students from local F.E. or another school
Library								x		x		
Creative Writing								x		x		
Physics & Mathematics												
Physical Science		(1972) x								x		
Maths for Primary Teachers												
Environmental Studies		(1972) x										
Household Science		x		x								
Business Studies		x										
American Studies		x				x						
Economic History												
Latin American Studies		x										
Dress Design		(1972) x		x				x				
Design and Technology						x						
Pottery		x		x		x						
Craft/Sculpture		x		x		x						

1 Secretarial

2 All students have to do either French or German or Spanish

This college also provides: Physical Education of all kinds, Dance/Dance Drama/Mime, and Careers Guidance and Counselling.

Sixth Form College C (Mixed) — Page 3

Subject	'A' Level	Beginners' 'A' Level	'O' Level	Beginners' 'O' Level	C.S.E.	Beginners' C.S.E.	Examination other than G.C.E. or C.S.E. (specify)	Non-examination course	Compulsory for all students	Compulsory for some students	Studied by some students at local F.E. or another school	Studied by some students from local F.E. or another school
Psychology								x	x			
Philosophy								x	x			
Religious Knowledge	x	x	x	x	x	x		x	x			
Rural Studies				x	x	x						
Russian	(1972) x						Hoped for in 1972					
Sociology	(1972) x		x	x	x		x¹	x	x	x (Social Studies)		
Spanish	x	x	x	x	x		q	x		x (Fr.Sp. / Ger.)		
Statistics in A/O/CSE, SMP Maths and Pure Maths	x	x	x	x	x	x	x					
Technical Drawing		x	x	x	x	x		x	x			
Use of English	x		x	x	x			x	x			
Woodwork	x	x	x	x	x	x	x	x	x			
Zoology	x	x										
Other: please specify												
Typing/Shorthand/Office Pract Practice				x	x	x		x	x			
Drama	x			x		x						
20th Century Integrated English History ⎫									x			
Geography, Religious Knowledge ⎭												
Film								x	x			

Sixth Form College D — Page 2

Subject	'A' Level	Beginners' 'A' Level	'O' Level	Beginners' 'O' Level	C.S.E.	Beginners' C.S.E.	Examination other than G.C.E. or C.S.E. (specify)	Non-examination course	Compulsory for all students	Compulsory for some students	Studied by some students at local F.E. or another school	Studied by some students from local F.E. or another school
Geology	×	×		×				×				
German	×		×	×								
Greek	×	×		×								
Greek literature in translation				×	×	×		×				
History	×	×	×	×	×			×				
Home Economics	×	×	×	×								
Human Biology			×	×								
Italian												
Latin	×		×	×								
Latin literature in translation												
Law	×											
Mathematics (Applied)	×		×	×	×	×						
Mathematics (Pure)	×		×	×				×		×		
Mathematics (Pure & Applied)	×	×										
Mathematics with statistics	×	×		×	×			×				
Metalwork	×			×				×			×	
Music	×		×	×	×							
Physics	×		×	×				×				
Political Studies	×		×	×				×				

Sixth Form College D — Page 1

Subject	'A' Level	Beginners' 'A' Level	'O' Level	Beginners' 'O' Level	C.S.E.	Beginners' C.S.E.	Examination other than G.C.E. or C.S.E. (specify)	Non-examination course	Compulsory for all students	Compulsory for some students	Studied by some students at local F.E. or another school	Studied by some students from local F.E. or another school
Accounting												
Applied Mechanics												
Archaeology								×				
Art	×	×	×	×	×							
Biology	×		×	×				×				
Botany												
British Constitution		×						×				
Chemistry	×		×	×								
Commerce			×	×				×				
Computer Science								×				
Chemistry w. Physics												
Dressmaking and Needlework	×		×	×				×				
Economics	×	×	×	×								
Engineering Science	×	×	×	×	×			×		×		
English	×		×	×	×	×		×				
French	×			×	×	×		×				
General Science						×						
General Studies										×		
Geography	×		×					×				

Sixth Form College D — Page 4

Subject	'A' Level	Beginners' 'A' Level	'O' Level	Beginners' 'O' Level	C.S.E.	Beginners' C.S.E.	Examination other than G.C.E. or C.S.E. (specify)	Non-examination course	Compulsory for all students	Compulsory for some students	Studied by some students at local F.E. or another school	Studied by some students from local F.E. or another school
Pianoforte							×					
Strings								×				
Brass												
Woodwind												
Organ												

Sixth Form College D — Page 3

Subject	'A' Level	Beginners' 'A' Level	'O' Level	Beginners' 'O' Level	C.S.E.	Beginners' C.S.E.	Examination other than G.C.E. or C.S.E. (specify)	Non-examination course	Compulsory for all students	Compulsory for some students	Studied by some students at local F.E. or another school	Studied by some students from local F.E. or another school
Psychology	×	×		×				×				
Philosophy			×					×				
Religious Knowledge									×			
Rural Studies												
Russian												
Sociology	×	×		×		×		×				
Spanish	×		×	×								
Statistics			×									
Technical Drawing	×		×	×				×				
Use of English			×									
Woodwork	×			×				×				
Zoology	×		×									
Other: please specify												
Local Survey						×						
Business Studies			×	×				×				
Post-War Society		×				×						
Craft		×						×				
Oral Communication								×				

Non-selective Secondary School A (Girls) — Page 1

Subject	'A' Level	Beginners' 'A' Level	'O' Level	Beginners' 'O' Level	C.S.E.	Beginners' C.S.E.	Examination other than G.C.E. or C.S.E. (specify)	Non-examination course	Compulsory for all students	Compulsory for some students	Studied by some students at local F.E. or another school	Studied by some students from local F.E. or another school
Accounting												
Applied Mechanics												
Archaeology												
Art			×	×	×	×		×				
Biology			×		×							
Botany			×		×							
British Constitution								×				
Chemistry			×		×							
Commerce			×		×	×		×				
Computer Science												
Chemistry w. Physics			×		×							
Dressmaking and Needlework			×	×	×							
Economics			×		×							
Engineering Science								×				
English			×		×			×	×			
French			×		×			×				
General Science			×		×			×				
General Studies			×		×			×				
Geography			×		×			×				

Non-selective Secondary School A (Girls) — Page 2

Subject	'A' Level	Beginners' 'A' Level	'O' Level	Beginners' 'O' Level	C.S.E.	Beginners' C.S.E.	Examination other than G.C.E. or C.S.E. (specify)	Non-examination course	Compulsory for all students	Compulsory for some students	Studied by some students at local F.E. or another school	Studied by some students from local F.E. or another school
Geology								×				
German			×	×	×			×				
Greek			×		×			×				
Greek literature in translation												
History			×		×							
Home Economics												
Human Biology			×		×			×				
Italian												
Latin												
Latin literature in translation												
Law												
Mathematics (Applied)												
Mathematics (Pure)												
Mathematics (Pure & Applied)									×			
Mathematics with statistics												
Metalwork												
Music			×		×			×				
Physics			×									
Political Studies			×					×				

Non-selective
Secondary
School A (Girls)
Page 3

Subject	'A' Level	Beginners' 'A' Level	'O' Level	Beginners' 'O' Level	C.S.E.	Beginners' C.S.E.	Examination other than G.C.E. or C.S.E. (specify)	Non-examination course	Compulsory for all students	Compulsory for some students	Studied by some students at local F.E. or another school	Studied by some students from local F.E. or another school
Psychology												
Philosophy												
Religious Knowledge			X	X	X			X				
Rural Studies												
Russian												
Sociology			X	X				X				
Spanish			X	X	X			X				
Statistics												
Technical Drawing												
Use of English												
Woodwork												
Zoology												
Other: please specify												
P.E.					X			X				
Modern Educ. Dance								X				

Non-selective Secondary School B (Boys) — Page 2

Subject	'A' Level	Beginners 'A' Level	'O' Level	Beginners 'O' Level	C.S.E.	Beginners' C.S.E.	Examination other than G.C.E. or C.S.E. (specify)	Non-examination course	Compulsory for all students	Compulsory for some students	Studied by some students at local F.E. or another school	Studied by some students from local F.E. or another school
Geology												
German												
Greek												
Greek literature in translation								x				
History			x		x							
Home Economics												
Human Biology												
Italian												
Latin												
Latin literature in translation												
Law												
Mathematics (Applied)			x		x		x	x	x	x		
Mathematics (Pure)												
Mathematics (Pure & Applied)												
Mathematics with statistics												
Metalwork			x		x							
Music			x		x				x			
Physics			x		x							
Political Studies												

Non-selective Secondary School B (Boys) — Page 1

Subject	'A' Level	Beginners 'A' Level	'O' Level	Beginners 'O' Level	C.S.E.	Beginners' C.S.E.	Examination other than G.C.E. or C.S.E. (specify)	Non-examination course	Compulsory for all students	Compulsory for some students	Studied by some students at local F.E. or another school	Studied by some students from local F.E. or another school
Accounting												
Applied Mechanics												
Archaeology												
Art	x							x				
Biology			x		x							
Botany			x		x							
British Constitution												
Chemistry			x		x							
Commerce												
Computer Science												
Chemistry w. Physics												
Dressmaking and Needlework												
Economics												
Engineering Science												
English			x		x				x			
French			x		x							
General Science			x		x			x				
General Studies												
Geography			x		x			x				

Non-selective Secondary School B (Boys) — Page 4

Subject	'A' Level	Beginners' 'A' Level	'O' Level	Beginners' 'O' Level	C.S.E.	Beginners' C.S.E.	Examination other than G.C.E. or C.S.E. (specify)	Non-examination course	Compulsory for all students	Compulsory for some students	Studied by some students at local F.E. or another school	Studied by some students from local F.E. or another school
Aeronautics					×							

Non-selective Secondary School B (Boys) — Page 3

Subject	'A' Level	Beginners' 'A' Level	'O' Level	Beginners' 'O' Level	C.S.E.	Beginners' C.S.E.	Examination other than G.C.E. or C.S.E. (specify)	Non-examination course	Compulsory for all students	Compulsory for some students	Studied by some students at local F.E. or another school	Studied by some students from local F.E. or another school
Psychology												
Philosophy												
Religious Knowledge			×		×			×				
Rural Studies												
Russian												
Sociology												
Spanish												
Statistics												
Technical Drawing			×		×							
Use of English												
Woodwork			×		×							
Zoology												
Other: please specify												
Building Construction (Craft Practice)											×	
Auto-Engineering											×	
General Engineering											×	
Radio and T.V. Mechanics											×	
Environmental Studies												

Non-selective Secondary School C (Mixed) — Page 1

Subject	Studied by some students from local F.E. or another school	Studied by some students at local F.E. or another school	Compulsory for some students	Compulsory for all students	Non-examination course	Examination other than G.C.E. or C.S.E. (specify)	Beginners' C.S.E.	C.S.E.	Beginners' 'O' Level	'O' Level	Beginners' 'A' Level	'A' Level
Accounting												
Applied Mechanics												
Archaeology												
Art				x				x		x		x
Biology		"A" level						x		x		
Botany								x		x		
British Constitution										x		x
Chemistry		"A" level						x		x		
Commerce					x			x		x		
Computer Science												
Chemistry w. Physics										x		
Dressmaking and Needlework				all girls	x			x		x		
Economics										x		x
Engineering Science		Linked x course										
English				x (2 yrs.)				x		x		x
French				x				x		x		x
General Science				x				x		x		
General Studies												
Geography					x			x		x		x

Non-selective Secondary School C (Mixed) — Page 2

Subject	Studied by some students from local F.E. or another school	Studied by some students at local F.E. or another school	Compulsory for some students	Compulsory for all students	Non-examination course	Examination other than G.C.E. or C.S.E. (specify)	Beginners' C.S.E.	C.S.E.	Beginners' 'O' Level	'O' Level	Beginners' 'A' Level	'A' Level
Geology										x		x
German										x		x
Greek										x		
Greek literature in translation												
History				x				x		x		x
Home Economics				x	x			x		x		x
Human Biology										x		
Italian												
Latin												
Latin literature in translation												
Law												
Mathematics (Applied)												
Mathematics (Pure)				x				x		x		x
Mathematics (Pure & Applied)												
Mathematics with statistics												
Metalwork				All boys	x			x		x		x
Music				x				x		x		x
Physics								x		x		
Political Studies		"A" level										

Non-selective Secondary School C (Mixed) Page 3

Subject	'A' Level	Beginners' 'A' Level	'O' Level	Beginners' 'O' Level	C.S.E.	Beginners' C.S.E.	Examination other than G.C.E. or C.S.E. (specify)	Non-examination course	Compulsory for all students	Compulsory for some students	Studied by some students at local F.E. or another school	Studied by some students from local F.E. or another school
Psychology												
Philosophy												
Religious Knowledge	x		x		x				x			
Rural Studies								x		x		
Russian												
Sociology												
Spanish												
Statistics												
Technical Drawing	x				x			x				
Use of English	x		x		x			x	"A" level			
Woodwork	x		x		x			x	All boys			
Zoology												
Other: please specify									x			
P.E.									x			
Building Construction											Linked course x course	Linked course
Nursing												
Jewellery-making								x				
Printing								x				

APPENDIX III

STUDENTS' ASPIRATIONS AND SOCIAL BACKGROUND

IN SOME INDIVIDUAL ENGLISH SCHOOLS AND COLLEGES

a) BOYS' SIXTH FORM COLLEGE

Aspiration:	Number	%
University or equivalent	57	41.3
Employment involving non-professional studies or training	24	17.4
Full-time studies (other than University or College of Education)	14	10.1
College of Education	12	8.7
Employment involving professional studies or training	12	8.7
Armed Services	9	6.5
Do not know	7	5.1
Employment involving no further studies or training	3	2.2
(No reply)	4	(–)

Social Background (Father's Occupation):	Number	%
Social class I: Professional or higher managerial	11	8.0
Social class II: Managerial or senior technical	40	29.2
Social class III: Other non-manual (skilled)	30	21.9
Social class III: Skilled manual	32	23.4
Social class IV and V: Semi- and un-skilled	12	8.8
Dead/retired/not working	9	6.6
Do not know	3	2.2
(No reply)	5	(–)

b) GIRLS' SIXTH FORM COLLEGE

Aspiration:	Number	%
University or equivalent	58	43.9
College of Education	31	23.5
Employment involving non-professional studies or training	17	12.9
Full-time studies (other than University or College of Education)	10	7.6
Employment involving professional studies or training	9	6.8
Armed Services	2	1.5
None of these	2	1.5
Do not know	2	1.5
Employment involving no further studies or training	1	0.8
(No reply)	1	(–)

Social Background (Father's Occupation):	Number	%
Social class I: Professional or higher managerial	19	14.4
Social class II: Managerial or senior technical	50	37.9
Social class III: Other non-manual (skilled)	20	15.2
Social class III: Skilled manual	20	15.2
Social class IV and V: Semi- and un-skilled	13	9.8
Dead/retired/not working	6	4.5
Do not know	4	3.0
(No reply)	1	(–)

c) **MIXED SIXTH FORM COLLEGE: 1**

Aspiration:	Number	%
Employment involving non-professional studies or training	50	37.9
University or equivalent	29	22.0
Employment involving professional studies or training	20	15.2
College of Education	13	9.8
Full-time studies (other than University or College of Education)	11	8.3
Do not know	5	3.8
Employment involving no further studies or training	3	2.3
None of these	1	0.8
(No reply	6	—)

Social Background (Father's Occupation):		
Social class I: Professional or higher managerial	7	5.3
Social class II: Managerial or senior technical	32	24.2
Social class III: Other non-manual (skilled)	25	18.9
Social class III: Skilled manual	38	28.8
Social class IV and V: Semi- and un-skilled	10	7.6
Dead/retired/not working	13	9.8
Do not know	7	5.3
(No reply	6	—)

d) **MIXED SIXTH FORM COLLEGE: 2**

Aspiration	Number	%
University or equivalent	44	37.9
College of Education	27	23.3
Employment involving professional studies or training	19	16.4
Employment involving non-professional studies or training	14	12.1
Full-time studies (other than University or College of Education)	7	6.0
Armed Services	2	1.7
Do not know	2	1.7
Employment involving no further studies or training	1	0.9

Social Background (Father's Occupation):		
Social class I: Professional or higher managerial	9	7.8
Social class II: Managerial or senior technical	32	27.6
Social class III: Other non-manual (skilled)	20	17.2
Social class III: Skilled manual	25	21.6
Social class IV and V: Semi- and un-skilled	14	12.1
Dead/retired/not working	13	11.2
Not classifiable/Armed Services	1	0.9
Do not know	2	1.7

e) TECHNICAL COLLEGE: 1

Aspiration:	Number	%
University or equivalent	26	27.1
Employment involving professional studies or training	22	22.9
Employment involving non-professional studies or training	20	20.8
Employment involving no further studies or training	8	8.3
College of Education	7	7.3
Full-time studies (other than University or College of Education)	7	7.3
Do not know	4	4.2
Armed Services	1	1.0
None of these	1	1.0
(No reply)	1	(–)

Social Background (Father's Occupation):	Number	%
Social class I: Professional or higher managerial	4	4.2
Social class II: Managerial or senior technical	24	25.3
Social class III: Other non-manual (skilled)	11	11.6
Social class III: Skilled manual	34	35.8
Social class IV and V: Semi- and un-skilled	11	11.6
Dead/retired/not working	6	6.3
Not classifiable/Armed Services	3	3.2
Do not know	2	2.1
(No reply)	2	(–)

f) TECHNICAL COLLEGE: 2

Aspiration:	Number	%
University or equivalent	40	45.5
College of Education	12	13.6
Employment involving professional studies or training	12	13.6
Full-time studies (other than University or College of Education)	8	9.1
Employment involving non-professional studies or training	8	9.1
Employment involving no further training or studies	3	3.4
None of these	3	3.4
Armed Services	1	1.1
Do not know	1	1.1

Social Background (Father's Occupation):	Number	%
Social class I: Professional or higher managerial	16	18.6
Social class II: Managerial or senior technical	34	39.5
Social class III: Other non-manual (skilled)	14	16.3
Social class III: Skilled manual	13	15.1
Social class IV and V: Semi- and un-skilled	3	3.5
Dead/retired/not working	5	5.8
Do not know	1	1.2
(No reply)	2	(–)

g) **BOYS' GRAMMAR SCHOOL**

Aspiration:	Number	%
University or equivalent	63	77.8
Employment involving professional studies or training	11	13.6
Employment involving non-professional studies or training	3	3.7
Full-time studies (other than University or College of Education)	2	2.5
College of Education	1	1.2
Employment involving no further studies or training	1	1.2
(No reply	1	–)

Social Background (Father's Occupation):

	Number	%
Social class I: Professional or higher managerial	11	13.6
Social class II: Managerial or senior technical	41	50.6
Social class III: Other non-manual (skilled)	21	25.9
Social class III: Skilled manual	5	6.2
Social class IV and V: Semi- and un-skilled	1	1.2
Dead/retired/not working	1	1.2
Not classifiable/Armed Services	1	1.2
(No reply	1	–)

h) **GIRLS' GRAMMAR SCHOOL**

Aspiration:	Number	%
University or equivalent	59	60.8
Full-time studies (other than University or College of Education)	11	11.3
College of Education	8	8.2
Employment involving professional studies or training	7	7.2
Employment involving non-professional studies or training	7	7.2
Do not know	4	4.1
Employment involving no further studies or training	1	1.0

Social Background (Father's Occupation):

	Number	%
Social class I: Professional or higher managerial	29	30.2
Social class II: Managerial or senior technical	39	40.6
Social class III: Other non-manual (skilled)	13	13.5
Social class III: Skilled manual	5	5.2
Social class IV and V: Semi- and un-skilled	4	4.2
Dead/retired/not working	3	3.1
Not classifiable/Armed Services	2	2.1
Do not know	1	1.0
(No reply	1	–)

i)   MIXED NON-SELECTIVE SECONDARY SCHOOL:

Aspiration:	Number	%
Full-time studies (other than University or College of Education)	17	32.7
University or equivalent	11	21.2
Employment involving non-professional studies or training	10	19.2
Employment involving professional studies or training	4	7.7
Do not know	4	7.7
College of Education	2	3.8
Armed Services	2	3.8
Employment involving no further studies or training	2	3.8

Social Background (Father's Occupation):

	Number	%
Social class I: Professional or higher managerial	7	13.5
Social class II: Managerial or senior technical	15	28.8
Social class III: Other non-manual (skilled)	10	19.2
Social class III: Skilled manual	9	17.3
Social class IV and V: Semi- and un-skilled	4	7.7
Dead/retired/not working	2	3.8
Not classifiable/Armed Services	4	7.7
Do not know	1	1.9

**APPENDIX IV: A TECHNICAL NOTE ON THE
SOCIOLOGICAL QUESTIONNAIRES**

Questionnaire Design

Each of the three types of questionnaire (for principals or head teachers; for those concerned with the provision of counselling and guidance; and for students) contained a mixture of open-ended and fixed-alternative questions. The inclusion of open-ended questions was regarded as essential wherever the researcher did not wish to impose any framework — explicit or implicit — on individuals' replies. For example, one objective of the students' questionnaire was to discover what opportunities students thought would be available to them after upper-secondary and further studies. The researcher wanted to know whether students thought in terms of employment or educational opportunities, or both; of specific or broad types of opportunities, and what these were. Clearly, the wording of these questions had to ensure that no indication was given as to the type of reply expected from students.

Another example is found in the section of the students' questionnaire concerned with counselling and guidance. One major aim was to discover the types of information, advice and guidance that students wanted to receive. Again, because the researcher did not wish to suggest any possible replies, this question was made open-ended, and students were left to describe as fully as they wished the type or types of counselling and guidance that they would have found most helpful.

A final example from the students' questionnaire concerns father's occupation. In order to try to reduce the problems of classification always associated with this social class indicator, the researcher decided that in England, at least, — where there were no difficulties of translation — students would be asked to describe as fully as possible their father's occupation. This could afterwards be classified by the researcher, using the Registrar General's Classification of Occupations. It was thought that this method was preferable to relying on students' own classification, unless the latter was unavoidable.

Further examples can be found in the other two types of questionnaire. Open-ended questions were included wherever the researcher wanted to obtain as full and spontaneous a picture as possible of individuals' views, perceptions or opinions.

In other instances, fixed alternative questions were used wherever possible, the alternatives were chosen after pilot fieldwork and desk research. In most cases, a "None of these" or "Something else" or "Other" category was also included, so that individuals could write in their reply if they felt that none of the categories given were appropriate.

Finally, a space for additional comments was provided at the end of the questionnaires. Generally speaking, principals or head teachers and those concerned with counselling and guidance made little use of this, perhaps because many of them had had an opportunity to express their views fully during the course of an interview structured around the questionnaire. But many students *did* make additional comments, and these were carefully analysed along with their other replies.

Data Analysis

The task of analysis was greatest and most complex in the case of the student questionnaire. The number of principals' or head teachers' and counselling and guidance questionnaires was sufficiently small to enable analysis of replies to be done manually without any difficulty. But 5,419 student questionnaires could obviously be handled only with the help of computer techniques.

Even so, a considerable amount of preliminary work was required to prepare the material for the computer. Replies to all the open-ended questions had to be analysed and coded, and this involved a great deal of translation work.

When this preparatory stage was complete, the coded replies to all the questions on the student questionnaire were transferred on to punched cards and then on to computer tapes. Using S.P.S.S., *"The Statistical Package for the Social Sciences"*, (Nie, Bent and Hull, 1970), frequency counts and later cross tabulations of variables were obtained. It was decided that the nature of the sociological variables, and the research methods and objectives, did not warrant the use of more sophisticated statistical techniques, such as correlation coefficients and T-tests.

**LIST OF TABLES CONTAINED IN THE CURRICULUM AND
TEACHING/LEARNING RELATIONSHIPS SECTION**

CHAPTER 12

Tables in this chapter refer to *all* students, and are prefixed with a letter A.

CHAPTER 13

Tables in this chapter refer to teachers and are prefixed with a letter T.

LIST OF TABLES CONTAINED IN THE
SOCIOLOGICAL SECTION OF THE REPORT

CHAPTER 16

CHAPTER 17

CHAPTER 18

INDEX